THE LAW AND PRACTICE OF BANKING: VOL. II

Securities for Bankers' Advances

BY

J. MILNES HOLDEN, LL.B., Ph.D., A.I.B.

Of Lincoln's Inn, Barrister-at-Law

FIFTH EDITION

Pitman Publishing

1971

First published 1954
Second edition 1957
Reprinted 1959
Third edition 1961
Reprinted 1962
Fourth edition 1964
Reprinted 1965
Fifth edition 1971

SIR ISAAC PITMAN AND SONS LTD.
PITMAN HOUSE, PARKER STREET, KINGSWAY, LONDON, WC2B 5PB
P.O. BOX 6038, PORTAL STREET, NAIROBI, KENYA
PITMAN HOUSE, BOUVERIE STREET, CARLTON, VICTORIA 3053, AUSTRALIA
P.O. BOX 11231. Johannesburg. S. Africa

THE CARSWELL COMPANY LTD., TORONTO

ISBN: 0 273 31558 7

MADE IN GREAT BRITAIN AT THE PITMAN PRESS, BATH
G1—(B.855)

297517

Preface to Fifth Edition

THIS book was first published in 1954 under the title "Securities for Bankers' Advances." Subsequent editions were published in 1957, 1961, and 1964. The present (fifth) edition becomes Volume 2 of "The Law and Practice of Banking," Volume 1 of which has been published under the sub-title "Banker and Customer."

The primary object of Volume 2 is to explain the theory and practice relating to securities for bankers' advances. The plan throughout the work is first to state the law relating to the type of security under consideration and then to explain the practice of bankers, influenced as it necessarily is by the law.

Over the years I have had the great good fortune to receive help from lawyers and bank officials in the preparation of the successive editions of this book. As the prefaces to the earlier editions of the book are omitted, it is appropriate for me to acknowledge here my indebtedness to them—

Mr. G. F. R. Ashton, until his retirement a Manager of the Overseas Department, Lloyds Bank Limited.

Mr. D. B. Brooks, until his retirement Head of the Head Office Security Department, National Provincial Bank Limited.

Lord Chorley, Q.C., formerly Sir Ernest Cassel Professor of Commercial and Industrial Law in the University of London.

Mr. T. J. Cogar, until his death in September, 1966, an Inspector of Barclays Bank Limited.

Mr. J. H. Clemens, until his retirement Manager, Lloyds Bank Limited, 46 Victoria Street, London, S.W.1.

Mr. L. P. Galpin, until his retirement an Assistant General Manager, Westminster Bank Limited.

Mr. L. C. B. Gower, F.B.A., a Law Commissioner; formerly Sir Ernest Cassel Professor of Commercial and Industrial Law in the University of London.

Mr. E. S. Harvey, District Inspector, Foreign Branches Inspection, Barclays Bank Limited.

Mr. H. C. Horton, until his retirement Overseas Manager, Martins Bank Limited.

Mr. L. C. Mather, a director and the Chief General Manager, Midland Bank Limited.

Mr. P. I. Twelvetree, the General Manager, Surrey Trustee Savings Bank.

Preface

It is hoped that readers will consider that the lay-out of the text has been improved. Additional sub-headings have been introduced, and the whole of the type has been re-set. Furthermore, the subject-matter is now indexed by reference to paragraph numbers instead of to pages. It is thought that this will assist readers when using the general index, and the tables of cases and statutes. Instead of having to look through a whole page in order to find a particular point, their attention will be directed to a specific paragraph.

Finally, my thanks are due to Miss Joanna Hide, and Miss Christina Prout, both of the Inter-Bank Research Organisation, who have helped me with the proof reading, and with the preparation of the index, and the tables of cases and statutes.

J. MILNES HOLDEN

10 Lombard Street,
London, E.C.3.
1st November, 1970

Contents

viii   *Contents*

PART VI: GOODS

PART VII: OTHER TYPES OF SECURITY

PART VIII: SECURITIES GIVEN BY COMPANIES

PART IX: STAMP DUTIES

Table of Cases

*References to paragraphs in which some account of the facts
of a case is given are printed in bold type.*

Chao *v.* British Traders and Shippers Ltd. *See* Kwei Tek Chao *v.* British Traders and Shippers Ltd.

Charlesworth *v.* Mills [1892] A.C. 231; 61 L.J.Q.B. 830; 66 L.T. 690; 56 J.P. 628; 41 W.R. 129; 8 T.L.R. 484; 36 Sol. Jo. 411 . . 24-5

Church of England Building Society *v.* Piskor [1954] Ch. 553; [1954] 2 All E.R. 85; 104 L.J. 313; 98 Sol. Jo. 316 4-34

City Permanent Building Society *v.* Miller [1952] Ch. 840; [1952] 2 All E.R. 621; [1952] 2 T.L.R. 547; 102 L.J. 539; 214 L.T. 103 . 4-34

Clayton's Case (1816) 1 Mer. 572; Chorley and Smart's Leading Cases 148 . 4-17, 5-13, 10-38, 12-17, 15-13, 19-25, 19-32, 19-33, 20-34, 21-4, 26-20, 27-11, 31-10, 32-35, 32-54

Cole *v.* North Western Bank (1875) 44 L.J.C.P. 233; L.R. 10 C.P. 354; 32 L.T. 733 . . . . 25-1, 25-8

Coleman *v.* London County and Westminster Bank Ltd. [1916] 2 Ch. 353; 85 L.J. Ch. 652; 115 L.T. 152; 3 L.D.B. 142 . . **15-37**

Collier, *Re* [1930] 2 Ch. 37; 99 L.J. Ch. 241; 143 L.T. 329 . 12-29

Collins *v.* Martin (1797) 1 B. & P. 648 . . . . 16-6, 25-1

Colonial Bank *v.* Whinney (1886) 11 App. Cas. 426; 56 L.J. Ch. 43; 55 L.T. 362; 2 T.L.R. 747 15-36

Columbian Fireproofing Co. Ltd., *Re* [1910] 2 Ch. 120; 79 L.J. Ch. 583; 102 L.T. 835 32-34

Commercial Bank of Australia Ltd. *v.* Official Assignee of the Estate of John Wilson & Co. [1893] A.C. 181; 62 L.J.P.C. 61; 68 L.T. 540; 9 T.L.R. 307 21-16

Conley, *Re, Ex parte* Trustee *v.* Barclays Bank Ltd. [1937] 4 All E.R. 438; 54 T.L.R. 158; reversed, [1938] 2 All E.R. 127; 107 L.J. Ch. 257; 158 L.T. 323; 54 T.L.R. 641; 82 Sol. Jo. 292; Chorley and Smart's Leading Cases 311 . . . . . **31-15/16**

Cooper *v.* National Provincial Bank Ltd. [1945] 2 All E.R. 641; [1946] K.B. 1; 115 L.J.K.B. 84; 173 L.T. 368; 62 T.L.R. 36; 89 Sol. Jo. 477 . . . . **18-8**

Coppin *v.* Gray (1842) 1 Y. & C. Ch. Cas. 205; 11 L.J. Ch. 105; 6 Jur. 312 18-19

Coulthart *v.* Clementson (1879) 5 Q.B.D. 42; 49 L.J.Q.B. 204; 41 L.T. 798; 28 W.R. 355 . . . . . 18-29, 19-28

Cousins *v.* Sun Life Assurance Society [1933] 1 Ch. 126; 102 L.J. Ch. 114; 148 L.T. 101; 49 T.L.R. 12 12-26

Coutts & Co. *v.* Browne-Lecky and Others [1947] K.B. 104; [1946] 2 All E.R. 207; [1946] W.N. 144; 62 T.L.R. 421; 90 Sol. Jo. 489; Chorley and Smart's Leading Cases 172 . . **19-44**, 19-45, 19-49

Coventry Permanent Economic Building Society *v.* Jones [1951] 1 All E.R. 901; [1951] W.N. 218; [1951] 1 T.L.R. 739; 211 L.T. 221 4-34

Crerar *v.* Bank of Scotland [1922] S.C. (H.L.) 137; 59 Sc. L.R. 312; 3 L.D.B. 248 15-17

Crisp, *Ex parte* (1744) 1 Atk. 133 18-16

Crouch *v.* The Credit Foncier Co. (1873) L.R. 8 Q.B. 374; 42 L.J.Q.B. 183; 29 L.T. 259; 21 W.R. 946 22-15

Cutts, *Re* (a Bankrupt) *Ex parte* Bognor Mutual Building Society *v.* Trustee in Bankruptcy [1956] 1 W.L.R. 728; [1956] 2 All E.R. 537 19-53

xxii   *Table of Cases*

Table of Statutes

Table of Statutes

Table of Statutory Instruments

Table of Abbreviations

A.C. . . .	Appeal Cases . . .	. 1891—current
Ad. & E. . .	Adolphus and Ellis . .	. . 1834–40
All E.R. . .	All England Reports . .	. 1936—current
App. Cas. . .	Appeal Cases . . .	. . 1875–90
Asp. M.C. . .	Aspinall's Maritime Law Cases	. 1871–1943
Atk. . . .	Atkyns	. . 1736–55
B. & Ald. . .	Barnewall and Alderson	. . 1817–22
B. & C. . .	Barnewall and Cresswell .	. . 1822–30
B. & P. . .	Bosanquet and Puller . .	. 1796–1804
B. & S. . .	Best and Smith . . .	. 1861–70
Beav. . .	Beavan	. . 1838–66
Bli. (N.S.) . .	Bligh, New Series . .	. . 1827–37
Bro. C.C. . .	Brown (by Belt) . .	. . 1778–94
Buck . . .	Buck	. . 1816–20
C. & P. . .	Carrington and Payne .	. . 1823–41
C.B. (N.S.) .	Common Bench, New Series	. . 1856–65
Cas. in Ch. .	Cases in Chancery . .	. . 1660–97
Ch. . . .	Chancery Division . .	. 1891—current
Ch. App. . .	Chancery Appeal Cases .	. . 1865–75
Ch. D. . .	Chancery Division . .	. . 1875–90
Chorley and Smart's Leading Cases .	*Leading Cases in the Law of Banking*, by Lord Chorley and P. E. Smart	
Cl. & Fin. . .	Clark and Finnelly . .	. . 1831–46
Com. Cas. . .	Commercial Cases . .	. 1896–1941
Court of Sess. Cas.	Court of Session Cases, 4th series	. 1873–98
Cox C.C. . .	Cox's Criminal Cases .	. 1843–1943
Cox Eq. Cas. .	Cox's Equity . . .	. . 1783–96
C.P. . . .	Common Pleas Cases . .	. 1865–75
C.P.D. . .	Common Pleas Division .	. . 1875–80
Cro. Eliz. . .	Croke	. 1582–1603
De G. & Sm. .	De Gex and Smale, temp. Knight-Bruce and Parker . . .	. 1846–52
De G. F. & J. .	De Gex, Fisher and Jones, temp. Campbell	1860–62
De G. M. & G. .	De Gex, Macnaghten & Gordon	. 1851–57
Deac. . . .	Deacon	. 1836–39
Dow & Ry. (K.B.)	Dowling and Ryland, King's Bench	. 1821–27
Drewr. . .	Drewry Reports, temp. Kindersley	. 1852–59
E. & B. . .	Ellis and Blackburn . .	. 1851–58
East . . .	East's Term Reports . .	. 1801–12
Eq. . . .	Equity Cases . . .	. 1866–75
Esp. . . .	Espinasse . . .	1793–1807

Exch. . .	Exchequer Reports (Welsby, Hurlstone and Gordon) 1847–56	
Giff. . . .	Giffard 1857–65	
H. & C. .	Hurlstone and Coltman 1862–66	
Har. & W. .	Harrison and Wollaston . . . 1835–36	
Hare . . .	Hare 1841–53	
H.L.C. .	Clark's Reports, House of Lords . . 1847–66	
J.P. . . .	Justice of the Peace and Local Government Review 1837–1945	
Jur. . . .	Jurist Reports 1837–54	
Jur. (N.S.) .	Jurist Reports, New Series . . . 1855–66	
K. & J. .	Kay and Johnson 1854–58	
K.B. . .	King's Bench 1901–52	
L.D.B. .	*Legal Decisions Affecting Bankers*	
Ll.L. Rep. .	Lloyd's List Reports . . . 1919—current	
L.J. (Bcy.) .	Law Journal Reports, Bankruptcy . 1831–1880	
L.J. Ch. .	Law Journal Reports, Chancery . 1831–1949	
L.J.C.P. .	Law Journal Reports, Common Pleas . 1831–80	
L.J. Ex. .	Law Journal Reports, Exchequer . 1831–1875	
L.J.K.B. .	Law Journal Reports, King's Bench 1831–37, 1901–47	
L.J.O.S. (K.B.) .	Law Journal Reports, Old Series, King's Bench 1822–30	
L.J.P.C. .	Law Journal Reports, Privy Council 1831–1947	
L.J.Q.B. .	Law Journal Reports, Queen's Bench 1837–1900	
L.J.R. .	Law Journal Reports . . . 1947–49	
L.R.C.P. .	Law Reports, Common Pleas Cases . . 1865–75	
L.R. Eq. .	Law Reports, Equity Cases . . 1865–75	
L.R. Ex. .	Exchequer Cases 1865–75	
L.R.H.L. .	House of Lords, English and Irish Appeals 1866–75	
L.T. . .	Law Times Reports . . . 1859–1947	
L.T. News .	Law Times Newspaper . . . 1843–1965	
L.T.O.S. .	Law Times, Old Series 1843–59	
M. & Gr. .	Manning and Granger 1840–44	
M. & W. .	Meeson and Welsby 1836–47	
Mer. . .	Merivale 1815–17	
Moo. & M. .	Moody and Malkin 1826–30	
Moo. & R. .	Moody and Robinson 1830–44	
Nev. & M. (K.B.)	Neville and Manning 1832–36	
Peake Ad. Cas. .	Peake's Additional Cases. . . 1795–1812	
Q.B. . .	Queen's Bench . 1891–1900, 1952—current	
Q.B.D. .	Queen's Bench Division 1875–90	
R.S.C. .	Rules of the Supreme Court	
R.R. .	Revised Reports 1785–1866	
Russ. .	Russell 1823–29	
S.C. . .	Session Cases . . . 1906—current	
S.C. (H.L.) .	Session Cases (House of Lords) . 1907—current	
S.L.T. .	Scots Law Times . . . 1893—current	
Sc.L.R. .	Scottish Law Reporter . . . 1865–1924	
Scott (N.R.) .	Scott's New Reports 1840–45	

Part One

INTRODUCTORY

CHAPTER 1

Principles of Good Lending

1-1. Although the purpose of this book is to set forth the legal and practical considerations relating to securities for bankers' advances, it is appropriate to state briefly, by way of introduction, those canons or principles of good lending which guide bank officials in determining whether a proposed loan is desirable, irrespective of whether or not security is offered.[1]

1-2. When a request for a loan is received, it is important to ensure that the borrower has the necessary legal capacity to borrow; for example, if the customer is a limited company a careful study of its memorandum and articles of association must be made.[2] The other matters upon which information should be obtained are as follows: the purpose of the advance, the amount involved, the duration of the advance, the source of repayment, the profitability of the transaction, and the security offered, if any. These points will be examined briefly.

Purpose of the Advance

1-3. First, the purpose must be one which is satisfactory from the banker's aspect, and secondly, certain Government controls exist, which may make it impossible to grant a particular advance even though it is perfectly sound from the point of view of banking policy.

A. THE BANKER'S ASPECT

1-4. The traditional role of banks in the United Kingdom is to provide short-term capital for commerce and industry. Thus a loan to a manufacturer to enable him to buy raw materials, or to a trader for the purchase of additional stock, may be quoted as illustrating the primary function of the banks, whereas a loan to a customer for the purchase of a house, repayable over a period of, say, twenty years, would not be granted. Building societies and other specialised institutions make long-term loans.[3]

---

[1] For a useful series of articles, see L. S. Dyer, "A Practical Approach to Bank Lending," *Journal of the Institute of Bankers*, Vol. 90 (1969), pp. 443–49, Vol. 91 (1970), pp. 69–74, 142–48, 225–31, 309–18, 380–86.

[2] See Vol. 1, paras. 11-270/72.

[3] See *post*, paras. 1-25/31.

1-5. Furthermore, a bank is not a money-lender in the narrow sense of that term, and considerable care must be exercised with small unsecured advances to customers who are in salaried positions but who have no capital resources. With rare exceptions, loans of this sort should not be made. At the outset, they look harmless enough. A cheque is presented for payment which overdraws a customer's account to the extent of five or six pounds a few days before his salary is due. No arrangement for an overdraft has been made, but the banker, relying upon the expected payment of salary, may decide to honour the cheque. Next month, the account is ten or twelve pounds overdrawn, and, in this way, the position gradually deteriorates. Many small bad debts have been incurred through allowing accounts of this nature to get out of control. The soundest policy is usually to write to the customer when the account first becomes overdrawn requesting him to make a payment to credit and, at the same time, informing him that it is not the practice of the bank to pay cheques which overdraw an account, unless prior arrangements have been made and suitable security deposited.

1-6. Unsecured advances to professional men—such as solicitors, accountants, and surveyors—are usually to be avoided for similar reasons, unless, of course, it is known that they are men of substance. It is often a good plan to suggest to a young professional man the advisability of taking out an insurance policy on his life. When several premiums have been paid and the policy has acquired a surrender value, it may be deposited as security for temporary accommodation. As a general rule, the amount of the loan against the security of the policy should be sufficiently below its surrender value to leave some margin to cover (say) a year's premiums and a year's interest on the loan. It is true that, in the event of the customer's untimely death, the full amount of the policy would become payable, but the most serious risk which a banker runs when making advances to men in this position is that of prolonged illness. This causes an immediate drop in earning capacity and very often makes it impossible for future premiums to be paid—unless, indeed, the bank is prepared to lend more money for this purpose.

B. GOVERNMENT CONTROLS

1. *Lending to foreign undertakings*

1-7. Sect. 30 (3) of the Exchange Control Act, 1947, provides that, except with the permission of the Treasury, no person resident in the United Kingdom may lend any money, Treasury bills or securities to any company which he knows, or has reason to think, is controlled from somewhere outside the scheduled territories. By virtue of the Exchange Control (Scheduled Territories) Order, 1967, as amended,[4] these territories are as follows: the United Kingdom, the Channel Islands and the Isle of Man; the Commonwealth of Australia; Barbados; Botswana; Ceylon; the Republic of Cyprus; the Gambia; Ghana; Guyana; Iceland; India (including Sikkim); the Republic of Ireland; Jamaica; the Hashemite Kingdom of Jordan; Kenya; the State of Kuwait; Lesotho; the United Kingdom of Libya; Malawi; Malasia; Malta; Mauritius; New Zealand; Nigeria; Pakistan; Sierra Leone; Singapore; the Republic of South Africa and the territory of South West Africa; the People's Republic of Southern Yemen; the United Republic of Tanzania; Trinidad and Tobago; Uganda; Western Samoa; Zambia; any part of Her Majesty's dominions not mentioned above, except Canada and Southern Rhodesia; and any protectorate, protected state or trust territory within the meaning of the British Nationality Acts, 1948 and 1958. The main object of this control is to ensure that foreign undertakings wishing to expand their activities in the United Kingdom provide the bulk of the requisite funds in foreign currency rather than by borrowing in sterling.

2. *"Directives" and "Special Deposits"*

1-8. During the Second World War the banks agreed, at the request of the Chancellor of the Exchequer, not to grant advances for any purpose which was not in furtherance of the war effort. Since the war, the Chancellor has written to the Governor of the Bank of England from time to time asking him to draw the attention of the banks to the principles of lending which it is considered desirable that they should follow in the light of current economic conditions. Thus the banks are sometimes asked to reduce their advances to bring them down to a stated percentage of their advances on a prior specified date. The control may be applied selectively; for example, advances to the nationalised industries or to finance exports may be exempt. Those "directives" or "requests" are not legally binding, but in practice they are faithfully observed by the banks. If necessary, they could be enforced by a direction from the Bank of England under Sect. 4 of the Bank of England Act, 1946.[5]

1-9. In 1958 it was announced that a new device was to be used in future if a general restriction of bank credit became necessary.

---

[4] The amendment is by S.I. 1968, No. 333.

[5] For an article questioning the power of the Bank of England to issue directives for the purpose of implementing a credit squeeze, see E. C. Woods, "A Banking Myth," *The New Law Journal*, Vol. 119 (1969), pp. 207–8.

Briefly, the new system, which was brought into operation for the first time in 1960, is as follows.[6] Initially, each London Clearing bank was required to transfer to an immobilised special account at the Bank of England, by a specified date, the equivalent of one per cent, and each Scottish bank the equivalent of one-half per cent, of its gross deposits, while continuing to observe the accustomed cash ratio and minimum liquidity ratio. The amount deposited, which bears interest at the current Treasury bill rate rounded to the nearest one-sixteenth per cent, is adjusted each month to maintain it at the prescribed percentage; and the percentage itself is varied from time to time by further calls or releases. In effect, therefore, the Special Deposits scheme is, as Sir Ralph Hawtrey has expressed it, "a forced loan from the banks."[7]

1-10. In 1968 it was announced that a somewhat similar system of control would be extended to other banks, including the merchant banks, the British overseas banks and the American and other foreign banks.[8] These banks agreed to place with the Bank of England, when called upon to do so, cash deposits calculated as a percentage of their various deposit liabilities. A single ratio is normally to be used for all these banks, but the Bank of England reserves the right to demand a higher percentage for any single bank. The Bank will pay interest on the deposits at a rate equivalent to the rate on Treasury bills. However, this rate will only be paid so long as the Bank considers that the response to its guidance on lending is sufficient; a lower rate may be paid if the response is insufficient.

3. *Borrowing (Control and Guarantees) Act*, 1946

1-11. By virtue of this Act, certain bank advances require the express permission of the Treasury. Fortunately, the instances where this permission is required are comparatively rare. The combined effect of Sect. 1 of the Act and of the Control of Borrowing Order, 1958, is that a person must not borrow in Great Britain any amount exceeding £50,000 in any one year without the permission of the Treasury. This prohibition applies not only to borrowing from a bank but also to *borrowing from any other source*: in other words, a person's total borrowing must not exceed £50,000 a year without

[6] For useful articles, see Sir Ralph Hawtrey, "New Credit Measures and the Balance of Payments," *The Bankers' Magazine*, Vol. CLXXXVI (1958), pp. 91–6; "How the 'Special Deposits' Plan Originated," *The Banker*, Vol. CX (1960), pp. 323–36; Paul Bareau, "The Economic Scene," *Journal of the Institute of Bankers*, Vol. 81 (1960), pp. 159–65.
[7] See *The Bankers' Magazine*, Vol. CLXXXIX (1960), at p. 418.
[8] "Control of Bank Lending: the Cash Deposits Scheme." *Bank of England Quarterly Bulletin*, June, 1968, pp. 166–170.

Treasury permission. If the stipulated amount is exceeded, the borrower is liable to a fine and/or imprisonment, but the lender can still recover his money.

1-12. If the matter rested there, very many overdrafts would require Treasury permission. There are, however, exceptions, the most important of which (as far as the lending banker is concerned) are as follows—

1. Loans by a bank to a customer, other than a local authority, "in the ordinary course of his business." The vast majority of loans in excess of £50,000 by banks to their customers come within this exception and do not, therefore, require Treasury permission.

2. Loans to any person, other than a local authority, repayable on demand or not more than six months after demand which are either wholly unsecured or secured only by a bill of exchange or promissory note.

3. Loans to local authorities for the purpose of defraying expenditure pending the receipt of their revenues.

4. Loans to personal representatives for the payment of death duties.

1-13. Further changes were made in relation to the control of borrowing as from 6th February, 1959, when the control of borrowing by persons and companies resident in the United Kingdom virtually came to an end. Borrowers from outside the United Kingdom still have to apply for permission when seeking to raise more than £50,000 in any period of twelve months. Control on domestic borrowing is retained only on local authorities' borrowing on the stock market; for this, Treasury consent is still required. This relaxation of the controls was achieved by means of a "general consent" issued by the Treasury. The Control of Borrowing Order, 1958, has been kept in existence, so far as it affects domestic borrowing, and it is there ready to hand if at some future time the Government need to make use of it again. In 1970 the 1958 Order was amended by an Order which removed the exemption from control of the borrowing or raising of money by the issue of non-sterling securities by or on behalf of investment trust companies resident in the scheduled territories but outside the United Kingdom.[9]

1-14. In the rare cases where Treasury permission is still required, application should be made by letter to the Capital Issues Committee. The name and address of the borrower, the nature of his business, the amount and purpose of the proposed borrowing and

---

[9] Control of Borrowing (Amendment) Order, 1970.

the security offered must be stated in the application, which is usually prepared by the borrower's solicitor or accountant. If the Capital Issues Committee decides to grant permission, this is given in the form of a letter. When the debenture or other security is presented to the Stamp Office for *ad valorem* stamping, this letter is usually required by that office as evidence that the borrowing has been approved.

Amount of the Advance

1-15. An important matter for consideration is whether the amount is likely to be sufficient for the given purpose. Customers often underestimate their requirements and then find that additional borrowing is necessary.

1-16. Then one must consider whether the proposed amount is reasonable in relation to the customer's own resources. It is sometimes said that if a customer is in business on his own account—perhaps he is a farmer or a retail tradesman—the amount of the advance should not exceed a quarter of his own resources. But, in practice, this proportion is often exceeded, and every case must be dealt with on its merits.

1-17. It may be necessary to obtain from the customer a statement of his assets and liabilities. Often it will be found that his accounts are prepared annually by a qualified accountant. This makes it easier to ascertain his financial position, but even then it should be remembered that the accountant frequently has to rely upon his client's statements for a good deal of the necessary information. A professionally-prepared balance sheet, through no fault of the accountant, does not necessarily tell "the truth, the whole truth, and nothing but the truth."

1-18. When lending money to large trading concerns—partnerships or more usually limited companies—a much more detailed investigation is necessary. It is essential to obtain copies of the balance sheets and of the trading and profit and loss accounts for at least the three previous years. The interpretation of balance sheets is a matter calling for considerable skill and experience.[10] Broadly speaking, there are two methods of approach to any balance sheet; these should be regarded as complementary and not alternative.

[10] The subject is too extensive for detailed attention in this book. The reader is referred to specialised works and, in particular, to J. H. Clemens, *Balance Sheets and the Lending Banker* (4th ed., 1968); L. C. Mather, *The Lending Banker, A Review of the Principles of Bank Lending, Unsecured Advances and Balance Sheets and the Banker* (3rd ed., 1966); James Dandy, *The Branch Banker—Studies in Bank Lending* (1960).

1-19. First, the business should be viewed as a going concern. The primary object is to find out the amount of the customer's working capital. A list of those assets which are easily realisable (such as bank balances, investments, stock, and trade debtors) should be prepared, and the total should be compared with the total of the short-term liabilities, such as trade creditors. The working capital is the excess of easily-realisable assets over short-term liabilities. The larger this surplus, the healthier is the customer's position from the banking standpoint. If there is no surplus, the business is probably in need of a more permanent form of capital than that normally provided by a bank. Nevertheless, it is unwise to be dogmatic on this point, because circumstances vary so greatly. In practice, many small concerns suffer from lack of working capital, but advances can sometimes be arranged on a satisfactory basis. On the other hand, it is often more prudent for a banker to decline to grant accommodation in such a case and to draw his customer's attention to the need for more permanent capital.

1-20. Secondly, if the "going concern approach" shows a satisfactorily liquid position, the next step is to try to estimate the dividend likely to be paid to the bank in respect of its advance in the event of the customer's bankruptcy or liquidation. This involves valuing the assets on a break-up basis, ignoring fictitious assets such as formation expenses and an adverse balance on profit and loss account. It is, of course, important to find out whether any of the customer's present creditors are secured. This second approach is intended to provide a final guide to the risk which will arise if the business fails. The main difficulty is that it is frequently impossible to say how much the assets would fetch if a forced sale became necessary. The test does not provide conclusive evidence as to the advisability or otherwise of granting accommodation; it is merely a guide to be considered in relation to all the other circumstances.

1-21. A careful analysis of the trading and profit and loss accounts will help to show not only whether the business is expanding or contracting but also whether it is being run on sound lines. Thus—

1. Year by year the turnover of the concern (i.e. work done or goods sold) should be compared with the amount of debtors as shown in the balance sheets. It is often an unhealthy sign if the proportion of trade debts to turnover is rising; this may indicate that some of the customer's debtors are finding it difficult to meet their commitments.

2. Turnover should be compared with the amount owing to creditors. If the proportion of trade creditors to turnover is rising,

this probably means that the customer is not meeting his liabilities promptly and that some of his creditors are pressing for payment.

3. It is usually a danger signal if the proportion of stock to turnover rises year by year. An excessive amount of stock usually indicates either sales resistance or stockpiling beyond the customer's resources. Whether an excessive amount of stock is being carried depends to some extent upon the nature of the business. As one writer aptly said, "a whisky distillery advertising 'Not a drop sold till it's seven years old' will have a rate of stock turnover much slower than that of a fishmonger advertising 'Fresh fish daily'."[11]

Duration of the Advance

1-22. The general rule is that bankers' advances are repayable on demand, and some banks insist that their managers bring this fact to the notice of the borrower in every case. This occasionally leads to uneasiness on his part. Suppose that a customer has requested accommodation to the extent of £3,000, and promises to reduce the loan by £1,000 per annum. Let it be assumed that, in all respects, the transaction is considered to be satisfactory from the banker's standpoint. Does it serve any useful purpose to inform the customer that the bank retains the right to demand the repayment of *the whole sum at any time*? Probably the most convenient way of dealing with this problem is to inform the customer that the bank has a right to claim repayment at any time and that the agreed reductions over the specified period represent the bank's *minimum* requirements. Having said this, one is quite justified in then telling the customer that, as long as he honours his part of the transaction, it is most unlikely in practice that the bank will require the loan to be repaid at an earlier date.[12]

1-23. With their deposit liabilities repayable upon demand or at seven days' notice, the Clearing banks have always taken the view that bank finance for trade and industry should, as far as possible, be confined to the provision of working capital or to short-term bridging finance, pending the realisation of an asset or the raising of permanent capital. The banks have, however, co-operated in the setting up of specialist institutions which were formed for the purpose of providing medium and long-term finance. These institutions are listed below.[13] Moreover, there are some special categories of

---

[11] H. H. Hutchinson, "Interpretation of Balance Sheets," *Journal of the Institute of Bankers*, Vol. LXXV (1954), p. 305.

[12] See also Vol. 1, para. 1-69.

[13] *Post*, paras. 1-26/30.

borrowers to whom the banks are prepared to grant credit facilities well beyond the usual period. Thus medium-term credits of two to eight years are granted in order to finance the export of capital equipment manufactured in this country. Much of this finance for the export of capital goods is arranged at a fixed rate of $5\frac{1}{2}$ per cent against a guarantee from the Export Credits Guarantee Department.

1-24. The Shipbuilding Industry Act, 1967, laid the basis for a scheme for the provision by the Clearing banks and the Scottish banks of medium and long-term credit, at a fixed low rate of interest, for British shipowners placing orders for new tonnage in British shipyards. Bank loans, usually repayable over a period of eight years from delivery of the ship, are supported by guarantees from the Ministry of Technology, given on the recommendation of the Shipbuilding Industry Board.

1-25. Long-term loans for the purchase of dwelling-houses are primarily the function of building societies. Medium and long-term finance for industry is made available through the following specialist institutions—

A. INDUSTRIAL AND COMMERCIAL FINANCE CORPORATION LTD.

1-26. This company (usually known as "I.C.F.C.") normally deals with advances from £5,000 up to £200,000; its capital is subscribed by the principal English and Scottish banks.

B. FINANCE CORPORATION FOR INDUSTRY LTD.

1-27. This company (usually known as "F.C.I.") is concerned with larger proposals; its capital is owned by a group of insurance companies, investment trusts, and the Bank of England.

C. SHIP MORTGAGE FINANCE CO. LTD.

1-28. The capital of this company was subscribed by a number of insurance companies, the I.C.F.C., the Shipbuilding Conference, and other City interests. Its main object is to assist British ship-owners by providing finance, upon completion of construction, of ships being built in United Kingdom shipyards. Loans are made only on the security of first mortgages. In suitable cases, loans are also made on first mortgages of existing ships built in the United Kingdom. Subject to the approval of the Exchange Control, the company is prepared, in approved cases, to make loans to foreign

shipowners in respect of ships constructed or to be constructed in
the United Kingdom.

D. AIR FINANCE LTD.

1-29. The capital of this company was subscribed by the F.C.I., a
group of merchant banks and a number of leading firms in the aircraft industry. The primary object of the company is to enable
manufacturers of aircraft and aero engines to offer extended credit
facilities to foreign buyers.

E. AGRICULTURAL MORTGAGE CORPORATION LTD.

1-30. The capital of this company was subscribed by the Bank of
England and the joint-stock banks. Its primary purpose is to make
loans on first mortgages of agricultural or farming estates, properties,
or lands in Great Britain, and to make loans in accordance with the
Improvement of Land Acts, 1864 and 1899, for effecting or paying
for improvements for agricultural purposes. The company has no
power to grant loans on the security of crops or stock.

F. THE BANKS' FINANCE COMPANIES

1-31. During 1965–67 the Clearing banks set up subsidiary companies
(or, in the case of some of the banks, started to use existing subsidiary companies) for the purpose of accepting time deposits and
making term loans. These subsidiary companies are often referred
to as the banks' finance companies.[14]

Source of Repayment

1-32. The next point upon which information will be required before
a banker accedes to a request for accommodation is the source from
which repayment is promised. In some instances, repayment will
be effected by the sale of some specific asset in the near future; for
example, where a customer proposes to sell the house in which he
lives and to buy another, his banker may agree to finance the
purchase of the second house on the understanding that the loan
is repaid, in the course of the next three or four months, out of the
proceeds of sale of the first house. Temporary, self-liquidating
advances of this sort are often called "bridgeover" advances.
Other illustrations of such advances are: an advance against the
security of debentures which are to be redeemed in a few months'

---

[14] See Vol. 1, paras. 10-136/43.

time, an advance against the security of a life policy which is to mature in the near future, or an advance to a trading company for capital purposes pending the raising of permanent capital by the company. These self-liquidating advances give little or no trouble, and they afford a good illustration of the primary function of banks in this country—the provision of short-term finance.

1-33. Quite often a customer asks for accommodation to provide him with additional working capital for trading purposes, and he undertakes to repay the advance out of profits over a period. The rate at which the customer can reasonably hope to repay should be ascertained. Let us suppose that he asks for an overdraft of, say, £5,000 for the purchase of additional stock. An examination of his audited accounts may show an average annual profit of, say, £2,500. It is not unusual for a customer in this position hopefully to assert that he will be able to repay the bank in a matter of two or three years. But when, in the course of further conversation, he admits that his personal expenses amount to about £2,000 per annum, it becomes clear that the most he could do would be to offer repayment at the rate of £500 per annum. It does not follow that a transaction of this nature would necessarily be declined; so much would depend upon the circumstances of the particular case. However, it serves to emphasise that considerable care has to be exercised when interviewing prospective borrowers, for, as a class, they are notoriously sanguine concerning their ability to repay. In particular, they frequently forget to take taxation into account when making their calculations.

Profitability of the Advance

1-34. Interest on advances is, of course, the main source of a bank's revenue, and a bank official must ensure that the rate of interest agreed with the customer provides a satisfactory return to the bank. Banks in this country make a practice of lending money at an agreed rate per cent over Bank rate, subject to a minimum; for example, the terms agreed between the bank and the customer may be two per cent over Bank rate, minimum five per cent. The terms quoted in any particular case will depend upon various factors, including the size of the advance, the financial strength of the customer, and the nature of the security offered, if any.

1-35. The interest paid by the customer is not intended to remunerate the bank for services other than the loan of the money. One has to ensure that such services as the payment and collection of the customer's cheques, agency facilities, and so forth, are properly remunerated by way of commission or service charge.

Security for the Advance

1-36. Security for a proposed advance should normally be required, even though the borrower's financial position appears to be sound; a borrower's position can, and sometimes does, change very quickly. The appropriate time to obtain security is at the outset, when the loan is being negotiated. It follows, therefore, that a study of the law and practice relating to securities is an essential part of a banker's training.

1-37. In conclusion, however, it must be stressed that the most important qualification of a successful banker is, and always has been, the ability to judge the character and credit-worthiness of his customers. Natually, personal knowledge of the borrower is of less importance in granting secured advances than in making loans without security, but, in both types of lending, it is desirable to satisfy oneself, as far as is reasonably possible, from a careful consideration of all the relevant facts, that the borrower is capable of effecting repayment in accordance with his promise. In other words, any security should be regarded as a last line of defence to fall back upon in exceptional circumstances only. To lend money against security knowing full well that one is likely to have to realise that security is bad banking practice. The realisation of securities is sometimes a lengthy, costly, and complicated business.

Part Two

LAND

CHAPTER 2

Definition of Terms

2-1. THE word "land" when used by lawyers has a much wider meaning than it has in everyday speech. The general rule of English law on this matter is summed up by the maxim *quicquid plantatur solo, solo cedit* (whatever is attached to the soil becomes part of it). If, therefore, a building is erected upon land and chattels are attached to the building, the term "land" prima facie includes the soil, the buildings, and the chattels affixed thereto. Similarly, "land" includes growing crops and timber.

Tenures

2-2. The theory of English law is that all land in England is still owned by the Crown. In former times the Crown used to grant lands to its subjects in return for certain services. To some extent these services became standardised. The nature of the service to be rendered determined the type of "tenure," as it was called. For example, there was one set of services which became known as "grand sergeanty" where the tenant was obliged to perform in person some service for the king of an honourable nature, such as carrying his banner or leading his army. Another tenure, which was eventually to become the most important of all, was that of "common socage" where the tenant was, as a rule, bound to perform some agricultural service. Gradually, these agricultural services were commuted for money payments, which were usually called "quit rents," indicating that the tenant was "quit," or free, from his services. In the course of time these sums ceased to be paid, chiefly because, with the fall in the value of money, they were not worth collecting.

2-3. The complicated system of tenures was modified by legislation, and the present position is that, for all practical purposes, there is only one true example of the old tenures remaining to-day, namely, socage—more commonly called "freehold."[1] However, most

---

[1] The only other type of tenure of any practical importance in modern times was copyhold. All copyhold land was converted into land of freehold tenure by the Law of Property Act, 1922, Sect. 128 and 12th Sched. para. (1). For a fuller discussion of the history of tenures, see R. E. Megarry, *A Manual of the Law of Real Property* (4th ed., 1969), pp. 9–13.

modern writers regard leasehold as a tenure. From the historical aspect this is perhaps inaccurate, or at least, misleading, since leaseholds remained outside the feudal system of tenures. Nevertheless, there is something to be said in favour of treating leasehold as a tenure, on the ground that leaseholds present the only surviving example of the relationship of lord and tenant which has any practical significance. Finally, there is crownhold, a tenure invented by the Leasehold Reform Act, 1967[2] to denote land which has been compulsorily acquired by the Land Commission and regranted by the Crown subject to statutory restrictions. In this book, therefore, modern tenures will be classified as—

(i) freehold, in respect of which all the old feudal incidents have, with very minor exceptions, disappeared;

(ii) leasehold, in respect of which a rent is payable by the tenant to the landlord, the latter having power, as a general rule, to forfeit the lease if his tenant fails to fulfil his obligations; and

(iii) crownhold.

Estates and Interests in Land

2-4. It has been shown that tenure denotes the relation between lord and tenant. This doctrine of tenures implies that a person whom a layman would, in everyday language, call the "owner" of land does not actually own it. What in fact he owns is some right in the land called an "estate" or an interest. These rights in land vary according to the time during which they are to continue to exist. Thus, it may be said that the term "estate" denotes the duration of an interest in land. At the present day, there are three freehold[3] estates or interests—

A. THE ESTATE IN FEE SIMPLE

2-5. This is the largest estate known to the law and is the nearest approach to absolute ownership that English law permits. Thus when we say that X is "tenant in fee simple" of Blackacre, we mean that he is the person who, in popular language, is said to be the owner of the land.

B. THE FEE TAIL

2-6. This continues to exist only so long as the original tenant or

---

[2] Sects. 17–21.

[3] "Freehold" in this connection has nothing to do with freehold (or socage) *tenure*. It is merely that the same word is used to express sometimes the quality of the tenure, and sometimes the quantity of the estate." Megarry, op. cit., p. 14.

any of his descendants survives. As a result of Sect. 1 of the Law of Property Act, 1925, it is no longer possible for a legal fee tail to exist. After 1925, all entails must exist behind a trust. The legal estate in fee simple must be vested in some trustee or trustees on trust for the person entitled in tail and everyone else interested in the land. Accordingly, instead of referring to an "estate tail," one usually refers at the present day to an "entailed interest."[4]

C. LIFE INTERESTS

2-7. The two types of life estate came into existence where land was limited to a tenant for his own life or for the life of another person. Both types of life estate were estates of freehold. Like entails, they must now exist behind a trust, and they are usually referred to as "life interests."

2-8. In addition to the aforementioned freehold estates and interests, there are the various forms of leasehold estates. The commonest example is where a tenant holds land for a fixed term of years, as under a lease for 999 years.

Legal and Equitable Estates and Interests

2-9. The distinction between legal and equitable estates and interests can only be explained by a brief reference to legal history. In former times the law was administered, for the most part, by the Courts of Common Law on the one hand, and by the Court of Chancery on the other. The Court of Chancery administered a system of justice called Equity, and the rights and interests which it recognised became known as "equitable" rights and interests, as distinct from those recognised by the Common Law Courts, which were known as "legal" rights. In the sphere of land law, therefore, a legal estate was one protected by the Common Law Courts, whereas an equitable estate was one protected by the Court of Chancery.

2-10. It would serve little useful purpose to examine in detail how and why the Court of Chancery granted recognition to certain rights which were not recognised at common law. The classification of estates into legal and equitable was profoundly affected by the 1925 legislation, and much of the old learning on the subject has become obsolete. The only two legal estates which can exist to-day are (i) the estate in fee simple absolute in possession, and (ii) the term of

[4] Megarry, op. cit., p. 42.

years absolute.[5] Thus, the person whom the layman would call the owner of a freehold or leasehold property is the owner of a legal estate. There is, of course, nothing to prevent some other person or persons from enjoying equitable interests in such property at the same time. Suppose, for example, that the fee simple in Blackacre is vested in X and Y who hold it on trust for Z. X and Y own the legal estate, but Z, being a beneficiary under a trust, has an equitable interest in Blackacre.

2-11. Although, as shown above, there are only two legal *estates* which can exist in land, there are, in addition, certain legal *interests* therein which may be created.[6] Among these is the charge by way of legal mortgage. It is still possible (as it was prior to 1926) to create an equitable mortgage. The practical distinction, as will be seen later, consists in the different remedies available to the respective mortgagees, a legal mortgagee enjoying, as a rule, wider and more effective remedies than an equitable mortgagee.

Title Deeds

2-12. Except in the case of "registered land" (for which see Chapter 10), a landowner's title is evidenced by a bundle of documents known as title deeds. These documents show previous transactions in the land, such as sales and mortgages. The most recent document is usually the one which indicates how the present owner acquired the property. For example, if he obtained the land by purchasing it, there will be a deed called a *conveyance* executed by the vendor and transferring to the purchaser the vendor's interest therein; whereas, if he acquired the property as a gift under the terms of someone's will, there will be an instrument known as an *assent*, executed by the personal representatives of the testator, which has the effect of transferring the former interest of the deceased to the beneficiary. When land is offered to a bank as security for a loan, the customer's title deeds should be carefully examined either by the bank or by its solicitors; the general principles to be followed when investigating title are considered later.[7]

2-13. When title deeds are lost or destroyed, the question arises as to how title to the land can be established. The usual practice of conveyancers, in such a case, is to obtain a declaration under the Statutory Declarations Act, 1835, from the person last known to

---

[5] Law of Property Act, 1925, Sect. 1.
[6] Ibid.
[7] *Post*, paras. 3-15/20.

have had the documents in his custody.[8] The wording of the declaration must, of course, depend upon the circumstances, but it will, as a rule, identify the documents and state when they were last seen and whether they were examined and found to be complete. In addition, it is nearly always possible to obtain secondary evidence of some of the deeds, such as abstracts of them. In some cases, the solicitor who acted for the present owner may be able to make a declaration that he acted for the present owner when he purchased the property, that a good title was deduced at the time and that he completed the purchase on or about a certain date and passed the deeds to the purchaser after the conveyance had been duly stamped. When the necessary evidence has been obtained, it is quite usual for the owner to apply to the Land Registry for registration of his title.

Distinction between a Mortgage and a Charge

2-14. A mortgage is a conveyance of a legal or equitable interest in property as security for the payment of a debt or for the discharge of some other obligation. The borrower is called the "mortgagor" and the lender the "mortgagee."

2-15. A charge is frequently regarded as a particular type of mortgage. There is, however, one important difference between a mortgage and a charge. The former is a conveyance of an interest in property subject to a right of redemption (that is, a right to have the interest reconveyed upon repayment of the loan or discharge of the obligation), whereas the latter conveys nothing but merely gives the "chargee" certain rights over the property.

Land as Security

2-16. Bankers used to be very much averse to accepting land as security. "The rule of a banker," wrote J. W. Gilbart, "is never to make any advances, directly or indirectly, upon deeds, or any other dead security."[9] The prejudice against this form of security no longer exists, and, provided that a sound case for accommodation has been made out, a modern banker has no hesitation in taking, by way of security, a mortgage of land.

2-17. When stating the advantages and disadvantages of land as security, it is not easy to generalise, because so much depends upon the type of property offered. An advantage which land enjoys over

---

[8] For an informative article see E. O. Walford, "Missing Title Deeds," *The Conveyancer and Property Lawyer*, Vol. 13 (1949), pp. 349–62.

[9] J. W. Gilbart, *The Logic of Banking* (1859), p. 194. However, Gilbart admitted that there were certain exceptions to the rule which he laid down.

certain other forms of security is that, over a period of years, it tends to increase in value. As the value of money falls, so the value of property rises. Compare land, in this respect, with a guarantee. A guarantee for, say, one hundred pounds can never be worth more than that sum. However, it is said that there are the following drawbacks to land as security—

2-18. The main disadvantage is that property is not easily realisable. This can be a serious drawback from the bank's point of view, but it depends, to a large extent, upon the particular type of property involved. Good investment property—houses and shops—can usually be sold without much difficulty, whereas industrial buildings put to a specialised use may be difficult to realise.

2-19. Secondly, it is often difficult to make an accurate valuation of land and buildings.

2-20. Thirdly, there is the expense involved from the customer's standpoint. A mortgage deed attracts *ad valorem* stamp duty at the rate of 2s. (10p) per cent.[10] In addition to this, the customer will often have to pay the fee of the bank's solicitor for examining and reporting upon title. In some cases, he will also have to pay for a professional valuation of the property.

2-21. Fourthly, there is a risk that the bank may fail to get a good title under its mortgage. This would arise, for example, where, owing to some technical irregularity in connection with previous dealings with the property, the customer himself had failed to obtain a good title. However, this risk is very slight, because any such defects should normally be revealed if (as is usual) the title is examined by the bank's solicitors.

2-22. Fifthly, it is sometimes said that there is a tendency for borrowings against property to become long-term mortgage loans. But this is hardly a valid objection; loans against other types of security may equally become long-term advances, unless proper control is exercised.

2-23. Sixthly, if a customer mortgages to the bank the house in which he lives and subsequently makes default in repaying his overdraft, the bank is usually reluctant to obtain from the court an order for possession, i.e., in order to realise its security. Such a claim sometimes gives rise to unwelcome publicity if the case is reported in local newspapers.

2-24. Lastly, the making of improvement grants by local authorities

10 See *post*, para. 33-24.

may, oddly enough, prejudicially affect the value of dwelling-houses held as security by a bank. This is a complicated subject, which cannot be explained in detail here. Briefly, local authorities may make improvement grants under Sects. 30–42 of the Housing (Financial Provisions) Act, 1958. If they do so, certain conditions automatically apply to the houses for a period of twenty years, and these conditions may prejudicially affect a mortgagee. The main effect of the conditions is that the house must be kept available for letting to a tenant at a controlled rent during the next twenty years when it is not occupied by the owner or a member of his family or a person becoming entitled to it under his will or on his death intestate. The result is that a purchaser can only take the property as an investment and not for his own occupation. If, therefore, a customer obtains an improvement grant in respect of a house which is mortgaged to a bank, the bank should re-value the security on a "without vacant possession" basis.

CHAPTER 3

Taking the Security

3-1. WHEN a banker is offered land and premises as security for an advance, the first matter he normally ascertains is their value. If this is satisfactory, he will decide whether to take a legal or an equitable mortgage, and he will satisfy himself that the customer has a good title to the property. Finally, the mortgage has to be drawn up and executed, and, in some cases, it must also be registered.

Valuation of the Property

3-2. It is not within the scope of this book to make a detailed examination of valuation problems.[1] Attention will merely be drawn to some of the points to be borne in mind when valuing various types of land and premises.

3-3. Sometimes a mortgage of house property is taken without any actual inspection of the premises, particularly if the customer is of good standing and the house is in his own occupation. In many cases nothing could be more irksome to him than to be told that an official of the bank wishes to come to his home to make a valuation. Furthermore, care should be exercised if it is decided to inspect a house which the customer has let to a tenant and is mortgaging to the bank. Nothing should be said in the presence of the tenant to give the slightest indication that his landlord is about to mortgage the house. If an examination of the interior of the house *is* really essential, the safest course as a general rule is to arrange for the landlord to take an official of the bank to see it. Sometimes an inspection of the exterior of the property is sufficient.

3-4. The salient points to be considered when valuing house property are based upon common sense. Is the property freehold or leasehold? If leasehold, how much is the ground rent, and how long has the lease to run? When did the property last change hands, and

---

[1] For a series of useful articles, see A. Forrester Fergus, "Valuation of Real Property," *Journal of the Institute of Bankers*, Vol. LXXII (1951), pp. 91–7, 164–9, 215–21. See also L. C. Mather, *Real Property as Bank Security and the Finance of Building Development* (being the Spring Lectures delivered before the Institute of Bankers in 1955), pp. 11–21; and Dennis N. Byrne, *Valuations for Mortgage Purposes* (being the second of the Autumn Lectures delivered before the Institute of Bankers in 1966), pp. 19–36.

at what figure? Was a high price paid for the benefit of vacant possession? Is the house being kept in a good state of repair? Are water, gas, and electricity laid on? Has the road been taken over by the local authority, or will there be a liability for heavy road charges? Is the character of the neighbourhood rising or falling? Are transport facilities good? Is there a garage or, at any rate, room for one to be built? If the house is let, does it fall within the provisions of the Rent Act?[2]

3-5. The valuation of shops and industrial premises is a more complicated subject. One's approach to the problem depends, in the first instance, upon whether it is proposed to value the property at its worth to its present owner or at its forced sale value. Bankers have usually maintained that all securities should be valued on the assumption that the customer's business has failed and that the bank is obliged to sell the assets concerned in the open market. Logically, there is much to be said for this view.

3-6. When taking a mortgage of business premises as security for a large overdraft, banks sometimes employ a professional valuer. In fact, some banks have one or more surveyors in their own service. Although a valuer's report may be helpful, a word of caution is needed. Valuation methods do not constitute an exact science, and it implies no disrespect if one ventures to suggest that valuers differ from each other in their opinions even more widely than lawyers do. However elaborate a valuation of business premises may be, it serves but a limited purpose. The real security is not the land and buildings, but the stability of the business itself. A careful study of the customer's financial position—as revealed in his balance sheets and profit and loss accounts—is often worth a good deal more than any number of professional reports on the value of the business premises.

Legal or Equitable Mortgage?

3-7. If the bank is satisfied as to the value of the property, the next point to decide is whether the mortgage is to be legal or equitable. From the lender's point of view, the advantages of the legal mortgage are such that, unless the borrower raises strong objection to it, this is the type of mortgage which should, with rare exceptions, be insisted upon. Indeed, some banks make it a rule that branch managers must not take an equitable mortgage without the prior consent of a Head Office official; other banks leave the matter to the discretion of the branch manager.

[2] See *post* paras. 7-34/38.

3-8. The outstanding advantage of a legal mortgage is that, if the advance is not repaid, the banker, as legal mortgagee, is in a position to sell the property or to appoint a receiver to collect the rents arising from it. These powers can be exercised without any court proceedings. If a banker merely takes an equitable mortgage under hand, he is in a much less powerful position: to sell the property or to appoint a receiver, he needs the assistance of the court.[3] Unless, therefore, the advance is for a very short period and the customer is of undoubted integrity, it is clearly in the bank's interest to obtain a legal mortgage and so to be in a position, should occasion arise, to enjoy the speedier remedies of a legal mortgagee.

3-9. If a customer objects to executing a legal mortgage, he usually does so on one of two grounds. First, the *ad valorem* stamp duty on a legal mortgage is 2s. (10p) per cent as compared with only 1s. (5p) per cent on an equitable mortgage under hand.[4] Secondly, he is sometimes most reluctant to create a legal mortgage, because, even after the advance is repaid, the mortgage deed, duly discharged, forms part of his title to the property and is a clear indication to anyone who may purchase from him that he borrowed money upon mortgage. An equitable mortgage, on the other hand, does not come upon the title in the future. It is amazing how "touchy" a borrower sometimes is in this respect.

Equitable Mortgage under Seal

3-10. In order to enjoy most of the advantages of a legal mortgage without inflicting upon the customer the "stigma" of having it upon his title in the future, some banks make use of a special type of equitable mortgage *under seal* which virtually gives the bank the same powers as does a legal mortgage. The drafting of this type of equitable mortgage under seal may be the more easily understood by first examining the position of a legal mortgagee as compared with that of an equitable mortgagee whose mortgage is executed under hand. The equitable mortgagee has no power of sale and no power to appoint a receiver, because he has no legal estate or interest in the property. Not having a legal estate himself, he cannot convey one to a purchaser. The main object of the equitable mortgage under seal is to enable him to do so, and the desired result is achieved in practice by inserting either or both of the clauses mentioned below.

---

[3] The remedies of mortgagees are considered in detail in Chapter 7.

[4] But sometimes it is cheaper to execute a legal mortgage because of the advantages of collateral stamping: see *post*, para. 33-34.

3-11. The first clause embodies a power of attorney whereby the mortgagor irrevocably appoints someone (usually an official of the bank) to sell or grant leases of the property as his agent or to execute a legal mortgage thereof. This power of attorney should be filed at the Central Office, unless it relates to one property only and is to be handed over on the completion of the transaction.[5]

3-12. The second clause contains a declaration of trust wherein the mortgagor acknowledges that he holds the property upon trust for the bank and, at the same time, empowers the bank to remove him from the trust and to appoint some other person as trustee.

3-13. Either clause enables the bank to deal with the legal estate. This type of equitable mortgage, being under seal, requires stamping at the same rate as a legal mortgage.

Solicitors' Undertakings

3-14. Sometimes a bank advance is made for the purpose of enabling a customer to purchase property. The necessary funds are paid to the customer's solicitors, and it is quite usual to ask them to give their written undertaking to apply the money for the sole purpose of acquiring the property, and upon completion of the purchase to send the title deeds and/or the land certificate direct to the bank. The following is the usual form of undertaking which is addressed by the customers' solicitors to the bank—

> If you provide facilities to my/our client...
> for the purchase of the freehold/leasehold property.............................
> .... I/We undertake—
> (*a*) that any sums received from you or your customer for the purpose of this transaction will be applied solely for acquiring a good marketable title to such property and in paying any necessary deposit, legal costs and disbursements in connection with such purchase. The purchase price contemplated is £.................... gross and with apportionments and any necessary disbursements is not expected to exceed £...................., and
> (*b*) after the property has been acquired by ....
> and all necessary stamping and registration has been completed to send the title deeds and/or land certificate and documents to you and in the meantime to hold them to your order.

---

[5] Law of Property Act, 1925, Sect. 125. If, however, the land is registered under the Land Registration Act, 1925, filing at the Land Registry is sufficient. Where the power is to deal with both registered and unregistered land, it should be filed at the Central Office, and an office copy at the Land Registry.

Investigation of Title

3-15. As soon as the title deeds are available, the banker's first task is to arrange for them to be examined in order to ensure that the customer has, in fact, a good title to the property in question. The examination of title deeds requires, in many cases, specialised knowledge, and, as a general rule, the deeds should be sent to the bank's solicitors who should be requested to prepare a report on title. If the property has been purchased recently by the customer, some bankers ask the customer's solicitors, who have investigated the title for him, to sign a certificate of title for the bank. This saves expense and duplication of work.

3-16. Where the loan is made for a short period and the title does not appear to be complicated, it may be considered unnecessary to seek a professional report on title. In such cases some banks permit their managers to examine the deeds instead of the bank's solicitors. Even in other cases the customer may wish to have permission to overdraw his account before there is time for the bank's solicitors to examine the deeds and submit their report. For these reasons it is essential for bank officers to be familiar with the general principles relating to the examination of title deeds.

3-17. Normally, upon opening a parcel of deeds, one finds what is called an abstract of title. This important document is a summary or epitome of all the documents, such as wills and conveyances, which have dealt with the title; it also recites the events, such as births, deaths, and marriages, which affect the title. The abstract must start with a good root of title, which may be defined as "a document which deals with the whole legal and equitable interest in the land, describes the property adequately, and contains nothing to throw any doubt on the title."[6] This document ought to be at least fifteen years old, because a purchaser under an open contract (that is to say, a contract which, *inter alia*, prescribes no special length of title) can insist upon having a good root of title at least that old[7] and upon seeing all documents subsequent thereto which affect the legal estate.

3-18. A conveyance by way of sale is, in practice, the most usual root of title. A legal mortgage is equally satisfactory, since it may be assumed that the mortgagee was satisfied at the time that his mortgagor had a good title. An equitable mortgage is not a good root of title. A *general* devise of land is not a good root of title, and

---

[6] R. E. Megarry, *A Manual of the Law of Real Property* (4th ed., 1969), p. 62.
[7] Law of Property Act, 1925, Sect. 44 (1), as amended by Law of Property Act, 1969, Sect. 23.

never was so, because it does not identify the property. A *specific* devise, on the other hand, is a good root of title, provided that the testator died before 1926. In the case of a testator who died after 1925, it is the written assent of the personal representatives which passes the legal estate. That assent will constitute a good root of title, whether the devise was specific or general, but a purchaser or mortgagee should also inspect the probate to see that there are no endorsements thereon. When leaseholds are sold, the vendor is obliged to abstract the lease, however old it may be; but in an open contract he cannot be required to prove the title to the freehold.[8]

3-19. After the document which forms the root of title has been abstracted, the remaining documents which affect the legal estate are listed in chronological order, together with recitals of those births, deaths, and marriages which are necessary to trace the devolution of the property to its present owner. Legal mortgages must be abstracted even though they have been discharged. Equitable mortgages, on the other hand, should not be abstracted, provided they have been discharged. Furthermore, it is not the practice to abstract expired leases. The various documents should be carefully examined to see that they describe the property adequately, that they have been executed by the parties named therein, and that they are properly stamped.

3-20. Finally, when a lender is offered, as security, land which he believes is unregistered, he should apply, on Land Registry Form No. 96, for an official search of the index map of *registered* titles. This will show whether, unknown to the lender, title to the land has been registered. Many lenders omit this precaution, relying upon the practice of the Land Registry to mark with their stamp the last document in the chain of title immediately preceding registration.[9] The precaution of making a search of the public index map is more necessary in a compulsory than in a non-compulsory area.[10] The Land Registry have remitted all fees in connection with these official searches in compulsory areas.

Planning Legislation

3-21. The general rule laid down in Sect. 13 (1) of the Town and Country Planning Act, 1962 (re-enacting earlier legislation) is that no development of land may take place without planning permission. "Development" is very comprehensively defined by the Act as

---

[8] Law of Property Act, 1925, Sect. 44 (2).
[9] *Post*, para. 10-16.
[10] See T. B. F. Ruoff, *Concise Land Registration Practice*, (2nd ed., 1967), p. 60.

meaning "the carrying out of building, engineering, mining, or other operations in, on, over or under land, or the making of any material change in the use of any buildings or other land."[11] Thus the broad general principle is that, if an owner wishes to build upon his land or to make alterations, or to put his land to some different use, he must obtain the prior consent of the local planning authority. If, for example, he owns a house which he wishes to use as a café, he needs permission. Similarly, he requires consent before he may divide a house into flats.[12] There are, however, many exceptional cases which only a detailed study of the Act and of the various Orders made under it will reveal.

3-22. If it appears to a local planning authority that development has been carried out without the grant of the necessary permission, the authority may serve on the owner and occupier of the land an "enforcement notice."[13] This notice may require the land to be restored to its original condition; it may order the demolition or alteration of any buildings; and, finally, may require the discontinuance of an offending user.

3-23. The Act may affect a mortgagee prejudicially, unless he takes steps to ensure that its provisions have been complied with. In some cases an owner may have altered the use to which his property is put in complete ignorance of the Act. Suppose that an owner of a house commences to use it as a café without obtaining plannning permission. The property, with the goodwill, may become worth two or three times its value as a private house. He then offers to mortgage it to his bank as security for an advance. After the mortgage has been executed and the advance has been granted, the local planning authority discovers the change of user and serves an enforcement notice requiring the café to be discontinued. In such a case, the value of the security may drop by a half or even more.

3-24. When investigating a title a prudent mortgagee should, therefore, try to guard against the risk that some unauthorised development may have taken place. The Law Society and the Clearing banks have made recommendations on the extent of the planning investigation which a solicitor should ordinarily be expected to undertake when making a report to a bank on title. A list of the agreed questions normally to be answered has been published.[14]

---

[11] Sect. 12 (1).
[12] Sect. 12 (3).
[13] Town and Country Planning Act, 1968, Sect. 15.
[14] See *The Law Society's Gazette*, February, 1956, pp. 79–81, *Journal of the Institute of Bankers*, Vol. LXXVII (1956), pp. 92–4.

3-25. Another precaution which a mortgagee should take, when investigating title, is to examine the development plan for the area prepared by the local planning authority. The plan may show, perhaps, that the land has been designated for compulsory acquisition. Such a designation would almost certainly make the land unattractive from a purchaser's point of view: and one of the main objects of a mortgagee should always be to have a security which is easily realisable.

Searching the Land Charges Register

3-26. Another important step in the investigation of title is that of making any necessary "searches." The object of searching is to discover the rights, if any, of third parties which are enforceable against the land. The general principle is that a purchaser or a mortgagee of land is deemed to have actual notice of all third-party rights which are capable of registration and are in fact registered, whereas he acquires his interest in the land free from third-party rights which are capable of registration and are not in fact registered.

3-27. The most important search to make is that of the registers in the Land Charges Department of the Land Registry in London. Special considerations apply to (i) mortgages of *registered* land,[15] (ii) mortgages created by limited companies,[16] and (iii) mortgages of land in Yorkshire.[17]

3-28. There are two methods of searching these registers. By far the most usual practice is that of filling up Form L.C. 11 and sending it by post to The Superintendent, Land Charges Registry, Station Approach Buildings, Station Approach, Kidbrooke, London, S.E.3. This results in the issue of an official search certificate which shows whether or not there are any entries outstanding on the registers. Alternatively, one may visit the Department personally and conduct the search oneself. However this is seldom done, partly because of the time involved and partly because it is much safer to search by post: an official search certificate is "conclusive" in favour of a purchaser (including a mortgagee).[18] Thus an applicant will not be bound by any registered charges which are not referred to in the official certificate.

3-29. There are five registers kept in the Land Charges Department

[15] See Chapter 10.
[16] See *post*, paras. 32-19/22.
[17] See *post*, paras. 3-63/65.
[18] Land Charges Act, 1925, Sects. 17 (3) and 20.

under the provisions of the Land Charges Act, 1925,[19] but there is no necessity to send in separate requisition forms for each register. The one form is effective for securing an official search certificate in respect of all the registers.[20]

3-30. Practical difficulties arise because the registers in the Land Charges Department are registers of names and not of properties. Thus a charge affecting Blackacre, a freehold property situated in Deansgate, Manchester, and owned by John Smith, will be indexed under "John Smith" provided—and this is important—that he was the owner of Blackacre at the time when the charge was created. It is obvious, therefore, that if Smith is proposing to mortgage Blackacre, the mortgagee should search against the name of "John Smith." If the land is owned by partners, trustees, or other joint owners, search should be made against the names of them all. On the requisition form the mortgagee should enter the full names of the persons in respect of whom a search is desired.

3-31. The cost of searching by post in the usual way is 3s. (15p) per name. The fee is normally paid by purchasing from a post office the necessary fee stamp and affixing it to Form L.C. 11. The result of a search will be telegraphed or telephoned if desired; the additional fee for a telegram to any part of the country is 9s. (45p) per application, and for a reply by telephone to any part of the country 6s. (30p) per application. Personal searches cost 3s. (15p) per name.[21]

3-32. In the parcel of title deeds one normally finds an official certificate of search in respect of each change of ownership of the property. Suppose William Robinson was the owner of Blackacre in 1925 and that he sold to Smith in 1954. One would expect to find a certificate of search, dated 1954, against the name of William Robinson. However, when the banker (or his solicitor) examines the title deeds to-day, he may find no such certificate. Is he justified in assuming that, when Blackacre was conveyed to Smith in 1954, the necessary search was in fact made against the name of William Robinson? The risk is, of course, that this may not have been done and that there may still be some charge against the name of William Robinson which affects Blackacre to-day even though Robinson has long ceased to be the owner.

3-33. It is sometimes said that searches should be made against the name of every owner since 1st January, 1926. The practical difficulty is that, in cases where a property has changed hands frequently, the

---

[19] Sect. 1.
[20] For details of these registers see *post*, paras. 3-40/55.
[21] For the full list of fees, see Land Charges Fees Order, 1970.

number of missing search certificates may be considerable. The author suggests that it would be prudent to search against the names of all who have owned the land since the date of the transaction which constitutes the root of title[22]—but only, of course, in those instances where the appropriate certificate is missing from the parcel of deeds.

3-34. Sometimes it is argued that search should also be made against the names of all legal mortgagees (except banks and building societies) since 1st January, 1926. The theory is that, having acquired a legal estate or a legal interest in the property, the mortgagee might have sub-mortgaged it. The then owner might (it is said) have paid off his mortgage debt without the knowledge of the sub-mortgagee who would still retain an interest in the land.[23] This possibility is very remote. The sub-mortgagee would only have registered his interest if he had not obtained the title deeds, and this very seldom happens.

When to Search

3-35. Another practical question which is frequently raised is at what time the search should be made. If one searches *before* the mortgage is executed, there is a risk, albeit a very slight one, that some interest of a third party may be registered between the date of search and the date of execution. A special provision to overcome this difficulty was inserted in the Law of Property (Amendment) Act, 1926.[24] The present effect of the Act, as amended by the Land Charges Rules, 1940, is that, where a prospective mortgagee obtains a search certificate and the mortgage is executed within fourteen days after the date of the certificate, he is not affected by any entry made in the register between the date of the certificate and the date of execution, unless that entry is made pursuant to a "priority notice" on the register before the certificate is issued. Any person intending to make application for the registration of any charge or other interest under the Land Charges Act, 1925, may lodge a "priority notice" with the Registrar. This must be done at least fourteen days before the creation of the charge. Then, if the

---

[22] For "root of title," see *ante*, para. 3-17. If a purchaser or mortgagee suffers loss as a result of the existence of a registered land charge of which he did not know, he may be entitled to compensation under the Law of Property Act, 1969, Sect. 25. This compensation is paid by the Chief Land Registrar. To qualify for compensation, the purchaser or mortgagee must have made the usual searches for whichever is the longer of (*a*) a period starting with a good root of title at least fifteen years old, or (*b*) the period for which he stipulated.
[23] For sub-mortgages see Chapter 9.
[24] Sect. 4 (2).

chargee registers his charge within twenty-eight days of the entry of the priority notice in the register, the registration dates back to the date when the charge was created. The reason why the notice must be given fourteen days before the charge is created is to allow for the expiration of the fourteen days' period of protection available to anyone who may have made an official search before the priority notice was lodged.

3-36. If the provision of the 1926 Act applies to banking advances, its effect may be illustrated as follows: On 1st May a customer brings to the bank his title deeds of Blackacre and an agreement for overdraft is made, the loan to be secured by a mortgage of the property; the customer is asked to call on 10th May to execute the mortgage. In the intervening period the title is examined and the official search certificate dated, say, 4th May, shows "no subsisting entries." If the customer executes the mortgage on 10th May (or on any day up to 18th May), the bank will not be affected by any interest which may have appeared in the register during that period.

3-37. It has been doubted, however, whether this protection applies to bankers' advances by way of fluctuating overdraft. The late Mr. R. W. Jones drew attention to the special provisions in the Law of Property Act, 1925,[25] which apply to mortgages made expressly for securing a current account or other further advances. A mortgagee under such a mortgage who makes a further advance is not to be deemed to have notice of a second mortgage merely because it was registered at the time of such further advance, provided that it was not registered "at the time when the original mortgage was created or when the last search (if any) by or on behalf of the mortgagee was made, whichever last happened." If it was not for this rule, a banker would be obliged, as Mr. Jones pointed out, to search before he paid each cheque. Having considered this aspect of the 1925 Act, Mr. Jones reached the conclusion that the fourteen days' grace allowed by the 1926 Act does not apply to advances by way of fluctuating overdraft. His advice to bankers was, therefore, to ensure that the search certificate is dated after, or contemporaneously with, the mortgage—never before it.[26]

3-38. As against this view it might be urged that the provisions in the two Acts are designed to serve two entirely distinct purposes: the 1926 Act deals with the date of the search certificate in relation to the date of the mortgage, and the 1925 Act obviates the necessity

[25] Sect. 94 (2) as amended by the Law of Property (Amendment) Act, 1926, Sect. 7 and Sched. For further details of these provisions, see *post*, para. 5-12.

[26] R. W. Jones, *Studies in Practical Banking* (1947), p. 137. Mr. Jones omitted this advice in his last (1951) edition of the book.

to search each time a cheque is paid. On this basis it might be argued that there is no reason for regarding them as mutually exclusive. However, difficulty arises when one tries to apply the provisions to a specific problem. In the hypothetical case already stated the search certificate was dated 4th May, and the mortgage was executed on 10th May. Let it be supposed that, between those two dates, some charge in favour of a third party was registered. On these facts there seems to be little doubt that, in respect of the amount of the *initial* overdraft (i.e. the first cheque which overdraws the account) the bank is protected by the 1926 Act. But when the next cheque is presented, a further search would be necessary if it was not for the provision of the 1925 Act. And that Act only affords protection if the charge in question was not on the register at the time when the mortgage was executed or when the last search was made, *whichever last happened.* The charge *was* on the register before the mortgage was executed, and so it seems that the bank's claim to protection would fail.

3-39. For this reason it is the established practice of bankers to search *after* the mortgage has been executed. It would be more convenient for bankers to be able to follow the practice of mortgagees who are not lending on current account and to search a few days *before* the execution of the mortgage. The present position whereby bankers are denied the benefit of the fourteen days' grace is unfortunate, and there seems to be a case for remedial legislation to remove this anomaly.

Entries Revealed by the Search

3-40. In most cases, the search at the Land Charges Department reveals "no subsisting entries." A brief reference must, however, be made to what might come to light. As already indicated, there are five separate registers. They are—

A. REGISTER OF PENDING ACTIONS

3-41. These are actions pending in court relating to any interest in land. A person who claims that he is entitled to land and who brings an action to enforce his rights may register it as a pending action. The result is that, if the present owner tries to sell the land, the purchaser will have notice of the third party's claim. Similarly, a petition in bankruptcy may be registered in the register of pending actions.

3-42. It is very seldom indeed that a search reveals any entry in this register. Certain annuities charged upon land and created before 1926 required registration here, but no new entries have been made since then. Any annuities created after 1925 are registrable as Class C (iii) land charges (see below), provided that they do not arise under a settlement or a trust for sale.

C. REGISTER OF WRITS AND ORDERS AFFECTING LAND

3-43. This register contains entries of various writs and orders enforcing judgments and orders of the courts. Thus an order appointing a receiver is registrable therein, as also is a receiving order in bankruptcy.

D. REGISTER OF DEEDS OF ARRANGEMENT

3-44. A debtor who is being hard pressed by his creditors sometimes makes an arrangement with them whereby they agree to release him from his debts if he pays a certain proportion of the money owing to them—say 50p in the pound. For this purpose he assigns his property to a trustee who distributes it to the creditors. The arrangement, if reduced to writing, is known as a deed of arrangement.

E. REGISTER OF LAND CHARGES

3-45. There are six classes of land charges, A, B, C, D, E, and F. Classes C, D, and F are of greater practical importance than the others.

Class A
3-46. These consist of charges upon land created as a result of the application of some person under the provisions of an Act of Parliament. Thus a charge upon land under Sect. 72 of the Agricultural Holdings Act, 1948, is a Class A charge.[27]

Class B
3-47. These consist of certain charges imposed automatically by statute. They are rare.

[27] See *post*, para. 5-24.

Class C

3-48. These charges are subdivided thus—

C (i) *Puisne Mortgages.* Puisne mortgages are legal mortgages of a legal estate in land where the mortgagee does not obtain possession of the title deeds. As a first mortgagee nearly always obtains the deeds, puisne mortgages are almost invariably second or third mortgages.

C (ii) *Limited Owners' Charges.* A limited owner's charge is an equitable charge which a tenant for life or other statutory owner acquires by discharging, out of his own pocket, certain liabilities such as death duties.

C (iii) *General Equitable Charges.* These are equitable charges which (*a*) are not secured by a deposit of documents relating to the legal estate, (*b*) do not arise under a trust for sale or a settlement, and (*c*) are not included in any other class of land charge. An illustration is an equitable mortgage of a legal estate in land where the mortgagee does not obtain possession of the title deeds.

C (iv) *Estate Contracts.* An estate contract is defined as "any contract by an estate owner, or by a person entitled at the date of the contract to have a legal estate conveyed to him, to convey or create a legal estate." Thus if the owner of the legal estate in Blackacre enters into an agreement for the sale thereof, this contract is registrable as a C (iv) charge.

Class D

3-49. These charges are subdivided thus—

D (i) *Death Duties.* The Commissioners of Inland Revenue may register a charge for estate duty but, in practice, they seldom do so.

D (ii) *Restrictive Covenants.* Any covenants or agreements entered into after 1925 which restrict the user of land are registrable unless made between a lessor and lessee.

D (iii) *Equitable Easements*, if created after 1925. An illustration is a right of way. If the easement is perpetual and is created by deed, it is a legal interest and is not registrable.

Class E

3-50. These charges comprise annuities charged upon land created *before* 1926 but not registered until *after* 1925.

Class F

3-51. These charges are those affecting houses by virtue of the Matrimonial Homes Act, 1967. The rights of occupation given to a spouse by the Act are a charge on the estate, and this charge is registrable.

3-52. It remains to consider what steps one should take if the official search certificate indicates that a charge is subsisting on one of the registers in the Land Charges Department. The certificate will reveal only the type of charge, and, if it is thought desirable to find out the precise nature and terms of the charge, application must be made to the Department on Form L.C. 14 for an office copy of it. The fee is 3s. (15p). If it is necessary for a copy of a plan to be supplied, an additional fee, varying with the amount of work involved, will be payable.

3-53. The entries which might most prejudicially affect the bank are the Class C (i), C (iii), and F land charges. Thus, if the customer has, unknown to the bank, already mortgaged the property to a third party without depositing the deeds, that mortgagee should have registered his mortgage either as a C (i) charge or as a C (iii) charge, according to whether his mortgage is legal or equitable. This state of affairs involving a fraudulent concealment by the customer of a prior mortgage is, however, not the only possible explanation of the subsisting entry. It may be found to relate to a mortgage which has long since been discharged. If this is so, steps should be taken to ensure that the person in whose favour it was created has it removed.

3-54. If a search reveals a Class F charge, the Matrimonial Homes Act, 1967[28] provides that a spouse who is entitled to this type of charge may agree in writing that any other charge shall rank in priority to the charge to which he or she is entitled. Unless the spouse who is entitled to the charge is prepared to agree that the bank's charge is to rank in priority to his or her charge, the house will not usually be an acceptable security.

3-55. In practice the Class D (ii) charge is the one which is most frequently revealed. If the premises are being used for business or professional purposes, an office copy of the entry should be obtained to find out whether those purposes constitute a breach of the restrictive covenant in question. If, on the other hand, the property consists of dwelling-houses, there is not the same risk of breach of covenant, and whether or not an office copy should be obtained is a matter for individual discretion. In most cases, the abstract will reveal the nature of the covenant.

[28] Sect. 6 (3).

Searching the Registers of Local Land Charges

3-56. Registers of local land charges are kept by all district, borough, and county councils. Unlike the registers in the Land Charges Department at the Land Registry in London, the registers of the local authorities are registers of properties and not of persons. Thus no question arises of making a number of searches against successive owners. The fee for an official search certificate is 10s. (50p) in respect of each parcel of land; alternatively it is possible to make a personal search for a fee of 4s. (20p).[29] If the land is in the area of a county borough, one search only is necessary—in the register at the local Town Hall. If it is in the area of a county district (non-county borough, or urban or rural council) two searches are necessary—at the local district council offices, and also at the county council offices.

3-57. The charges which are capable of registration are those acquired by any local authority by Act of Parliament. They include such items as charges in respect of money spent on making up a road, or in respect of improvement grants made by local authorities, and various matters under the Town and Country Planning Act, 1968, such as enforcement notices,[30] tree-preservation orders, and buildings-preservation orders.

3-58. Whether or not a mortgagee should search the local land charges registers will depend to some extent upon the type of property offered as security. If it has been built recently, there is always the possibility that charges may have been registered in respect of expenditure on roads. But even so, if the amount of the loan as compared with the value of the property shows a considerable margin, there is little point in spending time and money on searching.

3-59. A graver risk is that arising from the registration of matters under planning law. Moreover, a search of the local authority registers will not reveal all planning matters which are important to lenders. A careful study should be made of the development plans of the various local planning authorities in whose areas one is lending, because those plans reveal many matters that are likely to be of importance to a potential lender with regard to the land: they show, for example, which land is designated for compulsory purchase. Provision is made by the Town and Country Planning (Development Plans) Regulations, 1965, for the plans to be available for inspection, free of charge, at a convenient place within the area

[29] Local Land Charges Rules, 1968.
[30] See *ante*, para. 3-22.

covered by the plan. It is also provided that copies of the plan are to be made available for sale to the public at a reasonable cost.

3-60. When submitting the form of requisition for an official search for local land charges, it is usual to send to the local authority, at the same time, a list of inquiries covering a wide variety of matters which may affect the land. Thus, it may be important to ask whether the highways (including footpaths) abutting the property are maintained by the council; if not, whether the council has resolved to make them up at the cost of the frontagers. Printed forms of inquiry are published by the Solicitors' Law Stationery Society Ltd. The Law Society advises solicitors to use these forms. Some banks have prepared somewhat similar forms of their own. Local authorities charge a fee for answering these inquiries. In the case of borough or district councils the fee for answering inquiries relating to one parcel of land is normally 15s. (75p). Where the inquiries relate to several contiguous parcels of land and they are delivered on a single form the fees are—

> For the first parcel of land . . 15s. (75p)
> For each additional parcel of land . 3s. 9d.

3-61. In the case of county councils the fee for answering inquiries relating to one parcel of land is normally 12s. (60p). Where the inquiries relate to several contiguous parcels of land and they are delivered on a single form the fees are—

> For the first parcel of land . . 12s. (60p)
> For each additional parcel of land . 3s. (15p)

Registration of the Mortgage

3-62. In the case of a mortgage (whether legal or equitable) which is protected by deposit of the title deeds, the general rule is that, unless the mortgagor is a limited company, no registration thereof is required in any register.[31] On the other hand, a mortgagee whose mortgage is not accompanied by a deposit of the deeds must register his mortgage as a land charge at the Land Charges Department of the Land Registry in London; such mortgages are almost invariably second or third mortgages and they are considered in Chapter 8.

Land in Yorkshire

3-63. Certain special rules apply to mortgages of land in Yorkshire, other than the City of York itself, in respect of which the procedure

---

[31] For mortgages of land by limited companies, see *post*, paras. 32-19/22.

is the same as for land outside Yorkshire. The county is divided into three Ridings, North, East, and West. In each Riding (at Northallerton, Beverley, and Wakefield respectively) there is a deeds registry in which are registrable all documents that create or transfer a legal estate. This means that all legal (but not equitable) mortgages of land in Yorkshire (except in York), whether or not they are protected by a deposit of the title deeds, require registration at the deeds registry covering the area in which the land is situated. Thus the outstanding difference between a legal mortgage of land in Yorkshire and land elsewhere is that, even though the mortgagee obtains the deeds, he must register his mortgage. If he fails to do so and the mortgagor creates a second mortgage in favour of a mortgagee who does register, the second mortgage takes priority over the first.[32] The Law of Property Act, 1969,[33] contains provisions which will eventually lead to the closure of the Yorkshire deeds registries. In each Riding of Yorkshire the relevant Deeds Registry will continue until it is closed either by the operation of an Order extending compulsory registration under the Land Registration Acts to that Riding, or by a statutory instrument made by the Lord Chancellor at the request of the county council. Until closure of a Deeds Registry, a puisne mortgage created on or after 1st January, 1970, should be registered in the appropriate Deeds Register, and it may be registered also in the land charges section of the Deeds Registry, no fee being payable for the latter registration. After the closure of a Deeds Registry, all new land charges should be registered in the Registry in London, and registration without fee may be made in the London Registry to protect those puisne mortgages created on and after 1st January, 1970 and before the closure of the Deeds Registry which were registered during that period in the Deeds Register and not in the land charges section of that Deeds Registry.

3-64. Equitable mortgages are on a rather different footing. The Land Charges Act, 1925,[34] as amended by the Law of Property (Amendment) Act, 1926,[35] provides that "in the case of a general equitable charge, restrictive covenant, equitable easement or estate contract affecting land within any of the three ridings . . . registration shall be effected in the prescribed manner in the appropriate local deeds registry" instead of being registered in the Land Charges Register in London. Thus an equitable mortgagee of land in Yorkshire who obtains the deeds (unlike a legal mortgagee in a similar case) does not need to register, but an equitable mortgagee

[32] Yorkshire Registries Act, 1884, Sect. 14.
[33] Sects. 16–22.
[34] Sect. 10 (6).
[35] Sect. 7 and Sched.

who does not obtain the deeds must register. The Law of Property Act, 1969,[36] makes provision for the eventual transfer of the registers of land charges from the Yorkshire deeds registries to the Land Charges Department of the Land Registry in London.

3-65. It follows from the foregoing account of land in Yorkshire that the searches to be made when investigating title to land there differ from the searches necessary in other cases. A search should be made in the appropriate local registry at Northallerton, Beverley, or Wakefield as the case may be. A personal search is possible, or, alternatively, postal application may be made for an official search certificate.[37] This search would reveal, for example, any legal mortgages, any equitable mortgages not accompanied by the title deeds, or any restrictive covenants affecting the land. A search should also be made in the registers in the Land Charges Department of the Land Registry in London.[38]

Insurance of the Property

3-66. If land which is being mortgaged to a bank has buildings upon it, they should be fully insured in respect of fire. If the insurance company is a member of the British Insurance Association, there is no need for the bank to send the policy to the company to have the bank's interest endorsed thereon. There is an arrangement between the banks and the British Insurance Association whereby the banks merely notify member companies of their interest in policies. Member companies inform the banks if policies in respect of which notice has been given, are not renewed. Furthermore, each company keeps the bank's interest in the policy covered, pending receipt of instructions from the bank. If the bank requires the cover to be continued, the bank is responsible for seeing that the renewal premium is paid; if further cover is not required, the bank gives formal notice of cessation of its interest in the policy. This scheme applies to policies issued by branches of the member companies situated within the United Kingdom (including the Channel Islands, the Isle of Wight and the Isle of Man) and Eire.

3-67. If the insurance company is not a member of the British Insurance Association, the bank usually sends the policy to the company for the bank's interest to be endorsed thereon. Alternatively, the bank may notify the company by letter of the bank's interest. The company will not notify the bank if the policy is not

[36] Sect. 17 (2).
[37] Yorkshire Registries Act, 1884, Sects. 19–21.
[38] See *ante*, para. 3-28.

renewed, and therefore the bank must make its own arrangements to ensure that this is done. The best course is to persuade the customer to sign a standing order authorising the bank to pay the premiums to the debit of his account.

3-68. It does not follow that the only type of policy on which the bank's interest as mortgagee should be endorsed is the fire policy. In the case of hotels and public houses, it is quite usual to find that the licence is insured. Moreover, plate glass in shop windows is sometimes the subject of insurance. Whether the bank will require to have its interest endorsed on these policies will depend upon the circumstances of each case.

Ground Rent or Chief Rent Receipts

3-69. In the case of leasehold property it is important to ensure that the ground rent has been paid up to date. The last receipt in respect of the rent should be produced by the customer, and he should be asked to forward subsequent receipts to the bank to be placed with the title deeds. As with insurance premiums, a suitable diary note should be made.

3-70. Generally no rent is payable in respect of freehold property, but in certain parts of the country—particularly in Manchester and Bristol—it has been a common practice for the purchaser of a fee simple, instead of paying a lump sum, to enter into a covenant to pay a perpetual annual rentcharge, usually called a chief rent, or, alternatively, a fee farm rent. The payment thereof is secured by a right of entry. If freehold property subject to chief rent is mortgaged to the bank, steps should be taken to ensure that the rent is duly paid.

Executing the Mortgage

3-71. All legal mortgages involve the execution of a deed, as also do equitable mortgages under seal. A deed is a document which requires to be signed, sealed, and delivered. Attestation by a witness, though not essential, is usual. In order to execute the deed, the customer should, strictly speaking, sign it, touch the wafer seal with his finger and say "I deliver this as my act and deed" or some other words to show that the deed is intended to be operative immediately. The reason for this requirement is that a deed which has been signed and sealed but not delivered is ineffective. Practice differs from branch to branch in this matter. Some bank officials require customers to go through the formalities described above.

There is, however, an increasing tendency to dispense with them, and there can be very little risk in doing so. If the customer signs the deed and leaves it with the bank, it would certainly be very difficult for him to evade liability on the ground that he had not delivered it.[39]

3-72. A question which is sometimes asked is whether it is necessary or desirable for a bank official to explain to a customer the clauses in the document that he is about to execute. Various clauses commonly incorporated in the mortgage forms of the banks are discussed in the next chapter. The highly technical nature of many of the clauses clearly makes it impossible to go through the mortgage with the customer clause by clause giving a detailed explanation of them. Nor is there any necessity to do so. So long as the customer is aware of the *nature* of the document that he is signing, he will be bound by its terms even though he has not read and understood all its clauses.[40]

3-73. On the other hand, the customer should be given every opportunity of examining the document and of asking questions. If he feels so inclined, he should be permitted to take the form away with him before executing it so that he can read it through and, if necessary, obtain independent legal advice. Furthermore, there is no reason why, having executed the mortgage, he should not be supplied with a copy of the instrument. In the vast majority of cases, however, the customer is content to sign the document without making a detailed examination of it. It is then that the question arises whether the banker should draw his attention to any particular clauses. To some extent this must depend upon the circumstances of the case. However, it is always sound policy to remind him that, in the mortgage, he undertakes to produce the fire insurance receipts —though this would be unnecessary if the bank is to pay the premiums in accordance with a standing order signed by the customer. Again, it is a wise precaution, in some instances, to point out to him that he is precluded from granting leases of the property without the bank's consent.

Mortgages by Joint Tenants and by Tenants in Common

3-74. A bank is sometimes offered a mortgage by co-owners. At the

[39] In *Stromdale & Ball Ltd.* v. *Burden* [1952] 1 All E.R. 59 at p. 62, Danckwerts, J., said: ". . . it appears to me that at the present day if a party signs a document bearing wax or wafer or other indication of a seal with the intention of executing the document as a deed, that is sufficient adoption or recognition of the seal to amount to due execution as a deed."
[40] See *post*, paras. 18-5/6.

present day the two principal types of co-ownership are (*a*) joint tenancy, and (*b*) tenancy in common—

A. JOINT TENANCY

3-75. The distinguishing feature of a joint tenancy is that, on the death of one joint tenant, his interest in the land passes to the other joint tenants by the *jus accrescendi* (that is, "the right of survivorship"). Trustees are invariably made joint tenants because of this rule. It is obviously convenient for the trust property to pass automatically to the surviving trustee or trustees. If a banker is offered as security a mortgage by trustees, he will naturally require to satisfy himself that the money is required for the purposes of the trust and that the borrowing is authorised by the trust deed or by the general law. In this connection Sect. 16 (1) of the Trustee Act, 1925, enacts that "where trustees are authorised by the instrument, if any, creating the trust or by law to pay or apply capital money subject to the trust for any purpose or in any manner, they shall have . . . power to raise the money required by . . . mortgage of all or any part of the trust property for the time being in possession." The section applies notwithstanding anything to the contrary contained in the instrument, if any, creating the trust, but does not apply to trustees of property held for charitable purposes.[41] In general, therefore, unless express powers to borrow money and to mortgage trust property are conferred upon trustees by the will or trust deed, a banker will have to turn to the somewhat limited powers conferred by the Trustee Act, as set out above. Some safeguard is provided for lenders by Sect. 17 of the Act, which provides that no mortgagee advancing money on a mortgage purporting to be made under any trust or power vested in trustees is to be concerned to see that such money is wanted, or that no more than is wanted is raised, or otherwise as to the application thereof.[42]

3-76. Quite frequently, husband and wife take a conveyance of a house as joint tenants, the intention being that the title will vest in the survivor. In this case, and indeed in all others where land is *beneficially* limited for a legal estate to joint tenants, the result is that the land is automatically split up into a legal and an equitable joint tenancy,[43] but the number of persons holding the legal estate

[41] Trustee Act, 1925, Sect. 16 (2).

[42] Instead of obtaining a mortgage of the trust property, a banker is sometimes content to rely upon the joint and several liability of the trustees. For a useful article, see James Dandy, "Finance for Trustees and Others," *Journal of the Institute of Bankers*, Vol. 80 (1959), pp. 92–102.

[43] Law of Property Act, 1925, Sect. 36 (1).

must not exceed four.[44] The parties concerned are trustees for sale
of the legal estate, but as they own all beneficial interest in the
property, a banker can take a mortgage from them without regard
to the legal limitations on trustees' powers of creating mortgages.

B. TENANCY IN COMMON

3-77. Unlike joint tenants, tenants in common have distinct fixed
shares in property which has not yet been divided. There is no *jus
accrescendi*, and so the share of each passes under his will or in-
testacy. If, therefore, two or more persons agree to purchase property which they are to enjoy beneficially, or if a testator leaves a
property to two or more persons in his will, the normal result is the
creation of a tenancy in common.

3-78. As a result of the provisions of the Settled Land Act, 1925,[45]
and the Law of Property Act, 1925,[46] a tenancy in common can only
exist in equity and behind a trust for sale. Thus, if A, B, and C
purchase Blackacre, the legal estate will be conveyed to them as
joint tenants upon the statutory trusts; that is to say, the legal
estate will be held by them upon trust to sell the same and to stand
possessed of the net proceeds of sale and of the net rents and profits
until sale upon such trusts as may be requisite for giving effect to
the rights of the persons interested in the land.[47] The result is that
if A, B, and C provide the purchase money equally, they will each
be entitled in equity to a one-third share of the net proceeds of sale
and to a one-third share of the net rents and profits until sale. The
legal estate which is vested in A, B, and C is indivisible, but there is
nothing to prevent one or more of them from mortgaging his
interest, which is necessarily an equitable interest. The drafting of
the mortgage is invariably left to the bank's solicitors, and it would
be inappropriate to explain here the technicalities involved.

[44] Ibid., Sect. 34 (2).
[45] Sect. 36 (4).
[46] Sect. 34 (1).
[47] Law of Property Act, 1925, Sect. 35.

CHAPTER 4

Bank Mortgage Forms

4-1. IN the preceding chapter an account was given of the practical steps to be followed when taking land as security for an advance. Fortunately for bank officers, the drafting of the mortgage is not their responsibility. All the banks use printed mortgage forms, and the bank officer's duty is to select the correct form, fill in the name of the mortgagor and the description of the land, have the mortgage duly executed and stamped, and finally enter it in the various security records of the bank.

4-2. Nevertheless, customers sometimes ask why a particular clause has been inserted, and, although it may be sound policy in certain cases to recommend them to consult their own legal advisers on these matters, it seems desirable for bank officers to possess at least a general knowledge of the clauses usually employed in bank mortgage forms, rather than to regard them as a meaningless conglomeration of legal nonsense.[1] The purpose of the present chapter is to examine the clauses usually found there and the reasons for their inclusion.

Legal Mortgage of Freeholds

4-3. Under the Law of Property Act, 1925,[2] there are two methods of creating a legal mortgage of freeholds: (*a*) by a demise for a term of years absolute, subject to what is called a provision for cesser on redemption, and (*b*) by a charge by deed expressed to be by way of legal mortgage—

A. MORTGAGE BY DEMISE

4-4. The word "demise," in this connection, means the grant of a lease. Thus the mortgagor grants a lease to the mortgagee for a long term, customarily for three thousand or four thousand years. There is, however, no magic in selecting a period of several thousand years; a term for one million years would have just the same

---

[1] The late Professor Maitland once described a mortgage deed as "one long *suppressio veri* and *suggestio falsi*" (one long suppression of the truth and suggestion of what is false). See F. W. Maitland, *Equity* (revised by John Brunyate, 1936), p. 182

[2] Sect. 85 (1).

practical result. The effect is that the mortgagee acquires a legal estate in the land. The mortgagor retains the legal fee simple, and this is important if he wishes to create further legal mortgages.[3]

4-5. The so-called provision for "cesser on redemption" is simply a clause which provides that the term of years shall cease as soon as the loan is repaid. Although it is still the invariable practice to insert this provision, it appears to be totally unnecessary, because the Law of Property Act, 1925,[4] enacts that on repayment the term becomes a satisfied term and ceases automatically.

4-6. The demise and the provision for cesser on redemption might be worded as follows[5]—

> The Mortgagor as Beneficial Owner hereby demises to the Bank all the property specified in the Schedule hereto to hold the same unto the Bank for the term of 3,000 years from the date hereof subject to the provision of cesser hereinafter contained
> Provided that if the Mortgagor shall on demand pay to the Bank all sums of money which now are or shall at any time be owing to the Bank by the Mortgagor whether alone or jointly with any other person and in whatever name style or firm the term hereby created shall cease

B. CHARGE BY WAY OF LEGAL MORTGAGE

4-7. The alternative method of creating a legal mortgage of freeholds is the charge by deed expressed to be by way of legal mortgage, sometimes called, for the sake of brevity, "a legal charge." This was an innovation of the Law of Property Act, 1925.[6] The wording of the legal charge is shorter and simpler than that of a mortgage by demise; there is, for example, no provision for cesser on redemption. The following is an illustration of the phraseology commonly employed—

> The Borrower as Beneficial Owner hereby charges by way of legal mortgage all the property specified in the Schedule hereto with the payment to the Bank of the principal money interest and other money payable by the Borrower under this Deed

The effect of the Law of Property Act, 1925,[7] is that the lender ("the chargee") obtains the same protection, powers, and remedies as are enjoyed by a legal mortgagee whose mortgage is created by demise.

---

[3] See *post*, paras. 8-6/10.
[4] Sects. 5 and 116.
[5] To save space, the actual wording of the clauses normally found in the banks' forms has been slightly shortened throughout this chapter.
[6] Sect. 87 (1).
[7] Ibid.

4-8. There are the following advantages of employing a legal charge as compared with a mortgage by demise—

1. The document means what it says. This makes it easier for a customer to understand the deed that he is executing. A mortgage by demise, on the other hand, is far from simple to explain to a layman. "Why," asks the customer, "should I have to lease my property to the bank for thousands of years?"

2. Precisely the same form may be used for mortgaging both freeholds and leaseholds. This saves unnecessary duplication of forms, and, furthermore, enables the bank, if it so desires, to take as security a number of freeholds and leaseholds by merely listing them in the schedule to the legal charge. This, in turn, will probably save stamp duty, because there will be only one document to stamp instead of several.

3. The legal charge has a special advantage in relation to leaseholds which is considered below.

4-9. In spite of the advantages of the legal charge, some banks still use the mortgage by demise.

Legal Mortgage of Leaseholds

4-10. Under the Law of Property Act, 1925,[8] there are two methods of creating a legal mortgage of leaseholds, namely, (*a*) by a sub-demise (that is to say, a sub-lease) for a term of years absolute, subject to a provision for cesser on redemption, the term being at lease one day shorter than the term vested in the mortgagor, and (*b*) by a charge by deed expressed to be by way of legal mortgage—

A. MORTGAGE BY SUBDEMISE

4-11. In the case of the mortgage by subdemise, it is the usual practice to make the sub-term ten days shorter than the lease, the object being, so it is said, to allow for second and subsequent mortgages. Thus, if a customer has a lease for ninety-nine years, the first mortgage would be created by a lease of ninety-nine years less ten days, the second by ninety-nine years less nine days, and so on. It seems clear, however, that this precaution of making the sub-term ten days less than the lease is unnecessary, because the Law of Property Act, 1925,[9] expressly confirms the old rule that a lease may take effect in reversion upon another lease of the same or

[8] Sect. 86 (1).
[9] Sect. 149 (5).

greater length.[10] A legal mortgage of leaseholds by subdemise might be drafted as follows—

> The Mortgagor as Beneficial Owner hereby demises to the Bank all the premises comprised in and demised by the Lease specified in the Schedule hereto to hold the same unto the Bank for the residue of the term granted by the said Lease except the last ten days thereof but subject to the provision of cesser hereinafter contained
>
> Provided that if the Mortgagor shall on demand pay to the Bank all sums of money which now are or shall at any time be owing to the Bank by the Mortgagor whether alone or jointly with any other person and in whatever name style or firm the term hereby created shall cease

B. CHARGE BY WAY OF LEGAL MORTGAGE

4-12. The alternative method of creating a legal mortgage of leaseholds, namely by a legal charge, has been explained above. As already indicated, the same wording is appropriate for both freeholds and leaseholds. In the case of leaseholds, there is very often a special advantage in employing a legal charge in preference to a mortgage by subdemise. If the mortgagor holds his term on condition that he will not sub-lease without his landlord's consent, it seems that he must obtain this consent in order to create a mortgage by subdemise; but the Law of Property Act, 1925, Sect. 86 (1) provides that this consent shall not be unreasonably refused. The legal charge, on the other hand, does not involve the granting of a sub-lease, and so the landlord's consent is unnecessary.

Leasehold Reform Act, 1967

4-13. This Act offers occupants of many leasehold houses the right either to buy the freehold of the property, or to have the lease extended by fifty years. The effects upon mortgages are as follows—

A. MORTGAGE OF THE FREEHOLD

4-14. If a leaseholder exercises his right to buy the freehold, the conveyance of the freehold to the leaseholder automatically discharges the premises from any mortgage, even though the mortgagee is not a party to the conveyance.[11] The leaseholder must apply the price payable for the freehold, in the first instance, in or towards the redemption of the mortgage.[12]

---

[10] *Re Moore and Hulm's Contract* [1912] 2 Ch. 105.
[11] Leasehold Reform Act, 1967, Sect. 12 (1).
[12] Sect. 12 (2).

4-15. A mortgage of a leaseholder's interest does not automatically extend to the freehold (if acquired by the leaseholder) or to any extended lease acquired by him. If it is desired that a mortgage should be extended to cover the freehold, this may be done by requesting the mortgagor to execute a deed of substituted security. If a tenant acquires an extended lease under the Act, a mortgagee is entitled to possession of the documents of title relating to the new tenancy.[13] Accordingly, a bank mortgagee should call for these documents when a mortgagor obtains an extended lease; the bank should also require the mortgagor to execute a mortgage of the extended lease.

Special Clauses in Bank Mortgage Forms

4-16. Probably the most striking feature about the mortgage forms used by the banks is that they are remarkably long and, at first sight, complicated documents. The main reason for this is that they have been drafted by the banks' legal advisers in such a way as to confer every possible advantage upon the banks and to deprive the customers (so far as it is legally possible to do so) of every conceivable benefit which would otherwise be secured to them at common law or by statute. In the following pages the more important clauses usually found in these forms will be examined—

A. CONTINUING SECURITY

4-17. In view of the fact that banks frequently lend money on current account by way of fluctuating overdraft, it is the usual practice to state expressly that the security is to be a continuing security. If this was not done, the Rule in *Clayton's* case[14] would apply, and so payments in would be treated as payments towards the discharge of the mortgage debt and payments out would constitute unsecured advances. A clause to exclude the operation of the Rule in *Clayton's* case might be worded thus—

> It is hereby declared that this security shall be a continuing security and extend to cover any sums of money which shall for the time being constitute the balance due from the Mortgagor to the Bank

If the advance was being made by way of loan account, there would, strictly speaking, be no necessity for this clause.

[13] Sect. 14 (6).
[14] (1816) 1 Mer. 572.

B. PERSONAL COVENANT TO REPAY

4-18. Most mortgages contain a covenant by the mortgagor to repay all sums due. In the case of a mortgage to a bank, the covenant may be worded as follows—

> The Mortgagor hereby convenants with the Bank that the Mortgagor will on demand pay to the Bank all sums of money which now are or at any time hereafter may be due from the Mortgagor to the Bank together with all interest commission discount and other Banker's charges

An advantage of inserting the clause is that the words "on demand" make it clear that before the bank can sue the mortgagor it must demand the money. The result is that the Limitation Act, 1939,[15] does not commence to operate against the bank until a demand is made.[16] In the absence of these words, it might be argued that time runs against the bank from the date of each advance.

C. COVENANTS TO REPAIR AND TO INSURE

4-19. These covenants cover a number of important points and may be drafted as follows—

> The Mortgagor hereby covenants with the Bank that at all times during the continuance of this security—
> (i) The Mortgagor will keep any buildings fixtures or machinery which may from time to time form part of the said premises in a good state of repair and in perfect working order and also insured against loss or damage by fire in their full value for the time being in such Office or Offices as the Bank shall approve:
> (ii) The Mortgagor will punctually pay all premiums necessary for the purposes of such insurance and will forthwith on demand produce to the Bank the Policy or Policies of such insurance and the receipt for every such payment:
> (iii) In the case of default by the Mortgagor in keeping any of the said buildings fixtures or machinery in repair the Mortgagor will permit the Bank to enter on the mortgaged property and effect such repairs as the Bank may consider necessary, and in case of default by the Mortgagor in insuring or keeping insured any of the said buildings fixtures or machinery the Bank shall be entitled to exercise the powers of insurance against fire conferred by Statute on Mortgagees and the Mortgagor will repay to the Bank every sum expended by the Bank on such repairs or insurance and every sum so expended by the Bank shall be a charge on the mortgaged property

4-20. This last sub-clause calls for comment on two points. The

---

[15] Sect. 4 (3).
[16] *Lloyds Bank Ltd.* v. *Margolis* [1954] 1 W.L.R. 644.

powers of insurance conferred by statute on mortgagees are to be found in the Law of Property Act, 1925.[17] The Act provides, in effect, that where the mortgagor fails to insure against fire and the mortgage is made by deed, the mortgagee may insure and charge the premiums on the property in the same way as the money lent. But the amount of the insurance must not exceed the amount specified in the mortgage deed, or, if no amount is specified, two-thirds of the amount required to restore the property in case of total destruction. In view of this somewhat limited power of insurance conferred by statute, some banks include in their forms of mortgage an express power to insure the premises "in such sum as the Bank shall think fit."

4-21. It will be noticed that sub-clause (iii) provides that every sum expended by the bank on repairs shall be a charge on the mortgaged property. This is a useful safeguard, because there is no statutory provision which gives a charge for money spent for this purpose.

4-22. The mortgage deed usually continues by providing that—

> The Bank may require money received on an insurance of the mortgaged property whether effected by the Mortgagor or by the Bank and whether or not it is one for the maintenance of which the Mortgagor is liable under this Deed to be applied towards making good the loss or damage in respect of which the money is received or towards the discharge of the mortgage money

This clause puts the bank in a stronger position than it would occupy under the Law of Property Act, 1925. It is therein enacted that money received on an insurance effected under the Act or on an insurance "for the maintenance of which the mortgagor is liable under the mortgage deed" is to be applied by the mortgagor, if the mortgagee so requires, in making good the loss or damage in respect of which the money is received.[18] In *Halifax Building Society* v. *Keighley*[19] the mortgagor effected an insurance of the mortgaged property apart from statute or the deed. The premises were damaged by fire, and it was held that the mortgagees were not entitled to claim the money paid by the insurance company to the mortgagor, one of the reasons being that the case did not fall within the words of the 1925 Act. It is to meet this decision that the clause quoted above expressly extends to any insurance "whether or not it is one for the maintenance of which the mortgagor is liable under this Deed."

[17] Sects. 101 and 108.
[18] Sect. 108 (3).
[19] [1931] 2 K.B. 248.

D. MONEY DUE ON DEMAND

4-23. The various powers of a legal mortgagee are considered in Chapter 7. For the moment it is sufficient to say that his two most important remedies are his power of sale and his power to appoint a receiver. The Law of Property Act, 1925,[20] provides that these powers arise "when the mortgage money has become due." It is the usual practice, therefore, to state in the mortgage deed that the money is due on demand. This is particularly important where the bank, as mortgagee, finds it necessary to exercise its power of sale, because a purchaser will always wish to ascertain that a power of sale has arisen. A clause drafted in the following terms provides complete protection for a purchaser who is buying the property from the bank—

> It is hereby declared that the moneys owing upon this security shall be deemed to have become due within the meaning of Section 101 of the Law of Property Act 1925 immediately on demand for payment being made by the Bank or any Manager or other Officer of the Bank or any Branch thereof and that such demand may be effectually made by notice in writing either served personally on the Mortgagor his heirs executors administrators or assigns or left for or sent by post to him or them either at his or their usual or last known place of abode or business in England or on any part of the said premises.
>
> It is further declared that in addition to all other protection afforded by statute every purchaser or other third party dealing with the Bank shall be entitled and bound to assume without inquiry that some mortgage money is owing on the security hereof and that a demand therefor has been duly made hereunder and that the said mortgage money has accordingly become due

E. POWER OF SALE AND POWER TO APPOINT A RECEIVER

4-24. Although the Law of Property Act, 1925, provides (as shown above) that a mortgagee has a power of sale and a power to appoint a receiver "when the mortgage money has become due," it further enacts[21] that a mortgagee must not exercise either of these powers unless and until one of three events has happened, viz. (i) notice to repay the mortgage money has been served on the mortgagor and default has been made in payment of part or all of it for three months thereafter, (ii) some interest under the mortgage is two months or more in arrear, or (iii) there has been a breach by the mortgagor of some provision in the Act or in the mortgage deed

---

[20] Sect. 101.
[21] Sects. 103 and 109 (1).

(other than the covenant for payment of the mortgage money or interest).

4-25. Bankers usually take the view that the postponement of the power of sale and of the power to appoint a receiver for a period of three months after notice given is too long. It is customary, there- fore, for the mortgage deed to make express provision as to the exercise of these powers. Some deeds stipulate for a period of, say, one month; others stipulate that the powers may be exercised at any time after payment of the moneys secured by the mortgage has been demanded and the mortgagor has made default. The following provisions are appropriate in order to achieve the second alter- native—

> Section 103 of the Law of Property Act 1925 regulating the exercise of the power of sale shall not apply to this security
> The statutory power to appoint a receiver may be exercised at any time after payment of the moneys hereby secured has been demanded and the Mortgagor has made default in paying the same

4-26. A purchaser from a mortgagee need not inquire whether the mortgagee's power of sale has become *exercisable*. The Law of Property Act, 1925, protects the purchaser by enacting that his title is not to be impeachable on the ground (*inter alia*) that due notice was not given to the mortgagor by the mortgagee.[22] This should not be confused with the rule that a purchaser must always ensure that a power of sale has *arisen*.[23]

F. CONSOLIDATION CLAUSE

4-27. The doctrine of consolidation may best be explained by a brief reference to its history. Before there was any legislation on this subject, it had been held by the courts that within certain limits a mortgagee of two or more properties could treat the securities as jointly charged with the repayment of the aggregate debt, so that a mortgagor could not repay one mortgage without redeeming them all. In other words the mortgagee could "consolidate" them, or, as Lord Selborne expressed it in *Jennings* v. *Jordan*,[24] he could "treat them as one, and decline to be redeemed as to any, unless he is redeemed as to all."

4-28. This rule was thought to be rather unfair to borrowers, with the result that Parliament abolished it by the Conveyancing Act,

[22] Sect. 104 (2).
[23] See *ante*, para. 4-23.
[24] (1881) 6 App. Cas. 698, at p. 700.

1881.[25] The position thus established was maintained by the Law of Property Act, 1925,[26] which provides that "a mortgagor seeking to redeem any one mortgage is entitled to do so without paying any money due under any separate mortgage made by him. . . ." Both Acts, however, permit the parties to a mortgage deed to exclude the statutory rule if they so desire. Banks, as mortgagees, invariably do so by inserting a clause on the following lines—

> It is hereby declared that Section 93 of the Law of Property Act 1925 shall not apply to this security and that the Mortgagor and his successors in title shall not be entitled to redeem this security without at the same time redeeming every or any existing or future mortgage for the time being held by the Bank on other property now or at any time hereafter belonging to the Mortgagor or his successors in title or to redeem any other such mortgage without at the same time redeeming this security

4-29. Although a clause to this effect is always to be found in bank mortgage forms, it is very rarely indeed that it serves any practical purpose. The statutory rule could only prejudicially affect the bank's position where *separate* loans had been granted by the bank against *separate* properties. This is seldom, if ever, done in practice. Indeed, each security is expressly stated to cover any sums of money which for the time being constitute the balance due from the mortgagor to the bank.

G. MORTGAGOR DEPRIVED OF POWER TO GRANT LEASES

4-30. The Law of Property Act, 1925,[27] provides that, subject to certain conditions, a mortgagor in possession may grant agricultural or occupation leases for any term not exceeding fifty years and building leases for any term not exceeding nine hundred and ninety-nine years.[28] The Act also provides that a mortgagor in possession may accept a surrender of any lease, if, and only if, his object in doing so is to grant a new lease that falls within his statutory powers.[29]

4-31. Once again, however, the parties to the mortgage are permitted to exclude or to modify the provisions of the statute,[30] and, since it

---

[25] Sect. 17 (1).

[26] Sect. 93 (1).

[27] Sect. 99, replacing the Conveyancing Act, 1881, Sect. 18.

[28] These leasing powers become vested in the mortgagee if he is in possession or has appointed a receiver who is still acting.

[29] Sect. 100 (1).

[30] Law of Property Act, 1925, Sect. 99 (13). But the statutory power of a mortgagor in possession to create a lease of agricultural land binding on a mortgagee cannot be excluded: see Agricultural Holdings Act, 1948, Sect. 95 and Sched. VII, para. 2.

is possible for the bank's position to be prejudiced if the customer is not deprived of his statutory powers of leasing and of accepting surrenders of leases, a clause to the following effect is usually inserted—

> It is hereby declared that neither the Mortgagor nor any of his successors in title shall except with the written consent of any Manager or other Officer of the Head Office of the Bank lease or agree to lease or accept surrenders of leases of the mortgaged property or any part thereof

4-32. If the mortgagor does, in fact, grant a lease to a third party without consent, such lease is not binding as against the mortgagee, who can say in effect[31]—

> There is here no contract which affects me in any way whatever. I am not a party to the tenancy, and the power which the Law of Property Act, 1925, would have given to the mortgagor to make a contract binding on me has been expressly and properly excluded . . . Therefore I, the mortgagee, am wholly unaffected by this transaction of demise.

4-33. The decision in *Dudley and District Benefit Building Society v. Emerson*[32] affords an illustration of the advantage of inserting in a mortgage a clause similar to that quoted above. A borrower had charged a house by way of legal mortgage to a building society. The statutory powers of leasing conferred on a mortgagor in possession had been expressly excluded. The borrower, however, granted a weekly tenancy of the house to a person who went into possession. The borrower defaulted on the instalments payable under the mortgage, and the building society started proceedings for delivery up of possession of the mortgaged premises. The house fell within the ambit of the Rent Restriction Acts, and the tenant claimed that he could not be evicted. Vaisey, J., decided that this claim was valid, but the Court of Appeal unanimously reversed his decision. The tenancy granted by the borrower conferred a good title as between the tenant and the borrower but not as against the mortgagee. Dealing with the object of the Rent Restriction Acts, Sir Raymond Evershed, M.R., pointed out that the Acts are designed to protect occupants of houses within the Acts against eviction by their landlords. The building society was not the tenant's landlord.

4-34. Although a clause depriving the customer of his power to grant leases without the bank's consent is adequate to protect the bank in circumstances similar to those outlined above, there is yet another risk which cannot, so it seems, be guarded against by any

[31] *Per* Sir Raymond Evershed, M.R., in *Dudley and District Benefit Building Society v. Emerson* [1949] 1 Ch. 707, at pp. 714–15.
[32] [1949] 1 Ch. 707.

form of words in the mortgage. This is illustrated by a later decision of the Court of Appeal—*Universal Permanent Building Society* v. *Cooke*[33]—where the facts were as follows: On 3rd November, 1948, a Mrs. Cooke entered into a contract for the purchase of certain premises. She had no right to possession until completion, but on 12th December, 1948, she purported orally to let part of the premises to a tenant, who went into occupation on 16th December, 1948. By a conveyance dated 28th December, 1948, the purchase by Mrs. Cooke was completed, and on the following day she mortgaged the premises to a building society. The mortgage excluded the mortgagor's power of leasing. The mortgagor having defaulted, the building society claimed possession of the whole premises. The Court of Appeal held that, having regard to the dates which the respective instruments bore, there was a period of one day when the fee simple was vested in Mrs. Cooke unencumbered by the mortgage, and during that period the tenant's title to a lease at law was completed by estoppel. The result was that the tenant was entitled to rely on the Rent Restriction Acts and that the building society failed to get an order for possession. In a later case the Court of Appeal decided that the result is the same even if completion is effected and the mortgage is executed on the same day.[34]

4-35. Although these decisions are of most interest to building societies, they are of considerable importance to bankers as well, because bankers sometimes make short-term advances to enable completion to take place pending a building society or other loan. The moral of the cases is that lenders who are relying upon the vacant possession value of their security should make sure that the premises are not let to a tenant on or before the date when the mortgage is executed. A banker will generally be content to rely upon his customer's assurance that he is buying the premises for his own occupation.

H. ATTORNMENT CLAUSE

4-36. It will often be found that a bank's form of legal mortgage

---

[33] [1951] 2 All E.R. 893; [1952] Ch. 95; 212 L.T. 267.
[34] *Church of England Building Society* v. *Piskor* [1954] Ch. 553. Observations to the contrary by Harman, J. in *Coventry Permanent Economic Building Society* v. *Jones* [1951] 1 All E.R. 901 were disapproved.

If the property in question is registered land, the principle appears to be that in cases where the tenant is in actual occupation at the date of the execution of the mortgage, the tenant's right to possession is protected as an "overriding interest" (see *post* para. 10-6) by the Land Registration Act, 1925, Sect. 70: see *Woolwich Equitable Building Society* v. *Marshall* [1952] Ch. 1; *City Permanent Building Society*

concludes with a clause worded as follows—

> The Mortgagor hereby attorns tenant to the Bank of such of the said premises as are in his occupation at the yearly rent of a peppercorn if demanded. Provided that the Bank may at any time hereafter enter into and upon such premises or any part thereof and determine the tenancy hereby created without giving to the Mortgagor or his successors in title any notice to quit and that neither the tenancy created by the said attornment nor any receipt of rent shall constitute the Bank Mortgagees in possession or render them liable to account as such

4-37. A mortgagor who reads this clause may well marvel at the peculiar ways of lawyers. He will most certainly agree with Lord Macnaghten's statement that "no one . . . by the light of nature ever understood an English mortgage of real estate."[35] What is the object of his attorning tenant to the bank, and does he really need to lay in a stock of peppercorns? The answer is that no rent is ever demanded and that the purpose of the clause was to enable the bank, in accordance with the Rules of the Supreme Court, to obtain a more speedy process (known as "a summary judgment") for the recovery of the land. This was particularly useful where the bank wished to exercise its power of sale and the customer refused to leave the premises. In fact, however, the Rules as amended have made the speedy procedure available to mortgagees as such.[36] Thus there is no longer any advantage in this respect in retaining an attornment clause in a mortgage and at least one of the Clearing banks has deleted this clause from its form of mortgage. It does, however, sometimes serve a useful purpose in that it enables a mortgagee to obtain from justices a warrant for possession under the Small Tenements Recovery Act, 1838.[37]

Equitable Mortgage under Hand

4-38. The equitable mortgage, or memorandum of deposit, as it is frequently called, is a comparatively simple document, and no detailed examination of its clauses is called for. The same instrument is used for both freeholds and leaseholds. It opens with a declaration by the customer that the deeds specified in the schedule are deposited as a continuing security for the payment to the bank

---

v. *Miller* [1952] Ch. 840; *Mornington Permanent Building Society* v. *Kenway* [1953] 1 Ch. 382.

[35] *Samuel* v. *Jarrah Timber and Wood Paving Corporation* [1904] A.C. 323, at p. 326.
[36] See Order 14, rule 3.
[37] Sect. 1. For a case where a mortgagee obtained such a warrant by employing an attornment clause, see *Dudley and District Benefit Building Society* v. *Gordon* [1929] 2 K.B. 105.

on demand of all advances, including interest, commission, discount, and other bankers' charges. Then there is an undertaking by the customer to execute a legal mortgage in the bank's favour whenever called upon by the bank to do so. The undertaking should provide that "every such mortgage shall be prepared by your Solicitors at my expense and shall contain such covenants, powers, provisions, and remedies, and be in such form as your Solicitors shall think proper." A declaration is usually incorporated to the effect that the property is free of all charges and incumbrances, and an undertaking is given not to create any further charge without the bank's written consent. As in the case of a legal mortgage, the borrower agrees to keep all buildings insured against fire and to produce the premium receipts. The borrower should further agree that if he fails to keep the buildings insured, the bank is to be entitled to insure them and charge the premiums to the borrower; the powers of insurance conferred on mortgagees by the Law of Property Act, 1925,[38] apply only to mortgages made by deed. Finally, the borrower agrees that the statutory leasing powers of mortgagors and the restriction on consolidation contained in the Law of Property Act, 1925, are to be excluded.

[38] See *ante*, para. 4-20.

CHAPTER 5

Priorities

5-1. WHERE a mortgagor has created more than one mortgage of his property, it is frequently important to determine the priority of those mortgages, that is to say, the order in which they shall rank for payment. This problem is of greatest practical significance where the amounts advanced against the security of the various mortgages exceed the value of the property. The purpose of this chapter is to state the legal rules which govern the priority of mortgages.

Successive Mortgages of a Legal Estate

5-2. The general rules relating to priority may be illustrated by assuming that the owner of a freehold or leasehold property creates three mortgages, in favour of M1, M2, and M3 respectively. The mortgage to M1 will almost certainly be accompanied by the title deeds and the mortgages to M2 and M3 will necessarily be without deposit of the deeds.

5-3. The first point is that it makes no difference whether any particular mortgage is legal or equitable. A mortgagee cannot "step in front" of any other mortgagee by deciding to take a legal mortgage; similarly, a person taking an equitable mortgage runs no risk that a subsequent mortgagee might "step in front" of him merely by taking a legal mortgage.

5-4. The legal rules necessary to determine the priority of the mortgages of M1, M2, and M3 are as follows: Mortgages protected by a deposit of documents relating to the legal estate are excepted from the provisions of the 1925 legislation requiring certain mortgages to be registered as land charges.[1] M1, therefore, does not need to register his mortgage. His priority is protected by the fact that he has obtained the deeds. As will be shown later, he may possibly lose his priority over later mortgagees if he parts with possession of the deeds.[2]

5-5. The mortgages in favour of M2 and M3, being mortgages not

[1] Land Charges Act, 1925, Sect. 10 (1), and Law of Property Act, 1925, Sect. 13 .
[2] See *post*, paras. 5-19/20.

protected by a deposit of documents relating to the legal estate, require to be registered as land charges. If their mortgages are legal, they should be registered as puisne mortgages, and, if equitable, as general equitable charges.[3] If, therefore, M2 and M3 register their mortgages at the time of execution, this preserves their priority.[4] M2 takes priority over M3, and M3 ranks before any subsequent incumbrancers. Both M2 and M3 are, of course, postponed to M1. This is the normal, straightforward case. If, however, M2 and M3 fail to register at all, or if M3 registers before M2, more difficult problems arise, the solution of which depends upon the relevant provisions of the 1925 legislation which must now be considered in detail.

5-6. Section 97 of the Law of Property Act, 1925, provides that—

> Every mortgage affecting a legal estate in land made after the commencement of this Act, whether legal or equitable (not being a mortgage protected by the deposit of documents relating to the legal estate affected) shall rank according to its date of registration as a land charge pursuant to the Land Charges Act, 1925.

Therefore, if M3 registers before M2, M3 will obtain priority over M2.

5-7. The same result is obtained by applying the provisions of Sect. 13 (2) of the Land Charges Act, 1925. This subsection declares, in effect, that a puisne mortgage or a general equitable charge is to be void as against a subsequent mortgagee, unless it is registered before the execution of the subsequent mortgage.[5] Therefore, if, when M3's mortgage is executed, M2 has not registered, M2's mortgage is void as against M3. Furthermore, the result is the same even if M3 had *actual* notice of M2's mortgage at the time when M3 acquired his interest.[6]

5-8. A much more difficult problem arises where the sequence of events is as follows. The owner of the legal estate grants a mortgage to M2. *Before* M2 registers, another mortgage is created in favour of M3. M2 registers his mortgage and then M3 does the same.

[3] For details of the charges registrable in the land charges register, see *ante*, paras. 3-45/51.

[4] Law of Property Act, 1925, Sect. 97, and Land Charges Act, 1925, Sect. 13 (2).

[5] The subsection declares it void "as against a purchaser of the land" and Sect. 20 (8) enacts that a purchaser 'means any person (including a mortgagee or lessee) who, for valuable consideration, takes any interest in land or in a charge on land."

[6] In this connection the Law of Property Act, 1925, Sect. 199 (1) provides that a purchaser (including a mortgagee) "shall not be prejudicially affected by notice of any instrument or matter capable of registration under the provisions of the Land Charges Act, 1925, or any enactment which it replaces, which is void or not enforceable as against him under that Act or enactment, by reason of the non-registration thereof."

According to Sect. 97 of the Law of Property Act, 1925, the order would be M2, M3. But, by virtue of Sect. 13 (2) of the Land Charges Act, 1925, the order would be M3, M2. It is impossible to say how the courts would resolve this conflict.[7]

5-9. Finally, let it be supposed that neither M2 nor M3 registers. There is no difficulty here. Under Sect. 13 (2) of the Land Charges Act, 1925, M2's mortgage is void as against M3 for want of registration, and so M3 has priority over M2. In fact, if there is a succession of registrable mortgages, none of which is registered, it will be found that the last will rank first and so on.

Mortgage to Secure a Current Account

5-10. Section 94 (1) of the Law of Property Act, 1925, lays down three exceptional cases where a prior mortgagee has a right to make further advances to rank in priority to subsequent mortgages, whether legal or equitable. They are (i) where an arrangement to that effect has been made with subsequent mortgagees, (ii) where the mortgage imposes an obligation on the prior mortgagee to make further advances, and (iii) where he has no notice of subsequent mortgages at the time when he makes the further advance.[8]

5-11. It is the last of these three which is of most importance to bankers. Suppose that a customer creates a first mortgage in favour of his bank and later, unknown to the bank, mortgages the property to M2 who registers. Section 198 (1) of the Law of Property Act, 1925, provides that—

> The registration of any instrument or matter under the provisions of the Land Charges Act, 1925, or any enactment which it replaces in any register kept at the land registry or elsewhere, shall be deemed to constitute actual notice of such instrument or matter, and of the fact of such registration, to all persons and for all purposes connected with the land affected . . .

5-12. This would mean that the banker would be fixed with notice of the second mortgage by the mere fact of its having been registered,

---

[7] For a lucid article see R. E. Megarry, "Priority after 1925 of Mortgages of a legal Estate in Land," *Cambridge Law Journal*, Vol. VII, pp. 243–60 where the learned author sums up by suggesting that Sect. 13 (2) of the Land Charges Act, 1925, would prevail.

[8] Where a prior mortgagee makes further advances ranking in priority to subsequent mortgages, this is sometimes known as the "tacking" of further advances. The doctrine of tacking applied in other ways before 1926. The Law of Property Act, 1925, sect. 94 (3), enacts that "save in regard to the making of further advances as aforesaid, the right to tack is hereby abolished."

and that, before paying every cheque drawn on a current account secured by a mortgage of land, a search of the land charges register would be necessary. In order to meet this type of problem, it is enacted in Sect. 94 (2) of the Law of Property Act, 1925,[9] that—

> In relation to the making of further advances after the commencement of this Act a mortgagee shall not be deemed to have notice of a mortgage merely by reason that it was registered as a land charge or in a local deeds registry, if it was not so registered at the time when the original mortgage was created or when the last search (if any) by or on behalf of the mortgagee was made, whichever last happened.

It should be emphasised that the benefit of this subsection extends only to mortgagees whose mortgages are made expressly for securing a current account or other further advances. Other mortgagees, before making a further advance, should search again. Furthermore, although the subsection makes it unnecessary for a banker to search each time he pays a cheque on a current account, it is clear that, if he *does* search again and finds a second mortgage on the register he is in just the same position (discussed below) as if he had received direct notice from the second mortgagee.

Notice of Second Mortgage

5-13. In practice it is very rarely indeed that Sect. 94 (2) of the Law of Property Act, 1925, comes into operation. The second mortgagee not only registers his charge: he gives notice to the first mortgagee as well. Once the first mortgagee (the bank, in the illustration above) knows of the second mortgage, he cannot, without the second mortgagee's consent, make any further advances to rank in priority to the second mortgagee. The banker's usual course in order to avoid the operation of the Rule in *Clayton's* case,[10] is to rule off the mortgagor's account and to pass future transactions through a separate account, which will, of course, be kept in credit unless the circumstances warrant unsecured accommodation or further security is deposited. It makes no difference that the bank's form of mortgage is drafted as a security for further advances, though it would be otherwise (as already shown above) if the mortgage to the bank imposed an obligation on the bank to make further advances. In fact, however, banks never place themselves under an obligation of this nature.

[9] As amended by the Law of Property (Amendment) Act, 1926, Sect. 7 and Sched. The protection afforded is not as comprehensive as it might have been. It protects the mortgagee as against subsequent *mortgages* only and not in respect of the other matters which are registrable under the Land Charges Act.

[10] (1816) 1 Mer. 572.

5-14. The leading case illustrating the loss which a bank may incur by not ruling off a current account upon receipt of notice of a second mortgage is the House of Lords' decision in *Deeley* v. *Lloyds Bank Ltd.*[11] A customer of Lloyds Bank mortgaged his business premises to the bank in 1893 to secure his overdraft on current account. In 1895 he created another mortgage in favour of a second mortgagee who gave notice of his mortgage to the bank. In spite of the fact that one of the bank's rules expressly provided that in such circumstances "the account must at once be ruled off and a separate account opened for subsequent transactions," this was not done. The customer from time to time made payments into and out of his current account which, if the Rule in *Clayton's* case was applicable, would have had the effect of paying off the sum due to the bank at the date of the second mortgage and of creating new advances ranking after the second mortgage. Counsel for the bank argued that the Rule was merely a rule of evidence of intention and that the facts of the case were inconsistent with an intention to appropriate according to the Rule. The House of Lords refused to accede to this argument and held that the second mortgage took priority over that in favour of the bank.

5-15. If a bank receives notice of a second mortgage and the second mortgage expressly states that it is subject to a first mortgage in favour of the bank to secure a named sum, the bank may lend up to that sum *by way of loan account* without losing its priority. If, however, the bank's advance is by way of overdraft, it must be specifically acknowledged by the second mortgagee (e.g. in his notice to the bank) that the bank is at liberty to make advances by way of fluctuating overdraft to an amount not exceeding at any one time the named sum.

5-16. The position is a little more complicated where the bank has lent money to a customer on loan account and the customer has a credit balance on current account. On receipt of notice of a second mortgage, should the bank at once combine the two accounts, and would the bank be justified in dishonouring cheques drawn by the customer thereafter? Sir John Paget expressed the view that the bank ought not to combine the accounts or refuse to honour cheques drawn on the credit balance.[12] His opinion, however, did not deal with the point that the customer may well have expressly agreed in the bank's form of charge not to create any further charge without the bank's written consent. In such case, it would seem that, if the customer acted in breach of that agreement, the bank would be

[11] [1912] A.C. 756.
[12] *Questions on Banking Practice* (10th ed., 1965), pp. 253/4.

justified in dishonouring cheques subsequently presented. Of course, the bank would usually try to obtain from the second mortgagee an acknowledgment that the bank's mortgage would take priority over the second mortgage in respect of the full amount of the bank's loan; no question would then arise concerning the credit balance on current account.

First Mortgage without Deposit of Deeds

5-17. It occasionally happens that a mortgagor who is creating a first mortgage is unable to deposit the relative title deeds. Suppose that he owns two properties, Blackacre and Greenacre, which were conveyed to him by one and the same deed. He has mortgaged Blackacre to X and has deposited with him the title deeds. In a case such as this, it is obvious that if he wishes to mortgage Greenacre to the bank, some, at least, of the deeds relating to Greenacre will have to remain in X's possession even though he has no mortgage in respect of Greenacre.

5-18. The bank will naturally wish to investigate its customer's title to Greenacre and so will arrange for its solicitor to examine the deeds in X's possession. At the same time X should be asked to sign a statement that he has no claim or interest of any sort on Greenacre. The mortgage in favour of the bank will then be executed and registered as a puisne mortgage or as a general equitable charge, according as to whether the mortgage is legal or equitable. The bank's priority is now effectively protected. If the mortgagor subsequently pays off his debt to X, takes the title deeds of both properties to Y and executes a mortgage in Y's favour, Y will be postponed to the bank so far as their respective interests in Greenacre are concerned, because the registration of the bank's mortgage in the land charges register is deemed to constitute "actual notice" thereof to Y.[13] Naturally Y does not need to register his mortgage in order to safeguard himself as against subsequent incumbrancers: his priority is protected by the deposit of the title deeds.

Temporary Release of Deeds

5-19. The legal position of a mortgagee who temporarily parts with the possession of the title deeds is not free from doubt. The problem may be illustrated by the following example. A customer creates a mortgage of Blackacre in favour of his bank and deposits the deeds. On a later occasion, and before the overdraft is paid off, he asks

[13] Law of Property Act, 1925, Sect. 198 (1). See *ante*, para. 5-11.

the bank to release the deeds to him for a short period. He may say that he is trying to sell the property and wishes to show the deeds to potential purchasers, or that he is involved in a dispute with a neighbour concerning a boundary fence or a party-wall, or that he wants his solicitor to advise him on certain restrictive covenants. The bank releases the deeds to the customer, whereupon, let us suppose, he takes them to M2 and fraudulently states that the property is free from mortgage. M2 agrees to take a mortgage of Blackacre *without* deposit of the deeds. He searches the land charges register, finds that there are no subsisting entries and has his mortgage registered. The customer then returns the deeds to the bank, which has, of course, no knowledge of the mortgage in favour of M2. Will the bank's mortgage rank before that of M2, or can it be argued that the bank's carelessness in parting with the deeds has deprived it of its priority?

5-20. Before the 1926 legislation there was authority for the view that a first mortgagee would not be postponed to a later mortgagee on the ground of mere carelessness or want of prudence. In fact, it was said that a first mortgagee would not lose his priority in such a case unless he had actually assisted in or connived at the fraud.[14] It is doubtful whether this is the law to-day. The new system of priorities seems clearly to recognise the principle that a mortgagee must protect himself either by keeping the deeds or by registering his interest, whereas prior to 1926 there was no provision for the registration of mortgages unprotected by a deposit of the deeds.

5-21. The ideal course, therefore, would be for the bank to decline to part with the deeds and to insist that any person wishing to examine them should do so on the bank's premises with the written authority of the customer. Nevertheless, in practice, it is quite usual to release deeds to a customer's solicitor against a written undertaking by the solicitor to hold the documents on behalf of the bank and not to permit any dealing with the property without the bank's written consent.

5-22. Most banks have a printed form for use in such cases. This form consists of two parts. The first is addressed by the customer to the bank, and reads as follows—

> I/We hereby request and authorise you to deliver on loan at my/our risk to . . . . . the title deeds and/or land certificate and documents relating to . . . . . in accordance with the Schedule hereto on his/their undertaking to hold them on your behalf and to return them to you

---

14 *Northern Counties of England Fire Insurance Co.* v. *Whipp* (1884) 26 Ch. D. 482. See also *Martinez* v. *Cooper* (1826) 2 Russ. 198.

on demand in the same condition in which they now are and without the property to which they relate or any interest therein being in any way charged, conveyed, assigned, leased, encumbered, disposed of, or dealt with.

The other part of the form is addressed by the solicitors to the bank, and reads as follows—

> I/We hereby acknowledge to have received on loan from you the title deeds and/or land certificate and documents relating to . . . . . in accordance with the Schedule hereto. I/We undertake to hold them on your behalf and to return them to you on demand in the same condition in which they now are and without the property to which they relate or any interest therein being, to our knowledge, in any way charged, conveyed, assigned, leased, disposed of, or dealt with.

5-23. If this procedure is followed, the bank's position may depend upon the integrity of the solicitor concerned. If he practices in another town and is unknown to the bank, it is a wise precaution to ask one's manager or agent in that town for a confidential report as to his standing. Finally, if there is any cause for uneasiness concerning the respectability of the persons who will have access to the deeds, there is no reason why the bank, when parting with them, should not register its mortgage either as a puisne mortgage or as a general equitable charge, as the case may be. This would afford complete protection, but it is a precaution which is seldom necessary.

Agricultural Holdings Act, 1948

5-24. There is a possible exception to the normal rules relating to priorities when the land mortgaged is an agricultural holding. The term "agricultural holding" is defined by the Agricultural Holdings Act, 1948, Sect. 1, as being "the aggregate of the agricultural land comprised in a contract of tenancy"; and agricultural land means "land used for agriculture which is so used for the purposes of a trade or business." The problem arises where the owner of agricultural land grants a lease to a tenant and borrows money on the security of a mortgage of the land. The tenant is often entitled on the termination of his tenancy to compensation from his landlord in respect of various items, such as improvements which he has effected. The Agricultural Holdings Act, 1948,[15] provides that—

> Where a sum becomes due to a tenant of an agricultural holding in respect of compensation from the landlord, and the landlord fails to discharge his liability therefor within the period of one month from the

[15] Sect. 72.

date on which the sum becomes due, the tenant shall be entitled to obtain from the Minister [of Agriculture and Fisheries] an order charging the holding with payment of the amount due.

The statute also enacts that such a charge "shall rank in priority to any other charge, however and whenever created or arising."[16]

5-25. The effect of these provisions is that a tenant may obtain a charge on the land which will rank in priority to a previous mortgage. In cases where the compensation payable is substantial, a banker who has taken a mortgage of agricultural land may find that his position is prejudicially affected. In fact, however, the provision is not so detrimental to the banker as it appears to be, because the money secured by the tenant's charge will have been spent in improving the bank's security. Nevertheless, the possibility that such a charge may be created is a factor which should be taken into account when valuing agricultural land.[17]

Successive Mortgages of an Equitable Interest

5-26. So far it has been assumed that the mortgagor has a legal estate in the land which he is mortgaging; in other words he is the person whom the layman would regard as the "absolute owner" of a freehold or leasehold property. It may be, however, that he has merely a life interest or a reversionary interest in the property. Special rules govern the priorities of equitable interests of this nature. They are considered in Chapter 28.

[16] Sect. 83 (5).
[17] For an example of another Act under which a charge may be created to take priority over prior mortgages, see the Improvement of Land Act, 1864, Sect. 59.

CHAPTER 6

Discharge of the Mortgage

6-1. WHEN the advance secured by a legal mortgage of land is repaid, some formalities are necessary to show that the bank's interest therein has come to an end. This chapter deals with the procedure to be followed when it is desired to discharge a first mortgage. A further point for consideration when a second mortgage is released is dealt with in a later chapter.[1]

The Statutory Receipt

6-2. In order to discharge a mortgage a bank usually endorses on the mortgage deed a receipt for the money secured by the mortgage. The same wording may be used for both freeholds and leaseholds, and it makes no difference whether the mortgage was created by a legal charge or by a demise (or a subdemise in the case of leaseholds). Most bank mortgages have a form of receipt already printed on the back.

6-3. The Third Schedule to the Law of Property Act, 1925, sets out a specimen form of receipt. The Act provides that a receipt in that form "may be given . . . with such variations and additions, if any, as may be deemed expedient."[2] No special technicalities need to be observed when drafting such a receipt, except that the name of the person who pays the money must be stated.[3] The following is an illustration—

> We the within-named London Bank Limited hereby acknowledge that we have this   day of   19   received all the money secured by the within-written Mortgage (including interest commission and costs) the payment having been made by A. B. of

The mortgage itself, with the receipt endorsed thereon, forms a link in the title to the land. When it is handed to the customer (together with the title deeds which he deposited when creating the mortgage), he should be advised to keep it safely with the deeds, so that, when he wishes to sell the property, his solicitor may abstract the mortgage and the statutory receipt.

---

[1] See *post*, para. 8-24.
[2] Sect. 115 (5).
[3] Sect. 115 (1).

6-4. The receipt attracts stamp duty at the rate of 1s. (5p) for every £200, or fractional part of £200, of the total amount or value of the money at any time secured, with a maximum duty of 10s. (50p).[4] Some banks leave it to the customer to attend to the stamping, whereas others prefer to see that the instrument is stamped before it leaves their possession. Probably the latter course is the safer, because, if the customer neglects to have the instrument stamped, he may find at a later date that he will only be permitted to have it stamped upon payment of a penalty.

6-5. If the security comprised buildings covered by fire insurance and the bank duly notified the company of its interest in the policy, a letter should be sent to the company informing them that the bank no longer has any interest in the policy.

6-6. Finally, the Law of Property Act, 1925, provides[5] that where the receipt acknowledges that the money has been paid by some third party, it operates "as if the benefit of the mortgage had by deed been transferred to him" unless it is otherwise expressly provided. This section applies where, for example, a guarantor pays off the whole debt and is therefore entitled to have transferred to him all securities deposited to secure the customer's account.[6]

An Alternative Method—Reconveyance or Surrender

6-7. The method of discharging a mortgage outlined above is the one most commonly used at the present day. Nevertheless, some banks still discharge a mortgage by endorsing thereon a reconveyance worded as follows—

> This Reconveyance made the   day of   19   between the within-named City Bank Limited (hereinafter called "the Bank") of the one part and the within-named A.B. of   (hereinafter called "the Mortgagor") of the other part Witnesseth that the Bank as Mortgagees hereby surrender and convey unto the Mortgagor All the property vested in the Bank subject to redemption by virtue of the within-written Mortgage To hold the same unto the Mortgagor freed and discharged from all moneys secured by and from all claims and demands under the within-written Mortgage

6-8. This was the mode of discharging a mortgage in use prior to 1926. The 1925 legislation did not make the new method compulsory: the section which introduced it expressly provides that "the right of any person to require a reassignment, surrender,

---

[4] Finance Act, 1970, Sect. 32 and Sched. 7.
[5] Sect. 115 (2).
[6] See *post*, para. 18-16.

release or transfer to be executed in lieu of a receipt" is not to be affected.[7] The method of discharge by way of reconveyance or release is appropriate where the whole of the sum secured by the mortgage is not being repaid. Strictly, a statutory receipt should not be used in such cases.

6-9. The stamp duty on a reconveyance is at the same rate as on a statutory receipt. It seems that it is possible to avoid payment of this *ad valorem* duty. The Law of Property Act, 1925,[8] provides, in effect, that, when a mortgage is created by demise and the money secured thereby has been repaid, the term of years shall automatically cease. Presumably, if the mortgage takes the form of a legal charge, repayment of the debt likewise puts an end to the charge.[9] Thus a mere receipt for principal, interest, and costs operates indirectly to discharge a mortgage in the sense that it furnishes evidence that the mortgage debt has been repaid. Such a receipt is exempt from stamp duty.[10]

No Seal Required on Receipt

6-10. An advantage of a statutory receipt as compared with a reconveyance is that it does not require to be executed under seal.[11] Nevertheless, it is the invariable practice of the banks to execute these receipts under seal, and this involves a delay of several days whilst the instrument is sent to Head Office. The only advantage of this procedure is that it enables Head Office officials to ensure that no irregular releases are permitted, and it would certainly save a good deal of time if the banks were to authorise their branch managers to give the receipt under hand.

6-11. The delays which the present system involves are sometimes a source of irritation to customers. When an overdraft has been repaid, the customer often asks his bank manager for the immediate return of his deeds. Under these circumstances a refusal to return them on the ground that the mortgage requires discharging under the bank's seal might give rise to an action for damages against the bank. This might happen where the customer is arranging a sale of the property and requires his deeds for this purpose. In practice, one would deal with the problem by allowing him to take all the deeds, except the mortgage deed, straightaway, and by giving an

---

[7] Law of Property Act, 1925, Sect. 115 (4).
[8] Sect. 116.
[9] See the Law of Property Act, 1925, Sect. 87 (1).
[10] Finance Act, 1970, Sect. 32 and Sched. 7.
[11] *Simpson* v. *Geoghegan* [1934] W.N. 232.

undertaking to the purchaser's solicitor to send on the discharged mortgage as soon as it is available. A few days later, the mortgage deed duly discharged can be sent on to him. But this difficulty would be avoided if branch managers were authorised to sign statutory receipts on the bank's behalf.

Claims of Subsequent Mortgagees

6-12. If a customer creates a second mortgage of his property, and the second mortgagee gives notice thereof to the bank as first mortgagee, the bank must not return the deeds to the customer upon repayment of the advance. They should be delivered instead to the second mortgagee, because he has a better right to them than the customer has.

6-13. If the second mortgagee has failed to give direct notice to the bank and has merely registered his interest in the land, the question arises whether the bank ought to search the land charges register before returning the deeds to its customer in order to discover whether there are any entries therein affecting the land. This was a matter which caused considerable doubt after the passing of the Law of Property Act, 1925. Section 96 (2) of that Act provided that—

> A mortgagee, whose mortgage is surrendered or otherwise extinguished, shall not be liable on account of delivering documents of title in his possession to the person not having the best right thereto, unless he has notice of the right or claim of a person having a better right . . .

This section, when read in conjunction with Sect. 198 (1), gave rise to difficulties, because the latter section enacted that registration of any matter under the provisions of the Land Charges Act, 1925, was to be "deemed to constitute actual notice" to all persons connected with the land affected.

6-14. In order to overcome this difficulty the Law of Property (Amendment) Act, 1926,[12] added the following words to Sect. 96 (2) of the 1925 Act: "In this subsection notice does not include notice implied by reason of registration under the Land Charges Act, 1925, or in a local deeds register." The generally accepted view is, therefore, that a mortgagee, when paid off, may safely hand over the deeds to the mortgagor without searching.[13] This should

---

[12] Sect. 7 and Sched.

[13] Mr. Cyprian Williams expressed the opinion that the amendment does not afford complete protection. He argued that it alters the law "with respect solely to a mortgagee's liability for not delivering over the title deeds, on payment off, to the person

be contrasted with the procedure to be followed when a mortgagee has exercised his power of sale and has a surplus in his hands after discharging the mortgage debt: in this case, search is essential.[14]

Discharge of Equitable Mortgage under Hand

6-15. The method of discharging an equitable mortgage varies considerably from one bank to another. Since such a mortgage does not create any legal estate or intersst in the land, there is no necessity for a formal surrender under seal, or for a statutory receipt in the form indicated in the Third Schedule to the Law of Property Act, 1925. Furthermore, when once an equitable mortgage has been discharged, it does not come upon the title to the land and should not be abstracted.[15]

6-16. Some banks discharge an equitable mortgage by merely writing "cancelled" across the memorandum of deposit and handing back the deeds to the customer. This is quite sufficient. Occasionally, however, the customer wishes to have a receipt, and this may be written either on the memorandum of deposit or on a separate form of receipt. If the receipt is endorsed on the memorandum, it is exempt from duty by the Stamp Act, 1891.[16] Some banks authorise their branch managers to sign these receipts, whereas others require them to be signed by a Head Office official.

Discharge of Equitable Mortgage under Seal

6-17. An equitable mortgage under seal[17] should be discharged in precisely the same way as an equitable mortgage under hand. Nevertheless, some customers (or, in practice, their solicitors) are under the mistaken impression that, since the mortgage itself is under seal, the same formalities are necessary to discharge it as in the case of a legal mortgage. This is not so.

6-18. However, if the customer insists upon having the type of

---

who has the best right thereto." Therefore, Mr. Williams maintained that "no mortgagee can with absolute security receive payment of the mortgage money from the mortgagor, or any other person, without first searching in the appropriate registers to see if the presentation of a bankruptcy petition or a receiving order, has been registered against the name of the person about to make the payment." *The Law Journal Newspaper*, 5th June, 1926.

[14] See *post*, para. 7-11.

[15] See *ante*, para. 3-19.

[16] Sched. 1, "Receipt" Exemption (11). If a separate form of receipt is employed, this used to require a twopenny stamp, but the duty was abolished as from 1st February 1971, by the Finance Act, 1970, Sect. 32 and Sched. 7.

[17] See *ante*, para. 3-10.

discharge applicable to a legal mortgage, there is no harm in obliging him. Even if the receipt is executed under seal on the mortgage itself and follows the wording given in the Third Schedule to the Law of Property Act, 1925, the receipt is exempt from stamp duty.[18]

Releasing the Deeds upon Sale of the Property

6-19. If the customer wishes to sell the property which he has mortgaged to the bank, his solicitors will, of course, require the title deeds in order to prepare an abstract of title. In such cases, it is the usual practice for the bank to release the deeds to his solicitors against their undertaking to pay the proceeds of sale to the bank. Most banks have a printed form for use in such cases. This form consists of two parts. The first is addressed by the customer to the bank, and is worded as follows—

> I/We hereby request and authorise you to deliver at my/our risk to ....the title deeds and/or land certificate and documents relating to....................in accordance with the Schedule hereto for the purpose of the sale/mortgage of this property on his/their undertaking to hold them on your behalf and to return them to you on demand in the same condition in which they now are, pending completion of such transaction, and if the transaction is complete—
>
> (*a*) to pay to you the amount of the purchase/mortgage money, not being less than £....................gross subject only to the deduction therefrom of the deposit (if held by the estate agents) the estate agents' commission and the legal costs and disbursements relating to the transaction, and
>
> (*b*) if the title deeds and/or land certificate and documents also relate to other property in addition to that referred to above, to return same to you suitably endorsed or noted.

The other part of the form is addressed by the solicitors to the bank, and reads as follows—

> I/We hereby acknowledge to have received from you the title deeds and/or land certificate and documents *together with a charge to the bank* relating to............................in accordance with the Schedule hereto for the purpose of the sale/mortgage of this property. I/We undertake to hold them on your behalf and to return them to you on demand in the same condition in which they now are, pending completion of such transaction. If the transaction is completed, I/We undertake—

[18] The Law of Property Act, 1925, Sect. 115 (5), which specifies the stamp duty for statutory receipts, applies only to the discharge of *legal* mortgages. The Inland Revenue agree that the receipts mentioned in the text above are exempt from duty; see *Journal of the Institute of Bankers*, Vol. LXXIV (1953), p. 222.

(*a*) to pay to you the amount of the purchase/mortgage money, not being less than £.................gross subject only to the deduction therefrom of the deposit (if held by the estate agents), the estate agents' commission and the legal costs and disbursements relating to the transaction, and

(*b*) if the title deeds and/or land certificate and documents also relate to other property in addition to that referred to above, to return same to you suitably endorsed or noted.

Notes: 1. If there are likely to be any deductions from the purchase price other than those shown above, these must be specifically mentioned.

2. Delete the words printed in italics if no charge form has been taken.

6-20. When releasing deeds in this way, some banks made a practice of retaining the mortgage executed by the customer. The result was, in some cases, that the bank's mortgage was not included in the abstract of title—a serious matter if the bank's mortgage was a legal one. In order to remedy this, an arrangement was made between the Law Society and the Committee of London Clearing Bankers, whereby the bank concerned will either hand over the mortgage, with the other title deeds, to the customer's solicitors, or, alternatively, will notify the solicitors of the existence of the mortgage either on a special form included with the deeds and listed in the schedule to be receipted by the solicitors, or in some other appropriate way.[19]

Release of Part Only of the Mortgaged Property

A. WHERE THE MORTGAGE IS A LEGAL ONE

6-21. If a customer has mortgaged to the bank two or more properties by means of one deed and wishes to redeem only one of them, it is clear that a discharge cannot be effected by endorsing a receipt on that deed. An express release must be executed. This instrument will recite the mortgage and will then release the interest of the bank in the following terms—

This Deed Witnesseth that the Bank as Mortgagees hereby surrender and release unto the Mortgagor all the property specified in the Schedule hereto

The instrument attracts stamp duty at the rate of 1s. (5p) per £200 on the amount at any time secured, with a maximum of 10s. (50p).

[19] See *Journal of the Institute of Bankers*, Vol. LXXI (1950), p. 222.

B. WHERE THE MORTGAGE IS AN EQUITABLE ONE

6-22. Since such a mortgage does not create any legal estate or interest in favour of the bank, there is no need for a formal release under seal to be executed. Nevertheless, the customer must be supplied with some document to prove that the bank no longer has any interest in part of the property. This is particularly important if the customer is proposing to sell it, e.g. where he is a builder and is selling houses to various purchasers. In practice the branch manager of the bank usually signs a letter stating that the bank has no charge on the house that is being sold. This is sufficient to release it from the equitable mortgage. Occasionally the bank is asked to join in the conveyance by the customer to the purchaser, but, strictly, this is unnecessary.

CHAPTER 7

Remedies of Mortgagees

7-1. IF a customer fails to discharge his debt, the bank will be forced to look to its security for repayment of the advance. The remedies available to a mortgagee depend to a large extent upon whether his mortgage is legal or equitable, though a suitably drafted equitable mortgage under seal places the mortgagee, for all practical purposes, in just as strong a position as that occupied by a legal mortgagee.[1] A knowledge of the practical considerations which guide bankers in deciding which remedy is likely to be the most effective is at least as important as a study of the legal aspects of the subject. The remedies to be examined are: (*a*) an action against the mortgagor for the amount of the debt, (*b*) sale of the property, (*c*) appointment of a receiver, (*d*) foreclosure, and (*e*) taking possession of the property. Of these, two are derived from the common law (the right to sue and the right to take possession), two are solely the result of statute (sale and the appointment of a receiver) and one is equitable in origin but is now largely regulated by statute (foreclosure). The remedies of a second mortgagee are treated separately in the next chapter.

A. ACTION FOR THE DEBT

7-2. Every creditor, whether secured or not, has, of course, a right to sue his debtor if the latter fails to pay his debt.[2] In the case of mortgages by deed it is usual for the mortgagor to covenant expressly with the bank to pay on demand all sums due.[3]

7-3. In the vast majority of cases, however, it is a waste of time for a secured creditor to obtain judgment against his debtor. The main reason why an *unsecured* creditor proceeds to judgment is to enable him to levy execution against the debtor's property.[4] In view of the

---

[1] See *ante*, para. 3-10.

[2] For a useful account of this subject, see John Howgate, "The Recovery of Debts," *Journal of the Institute of Bankers*, Vol. LXXI (1950), pp. 227–35 and Vol. LXXII (1951) pp. 13–20.

[3] See *ante*, para. 4-18.

[4] The commonest form of execution is by writ of *fieri facias*. The judgment creditor takes out this writ, which commands the sheriff to *cause to be made* out of the goods and chattels of the debtor the amount of the judgment debt with interest at four per cent per annum. A judgment creditor may obtain a charging order on his debtor's land by applying to the court under the Administration of Justice Act, 1956, Sect. 35; this procedure replaces the old writ of *elegit* (which was abolished by Sect. 34 (1) of the

fact that a secured creditor already has a measure of control over some of his debtor's property, there is, as a general rule, no point in trying to levy execution over other of his assets.

7-4. In one type of case, however, it is sometimes profitable for a partly-secured creditor to proceed to judgment. Another result of obtaining judgment is that the creditor is able to serve on the debtor a bankruptcy notice requiring him to pay the debt or to secure or compound for it to the satisfaction of the creditor or the court.[5] If the debtor does not comply with the requirements of that notice within seven days or satisfy the court that he has a counterclaim or set-off which equals or exceeds the amount of the judgment debt, he commits an act of bankruptcy on which a petition may be presented and he may be adjudicated bankrupt.[6] Therefore, if the bank has any reason to think that the debtor could, if hard-pressed, repay the overdraft (e.g. by borrowing money from his relatives) it is occasionally a good plan to hold the threat of bankruptcy proceedings over his head. This course, in suitable instances, may prove to be simpler and more effective than an attempt to realise the security. Nevertheless, it is a course which should be followed with caution; as a rule, it is better to accept a loss than to adopt intimidatory methods which will, in the long run, injure the bank's reputation.

B. SALE OF THE PROPERTY

7-5. At common law a mortgagee had no power of sale, and so an express power was generally inserted in mortgage deeds.[7] Then an Act passed in 1860—usually referred to as Lord Cranworth's Act—gave a somewhat restricted and unsatisfactory power of sale. The mortgagee's position was improved by the Conveyancing Act, 1881, and the provisions of that Act have been replaced, with slight modifications, by the Law of Property Act, 1925.

7-6. The 1925 Act provides that every mortgagee whose mortgage is made by *deed* shall have power (subject to any contrary stipulation in the mortgage deed) to sell the mortgaged property, or any part thereof, either together or in lots, by public auction or by private contract.[8] When mortgages of freeholds are realised, the conveyance

---

Act), and an order thus obtained has the same effect as an equitable charge created by the debtor under hand.

[5] See the Bankruptcy Act, 1914, Sect. 2.

[6] Sect. 1 (1).

[7] Though it seems that express powers of sale were not usually inserted until about 1820–30: see *Stevens* v. *Theatres Ltd.* [1903] 1 Ch. 857, at p. 860.

[8] Law of Property Act, 1925, Sect. 101 (1) and (4). All legal mortgages are necessarily made by deed. For equitable mortgages, see *post*, paras. 7-25/28.

to the purchaser by the mortgagee operates to pass to the purchaser the legal fee simple in the land and to extinguish the mortgage terms vested both in the selling mortgagee and in any subsequent mortgagees.[9] When mortgages of leaseholds are realised, the conveyance to the purchaser by the mortgagee operates to pass to the purchaser, not only the mortgage term, but also the reversion which is vested in the mortgagor.[10] The power of sale *arises* only when the mortgage money has become due, and bank mortgage forms declare that the moneys secured by the mortgage are to be deemed to have become due on demand.[11] The power does not become *exercisable* under the Act unless, *inter alia*, notice to repay the mortgaged money has been served on the mortgagor and default has been made in payment of part or all of it for three months thereafter, but this period is very frequently reduced by express provision in the mortgage deeds used by the banks.[12]

7-7. The actual steps to be taken upon a sale by a legal mortgagee are, therefore, quite straightforward. The bank (or its solicitor) sends a letter by registered post to the customer demanding immediate repayment of the debt and warning him that, in the event of default, the bank will proceed to exercise its rights in relation to the security. The general rule is that the sale may be effected without any order of the court, but the Law of Property Act, 1925, Sect. 110 (1), provides that—

> Where the statutory or express power for a mortgagee either to sell or to appoint a receiver is made exercisable by reason of the mortgagor committing an act of bankruptcy or being adjudged a bankrupt, such power shall not be exercised only on account of the act of bankruptcy or adjudication, without the leave of the court.

This section does not affect the exercise of the power to sell or to appoint a receiver when an event within Sect. 103 has occurred,[13] notwithstanding that the mortgagor may also be a bankrupt.

7-8. The mortgagee is not a trustee for the mortgagor of his power of sale. The power is given to him for his own benefit, and, provided that he exercises the power bona fide, the court will not interfere even though the sale may be disadvantageous. When a building society is selling as mortgagee, the society is obliged by statute to exercise "reasonable care" to obtain "the best price which can reasonably

---

[9] Law of Property Act, 1925, Sect. 88 (1).
[10] Ibid., Sect. 89 (1).
[11] See *ante*, para. 4-23.
[12] See *ante*, paras. 4-24/25.
[13] See *ante*, para. 4-24.

be obtained."[14] There is no such provision relating to sales by banks as mortgagees, but a banker, in common with any other mortgagee, must act prudently. Thus a mortgagee must, as Sir George Jessel, M.R., observed, "conduct the sale properly, and must sell at a fair value."[15] If the sale is by private treaty, it is prudent (though not legally essential) to obtain either a professional valuation or the customer's approval of the transaction. It may be added that, once a mortgagee has entered into a contract to sell the property, the mortgagor cannot prevent the sale by tendering the mortgage money to the mortgagee.[16]

7-9. If (as is usual) the assistance of an estate agent or an auctioneer is sought to find a purchaser, it is preferable to instruct him that the bank's name must not appear in any notice offering the property for sale. There are two reasons for this. First, if it becomes known that the bank is selling as mortgagee, the impression is sometimes created that the bank may be willing to accept a very low figure in order to liquidate its advance, and, secondly, it is not considered "good policy" to advertise that the bank is realising securities.

7-10. It is often desirable to obtain vacant possession of the premises before effecting a sale. Where the customer is in occupation and refuses to quit, the bank may take steps to obtain "a summary judgment" for the recovery of the land.[17] If the premises are a matrimonial home, a deserted spouse (usually the wife) who is living there may insist upon being joined as a defendant in legal proceedings brought against her husband as owner of the house by a mortgagee to recover possession thereof. This is because she has a right to pay off the mortgage debt under Sect. 1(5) of the Matrimonial Homes Act, 1967.[18] If the premises are let, the bank will usually be obliged to sell them subject to tenancy. But if the lease had been granted after the execution of the mortgage and without any necessary consent of the bank, the lease would not be valid as against the bank. This applies—as was shown in *Dudley and District Benefit Building Society* v. *Emerson*[19]—even though the property falls within the Rent Restriction Acts.

7-11. When the sale has taken place, any surplus after discharging the customer's debt to the bank must not be placed to the credit of his account if there are any subsequent mortgages outstanding.[20]

[14] Building Societies Act, 1939, Sect. 10.
[15] *Nash* v. *Eads* (1880) 25 Sol. Jo. 95.
[16] *Waring* v. *London and Manchester Assurance Co. Ltd.* [1935] 1 Ch. 310.
[17] See *ante*, para. 4-37.
[18] *Hastings and Thanet Building Society* v. *Goddard* [1970] 2 All E.R. 737.
[19] [1949] 1 Ch. 707, *ante*, para. 4-33.
[20] Law of Property Act, 1925, Sect. 105.

Subsequent mortgagees, if any, will in the normal course of events have given direct notice to the bank of their interests. However, there is always the possibility that later mortgages, although registered, have not been notified to the bank. Thus the bank should always search the land charges register, because registration is equivalent to notice;[21] if the bank paid the surplus to the customer, it would be liable to any subsequent registered mortgagee who was thereby prejudiced. Where the bank discovers the existence of second *and subsequent* mortgages, the question may arise whether the bank holds any surplus (if sufficiently substantial) in trust for *all* those mortgagees or whether the entire surplus may be paid to the second mortgagee. As yet this point does not appear to have been finally decided, though Eve, J., once expressed the opinion that the whole surplus should be handed over to the second mortgagee.[22]

7-12. Finally, in cases where the customer has created a second mortgage, the bank will usually ask the second mortgagee if he would care to take over the first mortgage by paying off the customer's debt to the bank. This policy (if successful) makes it unnecessary for the bank to exercise its power of sale or any other remedy. Although the bank cannot compel the second mortgagee to take this course, it sometimes helps if one informs the second mortgagee in appropriate instances that, if the bank was to sell the property, the proceeds might not be sufficient to repay both the bank and the second mortgagee. Of course, if the second mortgagee declines to take over the first mortgage, the bank's positon is not in any way prejudiced. The bank, as first mortgagee, is in a position to convey the property to a purchaser "freed from all estates, interests, and rights to which the mortgage has priority."[23]

C. APPOINTMENT OF A RECEIVER

7-13. In just the same way as, at common law, a mortgagee had no power of sale, so too he had no power to appoint a receiver, with the result that it was usual to insert an express power in mortgage deeds enabling him to do so. Then Lord Cranworth's Act, 1860, gave a mortgagee a rather unsatisfactory statutory power of appointing a receiver. The mortgagee's position was strengthened by the Conveyancing Act, 1881, and the rules laid down in that Act have been replaced, with amendments, by the Law of Property Act, 1925.

---

[21] Ibid., Sect. 198 (1) *ante*, para. 5-11.
[22] *Re Thomson's Mortgage Trust, Thomson* v. *Bruty* [1920] 1 Ch. 508. Eve, J., based his opinion upon the Conveyancing Act, 1881, Sect. 21, now replaced by the Law of Property Act, 1925, Sect. 105, but he admitted that the matter was not free from doubt.
[23] Law of Property Act, 1925, Sect. 104 (1).

7-14. The effect of the 1925 Act is that the statutory power to appoint a receiver arises and becomes exercisable in precisely the same circumstances as the power of sale.[24] The typical case where, in practice, it is advisable to appoint a receiver is where the property is let and a sale subject to tenancy is considered unwise in the immediate future. It may not be possible to find a purchaser for some time, and the appointment of a receiver is very often an interim measure taken with the object of ensuring that the rents of the property are collected by the receiver and applied in discharge of the mortgage interest and reduction of the debt outstanding.

7-15. A mortgagee may appoint a receiver by writing under hand,[25] though the banks sometimes make the appointment under seal. The stamp duty in either case is 10s. (50p).[26] The instrument will be exhibited to the tenant, who must thereafter pay the rent to the receiver. In small receiverships a bank will occasionally appoint one of its own officials, but in relation to large properties it is advisable to appoint an estate agent or accountant who will, of course, be remunerated for his services. A receiver is entitled to retain out of any money received by him, for his remuneration, and in satisfaction of all costs, charges, and expenses a commission at such rate, not exceeding five per cent on the gross amount of all money received, as is specified in his appointment, and if no rate is specified, then at the rate of five per cent on that gross amount, or at such other rate as the court, on his application, thinks fit to allow.[27] In the case of an express power to appoint, the instrument of appointment may fix a rate of commission higher than five per cent; e.g. commission of five per cent per annum as remuneration, plus all costs, charges, and expenses properly incurred.[28] In practice it is often desirable to fix the remuneration in this way in order to give the receiver a clear five per cent. This is especially important where the cost of collecting the rents is high; for example, where there are numerous properties yielding small rentals.

7-16. A receiver has power to recover the income of the property, by action, distress, or otherwise, and to give receipts in respect thereof;[29] and he can exercise the powers of leasing and accepting surrender of leases if these powers are delegated to him in writing by the

---

[24] Sects. 101 (1) and 109 (1).

[25] Sect. 109 (1).

[26] Stamp Act, 1891, Sched. I, heading "Letter or Power of Attorney"; E. N. Alpe *Law of Stamp Duties* (25th ed., 1960), p. 272.

[27] Law of Property Act, 1925, Sect. 109 (6).

[28] *Re Greycaine Ltd.* [1946] Ch. 269, *post*, para. 32-61.

[29] Sect. 109 (3). "Distress" is the right of a landlord, whose tenant is in arrears with his rent to seize goods which he finds on the premises and to sell them.

mortgagee.[30] In all matters he is deemed to be the agent of the mortgagor, who is solely responsible for his acts or defaults unless the mortgage otherwise provides.[31]

7-17. It is the duty of the receiver to apply the rents received by him as follows: (i) in discharge of outgoings in respect of the property, such as taxes and rates, (ii) in payment of interest on prior incumbrances, (iii) in payment of insurance premiums, repairs, and of his own commission, (iv) in payment of interest due under the mortgage, and (v) if so directed in writing by the mortgagee, towards discharge of the principal money lent on mortgage.[32] In practice a bank, when appointing a receiver, invariably does direct him to apply the surplus towards reduction of the principal sum; otherwise, it would be payable to the person who would have been entitled to it if the receiver had not been appointed—usually the mortgagor.

D. FORECLOSURE

7-18. Although the remedy of foreclosure was created by the courts of equity, its present effect is largely governed by the Law of Property Act, 1925.[33] Briefly, the result of a foreclosure order absolute is to vest the mortgagor's fee simple or (if the property is leasehold) his term of years in the mortgagee, regardless of the relation between the value of the property and the amount of the debt. Thus, theoretically, a mortgagee might be able to become "absolute owner" of property worth £1,000 if the mortgagor failed to repay his debt of £500, though in practice this would never happen, because the mortgagor would always be able to borrow £500 from another lender to repay the mortgagee who was threatening to foreclose. If there are prior incumbrances, the mortgagee takes the property subject to them, but free from any subsequent ones.

7-19. It is, perhaps, a little strange that the remedy was not abolished by the 1925 legislation, though probably there is little harm in retaining it, because the court has power, at the request of any person interested either in the mortgage money or in the right of redemption, to direct a sale of the property instead.[34] Banks seldom, if ever, foreclose, and the procedure will be explained in outline only. The mortgagee obtains from the court a foreclosure order *nisi*. This states that if the mortgage debt is repaid by a certain day—usually six months hence—the mortgage will be discharged,

[30] Sect. 99 (19).
[31] Sect. 109 (2).
[32] Sect. 109 (8).
[33] Sects. 88 (2) and 89 (2).
[34] Law of Property Act, 1925, Sect. 91 (2).

but that, if the money is not paid, the mortgage will be foreclosed. If, when the date comes, the debt is still outstanding, a foreclosure order absolute is made, and the property becomes that of the mortgagee. Although this is in its terms final, the court will occasionally open a foreclosure absolute, as for example when an unforeseen circumstance prevented the mortgagor, at the last moment, from raising the money.

7-20. A mortgagee who has started foreclosure proceedings is not permitted, without the court's consent, to exercise his power of sale after the foreclosure order *nisi* has been made but before the order absolute, because this would deprive the mortgagor of the right to redeem given by the court. This is an exception to the general rule that a mortgagee's remedies are concurrent. He can, for example, in a single action claim foreclosure and judgment on the mortgagor's covenant to repay. Failure to obtain the court's consent does not invalidate a conveyance to a purchaser, provided that he takes bona fide and for value.[35]

E. TAKING POSSESSION OF THE PROPERTY

7-21. The mortgagee's right to take possession of the mortgaged property (unlike his powers to sell and to appoint a receiver) is not statutory.[36] Nor does it depend upon any express authority conferred by the mortgage deed. It results from the fact that a legal mortgage by demise (or by subdemise in the case of leasehold property) gives the mortgagee a term of years. Thus he is entitled to take possession of the property, peaceably if he can, or failing that by means of an action for recovery of the land against the mortgagor; and a mortgagee under a legal charge enjoys "the same protection, powers, and remedies" by virtue of the Law of Property Act, 1925.[37] In many cases, however, a mortgagee covenants that he will not take possession until the mortgagor defaults. Furthermore, if the mortgagor has attorned tenant to the mortgagee,[38] the tenancy must be determined before entry is made.

7-22. If a mortgagee brought an action for recovery of the land against the mortgagor, who was in default, the mortgagee used to be

[35] *Stevens* v. *Theatres Ltd.* [1903] 1 Ch. 857. The point appears to be covered by a new provision in the Law of Property Act, 1925, Sect. 104 (2) (*c*).
[36] The right to take possession is preserved, but not conferred, by the Law of Property Act, 1925, Sect. 95 (4).
[37] Sect. 87 (1), and see Sect. 95 (4) *supra*.
[38] See *ante*, para. 4-36.

entitled to an order for possession forthwith, subject to the exception that if there was any reasonable prospect of a short adjournment enabling the mortgagor to find the money to pay off the mortgagee, the court might grant such an adjournment.[39] However, in regard to mortgages of dwelling houses, Sect. 36 of the Administration of Justice Act, 1970, now gives the mortgagor an opportunity to make good his default, if there is a reasonable prospect that he can do so.

7-23. If the mortgagor is occupying the property himself, the mortgagee takes possession by evicting him; the mortgagee then enjoys the leasing powers conferred by the Law of Property Act, 1925, Sect. 99, upon mortgagees in possession. Their powers of leasing are the same as those of mortgagors in possession.[40] The mortgagee may, if he wishes, occupy the premises himself, in which case he will be liable for an occupation rent based on the highest possible rental value of the premises.[41] If the property is already lawfully let to a tenant, the mortgagee obviously cannot take physical possession: in this case, he takes possession by directing the tenant to pay his rent to him instead of to the mortgagor. The rent which the mortgagee receives must be applied by him in satisfaction of his claim for principal and interest.

7-24. In practice it is very rare indeed to find a mortgagee exercising his remedy of taking possession. The most important practical reason for this is that it is much simpler to appoint a receiver and to remunerate him for collecting the rents. Another reason is that mortgagees seem to fear the application of the rule that a mortgagee in possession is liable to account to the mortgagor for the rents and profits on the footing of "wilful default," that is to say, he must account not only for the sums which he actually receives, but also for those sums which, but for his own default, he might have received. Thus, in *White* v. *City of London Brewery Co.*,[42] a mortgagee of a public house took possession and let it as a tied house, that is, subject to a covenant to take only the mortgagee's beers. The Court of Appeal held that he was accountable not for the rent which he actually obtained but for the higher rent which he might have obtained if he had let the house as a "free house." There is no doubt, however, that the risks involved in taking possession are often exaggerated. If the property is already let, there is virtually no risk, and even in other cases the danger is very slight provided that the mortgagee exercises common sense.

---

[39] *Birmingham Citizens Permanent Building Society* v. *Caunt* [1962] Ch. 883.
[40] For these powers see *ante*, para. 4-30.
[41] *Marriott* v. *The Anchor Reversionary Co.* (1861) 3 De G.F. & J. 177.
[42] (1889) 42 Ch. D. 237.

Remedies of Equitable Mortgagee: Mortgage under Hand

7-25. The remedies available to an equitable mortgagee whose mortgage has been executed under hand are not nearly so comprehensive as those enjoyed by a legal mortgagee. He can, if he wishes, sue the mortgagor for the amount of the debt, and he may foreclose in the same way as a legal mortgagee. The memorandum of deposit which the mortgagor will have signed will normally include an undertaking by him to execute a legal mortgage when called upon to do so. If he honours his undertaking, all is well. If, however, he declines to do so, the assistance of the court will be required before the mortgagee can sell the property or appoint a receiver. With regard to the former remedy, the Law of Property Act, 1925,[43] provides that—

> Where an order for sale is made by the court in reference to an equitable mortgage on land . . . the court may, in favour of a purchaser, make a vesting order conveying the land or may appoint a person to convey the land or create and vest in the mortgagee a legal term of years absolute to enable him to carry out the sale, as the case may require, in like manner as if the mortgage had been created by deed by way of legal mortgage pursuant to this Act . . .

7-26. Finally, it is the generally accepted view that an equitable mortgagee has no right to take possession of the mortgaged property without an order of the court.[44]

Remedies of Equitable Mortgagee: Mortgage under Seal

7-27. An equitable mortgagee whose mortgage has been executed under seal is in a much stronger position than a mortgagee holding a memorandum of deposit under hand. The Law of Property Act, 1925,[45] expressly provides that the power of sale and the power to appoint a receiver are available to those mortgagees whose mortgages are made by *deed*. As these remedies are undoubtedly the ones which mortgagees find most useful in practice, it means that an equitable mortgagee by deed is in very much the same position, at any rate with regard to the remedies available to him, as a legal mortgagee.

7-28. Although an equitable mortgagee by deed has a statutory

---

[43] Sect. 90 (1).
[44] See, for example, the judgment of Harman, J., in *Barclays Bank Ltd.* v. *Bird* [1954] Ch. 274, at p. 280. For an article challenging this view, see H. W. R. Wade, "An Equitable Mortgagee's Right to Possession," *Law Quarterly ev ew*, Vol. 71 (1955), pp. 204–22.
[45] Sect. 101.

power to sell the property, it would seem that this, of itself, does not enable him to convey the legal estate to a purchaser. This difficulty may be overcome by inserting in the deed an "irrevocable power of attorney" clause and/or a "declaration of trust" clause.[46] Even if the mortgagor dies or is adjudicated bankrupt, a mortgagee in such a case can make title without the co-operation of the mortgagor's executor or trustee in bankruptcy, because the Law of Property Act, 1925,[47] provides that an "irrevocable" power of attorney given to a mortgagee is not revoked by the mortgagor's death or bankruptcy. In spite of the protection afforded by the statute, some banks as a matter of practice do not act under the power of attorney in cases where it is known to the bank that the mortgagor has died or has been adjudicated bankrupt.

Mortgagee's Right to Fixtures

7-29. It is obviously of the greatest importance to a bank, as mortgagee, to known precisely what is included in a mortgage of land. The general rule has been stated in an earlier chapter that the term "land" as used by lawyers includes the soil, the buildings on the soil and the chattels ("fixtures") attached to the building.[48] This principle is of general application in the law relating to mortgages and so, for example, a mortgagee obtains rights over the buildings even though the mortgage makes no reference to the presence of any buildings on the land.

7-30. Similarly, fixtures pass with the land to the mortgagee, unless the mortgage shows a contrary intention; and the same rule applies to fixtures which are added by the mortgagor after the mortgage has been executed. It follows from this that the mortgagor is not entitled to remove fixtures, without the mortgagee's consent, whether they have been annexed to the land before or after the date of the mortgage. These principles apply to all mortgages, whether legal or equitable, and irrespective of whether the property is freehold or leasehold.

7-31. In spite of this, the lawyers who draft the mortgage forms used by the banks often make express reference to fixtures. Thus the property which is the subject of the mortgage is sometimes described thus—

all the property specified in the Schedule hereto together with all fixtures whatsoever now or at any time hereafter affixed or attached to the said

[46] See *ante*, paras. 3-10/13.
[47] Sect. 126 (1).
[48] See *ante*, para. 2-1.

premises or to any part thereof other than trade machinery as defined
by Section 5 of the Bills of Sale Act, 1878

Trade machinery is excluded because such machinery is, by the
Act, deemed to be personal chattels and is taken out of the category
of fixtures.[49] Consequently, if such machinery is assigned by *separate
words* in an instrument creating a mortgage of the land to which it is
affixed, the instrument requires registration as a bill of sale.[50] It is
often wiser to omit from the mortgage all reference to fixtures,
because it has been held that trade machinery as defined by the Act
is capable of passing with other fixtures as part of the security
although the mortgage contains no express mention of fixtures.[51] In
other words, "the trade machinery passes as a portion of the land,
not as personal chattels."[52]

7-32. There is an exception to the general rule that chattels attached
to a building become fixtures and so pass with the land to a mortgagee, namely, that when chattels are annexed to land by a third
party under an agreement between him and the mortgagor which
permits him to remove them in certain circumstances, his right to
remove them cannot, as a general rule, be defeated by the mortgagee. A clear illustration of the risks to which banks may be
exposed as a result of this exception is provided by the case of *Lyon
& Co.* v. *London City and Midland Bank*.[53] Some chairs had been
hired from the plaintiffs by the owner of a place of public entertain-
ment in Brighton. The Brighton Town Council required the chairs
to be fastened to the floor, and this was done. The building and
fixtures were then mortgaged to the London City and Midland Bank.
The bank exercised its remedy of taking possession of the property
and claimed the chairs. However, the court held that they did not
form part of the property mortgaged and that the bank's claim must
fail.

7-33. Other decisions on this topic have made it extremely difficult
to determine whether, on the facts of any given case, a mortgagee
will succeed or fail in his claim to fixtures in which third parties
are interested. On one occasion Lord Lindley said that he did
"not profess to be able to reconcile all the cases on fixtures, still less

---

[49] Not all trade machinery is affected by these provisions. Trade machinery as
defined by the Act does not include, for example "fixed motive-powers" such as
steam-engines and steam-boilers. Machinery of this nature, therefore, falls within
the category of fixtures and passes with the land to the mortgagee.
[50] *Small* v. *National Provincial Bank of England* [1894] 1 Ch. 686.
[51] *Re Yates, Batcheldor* v. *Yates* (1888) 38 Ch. D. 112.
[52] Ibid., at p. 124, *per* Lindley, L.J. For a more detailed discussion see Key and
Elphinstone's *Precedents in Conveyancing* (15th ed., 1953) Vol. II, p. 185.
[53] [1903] 2 K.B. 135.

all that has been said about them."[54] The only prudent course for a banker to take is to make very careful inquiries with a view to ascertaining whether any third party has any interest in fixtures which may prejudicially affect the bank as mortgagee.

The Rent Act, 1968

7-34. There is an important restriction on the mortgagee's power to exercise his remedies which applies only to mortgages of certain dwelling-houses. This arises by virtue of the provisions of the Rent Act, 1968. The control of mortgages does not, however, afford any protection to owner-occupiers who have mortgaged their houses. The purpose of the control is to relieve those mortgagors who have let their houses to tenants and are restricted as regards increasing the rent paid by those tenants.

7-35. The control does not apply to all dwelling-houses.[55] At present there are two systems of control in operation, namely (i) "controlled tenancies" i.e., tenancies existing before 6th July, 1957, of houses with a rateable value which on 7th November, 1956, did not exceed £40 in London and £30 elsewhere, and (ii) "regulated tenancies," i.e., all other tenancies of houses with a rateable value which on 23rd March, 1965, did not exceed £400 in Greater London and £200 elsewhere.[56]

7-36. As far as mortgages are concerned, there are likewise two systems of protection, one where the property was on 7th December, 1965, subject to a controlled tenancy, and the other where the tenancy was regulated. The mortgages will be referred to hereafter as (*a*) controlled mortgages, and (*b*) regulated mortgages.

A. CONTROLLED MORTGAGES

7-37. The Rent Act, 1968,[57] applies, with certain exceptions, to prevent the mortgagee from taking any steps to enforce his security, until interest is twenty-one days in arrear, or the mortgagor is guilty of breach of covenant (other than for repayment of principal) or has failed to keep the property in proper repair or to pay some

---

[54] *Reynolds* v. *Ashby & Son* [1904] A.C. 466, at pp. 473–4. In this case, although the facts bore a close resemblance to those in *Lyon & Co.'s* case, the House of Lords gave its decision in favour of the mortgagee; and yet the House expressly approved the decision in *Lyon & Co.'s* case.

[55] This is a complex subject, which can only be considered briefly in this book. Reference should be made to the specialised works on the subject, e.g., R. E. Megarry, *The Rent Acts*.

[56] Rent Act, 1968, Sects. 1, 6, 7, 2nd Sched., Part I.

[57] Rent Act, 1968, Sect. 96 (1), 12th Sched., Part II.

interest or instalment of principal recoverable under a prior incumbrance. In addition to this restriction, no increase in the mortgage interest above the standard rate of interest can, in general, be made.[58] The author does not know of any case where a customer has claimed that the rate of interest on his overdraft could not be increased by virtue of these provisions.

B. REGULATED MORTGAGES

7-38. There is no automatic protection of a mortgagor under a regulated mortgage, but he may apply to the court for relief if he will be caused "severe financial hardship" by an increase in mortgage interest, the enforcement of the mortgage, or the registration of a reduced rent.[59]

---

[58] Rent Act, 1968, Sect. 96 (1), 12th Sched., Part I. The standard rate of interest is the rate payable on 3rd August, 1914, for old control, or 1st September, 1939, for new control, or, if the mortgage was created subsequently, the original rate of interest.

[59] Rent Act, 1968, Sect. 95.

CHAPTER 8

Second Mortgages

8-1. SECOND mortgages are frequently frowned upon as a banking security. Indeed, some banks make it a rule that they must not be accepted without the prior consent of a Head Office official. Nevertheless, there are circumstances where it is perfectly sound banking practice to take a second, or even a third, mortgage. If those circumstances exist and no other security is available, a second or third mortgage should not be refused.

Risks of Second Mortgages

8-2. The main determining factor when considering the suitability of a second mortgage is the relation between the value of the property and the amount of the advance made by the first mortgagee. Suppose, for example, that a customer is asking for accommodation to the extent of £750 against the security of a second mortgage of property valued at £5,000 where a first mortgagee has advanced only £1,000. In circumstances such as these, there is virtually no risk in accepting a second mortgage, provided that the appropriate steps are taken to safeguard the bank's legal position. As a matter of practice, however, it might well be sound policy for the bank to try to arrange for the first mortgagee to be paid off—the bank lending an extra one thousand pounds for this purpose and taking a first mortgage of the property.

8-3. The most important practical disadvantage of a second mortgage is that the second mortgagee is, to some extent, at the mercy of the first mortgagee. Thus, if the first mortgagee decides to exercise his power of sale, it may be that the price obtained will be insufficient to repay both debts. In this connection it should not be overlooked that any arrears of interest due to the first mortgagee will be added to the capital sum owing to him. Of course, the first mortgagee must exercise his power bona fide,[1] but he is under no duty to delay the sale to obtain a better price and so to improve the position of the second mortgagee; hence the importance of seeing that a wide margin exists between the value of the property and the amount of the first mortgagee's loan.

---

[1] See *ante*, para. 7-8.

8-4. Another risk is that the first mortgagee might commence foreclosure proceedings, which, if successful, would have the effect of extinguishing the second mortgage. But this danger is not as great as it seems. The second mortgagee has to be made a party to the action—if this is not done, his mortgage is not foreclosed—and when the order *nisi* is made, the second mortgagee is given the alternative of either losing his security or paying off the first mortgage. Furthermore, the Law of Property Act, 1925,[2] enables the court, at the request of the mortgagor or the second mortgagee, to direct a sale of the property instead of foreclosure.

8-5. Finally, a second mortgage suffers from the disadvantage that the first mortgagee may be under an obligation to make further advances. This point is considered later.[3]

Second Legal Mortgage

A. FREEHOLDS

8-6. A second legal mortgage of freehold property may be created in either of two ways—

(i) By a charge by deed expressed to be by way of legal mortgage. The same wording may be employed as in the case of a first mortgage,[4] though it is usual to add a clause to the effect that the mortgage thereby created is subject to a first mortgage dated . . . in favour of . . .

(ii) By a demise for a term of years absolute. When a mortgagor creates a first mortgage by granting a lease to the mortgagee for a long term, say three thousand years, the mortgagor retains the legal fee simple.[5] He has, therefore, a legal estate out of which further terms of years may be created. In practice he creates a second legal mortgage by granting to the second mortgagee a term one day longer than that in favour of the first mortgagee.

B. LEASEHOLDS

8-7. Similarly, a second legal mortgage of leasehold property may be created either—

(i) By a charge by deed expressed to be by way of legal mortgage; or

[2] Sect. 91 (2).
[3] See *post*, para. 8-13.
[4] See *ante*, para. 4-7.
[5] See *ante*, para. 4-4.

(ii) By a subdemise for a term of years absolute. This method has already been explained.[6] Normally, the term granted to the second mortgagee will, as in the case of freeholds, be one day longer than that granted to the first mortgagee.

Second Equitable Mortgage

8-8. A second equitable mortgage is a very rare form of banking security. If a banker feels obliged to accept a second mortgage at all, he nearly always insists upon having a legal mortgage so as to enjoy the more effective remedies of a legal mortgagee. The only type of case within the author's knowledge in which a bank was prepared to accept a second equitable mortgage was where property (subject to a first mortgage) was almost certain to be sold by the mortgagor during the next few months. In circumstances such as these—and particularly if some form of security is necessary to bolster up an unsecured overdraft—a second equitable mortgage is useful in that it prevents the customer from paying his other creditors out of the net proceeds of sale of the property in preference to the bank. The same rates of stamp duty apply to second mortgages as to first: hence it is cheaper to take an equitable mortgage than a legal one, unless advantage can be taken of collateral stamping.[7]

8-9. The wording of a second equitable mortgage closely follows that of a first equitable mortgage,[8] except, of course, that there is no deposit of the title deeds. The instrument should incorporate the usual undertaking by the customer to execute a legal mortgage when called upon.

8-10. Theoretically it would be possible to execute a second equitable mortgage under seal embodying either an irrevocable power of attorney and/or a declaration of trust. It is doubtful whether this is ever done in practice.

Creation of a Second Mortgage

8-11. The various steps to take when accepting a second mortgage of land may now be summarised briefly. In the normal course of events the deeds will be in the possession of the first mortgagee. In many cases it will be necessary to arrange for an official of the bank or its solicitor to examine them and to report upon title in

---

[6] See *ante*, para. 4-11.
[7] See *post*, para. 33-34.
[8] See *ante*, para. 4-38.

the usual way. Furthermore, the customary searches should be made at the Land Charges Department (or in one of the local registries in Yorkshire) and also in the registers of the appropriate local authorities.[9] In practice, however, one sometimes dispenses with investigation of title on the assumption that the first mortgagee has attended to this matter. Thus a bank which is taking a second mortgage often dispenses with investigation of title when the first mortgagee is a building society.

8-12. In view of the fact that the second mortgage will not be protected by a deposit of the deeds, the second mortgagee must register his interest in the Register of Land Charges. If his mortgage is legal, it will be registered as a Class C (i) charge ("puisne mortgages"), and if equitable, as a Class C (iii) charge ("general equitable charges"). This will secure his priority as against subsequent incumbrancers. The receipt of an application for registration is acknowledged by the Registry quoting the reference number under which the application is registered. This should be retained with the mortgage. If, however, the land is situated in Yorkshire, registration may have to be effected in the appropriate local deeds registry instead.[10]

8-13. Formal written notice of the second mortgage should be served on the first mortgagee, who should be asked to state the amount of his loan and to confirm that his mortgage does not impose upon him an obligation to make further advances. There are two reasons for giving this notice to the first mortgagee—

1. It prevents him from making further advances which will rank in priority to the bank as second mortgagee. This is particularly important if the first mortgage has been created to secure a current account or other further advances, because in such a case registration is not deemed to be notice.[11] If the first mortgage imposes an obligation upon the mortgagee to make further advances, this fact will be stated in the answer to the bank's question. Such advances, when made, will rank in priority to the bank's second mortgage.[12]

2. The giving of notice to the first mortgagee places him under a duty, when his mortgage is discharged, to hand over the deeds to the second mortgagee. Mere registration without notice would

[9] See *ante*, paras. 3-26/65.
[10] See *ante*, para. 3-63.
[11] See *ante*, para. 5-12.
[12] Law of Property Act, 1925, Sect. 94 (1), *ante*, para. 5-10.

be insufficient to achieve this result, because, when a mortgagee releases a mortgage, he is under no obligation to search.[13]

8-14. In order to complete his security, all that remains for the banker to do is to have the mortgage duly stamped and to ensure that the premises are properly insured. Notice of the bank's interest as second mortgagee should be given to the insurance company.[14] As in the case of a first mortgage the bank should make sure that the premiums are paid promptly. Finally, if the property is leasehold, the customer should be asked to exhibit the ground rent receipts periodically.

Remedies of Second Mortgagee

8-15. The remedies of a second mortgagee are very similar to those available to a first mortgagee—

A. ACTION FOR THE DEBT

8-16. A second mortgagee may sue the mortgagor if the latter fails to repay his debt.[15]

B. SALE OF THE PROPERTY

8-17. If his mortgage is by deed and does not contain any contrary stipulation, a second mortgagee has statutory power to sell the property in the same circumstances which enable a first mortgagee to exercise this remedy.[16] The second mortgagee may, if he wishes, sell the property without the concurrence of the first mortgagee. In other words he may sell the property subject to the first mortgage, which will still continue to subsist. In practice this is rarely done, because it is not easy to find a purchaser who is willing to buy land subject to an existing mortgage.

8-18. Usually, therefore, the second mortgagee will try to persuade the first mortgagee to join in the sale, the proceeds of sale being applied to discharge both their debts. In this event the purchaser obtains the property free from mortgage. If the first mortgagee is obstinate and refuses to release his security, there is a useful provision in the Law of Property Act, 1925,[17] whereby the second mortgagee may apply to the court which may, if it thinks fit, declare the property

[13] See *ante*, para. 6-13/14.
[14] See *ante*, paras. 3-66/67.
[15] See *ante*, para. 7-2.
[16] See *ante*, paras. 7-5/7.
[17] Sect. 50.

to be free from incumbrance upon sufficient money being paid into court. In effect the court compels the first mortgagee to be paid off.

8-19. If the second mortgage is not by deed, the mortgagee has no statutory power of sale. He can, however, apply to the court for an order for sale.

C. APPOINTMENT OF A RECEIVER

8-20. A second mortgagee has statutory power to appoint a receiver in just the same way as a first mortgagee, provided that his mortgage is by deed and does not expressly exclude the power.[18] Similarly, he may delegate to the receiver his leasing powers. The receiver must apply all rents received by him as stated in Chapter 7.[19] Thus interest on the first mortgage must be paid before any payments are made to the second mortgagee. It may be, however, that the mortgagor is not in default on the first mortgage, in which case the first mortgagee will have no claim on the amounts collected by the receiver.

8-21. If the second mortgage is not by deed, the mortgagee has no statutory power to appoint a receiver, though he may apply to the court, which will make an appointment in suitable cases.

D. FORECLOSURE

8-22. A second mortgagee, whether legal or equitable, may apply to the court for a foreclosure order. When the order absolute is made the property becomes his, subject to any prior incumbrances.[20]

E. TAKING POSSESSION OF THE PROPERTY

8-23. A second mortgagee under a legal mortgage may take possession of the property, unless the first mortgagee has already done so or a receiver has been appointed. As in the case of a first mortgagee, he is liable to account to the mortgagor for the rents and profits on the footing of "wilful default."[21] He will be obliged to apply the rents, in the first instance, in payment of interest on the first mortgage if the mortgagor is in default on that mortgage.

[18] See *ante*, paras. 7-13/14.
[19] See *ante*, para. 7-17.
[20] See *ante*, para. 7-18.
[21] See *ante*, para. 7-24.

Discharge of Second Mortgage

8-24. A second mortgage is discharged in the same way as a first mortgage (see Chapter 6). In the normal course of events the second mortgagee will not have obtained the title deeds, these being in the possession of the first mortgagee. He will therefore have protected his priority by registering his mortgage in the Register of Land Charges.[22] Upon discharging his mortgage he should remove the entry from the register. This is usually done by sending in Form L.C. 8, which, in the case of a limited company mortgagee (for example, a bank), must be completed under the company's seal. A new form, L.C. 8 (combined with L.C. 6) may be sealed by the bank or signed by the bank's solicitors. There is, moreover, a useful arrangement with most banks permitting certain officials to sign either the old or new Form L.C. 8 on behalf of the bank, in lieu of the form being sealed. The officials are nominated by the head office of the bank. Finally, the bank should notify the first mortgagee that its mortgage has been discharged.

[22] See *ante*, para. 8-12.

CHAPTER 9

Sub-Mortgages

9-1. A SUB-MORTGAGE may be defined briefly as "a mortgage of a mortgage," or, more accurately, as "a mortgage of a mortgage debt and of the security for that debt." Its use may best be explained by an illustration. B has borrowed from L the sum of £10,000 and, as security for the loan, has mortgaged Blackacre to L. L, who has an account at the London Bank, finds that he requires to borrow £1,000. Clearly it would be inadvisable for him to call in the whole of his loan, so he decides to raise the money by mortgaging his mortgage to the London Bank, that is to say, by creating a sub-mortgage. In this transaction L becomes the sub-mortgagor, and the London Bank the sub-mortgagee. The mortgage executed by B in favour of L is then often referred to as "the head mortgage."

Creation of a Sub-mortgage

9-2. The correct way of drafting a legal sub-mortgage depends upon the nature of the head mortgage. If the head mortgage is a mortgage by demise or subdemise, the mortgagee's legal estate is a term of years absolute and so a legal sub-mortgage can be effected in one of two ways[1]—

(*a*) by a charge by way of legal mortgage; or
(*b*) by a subdemise for a term less by at least one day than the term held by the sub-mortgagor.

9-3. In either case the sub-mortgage should contain an express assignment of the mortgage debt due under the head mortgage, followed by the usual proviso for redemption on repayment by the sub-mortgagor of all sums due to the sub-mortgagee.

9-4. If the head mortgage is a charge by way of legal mortgage, the mortgagee has no estate for a term of years and it would seem that the sub-mortgage should be effected by a transfer of the benefit of the head mortgage under Sect. 114 of the Law of Property Act, 1925.[2] This operates to transfer to the sub-mortgagee (i) the right

---

[1] Law of Property Act, 1925, Sect. 86 (1). Sect. 86 (2), in effect, prevents such a sub-mortgage being made by assignment. A purported assignment operates as a subdemise.
[2] See *Encyclopaedia of Forms and Precedents* (4th ed., 1967), Vol. 14, p. 774.

to recover the debt due under the head mortgage, and (ii) the right to enforce the legal charge thereby created. Then follows a clause which provides that, on the repayment by the sub-mortgagor of all sums due to the sub-mortgagee, the benefit of the head mortgage is to be re-transferred to the sub-mortgagor. This method of creating a sub-mortgage (i.e. by transferring the benefit of the head mortgage) is not invariably followed: some banks use their ordinary charge by way of legal mortgage. The argument is that as the head mortgage is a charge by way of legal mortgage, the mortgagee has under Sect. 87 (1) of the Law of Property Act, 1925, the same powers as if the mortgage was created by demise. Therefore, it is said, the sub-mortgage may be created by the same methods as those which apply when the head mortgage is a mortgage by demise. There is considerable force in this argument, but the better view is that when the head mortgage is a charge by way of legal mortgage, a sub-mortgage should be created by a transfer under Sect. 114 of the Law of Property Act, 1925.

9-5. It is possible to create an equitable sub-mortgage even though the head mortgage is a legal one, and this is, in fact, sometimes done by building societies. If the head mortgage is equitable, any sub-mortgage will necessarily be equitable, because the sub-mortgagor has only an equitable interest in the land.

A Sub-mortgage as Security

9-6. When a sub-mortgage is offered as security, the first step to take is to find out how much is still owing by the mortgagor to the mortgagee under the head mortgage; and secondly the property itself should be valued in order to ascertain whether the mortgage debt under the head mortgage is adequately secured. Even if the debt is not fully secured, a banker may still be prepared to accept a sub-mortgage, provided that the standing of the mortgagor under the head mortgage is undoubted. The threefold nature of the security in the case of a sub-mortgage should be noted. There is the personal obligation of the customer (the sub-mortgagor), together with the personal liability of the mortgagor, which is itself supported by a mortgage of the land.

9-7. Next, the bank will arrange for one of its officials or for its solicitors to examine the deeds, including, of course, the mortgage, and to report upon title. As a counsel of perfection one should search at the Land Charges Department against the name of the sub-mortgagor to discover whether he has already created a sub-mortgage without depositing the deeds—a very remote possibility.

If the proper searches were made by the mortgagee at the time when he took his mortgage, no further searching will be necessary in most cases. But, if the mortgagee has advanced additional sums since then and failed to search again, a further search should be made against the mortgagor to make quite sure that he has not created a second mortgage which would rank in priority to the later advances of the first mortgagee; though this could not happen if the first mortgage was made expressly for securing a current account or other further advances.[3]

9-8. The drafting of a sub-mortgage has already been considered.[4] As soon as the instrument has been executed, formal notice thereof should be served on the mortgagor under the head mortgage. He should be asked to acknowledge receipt and to confirm the amount of his debt; he should also be informed that any repayments of his debt must be made direct to the bank and not to his mortgagee.

9-9. The sub-mortgage should be duly stamped—the same rates of duty apply as in the case of a mortgage, namely, 2s. (10p) per cent if legal, 1s. (5p) per cent if equitable. All the deeds should be deposited with the bank, and the usual precautions should be taken to ensure that any premises are adequately insured and that the ground rent (if the property is leasehold) is promptly paid. These last points should be watched by the mortgagee under the head mortgage, but it is advisable for the bank, as sub-mortgagee, to make sure that everything is in order. If the land is situated in Yorkshire and the sub-mortgage creates or transfers a legal estate, registration may have to be effected in the appropriate local deeds registry.[5] Finally, if a sub-mortgage is executed by a company, it must be registered with the Registrar of Companies pursuant to Sect. 95 of the Companies Act, 1948.[6]

Remedies of Sub-mortgagee

The remedies of a legal sub-mortgagee are as follows—

A. ACTION FOR THE DEBT

9-10. The sub-mortgagee may sue the sub-mortgagor for the amount of the debt.

[3] See *ante*, para. 5-12.
[4] See *ante*, paras. 9-2/5.
[5] See *ante*, para. 3-63.
[6] See *post*, para. 32-4.

B. SALE OF THE DEBT

9-11. The sub-mortgagee may exercise the power of sale conferred by the sub-mortgage and sell the mortgage debt itself, if he can find anyone who is willing to purchase it. He can exercise this power whenever default has been made under the sub-mortgage, even though no default has been made under the head mortgage. Naturally the interest in the land which the purchaser obtains will be subject to redemption under the head mortgage. This is because the purchaser buys, not the land, but the right to receive payment of a debt which is secured on the land.

C. POWERS CONFERRED BY THE HEAD MORTGAGE

9-12. If default has been made under both the head mortgage and the sub-mortgage, the sub-mortgagee may exercise the powers conferred by the head mortgage. A bank, as sub-mortgagee, should ascertain what those powers are. It is very likely that they are not so extensive as those incorporated in the usual form of mortgage employed by the banks; for example, it is possible that Sect. 103 of the Law of Property Act, 1925, regulating the exercise of the power of sale, may apply without modification.[7]

9-13. If the sub-mortgagee exercises the power of sale conferred by the head mortgage, the purchaser will obtain the land freed from all claims of the mortgagor and the sub-mortgagor. This is the power which a sub-mortgagee normally wishes to exercise, but it can be resorted to only if the mortgagor under the head mortgage is in default. Fortunately one often finds that if the sub-mortgagor is in default, the mortgagor has defaulted also: indeed, it is usually the mortgagor's default that has brought the sub-mortgagor into difficulties.

9-14. In the case of an equitable sub-mortgage under hand, the legal position of the sub-mortgagee is analogous to that of a mortgagee whose mortgage consists of a memorandum of deposit under hand.[8] Thus, unless his sub-mortgagor is prepared to execute a legal sub-mortgage when called upon, the assistance of the court will be required before he can sell either the mortgage debt or the property.

Discharge of Sub-mortgage

9-15. When the advance secured by a legal sub-mortgage is repaid,

---

[7] See *ante*, para. 4-24.
[8] See *ante*, paras. 7-25/26.

the bank should endorse on the sub-mortgage a receipt in the following terms—

> We the within-named London Bank Limited hereby acknowledge that we have this   day of   19   received all the money secured by the within-written Sub-mortgage (including interest commission and costs) the payment having been made by A.B. of

The receipt must be stamped at the rate of 1s. (5p) per £200, with a maximum of 10s. (50p). All the deeds will be returned to the sub-mortgagor, and notice in writing of the discharge of the sub-mortgage should be sent to the mortgagor under the head mortgage.

9-16. The method outlined in an earlier chapter of discharging an equitable mortgage under hand applies, *mutatis mutandis*, to the discharge of an equitable sub-mortgage under hand.[9]

[9] See *ante*, paras. 6-15/16.

CHAPTER 10

Registered Land

10-1. THE main object of registration of title to land is to replace the relatively complicated investigation of title that is necessary on every purchase or mortgage of unregistered land by a title which, in a sense, is guaranteed by the State. Thus the system involves the substitution of the inconclusive, expensive, and constantly repeated examination of title by private individuals by one final and authoritative examination by the State. In this way a register of proprietors of land is compiled. It should be noted, however, that a registered proprietor is not necessarily entitled against all the world to remain proprietor. He is assumed to be the owner of the interest in respect of which he is registered, but this may prove on very rare occasions not to be the case. The register may then be rectified by removing his name, whereupon he will lose all interest in the land. If this happens, he may then be entitled to claim indemnity from a fund established by the State. The result is that the "State guaranteed title," as it is sometimes called, is not so much a guarantee of a right to an interest in land as an alternative claim to the interest or to compensation for loss of it.

10-2. A purchaser or mortgagee of registered land is able to discover, by making an inspection of the land register, whether the vendor or mortgagor has power to deal with the land and, furthermore, whether the land is subject to certain incumbrances. So far as is practicable the machinery for the purchase and sale of registered land has been assimilated to that of stocks and shares. Thus, when registered land is transferred, the registered proprietor executes an instrument of transfer which closely resembles a transfer of shares. Nevertheless, the inherent complexity of rights in land makes it impossible for the transfer of registered land to be quite as simple as a transfer of shares in the books of a company.

10-3. The present Acts governing registration of title are the Land Registration Acts, 1925, 1936, and 1966, but the system itself is much older than these statutes. Land Transfer Acts passed in 1862 and 1875 had provided for voluntary registration of title, and, under the Land Transfer Act, 1897, the system became compulsory in the county of London. Under the Land Registration Act, 1925, Sect. 120 (1), compulsory areas may be designated by Order in Council and many counties, cities, and boroughs have been so designated. When a county, city or county borough is made a compulsory area, this does not mean that all land there has to be registered forthwith. Registration only becomes obligatory when there is (i) a conveyance on sale of the fee simple, or (ii) a grant of a lease for forty years or more, or (iii) the assignment on sale of a lease with forty or more years unexpired.[1] In addition it is obligatory to register a lease for more than twenty-one years in cases where the freehold out of which the lease is granted has been registered; this is so because "dispositions" by registered proprietors as defined by the Act must themselves be registered.[2]

10-4. Applications for registration of title in regard to land *outside* the compulsory areas are entertained at present only in those classes of cases which the Registrar from time to time specifies.[3] Thus, applications will be entertained in cases where the entire set of title deeds has been lost or destroyed whilst in the custody of solicitors.[4]

Types of Title to Registered Land

10-5. It is beyond the scope of this book to examine exhaustively the way in which all the various types of interests in land may be protected by entries in the land register.[5] It is sufficient to examine such part of the system as is of direct interest to mortgagees, with particular reference to the practice of bankers. A proprietor who owns an estate capable of registration will be registered with one of the four following types of title: (*a*) absolute, (*b*) good leasehold, (*c*) possessory, and (*d*) qualified. All four classes are applicable to leaseholds, though the second is not, of course, applicable to a freehold title. In practice most freeholds are registered with an absolute title, and most leaseholds with a good leasehold title. The decision as to which type of title shall be granted rests with the Registrar, and the courts of law will not interfere.[6]

---

[1] Land Registration Act, 1925, Sect. 123 (1). But the registration of a lease is prohibited if it is a mortgage term still subject to a right of redemption: ibid., Sects 8 (1), 19 (2), and 123 (3).

[2] Ibid., Sect. 19 (2).

[3] Land Registration Act, 1966, Sect. 1 (2).

[4] See Practice Leaflet for Solicitors, No. 12, issued by the Registrar.

[5] For a detailed discussion the reader is referred to the specialised works on the subject, such as George H. Curtis and Theodore B. F. Ruoff, *The Law and Practice of Registered Conveyancing* (2nd ed., 1965); Theodore B. F. Ruoff, *Concise Land Registration Practice* (2nd ed., 1967); and J. Anthony Holland and J. R. Lewis, *Principles of Registered Land Conveyancing* (1967), a useful book for students.

[6] *Dennis* v. *Malcolm* [1934] Ch. 244.

A. ABSOLUTE TITLE

10-6. The effect of registration of an owner of freehold property with an absolute title is to vest in him an estate in fee simple in possession in the land subject to—

(i) Any incumbrances or other entries on the register.

(ii) "Overriding interests." These are a miscellaneous collection of interests which are not registrable and yet bind the legal estate without notice. Most of them are unimportant from a mortgagee's point of view. They are listed in the Land Registration Act, 1925, Sect. 70. Examples are rights of way and leases for not more than twenty-one years at a rent without a fine.

(iii) "Minor interests." These, unlike overriding interests, require to be protected by an entry on the register. The term "minor" is misleading: some minor interests may be important to an intending mortgagee. Restrictive covenants fall within the category. Similarly, when a receiving order in bankruptcy is made, "a bankruptcy inhibition" is entered preventing the registered proprietor from disposing of the land.

10-7. An absolute title to a leasehold interest is granted only in cases where the title to the freehold, the leasehold, and any intermediate leasehold has been approved. The effect of registration is to vest in the proprietor the leasehold subject to the various items set out above and subject also to all the liabilities of the lease. Registration guarantees not only that he is the owner of the lease but also that the lease was validly granted.

B. GOOD LEASEHOLD

10-8. This title applies only to leaseholds, and confers upon the proprietor the same rights as an absolute title except that it does not guarantee the lessor's right to grant the lease. The rule is that a lessee, when taking a lease, is not permitted to investigate the freehold title unless he expressly stipulates for this right.[7] Thus a lessee, when registering his title, cannot usually give the Registrar evidence of the freehold title, and so he can apply only for a good leasehold title and not for an absolute title.

C. POSSESSORY TITLE

10-9. Registration with this title has the same effect as registration with an absolute title, with the very important exception that the

[7] Law of Property Act, 1925, Sect. 44 (2).

title is subject to all rights subsisting or capable of arising at the time of registration.[8] In other words, the title is guaranteed in respect of dealings after registration, but no guarantee is given concerning the title prior to registration. This is a serious drawback from the point of view of a purchaser or mortgagee, who has to investigate the prior title as if the land was unregistered. Provision is made for the Registrar to convert a possessory title into absolute or good leasehold after the lapse of fifteen years and ten years respectively, provided that the Registrar is satisfied that the proprietor is in possession. Furthermore, where the Registrar is satisfied as to title, he may, on a transfer for valuable consideration of land registered with a possessory title, enter the title of the transferee or grantee as absolute or good leasehold, as the case may require, whether the transferee or grantee consents or not.[9]

D. QUALIFIED TITLE

10-10. This has the same effect as an absolute title subject to any flaws specified in the register, and is very uncommon. It is granted in cases where an absolute or good leasehold title has been applied for, but the Registrar has been unable to grant it.

The Land Register

The land register is divided into three parts—

A. THE PROPERTY REGISTER

10-11. This gives the title number, together with a short description of the land and states whether it is freehold or leasehold. It also quotes the appropriate reference to the Land Registry General Map.

B. THE PROPRIETORSHIP REGISTER

10-12. This states the nature of the title (absolute, good leasehold, qualified, or possessory), the name, address, and description of the registered proprietor, the date when he was registered and the price which he paid. It also sets forth various matters which may affect his right of dealing with the land, as, for example, bankruptcy inhibitions.

[8] Land Registration Act, 1925, Sects. 6 and 20 (3).
[9] Ibid., Sect. 77.

C. THE CHARGES REGISTER

10-13. This contains entries of such matters as mortgages and restrictive covenants.

10-14. The card-index system is employed, and the three parts of the register in respect of each property are usually filed on a single card. The register is not open to inspection by the public. It is available only to registered proprietors of the land or a charge on the land and any person authorised by them.[10]

District Land Registries

10-15. The District Land Registries referred to in the following list, are the proper offices for the registration of title to land within the areas which they serve. Applications of all kinds, whether for the first registration, dealings with registered land, office copies, or official searches, should be sent to the proper office. The Headquarters office of the Land Registry at Lincoln's Inn Fields, London, W.C.2, is no longer responsible for any registration work. However, personal searches of the registers and index maps held at one District Land Registry may be made at any of the other District Land Registries, or at the Headquarters office, on the applicant giving not less than four days' notice of his desire to do so at the office where inspection is sought.

District Registry	*Administrative Counties*	*County Boroughs, London Boroughs, etc.*
The Croydon District Land Registry, Sunley House, Croydon CR9 3LE		Bexley
		Bromley
		Croydon
		Greenwich
		Kingston upon Thames
		Lambeth
		Lewisham
		Merton
		Richmond upon Thames
		Southwark
		Sutton
		Wandsworth

[10] Sect. 112.

District Registry	*Administrative Counties*	*County Boroughs,* *London Boroughs,* *etc.*
The Durham District Land Registry, Aykley Heads, Durham	Durham Northumberland Yorkshire, East Riding Yorkshire, North Riding	Darlington Gateshead Hartlepool Kingston upon Hull Newcastle upon Tyne South Shields Sunderland Teesside Tynemouth York
The Gloucester District Land Registry, Bruton Way, Gloucester GL1 1DQ	Berkshire Gloucestershire Hampshire Isle of Wight Oxfordshire Staffordshire	Bournemouth Bristol Gloucester Oxford Portsmouth Reading Southampton Burton upon Trent Dudley Stoke-on-Trent Walsall West Bromwich Wolverhampton
The Harrow District Land Registry, Lyon House, Lyon Road, Harrow, Middx. HA1 2EU		The City of London The Inner Temple and the Middle Temple Barking Barnet Brent Camden City of Westminster Ealing Enfield Hackney Hammersmith Haringey Harrow Havering Hillingdon Hounslow Islington

District Registry	*Administrative Counties*	*County Boroughs, London Boroughs, etc.*
		Kensington and Chelsea
		Newham
		Redbridge
		Tower Hamlets
		Waltham Forest
The Lythan District Land Registry, Lytham St. Annes, Lancs. FY8 5AB	Cheshire Cumberland Herefordshire Lancashire Monmouthshire Shropshire Westmorland All the counties in Wales	Barrow-in-Furness Birkenhead Blackburn Blackpool Bolton Bootle Burnley Bury Carlisle Chester Liverpool Manchester Newport Oldham Preston Rochdale St. Helens Salford Southport Stockport Wallasey Warrington Wigan All the county boroughs in Wales
The Nottingham District Land Registry, Chalfont Drive, Nottingham NG8 3RN	Derbyshire Leicestershire Nottinghamshire Warwickshire Worcestershire Yorkshire, West Riding	Barnsley Birmingham Bradford Coventry Derby Dewsbury Doncaster Halifax Huddersfield Leeds Leicester

District Registry	Administrative Counties	County Boroughs, London Boroughs, etc.
		Nottingham
		Rotherham
		Sheffield
		Solihull
		Wakefield
		Warley
		Worcester
The Plymouth District Land Registry, Railway Offices, North Road, Plymouth, Devon PL4 6AD	Cornwall Devon Dorset Somerset Wiltshire	Bath Exeter Plymouth Torbay
The Stevenage District Land Registry, Brickdale House, Stevenage, Herts.	Bedfordshire Buckinghamshire Cambridgeshire and Isle of Ely Essex Hertfordshire Huntingdon and Peterborough Lincoln, parts of Holland Lincoln, parts of Kesteven Lincoln, parts of Lindsey Norfolk Northamptonshire Rutland Suffolk, East Suffolk, West	Great Yarmouth Grimsby Ipswich Lincoln Luton Northampton Norwich Southend-on-Sea
The Tunbridge Wells District Land Registry, Tunbridge Wells, Kent	Kent Surrey Sussex, East Sussex, West	Brighton Canterbury Eastbourne Hastings

The Land Certificate

10-16. When title is registered, the proprietor is supplied with a document known as a land certificate, which contains a facsimile of the entries in the register and also a copy of the official plan identifying the land. In the case of a freehold title, the last conveyance is branded with the Land Registry stamp, and in the case of a leasehold title, it is branded on the lease and on the last assignment. This marking of the deeds is authorised by the Land Registration Act, 1925.[11] The deeds are then returned to the proprietor, and they should be carefully preserved, because they may contain references to certain matters which do not appear on the register and are not recorded on the land certificate. These matters are the "overriding interests" referred to earlier.[12]

10-17. The land certificate will be officially examined, and, where necessary, made to correspond with the register at any time without fee if sent to the registry. The date on which the certificate was last examined in the registry and made to correspond with the register is endorsed thereon. This is a useful service, because it enables a registered proprietor to obtain evidence of the state of the register without cost a day or two before he enters into negotiations for the sale of the land. When the price has been agreed upon, the vendor executes a transfer which is sent to the registry together with the land certificate. The register and land certificate are suitably amended, and the certificate handed to the purchaser, though in certain cases (e.g. where the vendor is not parting with all the land) a new certificate will have to be issued in favour of the purchaser.

10-18. If the certificate is lost, the Registrar is empowered to issue a new one after taking such indemnities as he may consider necessary and after giving such public notice in the *Gazette* and in such other manner as appears to him sufficient in each case. Furthermore, the Registrar normally requires a statutory declaration by a responsible person who is able to speak to the facts connected with the loss and the efforts which have been made to trace the certificate. The declaration must state, among other matters, that the certificate has not been deposited as security for an advance.[13]

Mortgages of Registered Land in General

10-19. The law relating to mortgages of registered land is not fundamentally different from that relating to mortgages of unregistered land. For example, a customer may create in favour of his banker either a legal mortgage or an equitable mortgage of registered land, and the banker will be in a position to exercise the same remedies as are available to mortgagees of unregistered land. Thus the new system remains dependent upon the old law of real property.

---

[11] Sect. 16.
[12] See *ante*, para. 10-6.
[13] Land Registration Act, 1925, Sect. 67 (2) and the Land Registration Rules, 1925, rule 271. See also *Practice Leaflet for Solicitors, No.* 3.

10-20. The first step to take when offered a mortgage of registered land is to obtain the land certificate. Whether the title deeds will be required as well depends upon the circumstances. If the land is registered with a possessory title, the title prior to registration will have to be examined in just the same way as if the land was un-registered. In the case of a good leasehold title, the original lease should normally be required. If the mortgagor has an absolute title, the land certificate unaccompanied by the deeds is generally sufficient. If the deeds are available, it may perhaps be advisable to see whether they disclose any overriding interests, though, as already stated, these interests are not of much practical importance to mortgagees.[14] Finally, in the unlikely event of the land being registered with a qualified title, the banker should require the same evidence as to the estate, right, or interest excluded from the effect of registration, by reason of which the title is qualified and not absolute, as he would have required if the land was unregistered.

10-21. Next the banker will have to decide whether to take a legal or an equitable mortgage. There are methods of taking an equitable mortgage which place the banker in virtually the same position as if he had taken a legal mortgage, and, from the customer's point of view, an equitable mortgage is preferable, because the compara-tively heavy fees payable upon registration of a legal mortgage are avoided. However, some banks are not content with obtaining an equitable interest, and it is proposed to outline first the procedure to be followed when it is desired to create a legal mortgage.

Legal Mortgage of Registered Land

10-22. A mortgagee must find out whether there are any adverse entries on the register. There are two ways of doing this, and in practice it may be advisable to employ both. The first is to send the land certificate to the registry to be brought up to date; this is done free of charge. Then there is likely to be a period of a week or so during which the mortgage is prepared and executed, and it is con-ceivable that during this time some adverse entry may appear un-known to the banker. To guard against this, the banker may use the scheme of free official searches on behalf of purchasers and mort-gagees. The bank's solicitors should fill in and send to the registry Form 94A (for a search of the whole of the land in a title) or Form 94B (search of part), accompanied in each case by the written authority of the mortgagor or his solicitors. This gives the bank, as mortgagee, priority for fifteen days subsequent to the date of the search to complete and register the charge. The bank will obtain

---

[14] See *ante*, para. 10-6.

priority over any entry made in the register during that period.[15] An official search also exonerates the bank's solicitors from the responsibility for any error made in searching, which in the case of personal searches would fall on them.[16] A somewhat similar "period of grace" is available to a mortgagee of unregistered land who obtains a search certificate.[17] Unfortunately that system does not appear to protect bankers when lending by way of fluctuating overdraft; the analogous provisions relating to registered land do not suffer from this defect.

10-23. If, in regard to registered land, the bank's solicitor has obtained an official certificate of search but finds that he is unable to deliver the application for registration within the priority period of fifteen days, he may apply for an extension of priority for a further period of fourteen days.[18] Application for this extension must be made on Form 95 and be accompanied by a fee of £1.[19]

10-24. In relation to registered land, no searches need be made in any place other than the land registry, except—

    (i) the registers kept by the local authorities should be searched if the nature of the property seems to render this course desirable;[20]

    (ii) if the mortgagor is a limited company, a search must also be made at Companies House.[21]

10-25. Having obtained the search certificate, the banker is ready to prepare the mortgage. It must be by deed but, apart from that, the Land Registration Act, 1925, Sect. 25 (2), enacts that it may be in any form, provided that "the registered land comprised in the charge is described by reference to the register or in any other manner sufficient to enable the Registrar to identify the same without reference to any other document." The charge may be taken, if desired, on Form 45. Another form (No. 47) is worded rather differently in order to secure future advances. But the use of these forms is optional, and in practice most banks prefer to use their

---

[15] Land Registration (Official Searches) Rules, 1969, rr. 2 (2) and 5. The rules also enable solicitors to make official searches by telephone or teleprinter. These must be followed up by a normal application in Form 94A or 94B, thus overcoming the problem that the inability to transmit a signed authority to inspect the register would present.

[16] There is a fee of 5s. (25p) for making a personal search: Land Registration Fee Order, 1970, para. 2 and Sched. para. XII. A bank may conduct its own personal search provided that the customer's written consent is obtained; at least one of the Clearing banks searches in this way.

[17] See *ante*, para. 3-36.

[18] Land Registration (Official Searches) Rules, 1969, rr. 6 and 7.

[19] Land Registration Fee Order, 1970, para. 2 and Sched. para. XII.

[20] See *ante*, paras. 3-56/59.

[21] See *post*, para. 32-20.

ordinary legal mortgage forms applicable to unregistered land, because they contain various clauses designed to strengthen the bank's position. Some banks have a separate set of forms, suitably headed, for registered land. The description of the land on the mortgage form should include a reference to the title number. If the charge is to affect part only of the land comprised in a title, a description by plan or reference to the Land Registry General Map is required. A charge of two or more titles may be effected by the one instrument.

10-26. When the customer has executed the mortgage, the bank should have it registered within the priority period or the extended priority period in order that the bank's priority may be protected.[22] The following documents must be sent to the registry: (i) the charge, (ii) a copy thereof, (iii) the search certificate, and (iv) the land certificate. The land certificate, the search certificate, and the copy of the charge are retained in the registry, and the appropriate entry is made in the charges register. An instrument called a charge certificate is issued to the bank and within it is stitched the charge itself.

10-27. The appropriate fee for registration of the charge must accompany the aforementioned documents. The fees are prescribed by the Land Registration Fee Order, 1970[23]—

Amount of Charge or Mortgage	*Fee*
Not exceeding £5,000	£1 6s. (£1.30) for every £500 or part of £500
Exceeding £5,000 but not exceeding £100,000	£13 for the first £5,000 and £1 2s. (£1.10) for every £500 or part of £500 over £5,000
Exceeding £100,000	£222 for the first £100,000 and 10s. (£0.50) for every £1,000 or part of £1,000 over £100,000 with a maximum fee of £422

10-28. If the charge is one to secure further advances—as are most charges in favour of the banks—the registration fee is as follows[24]—

(*a*) Where the total amount of the advances or of the money to be owing at any one time is in any way limited, the same as that for the registration of a charge to secure the amount so limited.

(*b*) Where the total amount is unlimited the same as that for the registration of a charge to secure the amount for which stamp duty on the charge has been paid.

[22] See *ante*, paras. 10-22/23.
[23] Para. 2 and Sched. para V.
[24] 1970 Order, para. 14.

10-29. No registration fee is payable where the charge accompanies an application for first registration; and half the normal fee is payable where the charge accompanies a transfer for value.[25]

Legal Mortgage of Registered Land—An Alternative Method

10-30. There is an alternative method of creating a legal mortgage of registered land. By virtue of the Land Registration Act, 1925,[26] the proprietor of registered land may "mortgage, by deed or otherwise, the land or any part thereof in any manner which would have been permissible if the land had not been registered and with the like effect," provided that the land is described in the mortgage by reference to the register or in any other manner sufficient to enable the Registrar to identify it without reference to any other document.

10-31. The Act continues by declaring that, if the mortgage is by deed (which is, of course, essential for the creation of a legal mortgage), it may be protected by "a caution in a specially prescribed form."[27] The 1925 Rules[28] provide that this "mortgage caution" must be accompanied by the land certificate, the mortgage on which it is founded, and a copy thereof. The Registrar must then enter the mortgage caution in the proprietorship register (*not* the charges register) and give notice to the proprietor of the land that he has done so. The fees payable for entering a mortgage caution are the same as those for registration of a charge.[29] The Registrar retains the land certificate and the copy of the mortgage in the registry. He marks the original with a note of the registration and returns it to the mortgagee. At any time in the future the mortgagee who has availed himself of this procedure may require his mortgage to be registered as a charge with the same priority as the caution.[30] This method of mortgaging registered land is seldom, if ever, resorted to by bankers.

Equitable Mortgage of Registered Land

10-32. The creation of an equitable mortgage of registered land is easy and inexpensive: in particular, the heavy fees payable upon registration of a legal mortgage are avoided. The Land Registration Act, 1925,[31] provides that the proprietor of registered land may

[25] 1970 Order, para. 5.
[26] Sect. 106 (1).
[27] Sect. 106 (2).
[28] L.R. Rules, 1925, r. 223 (1), (2), (3), and (5).
[29] See *ante*, para. 10-27.
[30] Land Registration Act, 1925, Sect. 106 (5).
[31] Sect. 66.

"create a lien on the registered land" by deposit of the land certificate and that such lien shall, subject to any interests registered or protected on the register at the date of the deposit, "be equivalent to a lien created in the case of unregistered land by the deposit of documents of title." The equitable mortgagee should then give notice in duplicate on Form 85A to the Registrar, who will enter such notice in the charges register and send back the duplicate notice to the mortgagee by way of acknowledgment.[32] No fee is payable.[33] The lender's position is now adequately secured, because once the notice is put on the register it is complete protection against subsequent encumbrancers, since they cannot claim to be without notice.[34] Furthermore, if the registered proprietor should attempt to make any disposition of the land (which in most cases he could only do by using a duplicate or a forged land certificate), notice thereof would be sent to the equitable mortgagee who would have fourteen days in which to appear and oppose the transaction.[35]

10-33. A banker who decides to take an equitable mortgage will, of course, wish to ensure that there are no adverse entries on the register which might prejudicially affect him. The usual practice is to send the land certificate to the registry with Form 85A. The land certificate will be entered up to date including the notice of deposit. When the certificate is returned to the banker, he will see whether there are any entries on the register detrimental to him.

10-34. Occasionally a customer objects to having notice of deposit entered on the land certificate. In this event there is virtually no risk in having the certificate brought up to date first, and then, immediately it is returned by the Registrar, notice of deposit may be sent in, i.e. without the certificate. This keeps the entry off the certificate. There is another method adopted by one of the Clearing banks which keeps the entry off the certificate: the bank makes a personal search and lodges notice of deposit immediately the search discloses a clear title.

10-35. Although the mere deposit of the land certificate followed by the giving of notice to the Registrar is sufficient to create an equitable mortgage, a bank invariably obtains the mortgagor's signature to a form of charge containing the usual clauses found in bank security forms. For this purpose some banks use a memorandum of deposit under hand, but this cannot confer power upon the bank to sell the

[32] L.R. Rules, 1925, r. 239.
[33] Land Registration Fee Order, 1970, para. 4.
[34] *Re White Rose Cottage* [1965] Ch. 940.
[35] Land Registration Act, 1925, Sects. 54-6 and L.R. Rules, 1925, rr. 215-21.

property in the event of the mortgagor's default. Other banks ask
the mortgagor to execute an equitable mortgage *under seal* embodying the special clauses which enable the bank to sell the property
upon default.[36] Another method, which is quite frequently adopted,
is to ask the mortgagor to execute a *legal* mortgage. Instead of
registering it, however, and incurring a fairly heavy registration fee,
the bank merely gives notice of deposit of the land certificate. If
necessary, the mortgage may be registered at a later date, and the
bank will then be able to exercise all the powers of a legal mortgagee.

10-36. The Land Registration Rules, 1925, make provision for the
type of case where a borrower, who has agreed to buy land and who
wishes to obtain a loan to enable him to complete, cannot deposit
the land certificate with the lender because it has not yet been
issued to him. The procedure available is for the purchaser to give
notice to the Registrar that "he intends to deposit the land certificate,
when issued, with another person as security for money."[37] Notice
should normally be given on Form 85B when the intended deposit
relates to an application for first registration, and on Form 85C
when it relates to an uncompleted dealing with registered land.

Priorities

10-37. The rules relating to priorities where a mortgagor of registered
land creates more than one mortgage thereof are less complicated
than the rules governing similar competing interests in unregistered
land, which are discussed in Chapter 5. The main principle laid
down on this matter in the Land Registration Act, 1925,[38] is that
"registered charges on the same land shall as between themselves
rank according to the order in which they are entered on the register,
and not according to the order in which they are created."[39] This
section must be read in conjunction with another provision that is of
first importance to bankers, because it deals with registered charges
to secure further advances. It enacts[40] that—

> When a registered charge is made for securing further advances, the
> registrar shall, before making any entry on the register which would
> prejudicially affect the priority of any further advance thereunder, give
> to the proprietor of the charge at his registered address, notice by
> registered post of the intended entry, and the proprietor of the charge

[36] *Ante*, paras. 3-10/13.
[37] L.R. Rules, 1925, r. 240.
[38] Sect. 29.
[39] But occasionally absolute priority is given to charges ecrated under particular
statutes. Examples are to be found in the Improvement of Land Act, 1864, Sect. 59,
and the Agricultural Holdings Act, 1948, Sect. 83 (5), *anei*, para. 5-24.
[40] Land Registration Act, 1925, Sect. 30 (1).

shall not, in respect of any further advance, be affected by such entry, unless the advance is made after the date when notice ought to have been received in course of post.

This is followed by a provision that, if the proprietor of the charge suffers loss in relation to a further advance as the result of any failure on the part of the Registrar or the post office, he is entitled to be reimbursed out of an insurance fund established by the Land Registration Acts; but this does not apply if the loss occurred because the proprietor of the charge changed his address without notifying the Registrar.[41] Accordingly, when an overdraft secured by a registered charge is transferred from one branch to another, the Registrar should be informed.

10-38. The operation of these rules may be illustrated by the following example. A customer creates a legal mortgage of registered land to secure further advances in favour of his banker. The charge is duly registered. Then he creates a second mortgage in favour of M2 who applies to the Registrar for registration thereof. The Registrar gives notice to the banker who must then rule off the mortgagor's account in order to avoid the operation of the Rule in *Clayton's case*.[42]

10-39. To these general rules there is but one exception. The Law of Property (Amendment) Act, 1926,[43] provides that—

Where the proprietor of a charge is under an obligation, noted on the register, to make a further advance, a subsequent registered charge shall take effect subject to any further advance made pursuant to the obligation.

A similar rule applies to mortgages of unregistered land.[44]

10-40. So far, attention has been paid to the relative priorities of registered charges. If a first mortgagee does not register his charge, either because it is equitable and is therefore not registrable, or because it is legal and he decides to protect himself by a mortgage caution, his priority is secured, as we have already seen, by some form of entry on the register. The most important example of an unregistered first charge is that created by deposit of the land certificate, and the machinery for securing the priority of the chargee has already been noted.[45]

[41] Sect. 30 (2).
[42] (1816) 1 Mer. 572.
[43] Sect. 5.
[44] See *ante*, para. 5-10.
[45] See *ante*, para. 10-32.

Discharge of Mortgage of Registered Land

A. DISCHARGE OF REGISTERED CHARGE

10-41. Form 53 should be completed by the mortgagee and sent to the registry together with the charge certificate.[46] If a reconveyance is added to the form, stamp duty at the rate of 1s. (5p) per £200, with a maximum of 10s. (50p) must be paid. No fee is payable to the registry for the discharge of a registered charge. If there is no other charge on the register, the land certificate (retained in the registry during the subsistence of the charge) will be made up to date and returned to the proprietor of the land on application being made for this to be done. In the case of the joint-stock banks, the Registrar is willing to accept a discharge in Form 53 signed by a general manager or assistant general manager or someone of comparable rank. A branch manager's signature is accepted if the sum secured is less than £2,000.

10-42. Form 53 may also be used if the discharge relates to part only of the land. The following words should be added at the end of the form: "As to the land shown and edged with red on the accompanying plan, signed by me, being part of the land comprised in the said charge."

10-43. If the mortgagor has sold the property, it is convenient to use Form 55, which is a combined form of transfer and discharge. The form has to be executed by the mortgagor as proprietor of the land and by the mortgagee as proprietor of the charge, with the result that the purchaser obtains the land freed from the charge.

B. DISCHARGE OF UNREGISTERED CHARGE

10-44. Where an equitable mortgage has been created by the deposit of the land certificate, notice of which has been given to the Registrar, the notice of deposit may be withdrawn from the register on the written request of the person entitled to the lien created by the deposit; the land certificate must accompany this request.[47] For this purpose one may use the form on the back of the Registrar's acknowledgment of the notice of deposit. In the case of a bank the signature of a branch manager will be accepted. No fee is payable. The land certificate will be returned with the notice of deposit deleted therefrom.

10-45. Apparently it is impossible to withdraw notice of deposit as to part of the land in a title, unless that part is being sold.[48] In the

---

[46] Land Registration Act, 1925, Sect. 35 and L.R. Rules, 1925, rr. 151 and 267.
[47] L.R. Rules, 1925, r. 246.
[48] George H. Curtis and Theodore B. F. Ruoff, op cit., p. 636.

latter event the mortgagee may give his consent to a dealing with part of the land, and, when writing to the Registrar, he should state whether or not the dealing is to be registered free from his lien.

10-46. If the bank, when taking the deposit of the land certificate, obtained its customer's signature to a form of legal mortgage,[49] this form may be destroyed when the notice of deposit of the land certificate is withdrawn: it will not be required for the purpose of establishing the proprietor's title in the future. However, it seems that some solicitors like to have a release executed on the mortgage which will, of course, attract *ad valorem* stamp duty as in the case of unregistered land.

10-47. If the bank has taken an unregistered legal mortgage which it has protected by a mortgage caution, the caution should be withdrawn by the bank when it is desired to vacate the security. Application should be made on Form 71 which must either be sealed by the bank or made by its solicitor.[50] The caution will then be removed from the proprietorship register.

Remedies of Mortgagees of Registered Land

10-48. A legal or equitable mortgagee of registered land enjoys the same remedies as a legal or equitable mortgagee of unregistered land.[51] The only way in which their respective positions may differ arises from the fact that, in the case of a registered charge, the following covenants by the mortgagor are implied[52]—

(i) to pay the principal and interest at the appointed time and rate;

(ii) if the principal sum or any part thereof is unpaid at the appointed time, to pay interest half-yearly at the appointed rate on so much of the principal sum as remains unpaid;

(iii) in the case of leasehold titles, to pay the rent and perform the covenants of the lease and to keep the lender indemnified for non-payment or non-performance.

10-49. Although no such covenants are implied in mortgages of unregistered land, these mortgages invariably contain express covenants to the like effect and so the practical result is the same. Thus the mortgagee of unregistered land may sue the borrower on his *express* covenant to repay, whereas the mortgagee of registered land may sue on an *implied* covenant to do so.

---

[49] See *ante*, para. 10-35.
[50] L.R. Rules, 1925, rr. 222 and 224.
[51] See Chapter 7.
[52] Land Registration Act 1925 Sect. 28.

10-50. The other remedies call for little comment. A mortgagee who has registered his mortgage is able (subject to any entry on the register to the contrary) to exercise "all the powers conferred by law on the owner of a legal mortgage."[53] If he decides to exercise his power of sale, he will make use of Form 31.[54] On registration of the transfer, the charge is cancelled and so are all charges of inferior priority. If, however, the sale does not realise the full amount of the debt, the registration of the charge may be kept alive for the purpose of continuing the implied covenant to pay referred to above. A special application in writing must be made, stating the facts.

10-51. A mortgagee must have his mortgage registered before he is in a position to effect a sale. Thus, if his security consists of a legal mortgage protected by a mortgage caution, he must have his mortgage registered before he can sell. Similarly, if he has been content with an equitable mortgage by deposit of the land certificate but has taken the precaution of obtaining his mortgagor's signature to a form of legal mortgage, this must be registered before a sale can be effected. If the security consists simply of the deposit of the land certificate, application will have to be made to the court to order a sale.

Mortgage of An Equitable Interest in Registered Land

10-52. Let it be assumed that Blackacre, a plot of registered land, is held by T1 and T2 upon trust for sale. L is the life tenant and R the remainderman. L wishes to mortgage his interest in Blackacre to the bank. As L's life estate is a minor interest under the Land Registration Act, 1925,[55] no registered charge thereof can be made.

10-53. The Land Registry keeps a "Minor Interests Index," and the priority of mortgages of equitable interests in registered land is regulated by the order of priority cautions entered in that Index.[56] This Index is wholly extraneous to the general purposes of the Land Registration Acts, and persons dealing with a registered interest in the land are not concerned with it. It forms no part of the register and is, therefore, not referred to in the land certificate.[57] It will, of course, be necessary for the banker to search this Index to find out whether the customer has already mortgaged his life interest. Inquiry should be made by post, and a fee of £1 for the reply be

---

[53] Ibid., Sect. 34 (1).
[54] L.R. Rules, 1925, r. 114.
[55] Sect. 3 (xv).
[56] Land Registration Act, 1925, Sect. 102 (2) and L.R. Rules, 1925, r. 229.
[57] See L.R. Rules, 1925, r. 11.

payable.[58] He should also register a priority caution in respect of his mortgage and, for this purpose, application should be made on Form 72.[59] As soon as the caution is entered in the Index, notice thereof is given to the proprietor of the land, that is (in the example given above) to T1 and T2. When a mortgagee of an equitable interest lodges a priority caution in this way, he is not entitled to notice of any intended disposition of the land: his charge is not upon the land itself but upon the proceeds of sale in the hands of T1 and T2.

Second Mortgages of Registered Land

10-54. When a registered proprietor creates a first mortgage, whether legal or equitable, he has to give up possession of his land certificate. Where the mortgage is registered or is protected by a mortgage caution, the land certificate is deposited at the registry. In the event of an equitable mortgage by deposit of the land certificate with the lender, the certificate remains with him. Accordingly, if the borrower wishes to create a second mortgage, he must either give permission to his prospective lender to inspect his title in the registry, or alternatively, he may obtain an office copy of the subsisting entries in the register for a cost of 4s. (20p).[60]

10-55. The general observations in Chapter 8 concerning second mortgages of unregistered land apply also in the case of registered land. Thus notice should always be given to the first mortgagee, and an acknowledgment requested. If he is under an obligation to make further advances, this fact will have been recorded on the register. As in the case of a first mortgage, the Land Registration Acts prescribe no compulsory form which a second mortgage must take. A banker usually employs his ordinary legal mortgage form and adds a clause to the effect that it is subject to a first mortgage dated . . . in favour of. . . . If an office copy of the subsisting entries in the register has been obtained, the bank's solicitors should first apply for an official search on either Form 94A or Form 94B; for the purposes of these forms the office copy takes the place of the land certificate. The mortgage should then be completed and registered.[61] When the charge is sent to the registry, it must be accompanied by a copy thereof and by the search certificate. In due course the registry will issue to the bank a charge certificate which will contain a reference to the prior charge.

[58] Land Registration Fee Order, 1970, para. 2 and Sched. para. XIII.
[59] L.R. Rules, 1925, r. 229. By virtue of the 1970 Order, the fee is £1.
[60] Land Registration Fee Order, 1970, para. 2 and Sched. para. XII.
[61] See *ante*, para. 10-22.

10-56. The alternative method of creating a first legal mortgage of registered land may be used in order to create a second mortgage; that is to say, the banker may refrain from registering the mortgage and may protect his interest by a mortgage caution.[62]

Sub-mortgages of Registered Land

10-57. A sub-mortgage has been defined in an earlier chapter.[63] A mortgagee of registered land may create either a legal sub-mortgage or an equitable sub-mortgage, though, if the mortgage to him is equitable, any sub-mortgage which he creates will necessarily be equitable. Apart from the technical requirements arising from the fact that the land is registered, the banker should take the same steps as those which are necessary upon a sub-mortgage of unregistered land. Thus he must find out how much is still owing by the mortgagor under the head mortgage; the property should be valued; and, in due course, notice of the sub-mortgage must be given to the mortgagor under the head mortgage and an acknowledgment obtained. If the sub-mortgagor is a company, the sub-mortgage must be registered with the Registrar of Companies under Sect. 95 of the Companies Act, 1948.[64]

A. LEGAL SUB-MORTGAGE

10-58. The Land Registration Act, 1925, and the Rules made thereunder provide that the proprietor of a charge may charge the mortgage debt with the payment of money in the same manner as the proprietor of land may charge the land.[65] Such charges are known as "sub-charges." The Act does not prescribe any compulsory form of words for a sub-charge, and the usual method is to word it as a charge by way of legal mortgage. The sub-charge is usually headed with the title number, charge number, and short description of the property. It then continues: "I, A.B. of . . . hereby charge by way of legal mortgage the mortgage debt secured by the charge above referred to with payment to London Bank Limited of . . ." The next step is for the bank to have the sub-charge registered. For this purpose the charge certificate has to be produced at the registry, and a note of the sub-charge is entered therein.[66] The bank is then

---

[62] See *ante*, para. 10-31.
[63] See *ante*, para. 9-1.
[64] See *post*, para. 32-4.
[65] Sect. 36 and L.R. Rules, 1925, r. 163.
[66] L.R. Rules, 1925, r. 165.

issued with a certificate of sub-charge. The fees payable upon registration of a sub-charge are the same as those for the registration of a charge.[67]

10-59. The Land Registration Act, 1925,[68] provides that the proprietor of a registered charge may "create a lien on the charge" by deposit of the charge certificate and that such lien is equivalent to a lien created in the case of unregistered land by the deposit of the mortgage deed. A banker taking an equitable sub-mortgage in this way should give notice in duplicate on Form 85A to the Registrar, who will enter notice thereof in the charges register and send back the duplicate notice to the bank by way of acknowledgment. No fee is payable.[69]

10-60. It will be recalled that, when taking a deposit of a land certificate, a banker very frequently asks his customer to execute a form of *legal* mortgage without proceeding to register it.[70] Similarly, when a customer creates a sub-mortgage by deposit of the charge certificate, it is often advisable to ask him to execute a form of *legal* sub-mortgage. At any time in the future this instrument can be registered as a sub-charge.

[67] See *ante*, para. 10-27.
[68] Sect. 66.
[69] Land Registration Fee Order, 1970, para. 4.
[70] See *ante*, para. 10-35.

Part Three

LIFE POLICIES

CHAPTER 11

Contracts of Life Insurance

11-1. A CONTRACT of life insurance is "a contract by which the insurer, in consideration of a certain premium, either in a gross sum, or by annual payments, undertakes to pay to the person for whose benefit the insurance is made, a certain sum of money or annuity on the death of the person whose life is insured. . . . Sometimes the amount is made payable either at death, or at the expiration of a stated number of years, whichever shall first happen."[1]

11-2. It is sometimes said that the term life *assurance* should be used in preference to life *insurance*, on the principle that *insurance* refers exclusively to property risks, for example marine insurance and fire insurance. In practice, however, this distinction is not strictly observed and one frequently speaks of life *insurance* (though never, nowadays, of marine or fire *assurance*).[2]

A Contract "Uberrimae Fidei"

11-3. A contract of insurance is a contract *uberrimae fidei*, that is to say, a contract in which the utmost good faith must be observed. There must be a full disclosure of all facts and circumstances affecting the risk. The contract may be vitiated by their non-disclosure, whether innocent or fraudulent.

11-4. This principle was clearly illustrated in *London Assurance* v. *Mansel*.[3] The defendant wished to insure his life with the plaintiffs. He had filled in their proposal form which contained, *inter alia*, the following questions: "Has a proposal ever been made on your life at any other office or offices? If so, where? Was it accepted at the ordinary premium, or at an increased premium, or declined?"

[1] J. W. Smith, *A Compendium of Mercantile Law* (13th ed., 1931), p. 514.
[2] *Assurance* is the earlier term, used alike of marine and life insurance before the end of 16th century . . . *Insurance* occurs first in reference to fire, but soon became co-extensive with *assurance*, the two terms being synonymous in Magens 1755. *Assurance* would probably have dropped out of use but that Babbage in 1826 proposed to restrict *insurance* to risks of property, and *assurance* to life insurance. This has been followed so far that *assurance* is now rarely used of marine, fire, or accident insurance, and is retained in Great Britain in the nomenclature and use of the majority of life insurance companies. But in general popular use, *insurance* is the prevalent term." *The Oxford English Dictionary.*
[3] (1879) 11 Ch. D. 363.

His answer was: "Insured now in two offices for £16,000 at ordinary rates. Policies effected last year." The proposal was accepted, but the plaintiffs subsequently discovered that the defendant's life had been declined by several offices. It was held that the plaintiffs were entitled to have the contract set aside.

11-5. If insurers seek to avoid liability on the ground that there has been non-disclosure of a fact, they must prove the fact to be a material one. In other words, they must prove that it would tend to increase the risk or influence their decision regarding the proposal. Frequently, however, the parties agree that the statements contained in the proposal are the basis of the contract; in such cases, it is impossible for the assured to deny the materiality of the statements.[4]

Insurable Interest

11-6. The claimant on a life policy must be able to show that the person on whose behalf it was made had an insurable interest in the life. This is the result of the Life Assurance Act, 1774, which was passed to prevent persons from effecting insurances on lives in which they had no interest except as the basis of a gambling transaction. A person who has taken out a policy on the life of another in which he has no insurable interest cannot, as a general rule, repudiate the policy and recover back the premiums paid.[5] He may do so, however, if he was induced by the fraud of the insurers to believe that he was effecting a valid policy, because in such a case it is said that the parties are not *in pari delicto*, that is to say, in equal fault.[6]

11-7. Parliament has never enacted precisely when a person has an insurable interest, and so it has been left to the courts to determine whether, on the facts of a particular case, such an interest exists. The result of the decisions is that there are three categories of life insurance in relation to which insurable interest is presumed and where no proof of interest is necessary. These categories are (i) insurance by an individual on his own life,[7] (ii) insurance by a man on the life of his wife,[8] and (iii) insurance by a woman on the life of her husband.[9] Unless there is some pecuniary interest, a parent has no insurable interest in the life of a child,[10] nor the child in the lives of

---

[4] See, for example, *Stebbing* v. *Liverpool and London and Globe Insurance Co. Ltd.* [1917] 2 K.B. 433 (a decision on a policy of insurance against burglary).

[5] *Harse* v. *Pearl Life Assurance Co.* [1904] 1 K.B. 558.

[6] *Hughes* v. *Liverpool Victoria Legal Friendly Society* [1916] 2 K.B. 482.

[7] *Wainwright* v. *Bland* (1835) 1 Moo. & R. 481; (1836) 1 M. & W. 32.

[8] *Griffiths* v. *Fleming* [1909] 1 K.B. 805.

[9] *Reed* v. *Royal Exchange* (1795) Peale Ad. Cas. 70; Married Women's Property Act, 1882, Sect. 11.

[10] *Halford* v. *Kymer* (1830) 10 B. & C. 724.

its parents. In these and in other cases it is, of course, often possible to prove expressly that a pecuniary interest exists—for example, on the ground that the person whose life is insured is rendering domestic services to the assured and that his or her death would necessitate the employment of a servant. Finally it may be added that a creditor has an insurable interest in his debtor's life,[11] though it is not clear from the authorities what is the limit of this interest. Clearly it extends to the amount of the debt and interest thereon at the time the insurance is effected, but an insurance limited to this amount would not protect the creditor fully, because it would not provide for future interest.[12]

Effect of Suicide

A. SANE SUICIDE

11-8. Suicide used to be a crime in English law. Moreover, there was (and still is) a general legal principle that "no criminal can be allowed to benefit in any way by his crime."[13] From this it followed that, if he insured his life and committed suicide while sane, his personal representatives could not recover the policy moneys.[14] It made no difference that the policy provided for payment by the company in the event of sane suicide, because such a provision was held by the House of Lords in *Beresford* v. *Royal Insurance Co. Ltd.*[15] to be contrary to public policy. A certain Major Rowlandson had insured his life for £50,000, and the company had agreed with the assured to pay this sum to his executors or assigns on his death, even if he died by his own hand, whether sane or insane, provided that one year had elapsed from the commencement of the assurance. Some nine years later, a few minutes before the insurance was due to expire, Major Rowlandson shot himself. Letters and interviews on the day of his death made it clear that he took his life for the purpose of the policy moneys being made available for the payment of his debts. The deceased's administratrix claimed the moneys from the insurance company, which pleaded that, as the deceased died by his own hand, the policies became void. The House of Lords decided that the claim of the administratrix must fail.

[11] *Godsall* v. *Boldero* (1807) 9 East 72.
[12] See *MacGillivray on Insurance Law* (5th ed., 1961), para. 415.
[13] *Beresford* v. *Royal Insurance Co. Ltd.* [1938] 2 All E.R. 602, at p. 611, *per* Lord Macmillan.
[14] Nor can his personal representatives recover if he commits a capital offence and dies at the hands of justice. Similarly, a man who has insured the life of another cannot recover if he murders the person whose life he has insured: *Prince of Wales Assurance* v. *Palmer* (1858) 25 Beav. 605.
[15] [1938] 2 All E.R. 602.

11-9. Suicide is no longer a crime in English law: Sect. 1 of the Suicide Act, 1961, expressly so provided. Nevertheless, it is arguable that it would still be contrary to public policy for personal representatives to be allowed to recover policy moneys in circumstances similar to those in the *Beresford* case.

11-10. A question of considerable interest to bankers is whether a lender to whom a policy had been assigned by way of security would be allowed to recover in such circumstances. This point is still undecided, though there is a dictum of Lord Atkin in the *Beresford* case to the effect that the lender would be protected. He said[16]—

> Anxiety is naturally aroused, by the thought that this principle [of public policy] may be invoked so as to destroy the security given to lenders and others by policies of life insurance, which are in daily use for that purpose. The question does not directly arise, and I do not think that anything said in this case can be authoritative. I consider myself free, however, to say that I cannot see that there is any objection to an assignee for value before the suicide enforcing the policy which contains an express promise to pay upon sane suicide—at any rate, so far as the payment is to extend to the actual interest of the assignee.

Again, the old case of *Moore* v. *Woolsey*[17] is authority for the principle that a bona fide interest in a policy acquired by someone other than the assured will not be defeated by the life assured's suicide, where the policy contains a clause protecting such an interest.

B. INSANE SUICIDE

11-11. If a man insures his life and commits suicide while insane, the right of his personal representatives to recover will not be affected, unless there is an express term of the policy to the contrary. It is now common to find a clause in insurance policies worded thus: "The assurance shall be forfeited and become void if the assured shall within one year after such assurance shall have been effected die by suicide whether felonious or not." Often, however, the following proviso is added which protects the rights of third parties: "Provided always that no such assurance shall become void as regards any person who shall have a *bona fide* pecuniary interest therein under assignment charge or equitable lien but shall remain in force to the extent only of such interest."

---

[16] [1938] 2 All E.R., at p. 607.
[17] (1854) 4 E. & B. 243.

Types of Life Insurance

11-12. Competition for business between insurance offices has led to the introduction of life policies to cater for almost every conceivable need. The following are the principal types of policy—

A. ENDOWMENT POLICIES

11-13. These provide for the payment of a definite sum (with or without the addition of profits) at a certain date (for example, at the age of sixty-five) or at death, whichever occurs first. Some policies give the life assured the option, upon reaching the agreed age, of taking either a lump sum or an annuity.

B. WHOLE LIFE POLICIES

11-14. These are not nearly so popular nowadays as endowment policies. They provide for the payment of a lump sum (with or without the addition of profits) upon death. The premiums on whole life policies are lower than on endowment policies. If, therefore, the maximum amount of protection for the life assured's dependants is desired, a whole life policy should be taken out. The disadvantage of such a policy is that it cannot be used as a means of supplementing the life assured's income when he retires. The fact that most people like to benefit personally from their savings explains the popularity of endowment policies.

C. FAMILY PROTECTION POLICIES

11-15. These are designed to meet the requirements of a man with a young family. Some of these provide for payment of the principal sum on a sliding scale; e.g. £5,000 if the assured dies during the first five years of the policy, dropping eventually to (say) £1,000 at maturity date. Others entitle the widow to an annuity of so much per annum until her husband would have been (say) sixty-five had he lived, plus a lump sum at that date.

D. SETTLEMENT POLICIES

11-16. These policies fall within Sect. 11 of the Married Women's Property Act, 1882. This section enacts that a policy of assurance effected by any man on his own life, and expressed to be for the benefit of his wife, or of his children, or of his wife and children, or any of them, or by any woman on her own life and expressed to be for the benefit of her husband, or of her children, or of her husband and children, or any of them, shall create a trust in favour of the objects therein named, and that the moneys payable under any such policy shall not, so long as any object of the trust remains unperformed, form part of the estate of the insured or be subject to his or her debts. The assignment by way of security of policies of this type gives rise to special problems which will be considered in the next chapter.

E. INDUSTRIAL POLICIES

11-17. These are usually for small amounts, such as fifteen or twenty pounds. They are seldom accepted as a banking security. As a general rule they are assignable only with the company's consent, which is however usually given. Furthermore, the premiums are generally payable either weekly or monthly, and so an assignee is put to considerable trouble to see whether they are being promptly paid.

F. SHORT-TERM POLICIES

11-18. These become payable only if death occurs within a certain specified time. Such policies are sometimes effected by business men who are going abroad for a period. For obvious reasons these are not a suitable banking security.

Advantages of Life Policies as Security

11-19. J. W. Gilbart expressed the opinion that deeds were not a satisfactory banking security,[18] and he was equally emphatic about life policies[19]—

> A banker should never make advances upon life policies. They may become void, should the party commit suicide, or die by the hand of justice, or in a duel; or if he go without permission to certain foreign countries. The payment may be disputed, upon the ground that some deception or concealment was practised when the policy was obtained. And, in all cases, they are dependent upon the continued payment of the premiums.

11-20. At the present day, however, life policies are regarded by bankers as one of the most satisfactory forms of security. They are frequently accepted as cover for advances to those engaged in business or in the professions. Sometimes, too, the future success of a

---

[18] See *ante*, para. 2-16.
[19] J. W. Gilbart, *The Logic of Banking* (1859), p. 195.

business depends largely upon the manager or some other senior employee, and it is a good plan to hold a policy on his life as security. The following are the principal advantages of life policies as security.

11-21. First, the value of the security can easily be ascertained. After the first two or three annual premiums have been paid, the policy generally acquires what is called a "surrender value," that is, a sum which will be paid by the company upon the abandonment of the policy. This increases with the payment of each additional premium. Sometimes, the policy itself indicates how the surrender value is to be calculated; if it does not do so, the company will supply the information.

11-22. Secondly, a life policy can easily be realised. If, as is usual, the banker takes a legal mortgage of the policy, he is in a position to surrender it and to obtain payment of the surrender value, should the customer fail to repay his overdraft when called upon. Furthermore, instead of taking the drastic step of surrendering the policy the banker has other courses available to him; in particular, the company will probably be prepared to make a loan against the security of the policy.[20] Of course, if the customer dies, the full amount of the policy becomes payable.

11-23. Thirdly, a life policy is stable in value. Its surrender value continually increases, provided that the premiums are paid. There is, therefore, no necessity—as there is when valuing stocks and shares—to allow a margin for depreciation.

Disadvantages of Life Policies as Security

11-24. First, there is a risk that the customer may be unable to pay future premiums. This is probably the most important defect of a life policy as a security. It is particularly serious in cases where the banker has been unwise enough to allow the customer to overdraw to the full amount of the surrender value. In this event the banker may, if he wishes, pay the premiums and debit the amounts to the customer's account.[21] This keeps the policy alive and automatically increases its surrender value, though in most cases the overdraft will be increased by more than the addition to the surrender value.

11-25. Secondly, there is a slight risk that the policy may be vitiated by the assured's non-disclosure of all facts and circumstances

[20] See *post*, para. 13-8.
[21] See *post*, para. 12-18.

affecting the risk.[22] This rarely happens in practice, and there are no steps which the banker can take to safeguard himself.

11-26. Thirdly, there is a slight risk that the customer may die in circumstances that will not involve the company in liability, e.g. if he commits a capital offence and is hanged,[23] or if (subject to exceptions) he commits suicide.[24]

11-27. Fourthly, there is a slight risk that the policy may be vitiated if the life assured breaks one of the conditions contained therein. This is of small importance, because it is not usual for policies to contain stringent conditions. Occasionally, however, there may be restrictions on his going abroad or engaging in certain specified occupations such as aviation, mining, or the licensing trade.

11-28. Fifthly, there is a slight risk that the person taking out the policy may have had no insurable interest in the life assured.[25] This, too, is of small practical importance, partly because no reputable office would knowingly issue such a policy and also because, if it did so, it would almost certainly waive the illegality should a claim arise.

11-29. Finally it is sometimes said that a banker's reputation may be damaged if he is obliged to realise a policy which has been taken out to make provision for the assured's dependants.

[22] See *ante*, paras. 11-3/5.
[23] *Amicable Society* v. *Bolland* (1830) 4 Bli. (N.S.) 194. The death sentence for murder was suspended for five years by the Murder (Abolition of Death Penalty) Act, 1965, Sects. 1 and 4. In 1969 both Houses of Parliament voted in favour of the permanent abolition of the death sentence for murder: see *Hansard*, Commons Debates, Vol. 793, col. 1297, and Lords Debates, Vol. 306, col. 1321.
[24] For the distinction between sane and insane suicide, see *ante*, paras. 11-8/11.
[25] For the meaning of insurable interest, see *ante*, paras. 11-6/7.

CHAPTER 12

Taking and Releasing the Security

12-1. WHEN a banker is offered a life policy as security, he should make a careful examination of its terms and conditions. If they are satisfactory, he will decide whether to take a legal or equitable mortgage of the policy. When the mortgage has been executed, he will give notice thereof to the insurance company. This chapter deals in some detail with these matters, and then, quite shortly, with settlement policies and with the release of the security.

Examination of the Policy

12-2. The name of the company which issued the policy should be noted. Most British insurance companies are in an exceptionally strong financial position. If, however, the policy has been issued by a Dominion, Colonial, or foreign company, it may be necessary to make some inquiry concerning its standing. Policies issued by companies domiciled abroad and having no office in this country are not usually accepted because of the trouble involved when the policy becomes a claim.

12-3. The number of years during which the policy has been in force and the amount of the annual premium should be noted. This will give some guide as to the surrender value. As a general rule a policy acquires a surrender value after two or three annual premiums have been paid, and the amount of the surrender value is a percentage of the sums so paid. Sometimes, the policy itself indicates how the amount is to be calculated; if it does not do so, the company will supply the information.

12-4. Any special conditions attached to the policy should be examined. Occasionally, conditions are inserted because the assured is not "a first-class life." For example, in a policy for (say) £1,000 payable at the age of sixty or previous death, a special provision may be inserted that if the life assured dies within ten years after the issue of the policy, the amount payable will be limited to a sum equivalent to the premiums actually paid. Occasionally a special suicide clause is inserted, particularly if the assured has suffered from any nervous disorders. Thus the policy may contain a clause that, if the life assured dies by his own hand, whether sane or insane, *at any time* during the currency of the policy, the amount of the company's liability is to be limited to the premiums actually paid.[1] Policies containing conditions such as these are not necessarily unsatisfactory as a banking security, for, although the sum payable upon death may be reduced, the surrender value is usually unaffected.

12-5. The banker should ensure that the last premium receipt is with the policy and that the policy is properly stamped.[2]

12-6. One of the factors determining the annual premium to be paid is, of course, the life assured's age. He is required to supply this information to the company as one of the answers on the proposal form. Some companies, however, do not require him to furnish proof of his age before the contract is made and the policy is issued; but before any sums claimed under the policy will be paid, the company will require to satisfy itself that the life assured had stated his age correctly. This sometimes leads to difficulties when a claim is made, and one cannot help thinking that it would save trouble if all companies insisted upon proof of age before issuing their policies. It is surprising how many people are, apparently, under a mis-apprehension as to their age. This is more frequently under-stated than over-stated in proposal forms, particularly by women.

12-7. Hence it is that, in some of the policies offered to bankers as security, age has not been admitted. In such cases the bank should help the customer to have his age admitted. He will readily co-operate with the bank before the advance is made, though it may not be so easy to secure his co-operation afterwards. Age is usually proved by sending his birth certificate to the company. The necessary endorsement is then made on the policy, or a slip endorsement is issued by the company, which should be attached to the policy. There are other ways of proving a person's age if he has lost his birth certificate; for example, a baptismal certificate may be accepted, but this will usually need to be supported by direct evidence that the child was a young infant when baptised. In most cases, if the assured has lost his birth certificate, he should be advised to obtain what is called a "short" birth certificate by making application to the Registrar-General, General Register Office, Somerset House, London, W.C.2. Application should normally be made on form P.S.R.5. The fee is 3s. (15p). Short birth certificates show only the names, sex, date of birth, and (in most cases) place of birth of the person concerned.

---

1 Contrast this with the more usual suicide clause quoted, *ante,* para. 11-11.
2 See the table of duties, *post,* para. 33-17.

12-8. If the life assured is a woman who has married since the policy was issued, a certificate of her marriage should be obtained and registered with the company.

Equitable Mortgage of a Life Policy

12-9. A policy of life insurance is a chose in action[3] and no particular formality is necessary to create a mortgage of it. Thus a mortgage of a life policy may be created by an oral agreement between the parties or by a deposit of the policy accompanied by a written memorandum. A mortgage of this nature is perfectly valid as against the mortgagor's trustee in bankruptcy, but it gives the mortgagee an equitable interest only. When the policy moneys become payable, the company will require a discharge from the assured (or, if he is dead, from his personal representatives) as well as from the mortgagee.

12-10. Equitable mortgages of life policies are rare, but, if a banker is content with this security, the customer's signature to a memorandum of deposit should be obtained containing, *inter alia*, clauses whereby the customer agrees that the security is to be a continuing security, that he will pay the premiums when they become due and that he will execute a legal mortgage when called upon. The memorandum attracts stamp duty at the rate of 1s. (5p) per cent.[4]

12-11. Although there is no statutory provision governing the giving of notice to the company of *equitable* mortgages, this should be done to protect the mortgagee's priority. By giving notice, the mortgagee acquires priority over any previous mortgagees who have not given notice, unless he has actual or constructive notice of their rights at the time when he makes his advance. Non-production of the policy may amount to constructive notice of an earlier assignment.[5] If equitable mortgagees fail to give notice, their priorities are determined by the order of the dates of their charges.

Legal Mortgage of a Life Policy

12-12. By far the most usual way of creating a mortgage of a life

---

[3] The term "chose in action" is "a known legal expression to describe all personal rights of property which can only be claimed or enforced by action, and not by taking physical possession," *per* Channell, J., in *Torkington* v. *Magee*, [1902] 2 K.B. 427, at p. 430. Debts, life policies, stocks and shares, patents, copyrights, trademarks, and goodwill are examples of choses in action.

[4] *Post*, para. 33-30.

[5] *Spencer* v. *Clarke* (1878) 9 Ch. D. 137; followed in *Re Weniger's Policy* [1910] 2 Ch. 291.

policy in favour of a bank is the execution of a deed assigning the assured's right to recover the policy moneys. Before 1867 life policies were assignable in equity but were not assignable at law except to the Crown.[6] Legal mortgages of policies were first made possible by the Policies of Assurance Act, 1867. By that Act an assignee is enabled to sue in his own name, and accordingly is able to give a legal discharge, provided that—

(i) he has, at the time of action brought, the equitable right to receive the money;[7]

(ii) he has a properly stamped assignment in writing either by endorsement on the policy or by a separate instrument in the words or to the effect set forth in the Schedule to the Act;[8] and

(iii) notice has been given to the company in accordance with the Act.[9]

12-13. The position as regards the right to receive the policy money has been stated thus in a leading text-book[10]—

The company in considering who has the right in equity to receive the money, need not be concerned as to possible equitable claims of which they have no notice, formal or informal. But they must consider all equities of which they have any notice whatsoever, even though formal notice in accordance with the Act has not been given.

Form of Legal Assignment

12-14. The form of assignment in the Schedule to the Act is: "I, A.B. of, etc., in consideration of, etc., do hereby assign unto C.D. of, etc., his Executors, Administrators, and Assigns, the within Policy of Assurance granted, etc. [*here describe the Policy*]. In witness, etc." In practice bankers always use their own forms for the legal mortgage of a life policy. The principal clauses contained in the deed are as follows.

12-15. First, there is the assignment clause itself (which closely follows the wording given in the Schedule to the Act) coupled with a statement that the mortgage is to secure the payment of all sums owed by the customer, either solely or jointly with any other person or persons, whether on balance of account or on guarantees or in respect of bills of exchange, promissory notes, and other negotiable

---

[6] *Dufaur* v. *Professional Life* (1858) 25 Beav. 599.
[7] Sect. 1.
[8] Sect. 5.
[9] Sect. 3.
[10] *MacGillivray on Insurance Law* (5th ed., 1961) para. 1165.

instruments, and including interest with half-yearly rests and other banking charges.

12-16. This is followed by a proviso that, if the customer repays all sums which he owes to the bank as aforesaid, the bank will, at the customer's expense, re-assign the policy to the customer.

12-17. Thirdly, it is agreed that the security is to be a continuing one. This is to exclude the operation of the Rule in *Clayton's* case.[11]

12-18. Fourthly, the customer agrees to pay the premiums punctually and to produce the premium receipts to the bank. In the event of the customer failing to pay the premiums, it is agreed that the bank may pay them and debit the amounts to the customer's account. A card diary should be kept to ensure that premium receipts are brought in at the appropriate time; or, better still, the customer should be asked to sign a standing order authorising all the premiums to be paid by the bank and debited to his account. Normally insurance companies allow thirty days of grace for payment of premiums on life policies.

12-19. Fifthly, the customer agrees that, at any time and without his consent, the bank may sell and surrender the policy to the company or exchange the policy for a paid-up policy or sell the policy to any other person, and for the purpose of such surrender or sale may exercise all the powers of sale and other ancillary powers conferred upon mortgagees by the Law of Property Act, 1925, but free from the restrictions imposed upon a mortgagee's powers by Sect. 103 of the Act.[12]

12-20. Finally, there is a "consolidation clause" excluding Sect. 93 of the Law of Property Act, 1925.[13]

12-21. The *ad valorem* stamp duty, as in the case of other legal mortgages, is at the rate of 2s. (10p) per cent.[14]

Notice to the Company of the Assignment

12-22. As soon as the customer has executed a legal assignment of a life policy in favour of the bank, notice thereof should be given by the bank to the insurance company. If this notice is not given, the security is still perfectly valid as against the customer's trustee in

[11] (1816) Mer. 1572.
[12] For Sect. 103 see *ante*, para. 4-24.
[13] *Ante*, para. 4-28.
[14] *Post*, para. 33-24.

bankruptcy, but there are the following cogent reasons for giving notice—

1. It enables the bank to sue in its own name under the Policies of Assurance Act, 1867.

2. It binds the company so that if they pay to another claimant they may be held responsible.

3. It enables the bank to acquire priority over earlier assignees who have not given notice, provided that the bank had not received actual or constructive notice of the earlier assignments at the time when the bank made its advance. Non-production of the policy may amount to constructive notice of an earlier assignment; therefore the bank should always insist upon production of the policy. Thus in *Spencer* v. *Clarke*[15] a mortgagee accepted without further inquiry the mortgagor's statement that he "left it at home by mistake," whereas he had in fact executed a prior equitable mortgage in favour of a lender who did not give notice to the company. The later mortgagee gave notice to the company, but it was held that he had constructive notice of the earlier mortgage and could not acquire priority over it.

4. It preserves the bank's priority as against subsequent assignees.

12-23. In order to pass the legal title under the Policies of Assurance Act, 1867,[16] the notice must be in writing; it must give the date and purport of the assignment; and it must be addressed to the company's principal place of business or one of them if more than one is specified in the policy. It is the usual practice of bankers to request the company to acknowledge receipt of the notice by signing a duplicate notice sent to the company. The Act makes it obligatory for insurance companies to acknowledge receipt when requested to do so, and provides that they may charge a fee not exceeding 5s. (25p) for this service.[17] Most of the large companies do in fact charge 5s. (25p), though some companies charge less than this or make no charge at all. A list of their charges will be found in the Insurance Section of *The Bankers' Almanac and Year Book*.

12-24. When notice is given to the company of the bank's interest as assignee, the company should be asked to state whether they have received notice of any prior incumbrances or whether they have any charge on the policy themselves. If there has been an earlier assignment of the policy which has been duly discharged, the relevant document or documents should be deposited with the bank.

---

[15] (1878) 9 Ch. D. 137; followed in *Re Weniger's Policy* [1910] 2 Ch. 291.
[16] Sect. 3.
[17] Sect. 6.

At the time when notice of the bank's interest is given to the company it is often convenient to ask the company to quote the present surrender value of the policy in order that this may be entered in the bank's records. Most banks make a practice of writing to the company at regular intervals so as to keep up to date their records of surrender values. Some banks obtain up-to-date surrender values every six or twelve months, but the more usual practice nowadays seems to be to do this every third or fourth year, unless special conditions arise. The insurance companies make no charge for replying to these inquiries. Instead of writing to the company, it is often possible to ascertain the surrender value by referring to a table appearing on the policy itself, thereby saving both the bank and the company time and trouble.

Receipt of Banker of Notice of Second Charge

12-25. When once the assignment has been executed, the bank will, of course, keep the policy and the assignment in its custody until the policy matures or the advance is repaid. For this reason it is not easy for the customer to create any further assignments. If, however, a second assignment is executed and the assignee gives notice thereof to the bank, the customer's account must be ruled off in order to avoid the operation of the Rule in *Clayton's* case.[18] When the overdraft is repaid, the policy should be re-assigned; it should then be delivered, together with the assignment itself, not to the customer, but to the second assignee, if he so desires.

Settlement Policies

12-26. Settlement policies falling within the provisions of Sect. 11 of the Married Women's Property Act, 1882, were referred to in the previous chapter.[19] When such policies are offered as security, they give rise to special problems, because they create a trust in favour of the person or persons named or described therein. Some of these policies state that they are effected "for the benefit of" the persons designated as beneficiaries; others state that pursuant to the provisions of the Married Women's Property Act, 1882, the company will on the death of the assured pay the sum assured to the person or persons named or described. The most usual example of a policy of this type is one effected by a husband on his own life for the benefit of a named wife. This gives her an immediate vested interest

[18] (1816) 1 Mer. 572.
[19] *Ante*, para. 11-16.

in the policy so that, if she dies before her husband, it passes to her executors as part of her estate.[20]

12-27. If a banker is to obtain an effective assignment of a policy of this nature, the wife must be joined as a party thereto. Furthermore, in order to guard against the possibility that she may have been induced to sign under pressure from her husband (in which event she might be able to have the transaction set aside), it is desirable that her signature to the assignment should be witnessed by some independent person—preferably her own solicitor—who should explain the legal position to her.

12-28. Such is the effect of a settlement policy in favour of a *named* wife. Sometimes, however, policies are expressed to be in favour of the assured's wife (without naming her), and occasionally in favour of his children as well. The interpretation of these policies has given rise to a good deal of litigation, especially in cases where the assured married more than once and had children by more than one wife. The following is a summary of the decisions on the meaning of words which, from time to time, are used in settlement policies.[21]

12-29. "For the benefit of his wife." This means his widow, whether it be his wife living at the date of the policy or some future wife who shall survive him.[22]

12-30. "For the benefit of his wife and children." This means the person who at his death shall become his widow, and those of his children by any marriage and whenever born who shall survive him.[23]

12-31. "His widow or widow and children." This means the person who at his death shall become his widow, and those of his children by any marriage and whenever born who shall survive him.[24]

12-32. "For the benefit of his wife A.B. and the children of their marriage." This means the wife so named if she shall survive him, and such children of their marriage whenever born as shall survive him.[25]

---

[20] *Cousins* v. *Sun Life Assurance Society* [1933] 1 Ch. 126. But the husband is entitled to a lien on the policy moneys for premiums paid by him since his wife's death as being money expended by a trustee to preserve the property of a trust: *Re Smith's Estate, Bilham* v. *Smith* [1937] Ch. 636.

[21] The authorities are collected in *MacGillivray on Insurance Law* (5th ed., 1961), para. 1434.

[22] *Re Collier* [1930] 2 Ch. 37.

[23] *Re Browne's Policy* [1903] 1 Ch. 188.

[24] *Re Parker's Policies* [1960] 1 Ch. 526.

[25] *Re Seyton, Seyton* v. *Satterthwaite* (1887) 34 Ch. 511.

12-33. "For the benefit of his wife or, if she be dead, between his children in equal proportions." This means the wife at the time the policy was effected (and no other) if she shall survive him, or if she shall predecease him, his children by any marriage and whenever born who shall survive him.[26]

12-34. "For the benefit of his wife in the event of her surviving him, and failing her for the benefit of his children born or to be born or any of them." This means the wife at the time the policy was effected (and no other) if she shall survive him, or if she shall predecease him, his children.[27]

12-35. In most of the cases stated above, the policy would not be a suitable security, because it would be impossible to gather in all persons who might at some future date become beneficiaries. But a policy "for the benefit of his wife A.B. and the children of their marriage," could be accepted, provided that all the children were of full age and were prepared to join in the assignment together with their parents.

12-36. Certain policies which are not in fact settlement policies are sometimes mistaken for them. Thus, if a policy is effected by a wife on her husband's life for her own benefit, or if a policy is effected by a husband on his wife's life for his own benefit, neither policy falls within the Married Women's Property Act, 1882.[28] Therefore, the policy-holder may mortgage such a policy without his or her spouse joining as a party to the mortgage.

Policies on Lives of Minors

12-37. Policies on the lives of minors (that is, persons under eighteen years of age[29]) are sometimes offered as security. They may be divided into three classes—

A. MINORS' POLICIES

12-38. A minor may propose for and accept a policy of insurance provided that he is old enough to understand the nature of the transaction. However, he cannot, whilst still a minor, assign the policy as security for a loan. If he did so, the whole transaction would be void under the Infants Relief Act, 1874,[30] as being a contract for the

---

[26] *Re Griffith's Policy* [1903] 1 Ch. 739.
[27] *Watson and Others, Petitioners* (1944) Lord Patrick (Lord Ordinary) 18th July, unreported.
[28] See the terms of Sect. 11 of the Act, *ante*, para. 11-16.
[29] Family Law Reform Act, 1969, Sect. 1; see Vol. 1, para. 11-39.
[30] Sect. 1.

repayment of money lent or to be lent. The lender could neither sue the minor nor enforce his charge upon the policy.

B. PARENTS' POLICIES ON MINORS' LIVES NOT CREATING A TRUST

12-39. These policies are sometimes offered by a parent as security for a loan to himself. They may be illustrated by reference to the facts of *Re Engelbach's Estate*.[31] In that case there had been a proposal for an endowment policy in which the proposer described himself as the proposer "for his daughter Mary Noel, aged one month," and the policy issued on that proposal was expressed to be payable at the end of the endowment period to the daughter if she should survive the specified date, and if she should not survive that date all premiums were to be repaid without interest to the proposer. In fact she did survive the specified date and claimed the policy moneys. In the meantime her father had died, and his personal representatives claimed that the money belonged to his estate. Their claim was upheld by the court. It was pointed out that the daughter could not have enforced the contract in her own name against the insurance company because she was a stranger to the contract. She did not acquire any interest at law or in equity to the policy or the policy moneys merely by reason of the fact that the policy moneys were expressed to be payable to her. Furthermore, the father had not constituted himself a trustee for his daughter of the policy or of the moneys payable thereunder.

12-40. It follows from this decision that, if one can be quite certain that the particular policy offered is of the same nature as that in the *Engelbach* case, it may safely be accepted as security for the father's account. From a practical standpoint, however, it would nearly always be imprudent to do so, partly because the nature of the policy shows that it was taken out to make some provision for the child and partly because it is extremely difficult to distinguish such policies from those in the next group, which are definitely unacceptable as a banking security.

C. PARENTS' POLICIES ON MINORS' LIVES CREATING A TRUST

12-41. *Re Webb*[32] affords an illustration of policies of this type. There were two policies in identical terms, except for the names of

---

[31] [1924] 2 Ch. 348. See also *Re Sinclair's Policy* [1938] Ch. 799 and *Re Foster* (1938) 54 T.L.R. 993.
[32] [1941] Ch. 225.

the children, effected by a father on the lives of his two children. The proposal, which was signed by the father, stated that it was a proposal for a deferred assurance on the life "and for the benefit of" the child. In the schedule to the policy the grantee was stated to be the father "on behalf of and for the benefit of the life assured," and the child was named as the life assured. The sum assured was expressed to be payable to the personal representatives of the life assured provided that he died on or after his twenty-first birthday. The conditions of the policy, among other things, gave to the grantee "on behalf of the life assured" power to surrender it or to mortgage it for not more than the surrender value. On the life assured attaining the age of twenty-one the grantee's rights and powers were to cease, and the life assured was to become solely interested in and entitled to deal with the policy subject to any such mortgage. If the life assured died under twenty-one, part of the premiums was returnable to the grantee with interest.

12-42. The father paid all the premiums on the policies down to the time of his death, which occurred whilst the children were still minors. His executor took out a summons asking whether the policies formed part of his estate or were held by him and after his death by his executor in trust for the children. The court held that there was sufficient evidence in the present case to disclose the intention to create a trust. Hence a declaration was made that the two policies were held by the testator at his death and thereafter by his executor in trust for the two children respectively.

12-43. In policies falling within the second group the minor has no legal or beneficial interest in the policy or the policy moneys, whereas in the third group it is otherwise. The practical significance from a banker's point of view is that policies in the third group can never be regarded as a suitable security for the parent's account.

Releasing the Security

A. LEGAL MORTGAGE

12-44. The legal mortgage forms for life policies used by the banks generally have a form of re-assignment printed thereon. Technically, reassignment is no longer necessary, because the Law of Property Act, 1925,[33] provides that a receipt endorsed on a mortgage for all money thereby secured, which states the name of the person who pays the money and is executed by the person in whom the mortgaged property is vested and who is legally entitled to give a receipt for the

[33] Sect. 115 (1).

mortgage money, operates as a reconveyance without any formal reconveyance, surrender, or release. The re-assignment or endorsed receipt is executed under the bank's seal,[34] and the policy together with the discharged mortgage is handed back to the customer, unless the bank has received notice of a second mortgage. The instrument attracts stamp duty at 1s. (5p) per £200 with a maximum of 10s. (50p), and, for the reasons already given with reference to the discharge of legal mortgages of land,[35] it is usually advisable for the bank to attend to the stamping on behalf of the customer. He should be informed that the discharged mortgage ought to be carefully preserved, because it will be required by the company when the policy moneys become payable. Finally, the bank should write to the company informing them of the release of the policy.

B. EQUITABLE MORTGAGE

12-45. Since an equitable mortgage does not create any legal estate or interest in favour of the bank, there is no need for any re-assignment or for an endorsed receipt when it is desired to vacate the security. It is quite sufficient to write "cancelled" across the memorandum of deposit and to return it and the policy to the customer. If the company had been informed of the bank's interest, they should be advised that this interest has terminated.

[34] Though an advantage of the endorsed receipt is that legally it does not require sealing, *ante*, para. 6-10.

[35] *Ante*, para. 6-4.

CHAPTER 13

Enforcing the Security

13-1. THE procedure to be adopted when a life policy has been mortgaged to a bank and it is necessary to enforce the security depends upon whether or not the policy moneys have become payable. It also depends upon whether the mortgage of the policy is legal or equitable.

Legal Mortgage: Policy Moneys Payable

13-2. If a bank is a legal mortgagee of a life policy and the life assured has died or the policy has matured, it is a simple matter to claim from the company the sum payable. In the event of death, the company will, of course, require proof thereof. They will then prepare a form of receipt to be executed by the bank. When this is returned to the company, together with the policy and the mortgage deed, the company will forward its cheque to the bank in respect of the amount due.[1] In view of the fact that the legal interest in the policy vests in the bank, the personal representatives of the deceased are not required to join in the receipt.

13-3. A few weeks before a policy matures the company usually writes to the bank stating that the policy falls due on a specified date. This allows time for the receipt form to be completed in advance and lodged with the company together with the policy and the mortgage deed. The company will then dispatch its cheque in time to reach the bank on the maturity date. Some banks keep their own diary of maturity dates as an added safeguard.

13-4. In many cases the company asks the bank to sign a certificate to the effect that the total amount advanced under the deed of assignment has not at any time exceeded the amount for which the instrument has been stamped. Occasionally it will be found that a certificate in these terms cannot be given, because the deed of assignment was stamped to cover advances up to a certain sum and the current account subsequently exceeded that sum. This problem

---

[1] As the mortgage deed must be sent to the company, one should never take a mortgage in one deed of two policies issued by different companies. Even if both policies are issued by the same company, it is better to use separate deeds.

arose in *Re Waterhouse's Policy*,[2] where it was held that the assignment was a valid security for the sum in respect of which it had been stamped, but was unenforceable as to the excess. In such a case the bank's correct course is either (*a*) to claim from the company the sum covered by the stamping and allow them to pay the excess to the assured (or to his personal representatives as the case may be), or (*b*) to increase the stamping on the deed of assignment to cover the full amount—though this may involve stamping up under penalty.[3]

Equitable Mortgage: Policy Moneys Payable

13-5. If the bank is an equitable mortgagee of the policy, the legal title thereto remains in the assured or if he is dead, it vests in his personal representatives. Thus the assured or his representatives will have to join with the bank in the insurance company's form of receipt. In practice they are only too willing to do so, because every day's delay increases the amount of interest charged on the overdrawn account.

Legal Mortgage: Policy Moneys Not Yet Payable

13-6. Enforcing the security of a life policy before the policy moneys have become payable is a step which a banker is most reluctant to take. The surrender or sale of a policy always involves the assured in financial loss. Suppose, for example, that he has paid one hundred pounds in premiums. The surrender value may be only forty pounds. The assured whose policy was surrendered in such circumstances would probably regard this as sixty pounds "thrown away," though he has, of course, enjoyed the cover of the policy during the time when it was in force. For this reason a banker allows his customers the utmost latitude before enforcing the security. If enforcement becomes absolutely necessary, there are the following possible courses to be considered—

A. SURRENDER OF POLICY TO COMPANY

13-7. The usual form of legal mortgage expressly authorises the bank to surrender the policy to the company at any time without the consent of the customer. There are no special formalities to be observed. The policy and the mortgage deed should be forwarded to the company, which will provide a form of receipt to be executed by the bank.

---

[2] [1937] 1 Ch. 415.
[3] For a more detailed consideration of *In Re Waterhouse's Policy*, see *post*, paras. 33-25/28.

B. LOAN BY COMPANY AGAINST POLICY

13-8. The amount which a company is prepared to lend against the security of its own policies varies from company to company. Usually they will advance up to about ninety per cent of the surrender value. If this sum is sufficient to repay the bank overdraft, this course is usually to be preferred to surrender of the policy, because it keeps the policy alive. Obviously the customer's co-operation is required. He will make formal application to the company for a loan against the security of the policy and will authorise the company to pay the proceeds direct to the bank in exchange for the policy and the bank's mortgage duly discharged. Sometimes the amount which the company is prepared to lend just falls short of the sum required to repay the bank overdraft. In this event the customer may be able to persuade some friend or relative to make up the difference.

C. SALE OF POLICY

13-9. Before one takes the drastic step of surrendering a policy, it is always advisable to see whether it would not be more profitable to sell it. Friends or relations are sometimes prepared to purchase a customer's policy and to pay the premiums in the future. They will, of course, be entitled to the policy moneys in due course. Alternatively, there are various companies which specialise in the purchase of life policies and reversionary interests as an investment; their advertisements appear in the legal and financial press. If the policy is for a large sum, a sale of the policy to one of these companies is often the most satisfactory way of enforcing the security, because it will frequently be found that the purchase price is considerably in excess of the surrender value. The Life Assurance Act, 1774,[4] which prevents persons from effecting insurance on lives in which they have no insurable interest does not apply to a contract assigning the policy to a third party. If the policy is valid in its inception, it is not invalidated by assignment to a person who takes it merely as an investment or speculation.[5]

13-10. Before any steps are taken to sell the policy, one must ensure that the power of sale has become exercisable. If the deed of assignment contains no special provision to the contrary, Sect. 103 of the Law of Property Act, 1925, will apply, and the mortgagee

---

[4] *Ante*, para. 11-6.
[5] *Ashley* v. *Ashley* (1829) 3 Sim. 149; *M'Farlane* v. *The Royal London Friendly Society* (1886) 2 T.L.R. 755.

will be unable to exercise his power of sale until one of the events specified therein has occurred, e.g. the mortgagor has not complied with three months' notice to repay.[6] In practice, however, the usual form of mortgage of a life policy employed by the banks excludes Sect. 103 and empowers the bank to sell the policy at any time.[7]

D. CONVERSION INTO PAID-UP POLICY

13-11. This is a useful course where the customer finds that he is unable to pay the premiums. Insurance companies are nearly always prepared to issue a paid-up policy for a smaller sum in substitution for a policy which is not paid up. The surrender value is usually unaffected.

Equitable Mortgage: Policy Moneys Not Yet Payable

13-12. If the bank's mortgage is merely equitable and the customer has signed a memorandum of deposit promising to execute a legal mortgage when called upon, the first step towards realising the security is to ask the customer to implement his promise, or to consent to the surrender or sale of the policy. Should he fail to do so, the bank may apply to the court for a foreclosure order or for an order for sale. The procedure relating to foreclosure orders in regard to land was outlined in an earlier chapter,[8] and the procedure when applying for foreclosure of a life policy is similar. When the order is made absolute, the mortgagee becomes the owner of the policy (subject to any prior charges) and may surrender it. If the court orders the policy to be sold, it will require this to be done under its supervision to the best purchaser that can be found. The proceeds will be paid into court and then applied in discharge of the mortgagee's debt in accordance with the court's directions.

13-13. Instead of trying to surrender the policy or to sell it, a banker will usually find out first whether the insurance company is prepared to pay off the bank's loan and keep the policy alive.[9] Alternatively, the policy might be converted into a paid-up one.[10]

[6] *Ante*, para. 4-24.
[7] *Ante*, para 12-19.
[8] *Ante*, paras. 7-18/20.
[9] *Ante*, para. 13-8.
[10] *Ante*, para. 13-11.

Part Four

STOCKS AND SHARES

CHAPTER 14

The Nature of Stocks and Shares

14-1. MOST of the stocks and shares offered to a bank as security for an advance are dealt in on the London Stock Exchange or on one of the Provincial Stock Exchanges. These are often known as "quoted" securities to distinguish them from securities which are not quoted on any stock exchange. As cover for an advance, "unquoted" securities suffer from many disadvantages, which are discussed in Chapter 17.

Quoted Securities

The principal types of quoted securities are—

A. BRITISH GOVERNMENT STOCKS

14-2. These represent loans to the British Government. Long-dated stocks, i.e. those which are redeemable many years hence or are irredeemable (such as two-and-a-half per cent Consols), fluctuate in price with changes in the level of interest rates. Thus, when interest rates rise the price of long-dated Government stocks falls, and vice versa. Short-dated stocks, i.e. those which are drawing near to their redemption dates, are much more stable in value.

B. THE STOCKS OF COMMONWEALTH AND FOREIGN GOVERNMENTS

14-3. These fluctuate in value more than British Government stocks. Their suitability for security purposes naturally depends upon political and financial conditions in the country concerned.

C. MUNICIPAL STOCKS

14-4. The stocks of many local authorities in this country—county councils, boroughs, and a few urban district councils—are quoted on the stock exchange. For all practical purposes, they are as "safe" as British Government stocks. Some Commonwealth and foreign municipal loans are also quoted; whether or not they are a suitable security depends upon the financial reputation of the particular municipality.

D. THE STOCKS OF CERTAIN PUBLIC BOARDS

14-5. These include, for example, the stocks of the Agricultural Mortgage Corporation, the Metropolitan Water Board, and the Port of London Authority. These stocks rank almost as high as those of the British Government.

E. INDUSTRIAL AND COMMERCIAL STOCKS
AND SHARES

14-6. In this chapter the procedure which is followed in regard to the issue of shares by a company will be outlined, and an account will be given of the principal types of securities issued by companies. In the next chapter some of the factors affecting their suitability as security for advances will be considered.[1]

Issue of Shares by a Company

14-7. When a public company wishes to make an issue of shares, it usually prepares a document called a prospectus inviting members of the public to send in applications. Each application must be accompanied by a remittance of so much per share. Thus if the shares are one pound shares, the sum of 25p per share may be payable upon application. Sometimes, however, the whole amount is payable upon application. It is then the duty of the directors to proceed to allotment. Very often it will be found that the number of shares applied for exceeds the number to be issued. In this event the issue is said to be oversubscribed, and the directors will have to devise some method of scaling down the applications. Usually, though not always, allotment is made in full to small applicants whilst larger applications are scaled down.

14-8. The company informs the applicant of the number of shares allotted to him by sending him a "letter of allotment." Sometimes a further amount per share will be payable upon allotment—say, another 25p. Thereafter the balance may become payable in either one or two further instalments. If there are two instalments the first is usually about one or two months after allotment, and the second follows one or two months after the first. Each time an instalment is paid the letter of allotment is sent to the company to have the amount paid entered thereon. When all the instalments have been paid, the shares are said to be "fully paid up," and the letter of allotment is exchanged for a document called a share certificate which, as its name implies, certifies that the member

---

[1] *Post*, paras. 15-6/7.

named therein is registered in the books of the company as the holder of a specified number of shares.[2]

14-9. It has become the almost invariable practice for shares to be fully paid up. In former days it was quite common for shares to be issued on the terms that so much per share (say, ten shillings (50p) in the case of one pound shares) would remain uncalled until the directors decided otherwise. These "partly-paid" shares, as they are called, became unpopular largely because, in times of trade depression, shareholders found that calls made by the various companies of which they were members far exceeded their liquid resources. However, a few banks and insurance companies still have partly-paid shares, and in their case, the possibility of calls being made is regarded as very remote. Indeed, in the case of some of these partly-paid shares, part of the uncalled capital cannot be called up except upon liquidation.

14-10. Shares in a company are choses in action[3]. Except in the case of private companies the owner can usually transfer his shares to a purchaser without any restriction. Thus, in most cases a shareholder will have acquired his shares either by having had them allotted to him by the company or by having bought them from someone else. An owner of shares can create a legal mortgage of them by transferring them to a mortgagee; or he can retain the legal title to the shares and create an equitable mortgage[4]. If, however, the stocks or shares are in bearer form, they are made available as security by way of pledge[5].

14-11. By virtue of the Companies Act, 1948[6], a company may convert fully paid up shares into stock, provided that it is authorised to do so by its articles of association. Thus, instead of holding, for example, one hundred shares of one pound each, a member would hold one hundred pounds of stock. A company can never issue share capital in the form of stock in the first instance, though it can raise loan capital by issuing debenture stock.

Securities Issued by Companies

The principal types of securities issued by companies are—

[2] It used to be customary to exchange the letter of allotment for a scrip certificate to bearer upon payment of the amount due on allotment. Then the scrip certificate had to be exchanged for a share certificate when the calls had been paid. The usual modern practice is that stated in the text above, though scrip is still occasionally issued.
[3] *Ante*, para. 12–9.
[4] See *post*, Chapter 15.
[5] See *post*, Chapter 16.
[6] Sect. 61 (1). See also Vol. 1, paras. 10-104/106.

A. DEBENTURE STOCKS

14-12. The company security which offers the highest degree of safety is debenture stock. This is not part of the company's share capital. Persons who subscribe for debenture stock are in no sense the owners or part-owners of the company. They have, in effect, made a loan to the company—a loan which is generally secured by a charge on the company's assets. In return for their loan the lenders receive a fixed rate of interest. If unsecured, the stock is generally called "unsecured loan stock," rather than debenture stock. It is a rule of the London Stock Exchange that an official quotation will not be granted for a stock which constitutes an unsecured liability unless the stock is entitled "unsecured."[7] Sometimes, "convertible debenture stock" or "convertible unsecured loan stock" is issued. The holder has the option of surrendering his debenture or loan stock in exchange for ordinary stock at one or more stated dates and at stated rates.

B. PREFERENCE SHARES OR STOCK

14-13. These rank before the ordinary shares or stock with regard to the payment of dividend, and very often they carry a preferential claim to return of capital in the event of the company's liquidation. Usually, the preference shareholders receive a fixed rate of dividend. Occasionally, however, a company issues participating preference shares. The holders of these shares are entitled to a higher rate of dividend if the ordinary shareholders receive more than a stated return on their capital. All preference shares are either cumulative or non-cumulative, the distinction being important if in any particular year the company earns insufficient profits to enable the preference dividend to be paid.[8] If the shares are non-cumulative, that year's dividend will never be paid, but if they are cumulative, the dividend will be paid when profits are available.

C. ORDINARY SHARES OR STOCK

14-14. These rank for dividend, and often for capital repayment, after the preference shares, and accordingly they carry most of the risk. If a company prospers, the value of its ordinary shares may rise sharply; but if disaster overtakes a company, its ordinary shares may become worthless.

[7] Rule 159 (2) and Appendix 34, Sched. VII.

[8] Unlike debenture holders preference shareholders cannot appoint a receiver, though, if their dividend is not paid, they are sometimes given the right to vote at the company's general meeting.

D. DEFERRED SHARES OR STOCK

14-15. These are rarely issued today. They rank last for payment of dividend after the claims of all other types of shares have been satisfied.

Registered Stocks and Shares

14-16. Most securities are "registered," that is to say, the names and addresses of the stockholders or shareholders are entered in a register which shows the amount of stock or the number of shares which they hold. Each holder is given a stock or share certificate. He may transfer his ownership to a transferee by means of a signed transfer, which must be sent, together with the relevant certificate, to the person or body keeping the register. The appropriate entries are then made in the register, and a new certificate is issued in favour of the transferee.

14-17. The registers of British Government stocks are kept at the Bank of England, though there are also National Savings Stock registers for many of these stocks.[9] As regards the registers which have to be kept by companies, this work is performed by the secretary or registrar, though there is a growing practice of delegating the work to outside organisations which specialise in registration work, such as banks or firms of accountants.

14-18. The instrument of transfer which is normally used in order to transfer stocks and shares in companies and also to transfer most government stocks is the simplified stock transfer form which was introduced by the Stock Transfer Act, 1963.[10] This transfer form is executed under hand by the transferor, but does not require to be signed by the transferee. There are, however, still some cases where this simplified form cannot be used. Thus, when partly-paid shares in a company are transferred, the transferee's signature to a form of transfer is essential. The requisite form, as prescribed by the company's articles, may be either a deed or an instrument under hand. It has been held that where a transfer under hand is all that is required, the fact that it is actually executed under seal does not invalidate it.[11] Whatever form a transfer of stocks and shares in a company takes, it usually attracts *ad valorem* stamp duty on the consideration money.[12]

[9] See *post*, paras. 15-55/56.
[10] Sect. 1.
[11] *Ortigosa* v. *Brown, Janson & Co.* (1878) 47 L.J. Ch. 168.
[12] See the table "Conveyances or Transfers," *post*, para. 33-9. If the transfer is by way of security, a fixed duty of 10s. (50p) is payable: see *post*, para. 15-8.

Inscribed Stocks

14-19. A person who buys inscribed stock has his name entered in the inscription books of the registration authority, but he is not supplied with a stock certificate. Instead, he is given a "stock receipt" or a "certificate of inscription." This stock receipt (unlike a stock certificate) does not require to be produced when the stock is sold. The stock is transferable in the books of the registration authority on the personal attendance of the holder or of his duly appointed attorney, who is normally his solicitor or banker.

14-20. Prior to the Second World War, a person who invested in British Government stock or in certain other stocks was usually given the option of having his holding either "registered" or "inscribed." However, in 1943 all inscribed British Government stock was converted into registered stock by virtue of regulations made by the Treasury[13]. In 1949 regulations on similar lines were made by the Minister of Health with regard to all local authority stocks[14]. Thus inscribed stocks are rarely encountered today, though there are a few such stocks issued by Commonwealth Governments. However, even these stocks are now transferable in this country by an ordinary common form of transfer.[15]

Bearer Securities

14-21. The title to bearer securities passes by delivery. Moreover, as they are fully negotiable instruments, the property therein is capable of passing to a *bona fide* transferee for value, even though the transferor may have had no title or a defective title thereto.[16]

14-22. If expressly so authorised by its articles, a public limited company may issue, with respect to any shares which are fully paid up or with respect to stock, an instrument under its common seal stating that the bearer thereof is entitled to the shares or stock specified therein.[17] This instrument is called a "share warrant," and the shares may be transferred from one person to another by mere delivery of the warrant. It follows that the company does not know who is the owner of the shares at any particular time, because there

---

[13] Government Stock Regulations, 1943.

[14] Local and Other Authorities (Transfer of Stock) Regulations, 1949.

[15] Government and Other Stocks (Emergency Provisions) Act, 1939, Sect. 1, given permanent effect by the Emergency Laws (Repeal) Act, 1959, Sect. 6.

[16] Vol. I, para. 4-1.

[17] The Companies Act, 1948, Sect. 83; *Pilkington* v. *United Railways of the Havana and Regla Warehouses Ltd.* [1930] 2 Ch. 108. A *private* company cannot issue share warrants, because it must by its articles restrict the right to transfer its shares: see Companies Act, 1948, Sect. 28 (1).

is no registered holder; therefore it is usual for dividend coupons to be attached to the share warrant, which the bearer presents to the company or to its bankers when a dividend is declared. Share warrants have never been extensively issued by English companies, an important factor discouraging their use being the heavy stamp duty—now £3 per cent—which they attract.[18] Most foreign government loans are in bearer form, and the stocks of American and Canadian companies, though technically in favour of a registered holder, are transferable by delivery like bearer securities.[19] Moreover, the Finance Act, 1963, restored the right to exchange British Government registered stock for bearer bonds subject to certain conditions.[20]

14-23. The Exchange Control Act, 1947,[21] provided that, except with the permission of the Treasury, no person should, in the United Kingdom, issue any bearer certificate or coupon. The Act[22] further required existing bearer securities (with certain exceptions) to be kept with "authorised depositaries," and enacted that no payment of capital or interest in respect thereof was to be made except to or to the order of the authorised depositary. The depositary is not permitted to recognise any transfer unless there is produced to him evidence that by so doing he is not giving effect to an illegal transaction. The position of the authorised depositaries in relation to bearer securities is, therefore, analogous to that of registrars with regard to registered securities. For the most part the depositaries consist of the banks, together with a large number of solicitors and stockbrokers.[23]

Advantages of Stocks and Shares as Security

14-24. First, the value of the security can usually be ascertained without difficulty.

14-25. Secondly, it is said that in normal times stocks and shares enjoy stability of value. This point cannot be accepted without some qualification. Booms and recessions appear to be a permanent feature of our economy, and it is only to be expected that, in times of recession, prices of commercial and industrial shares will fall

---

[18] Stamp Act, 1891, Sched. I, as amended by the Finance Act, 1947, Sect. 52, and the Finance Act, 1963, Sect. 59. But bearer securities, once stamped, do not attract any further stamp duty upon transfer.
[19] For details, see *post* para. 16-9.
[20] Sect. 71.
[21] Sect. 10.
[22] Sects. 15 and 16.
[23] See the Exchange Control (Securities) Notices issued by the Bank of England.

considerably. "Gilt-edged" securities, such as British Government stocks, used to be less susceptible to violent price fluctuations, but in recent years even these stocks have reacted sharply.

14-26. Thirdly, there are few formalities to be observed when taking stocks and shares as security. Thus, there is no complicated investigation of title to make as there is when land is mortgaged to the bank. This in itself saves expense. Furthermore, the stamp duties payable upon a mortgage of stocks and shares are small.

14-27. Fourthly, stocks and shares can easily be realised if the customer is unable to repay his overdraft. The London and Provincial Stock Exchanges provide a ready market for such securities. Whether or not the bank will have power to sell them without the assistance either of the customer or of the court depends upon the way in which the security is taken. This is discussed in the next chapter.

14-28. Fifthly, in the case of fully negotiable securities (that is to say, those in favour of bearer) there are the following additional advantages: (i) the lender (the pledgee) is able to get a good title thereto even though his pledgor has a defective title;[24] (ii) the deposit of bearer securities as a pledge enables the banker to effect a sale without his customer's assistance; and (iii) neither the pledge nor the transfer by way of sale of bearer securities involves any stamp duty.

Disadvantages of Stocks and Shares as Security

14-29. First, there is the possibility of theft by the bank's employees. In view of the high standard of integrity of bank officers this point is of small practical importance. Nevertheless, in those rare cases when a member of the staff falls into temptation, he may choose stock exchange securities because they are easier to realise than, for example, title deeds or life policies. However, many companies and registration authorities make a point of writing to the transferor before registering a transfer—a practice which immediately reveals a fraud of this nature. This protection does not exist in the case of bearer securities.

14-30. Secondly, there are additional drawbacks to partly-paid shares as a banking security, though at the present day very few partly-paid shares exist. The possible disadvantages of these shares are: (i) a call may be made which the customer is unable to meet, and the banker may be faced with the alternative of advancing more

---

[24] See *London Joint Stock Bank* v. *Simmons* [1892] A.C. 201, *post*, para. 16-6.

money to enable the call to be paid or of allowing his customer to default, in which case the shares will probably be forfeited; (ii) even if the customer is able to pay the call himself, his cash resources will be reduced, and so he will be in a less favourable position to repay his overdraft; (iii) the market in partly-paid shares is sometimes narrower than that for fully-paid-up shares with the result that they may be liable to sharp fluctuations in price and may be more difficult to realise; and (iv) if the banker obtained a legal mortgage of partly-paid shares by having them transferred into his own name or that of his nominee, he would become liable to pay any calls that were made.

14-31. Finally, shares which are not quoted on a stock exchange are subject to certain special disadvantages which are explained in Chapter 17.

CHAPTER 15

Registered and Inscribed Stocks and Shares as Security

15-1. THIS chapter deals with the valuation of stocks and shares and the method of charging registered and inscribed securities; bearer securities are considered in Chapter 16, and unquoted shares in Chapter 17.

Valuation of Stocks and Shares

15-2. For the purpose of valuing quoted securities reference should be made to *The Stock Exchange Daily Official List*. This is a remarkable publication. It is published by the authority of the Council of the Stock Exchange and contains quotations for approximately ten thousand securities, which are grouped under various headings such as Banks and Discount Companies, British Funds, Investment Trusts, Shipping, and so on. In addition to providing a complete record of price movements from day to day, the *Official List* gives useful information concerning dividends recently paid.

15-3. If a security cannot be found in this list, reference should then be made to *The Monthly Supplement of Quoted Securities Temporarily Removed from the Stock Exhcange Daily Official List*. This monthly publication was started during the Second World War when the quotations of many securities in which there was little public interest were removed from the *Official List* in order to save paper.

15-4. Many small branches do not obtain the *Official List* or *The Monthly Supplement*. Reference may usefully be made to *The Times* or to *The Financial Times*, both of which publish daily markings. If the shares in question cannot be found there, it is usual to ask the bank's stockbroker to refer to his copy of the *Official List* or *The Monthly Supplement*.

15-5. Not all the shares offered as security will be found in one or other of these lists. A company which wishes to have its shares quoted on the London Stock Exchange must make application to the Council, which will require the company to comply with certain conditions. For various reasons a company may not wish to make application for a quotation, and the banker's next step will be to ascertain whether its shares are quoted one one of the Provincial Stock Exchanges. One or two of these exchanges specialise in the shares of local industries: for example, Oldham is the principal centre for dealings in cotton-spinning mill shares, and some of the shares dealt in on the Oldham Stock Exchange have no quotation on the London Exchange. The provincial exchanges publish their own Official Lists, and the usual way of obtaining the information one requires is by addressing a request to the bank's branch in the provincial town concerned.

15-6. The securities having been valued, it is possible to decide how much the bank would be prepared to lend against them. Clearly, it is not easy to generalise on this, because a good deal will depend upon the particular circumstances, such as the length and purpose of the proposed advance, the standing of the borrower, and the quality of the stocks and shares concerned. A mixed portfolio of "blue-chips" i.e., shares in leading companies, forms the most acceptable type of security. In all cases where the banker wishes the advance to be and to remain fully secured, it is obvious that there must be a reasonable margin between the agreed overdraft and the present worth of the securities. All manner of influences affect stock exchange prices—political tension at home or abroad, a General Election, devaluation, dividend limitation, claims for higher wages, rearmament, the possibility of trade depression, and so forth. Some stocks and shares are notoriously speculative, for example mining shares and the stocks of certain Foreign Governments, and in such cases a much wider margin should be allowed than when dealing with other securities. Again, there is only a nominal market in some shares, e.g. where the issue is a small one or where most of the shares are held by very few persons; under these circumstances the shares seldom change hands, and it may not be easy to find a buyer.

15-7. Sometimes it is advisable to obtain information concerning the capital structure of a company. This may be particularly important when ordinary shares are offered as security, and, although nothing in the nature of a detailed analysis of the company's financial position is called for, a banker should be sufficiently familiar with investment problems to realise that, as a general rule, the higher the proportion of preferential capital to total capital, the more speculative are the ordinary shares. As the late Mr. Hargreaves Parkinson observed: "The rule for shares is the same as that for cars; the high-geared share (i.e. the share with a high proportion of fixed-interest capital in front of it) gives the fastest running when the going is good, but the low-geared share is the best hill-climber in difficult times."[1] A careful investor therefore endeavours to sell high-geared shares immediately profits begin to fall, because in most cases these shares will drop much more heavily than low-geared shares. The moral for the prudent banker is to be very cautious of high-geared shares in times of prosperity.

Legal Mortgage of Registered Stocks and Shares

15-8. A legal mortgage of registered stocks and shares is effected by transferring them, usually by means of a stock transfer form,[2] to the lender or his nominees, subject to an agreement that the securities will be transferred back to the borrower when the advance is repaid. A purely nominal figure (say, 25p) should be inserted in the transfer as the consideration. This enables the transfer to be stamped with a 10s. (50p) stamp, instead of the usual *ad valorem* duty.[3] To establish that the transfer is liable to the fixed duty of 10s. (50p), it should bear the following certificate signed on behalf of the bank: "We hereby certify that this transfer is excepted from Sect. 74 of the Finance (1909–10) Act, 1910." When the transfer has been duly executed and stamped, it should be forwarded to the company together with the share certificate and the company's registration fee. The company will then issue a new certificate in favour of the transferee.

15-9. It used to be the invariable practice for banks to have the shares transferred to two of its officials, but this causes inconvenience if the officials die before the shares are transferred back to the customer. A more modern practice is for the bank to create a separate nominee company into whose name securities may be transferred. As a matter of convenience some banks have separate nominee companies for particular districts, e.g. Lloyds Bank (Bath) Nominees Ltd., Lloyds Bank (Birmingham) Nominees Ltd., and so on. It follows, of course, that dividends will be sent to the nominee company as the registered proprietor of the shares, and it is therefore necessary for the bank to keep careful records in order to be able to credit such dividends, when received, to the account of the correct customer and to forward to him other communications such as the annual balance sheet and directors' report. This involves a good deal of clerical work, and some banks still prefer to use personal nominees in many cases.

[1] Hargreaves Parkinson, *Scientific Investment* (4th ed., 1946), pp. 87–8.
[2] See *ante*, para. 14-18.
[3] Stamp Act, 1891, Sched. I, and the Finance (1909–10) Act, 1910, Sect. 74 (6) (and see *Inland Revenue Circular relating to Stamp Duties*, August, 1949).

15-10. So far it has been assumed that the stocks or shares to be mortgaged are those of a company. The procedure with reference to British Government stocks registered at the Bank of England or on the National Savings Stocks registers is very similar, except that transfers of Government stocks and of stocks issued by a local authority in the United Kingdom are exempt from all stamp duties.[4]

15-11. In addition to signing the instrument which transfers the stocks or shares into the name of the bank's nominee company, the customer is asked to sign a document which is usually called, perhaps not very accurately, a "memorandum of deposit." This is generally executed under hand, and the following are the principal clauses usually incorporated.

15-12. First, there is a statement that the stocks and shares (which are usually listed in a schedule) have been transferred to the bank or its nominees to the intent that such stocks and shares, together with all interest, dividends, and bonuses thereon, are to constitute a security in respect of all sums owed by the customer, either solely or jointly with any other person or persons, whether on balance of account or on guarantees or in respect of bills of exchange, promissory notes, and other negotiable instruments, and including interest with half-yearly rests and other banking charges.

15-13. Secondly, there is an agreement that the security is to be a continuing one. The purpose of this clause is to exclude the operation of the Rule in *Clayton's* case.[5]

15-14. Thirdly, there is an agreement that the bank may sell the securities at any time if the customer fails to repay his indebtedness on demand. If this clause is not inserted, it may be that the restrictions imposed upon a mortgagee's powers by Sect. 103 of the Law of Property Act, 1925, apply, with the result that three months' notice to repay would usually be required. On the other hand, there is much force in the argument that, as the mortgage is not by deed, the section is inapplicable. If this is correct, there would then (in the absence of express agreement) be merely an implied power to sell the shares after the expiration of a reasonable notice by the mortgagee.[6]

15-15. Fourthly, there is sometimes an undertaking to maintain a specified margin of cover.

[4] Stamp Act, 1891, Sched. I; Finance Act, 1967, Sect. 29(2)(b).
[5] (1816) 1 Mer. 572.
[6] See *Deverges* v. *Sandeman, Clark & Co.* [1902] 1 Ch. 579 (a decision on the Conveyancing Act, 1881, Sect. 20, now replaced by the Law of Property Act, 1925,

Stocks and Shares

15-16. Occasionally there is added a clause dealing with partly-paid shares whereby the customer agrees that the banker may pay any calls made and debit these sums to his account.

15-17. Finally it is a wise precaution to insert a clause whereby the customer agrees that, when the securities are transferred back to him, he will accept delivery of stocks or shares "of the same class or denomination" as those listed in the schedule. Without this clause the customer might be able to argue that he was entitled to have transfered to him the *identical* shares which he transferred to the bank. This result would be extremely inconvenient in practice, because large blocks of shares in a particular company are frequently held by the nominee companies of the banks in respect of advances to numerous customers, and it would involve much additional clerical work if all the holdings had to be kept separate and distinct.[7]

15-18. When the customer signs the memorandum, it is usual to ask him to initial the schedule of securities (if any) immediately underneath the last item. The document, if executed under the hand, is exempt from stamp duty as an agreement under hand.[8] If the agreement is executed under seal, it attracts the ordinary *ad valorem* deed duty, i.e. 2s. (10p) per cent, to be impressed within thirty days.[9] It is rare for these memoranda to be under seal. Even if the mortgagor is a limited company, the directors may pass a resolution authorising certain officials to execute the document under hand, unless the company's articles contain any provision to the contrary. The bank should obtain a certified copy of this resolution.

Equitable Mortgage of Registered Stocks and Shares

15-19. Instead of taking a legal mortgage of stocks and shares, a banker is often content with an equitable mortgage. This may be created quite informally, as, for example, where a customer deposits share certificates with his banker with the intention of creating a charge thereon. Strictly speaking, no transfer or memorandum needs to be signed by the customer. Cozens-Hardy, J., expressed the matter very clearly when he said: "The deposit of the certificate by way of security for the debt seems to me to amount to an equitable

---

Sect. 103). The court considered that a month, or even less, would be "reasonable notice."

[7] See *Crerar* v. *Bank of Scotland* [1922] S.C. (H.L.) 137, where, however, on the facts the court found that the customer had impliedly agreed to the bank's practice of not keeping the holdings separate.

[8] Finance Act, 1970, Sect. 32 and Sched. 7.

[9] *Post*, para. 33-24.

mortgage, or, in other words, to an agreement to execute a transfer of the shares by way of mortgage."[10]

15-20. In practice, however, a banker is unwilling to rely upon an informal mortgage of this nature, partly because the customer might try to advance the argument that he deposited the certificates for safe custody only and not by way of security, and partly because the various clauses contained in the memorandum of deposit which the customer is required to sign afford useful protection to the bank. This document is very similar in its terms to the so-called "memorandum of deposit" which the customer executes when he transfers securities to the bank's nominee company by way of legal mortgage.[11] There is, however, the obvious difference that, instead of stating that the stocks and shares listed in the schedule have been transferred by way of security, the customer undertakes to execute any necessary transfers, when called upon, either in favour of the bank's nominee company or in favour of a purchaser. The memorandum, like the one employed when the shares are transferred by way of legal mortgage, is exempt from stamp duty if executed under hand, but it attracts the usual *ad valorem* duty of 2s. (10p) per cent when under seal.

15-21. In cases where a customer is constantly changing his investment portfolio, it is tedious to have to ask him to sign a memorandum of deposit in respect of each new purchase of securities that he makes. To meet this situation, most banks make use of a special form of memorandum which does not refer specifically to any particular securities, but is expressed to cover all securities at any time lodged by the customer with the bank.

15-22. When the bank has obtained the deposit of the stock or share certificates and the customer has signed a memorandum of deposit, the question arises whether any further steps should be taken to protect the bank's position as equitable mortgagee. The actual procedure adopted varies somewhat in different banks. Some banks give notice of deposit to the company, and, at the same time, obtain the borrower's signature to a "blank" transfer. Other banks dispense with "blank" transfers altogether. Very occasionally, a notice in lieu of *distringas* is served on the company. These matters must be considered in some detail.

Notice of Deposit

15-23. When a banker takes as security an equitable mortgage of

---

[10] *Harrold* v. *Plenty* [1901] 2 Ch. 314, at p. 316.
[11] *Ante*, paras. 15-11/17. Some banks use the same memorandum for both legal and equitable mortgages.

stocks and shares, he must decide whether or not it is worth while to send to the company a letter in which he (i) informs the company that the bank has a charge over the securities in question, (ii) asks the company to acknowledge receipt of the bank's letter, (iii) inquires whether the company has received notice of any prior charges on the securities and, finally, (iv) whether the company has any lien thereon by virtue of its articles of association or otherwise. In the majority of cases the secretary of the company will return the bank's letter with the explanation that, by virtue of Sect. 117 of the Companies Act, 1948, the company cannot enter on its register notice of any trust, expressed, implied, or constructive.[12]

15-24. Nevertheless, notice to the company may serve a useful purpose. This may be illustrated by referring to the leading case of *Bradford Banking Co. Ltd.* v. *Henry Briggs, Son & Co. Ltd.*[13] In that case the articles of association of a company contained a clause which is very frequently met with, namely, that the company should have "a first and permanent lien and charge, available at law and in equity, upon every share for all debts due from the holder thereof." One of its shareholders, a Mr. Easby, deposited his share certificate with the Bradford Banking Company as security, and the bank wrote to the company informing them of its interest in the shares. The company acknowledged receipt but added: "We think it right to inform you that Mr. Easby is indebted to us, and that, under a clause in our articles of association we have a first and permanent lien upon all shares held by him." Subsequently Mr. Easby's indebtedness to the company was increased, and the main point at issue was whether the company could claim a lien on the shares in respect of these later advances in priority to the bank. The case was eventually decided in the bank's favour, for it was held by the House of Lords, reversing the decision of the Court of Appeal, that the company could not, in respect of moneys which became due from the shareholder to the company after notice of the deposit with the bank, claim priority over advances by the bank made after such notice. The House of Lords pointed out that the notice of deposit which the bank sent to the company was not a notice of trust within the meaning of the Companies Act, 1862.[14]

15-25. Accordingly, it is sound banking practice to send a notice of deposit to a company in cases where there is a possibility that the

---

[12] Similarly the Bank of England refuses and, by the National Debt Act, 1870, Sect. 30, cannot be compelled to notice any rights but those of the legal proprietors in whose names stock is standing in its books.

[13] (1886) L.R. 12 App. Cas. 29.

[14] Sect. 30, now replaced by Sect. 117 of the 1948 Act (*supra*).

company may have a lien on the shares. An instance where special care is needed is that of a licensee who mortgages to the bank his shares in a brewery company, because licensees are frequently indebted to their brewery. The existence of such a lien depends upon the company's articles; in the absence of any express provision, Article 11 of Table A of the Companies Act, 1948, gives the company a lien over its partly-paid shares, but not over shares which are fully paid.

15-26. Fortunately, a company cannot claim any lien on its fully-paid shares if they are quoted on the London Stock Exchange, because it is a rule of the Stock Exchange that an official quotation will not be granted for any fully-paid shares on which the company claims a lien.[15] In respect of these shares, therefore, there is little to be gained by serving the company with notice of deposit. Theoretically it could be argued that the customer might have obtained a duplicate share certificate by falsely stating that he had lost the original and, by making use of the duplicate certificate, he might have sold his shares. A notice to the company in such a case would be useful, because it would probably bring the reply that the person named was no longer a shareholder. This is a remote possibility, and the very slight risk of frauds of this nature does not warrant the trouble and expense of sending notices. The more general practice, therefore, is not to send a notice of deposit to a company in respect of its fully-paid shares if they are quoted on the Stock Exchange. However, even in the case of these shares, some banks send a notice to the company. The reason for so doing is that certain companies, while declining to accept notice, do in fact record it and, as a matter of courtesy, advise the bank if a transfer is presented for registration.

15-27. Before leaving this topic it is worth noting that some companies have inserted a special clause in their articles providing that the company shall have a paramount lien on its shares for debts incurred before *or after* notice of any equitable interest subsisting in any person other than the registered holder. The effect of such a clause has not yet been tested in the courts. It is clear, however, that there is nothing in the speeches in the House of Lords in the *Bradford Banking Company* case (*supra*) to indicate that there is any inexorable rule of equity making it impossible for the articles to relieve the company from noticing equities.

Notice in Lieu of Distringas

15-28. In view of the limited effect of sending to a company a notice of deposit of its shares, it may be thought advisable in some cases

[15] Rule 159 (2) and Appendix 34, Sched. VII.

to take the alternative and much more formal step of serving upon the company what is called "a notice in lieu of *distringas*." This peculiar phrase can only be explained historically. *Distringas* (meaning "that you distrain") was an old form of writ which had various uses both at Common Law and in Equity. An Act of Parliament passed in 1841[16] allowed a *distringas* to be issued whenever a transfer of stock by the Bank of England or other public company was sought to be restrained. The effect of the writ was temporary and merely prevented the stock from being dealt with until the person putting in the *distringas* had had an opportunity of asserting his claim. In 1883 this procedure by way of writ was abolished,[17] but machinery was created for the service of a notice upon the company in place of a writ; hence the phrase "notice in lieu of *distringas*."

15-29. The Rules of the Supreme Court at present in force provide that any person claiming to be interested in any stock standing in the books of a company may, on an affidavit by himself or his solicitor, and on filing the same in the Central Office or any district registry with a notice in a specified form, and on procuring an office copy of the affidavit and a duplicate of the filed notice authenticated by the seal of the Central Office or any district registry, serve the office copy and duplicate notice on the company.[18] If this procedure is followed by a banker who has taken an equitable mortgage of shares, the company must give the bank eight days' warning before registering any transfer of the shares. The bank, upon receiving this warning, can then proceed to obtain a restraining order or an injunction in a suit against the customer. There is a court fee of 10s. (50p) payable upon filing the notice, and Table A of the Companies Act, 1948, permits the company to charge a fee not exceeding 2s. 6d. ($12\frac{1}{2}$p) for the registration of the notice.[19] In addition, of course, there will be the fee of the commissioner for oaths when the affidavit is sworn.

15-30. Obviously the system provides complete, and reasonably cheap, protection against the risk that a dishonest customer may try to dispose of the shares without the bank's knowledge. The reason why it is so seldom resorted to is self-evident: the task of swearing an affidavit before a commissioner in respect of every deposit of stocks and shares would be almost an impossible one. Sometimes, however, a notice in lieu of *distringas* is useful if there is doubt as

[16] 5 Vict., c. 5, Sect. 15.
[17] By R.S.C. 1883, O. 46, r. 2.
[18] R.S.C., O. 50, r. 11.
[19] Article 28.

to the customer's integrity and for some reason it is impossible to take a legal mortgage by having the shares transferred to the bank's nominee company (e.g. because the company's articles impose some restriction on the right to transfer the shares).

"Blank" Transfers

15-31. When taking an equitable mortgage of stocks and shares, some banks obtain their customer's signature to a so-called "blank" transfer, though it would probably be more accurate to refer to it as an "undated, unstamped transfer." The following matters are filled in: details of the stock or shares concerned; the customer's name as transferor; and (as a rule) the names of the bank's nominees as transferee. The object is to enable the bank to complete its legal mortgage by transferring the securities into the name of its nominees whenever required and without recourse to the customer. Thereafter, the shares may be sold out of the name of the nominees.[20] Whether these transfers can usefully be taken depends upon whether the stocks and shares are transferable by instrument under hand, or the securities are transferable only by deed—

A. TRANSFERS UNDER HAND

15-32. The stocks and shares of the vast majority of companies are transferable by means of a stock transfer form executed under hand.[21] In relation to them there is no legal objection to "blank" transfers, and this holds good even though the transfers are in fact executed under seal.[22] Authority to fill up the blanks may be implied from the nature of the transaction.[23] But, in order to place the matter beyond doubt, those banks which make a practice of taking these transfers often include in their memoranda of deposit a clause whereby the customer agrees that the bank may complete and register the transfers at any time. The transfers should not be dated; otherwise they would have to be stamped within thirty days.

B. TRANSFERS BY DEED

15-33. In these cases transfers which are left blank in some material part are useless, because of the rule that, if a person seals and delivers

---

[20] At least one of the Clearing banks does not insert the name of its nominees as transferee. A direct sale to a purchaser can thus be effected, thereby saving the stamp duty of 10s. (50p) on the transfer to nominees.

[21] *Ante,* para. 14-18.

[22] *Per* Joyce, J., in *Ireland* v. *Hart* [1902] 1 Ch. 522, at pp. 527–8.

[23] *Re Tahiti Cotton Co., Ex parte Sargent* (1874) L.R. 17 Eq. 273.

a writing which is left blank in any material part, it is void for un-
certainty and is not his deed; nor can it be made his deed merely by
filling up the blanks after execution[24]; though it can, of course, be
filled in and executed by an agent of the transferor provided that the
authority is given under seal. The name of the transferee is certainly
a material part of the document, and so this cannot be inserted in a
deed after execution. Let it be supposed, however, that the names of
the bank's nominees have been inserted as transferee, but the date
has been left blank. There seems to be no decisive answer to the
question whether a date could be inserted subsequently. Probably
it is safer to assume that it could not. For this reason, some banks,
when dealing with transfers which have to be by deed, fill in the date,
together with the other details, and have the transfer executed by
the customer. They then stamp it, but refrain from registering it
unless the need arises. If the bank obtains a duly executed transfer
in this way, it might be said that there is no point in delaying its
registration, for by registering it the bank would obtain a legal
mortgage. It may be, however, that for various reasons the customer
objects to having the shares transferred out of his name (e.g. where
they comprise his qualification shares for holding office as a director
of the company), and in this event the method of holding a duly
executed and stamped transfer is useful. An alternative course
which is sometimes followed is for the customer to execute a power
of attorney whereby he irrevocably appoints an official of the bank
to sell the shares on his behalf and to execute the necessary transfers
by deed.

15-34. The danger of taking blank transfers in respect of stock which
is transferable only by deed was clearly illustrated in *Powell* v.
London and Provincial Bank.[25] In this particular case the bank
subsequently filled in its own name as transferee and had itself
registered as the owner of the stock. The company did not question
the transfer, because they had no knowledge of the fact that the
blanks had been filled in after execution. Later, it transpired that
the customer had been a trustee of the stock and should never have
deposited the certificate with the bank as security. New trustees
having been appointed, they claimed that they were entitled to the
stock and called upon the bank to transfer it to them. The Court
of Appeal held that they were entitled to succeed. The transfer to
the bank was inoperative, because there was no valid deed. Thus
the bank never obtained a legal interest in the stock, and, having
only an equitable interest, was necessarily postponed to the prior

---

[24] This is a very old rule laid down at least as early as *Markham* v. *Gonaston* (1598)
Cro. Eliz. 626.
[25] [1893] 2 Ch. 555.

equity of the plaintiffs. As the Court of Appeal pointed out, the bank would have obtained the legal interest in the stock if it had been authorised by deed to execute the transfer on its customer's behalf.

Disadvantages of Equitable Mortgages of Stocks and Shares

15-35. The following are the disadvantages of being content with an equitable, as opposed to a legal, mortgage of stocks and shares—

A. FRAUDULENT SALE OF SECURITIES

15-36. Cases where a customer fraudulently and without the bank's knowledge sells securities mortgaged to the bank are doubtless rare, but the possibility cannot be entirely ignored. The legal position was clearly illustrated in *Rainford* v. *James Keith & Blackman Co. Ltd.*[26] A shareholder named Casmey deposited his share certificate with the plaintiff as security for a loan and signed a transfer duly filled in except for the date. Casmey then sold the shares to a man called Younie and lodged a transfer with the company for registration, without the certificate, but with a declaration falsely stating that the certificate was in the possession of a friend, but not as security for a loan. The certificate had printed at its foot the words: "Without the production of this certificate no transfer of the shares mentioned therein can be registered." Nevertheless, the company registered the transfer and issued a share certificate to Younie. Later the plaintiff, learning that Casmey was in financial difficulties, sent his transfer and the original certificate to the company for registration. The company declined to register the shares in the plaintiff's name on the ground that they had been transferred to Younie. Whereupon the plaintiff brought an action against the company claiming (*inter alia*) damages for wrongfully registering the transfer to Younie and refusing to register his transfer. It was held that the company was not liable, because the note on the certificate did not amount to a representation that the shares would not be transferred without its production, but was merely a warning to the shareholder to take care of the certificate. In the course of argument in the Court of Appeal, Romer, L.J., said: "The only representation is that *at the date of the certificate* the person named therein was the owner of the shares."[27] In other words, it seems that a share certificate

---

[26] [1905] 1 Ch. 296; reversed on another ground, [1905] 2 Ch. 147.
[27] [1905] 2 Ch. at p. 154 (author's italics). If this is the law, it is difficult to see the need for the indemnity which companies usually require before they issue a duplicate certificate, and it is doubtful whether a company could insist upon an indemnity unless its articles expressly so provide (as does Article 9 of Table A of the Companie̦ Act, 1948).

is not a representation of continuing ownership, though the matter is not free from doubt.[28] The only really satisfactory way of guarding against this kind of risk is for the lender to serve the company with a notice in lieu of *distringas*,[29] though a limited protection may be obtained by giving the company notice of deposit of the certificate.[30]

B. PRIOR EQUITABLE INTEREST

15-37. Probably the greatest risk which a bank runs in being satisfied with an equitable mortgage is that there may already be other equitable interests in existence, for in this case the maxim "where the equities are equal, the first in time shall prevail" will apply, with the result that the bank's equitable mortgage will be postponed to the earlier equitable interests. For example, the customer may be a trustee of the securities and may be depositing them to secure an overdraft in breach of trust. In *Coleman* v. *London County and Westminster Bank Ltd.*,[31] Annie Coleman, the registered owner of certain debentures, executed a transfer thereof to Edward Coleman upon certain trusts. This transfer was never registered in the company's books. Thus Annie Coleman, though still registered as the legal owner of the debentures, was in fact holding them upon trust. One of the beneficiaries under the trust assigned his share therein to an assignee for value. At a later date Annie Coleman obtained possession of the debentures and, in her capacity as a director of the company she deposited the debentures with the company's bankers by way of equitable mortgage to secure the company's overdraft. About three years later the bank learned of the transfer which Annie Coleman had executed in favour of Edward Coleman, so they at once took a transfer of the debentures from Annie Coleman and registered it. The assignee for value then brought an action against the bank and claimed a declaration that the bank had no title to those debentures which one of the beneficiaries had assigned to her. This claim succeeded. The assignment had conferred an equitable interest upon her which was prior in time to the equitable mortgage in favour of the bank. Moreover, the bank could not improve its position by taking a transfer after they had notice of the assignee's equitable interest.

15-38. There is no method whereby a bank can protect itself against

---

[28] A dictum of Lord Blackburn in *Colonial Bank* v. *Whinney* (1886) 11 App. Cas. 426 at p. 438 suggests the contrary.

[29] *Ante*, para. 15-28.

[30] *Ante*, paras. 15-23/27.

[31] [1916] 2 Ch. 353. See also *Powell* v. *London and Provincial Bank* [1893] 2 Ch. 555, *ante*, para. 15-34.

this type of risk which an equitable mortgage of securities necessarily involves. It is only by securing a legal mortgage without notice of earlier equitable claims that the bank can obtain priority over such claims; for, in that case, the maxim is "where the equities are equal, the law prevails." In particular, when shares in joint names are offered as security, a banker should always insist upon a legal mortgage, unless he is perfectly certain that the parties are not trustees.

C. DIFFICULTY IN REALISING THE SECURITY

15-39. Unless "blank" transfers are obtained, the securities cannot be sold without the assistance of the court or the customer's co-operation. Even if blank transfers are taken, there may be difficulty in obtaining registration of the transfers if the customer notifies the company that they are not to be registered. Again, if the customer dies and the company receives notice of his death, it will not register the transfers without the concurrence of his personal representatives. Furthermore, there are cases where blank transfers cannot be used.[32]

D. ISSUE OF BONUS SHARES

15-40. If an issue of bonus shares is made to the customer without the bank's knowledge, this may have a serious effect upon the value of the bank's security, particularly in cases where free bonus shares are issued without a proportionate increase in profits. Suppose, for example, a company's shares are quoted at £4 per share. The directors decide to capitalise part of the reserves by issuing one bonus share for every existing share, but it is not expected that the total amount available for distribution by way of dividends will show any appreciable increase in the near future. Obviously, the value of the shares will fall to about £2, and unless the bank secures a deposit of the bonus shares half its security will have gone. Some banks have inserted a clause in their memoranda of deposit whereby the customer agrees that any future bonus shares are to be regarded as part of the security. The risk is, of course, that the bonus issue may be made without the bank's knowledge, and the customer may forget to deposit his new share certificate with the bank. A vigilant bank officer will watch the newspapers for details of bonus issues. Furthermore, it is usual for stocks and shares held as security to be revalued at least every six months, and a fall in the value of any particular security may indicate that bonus shares have been issued.

[32] *Ante*, para. 15-33.

E. LIEN ON SHARES BY COMPANY

15-41. There is a risk that the company may have a lien on the shares in respect of sums owing to it by its shareholder. In some cases, a notice of deposit may usefully be sent to the company in order to guard against this risk.[33]

15-42. The drawbacks to an equitable mortgage are such that bankers are generally well advised to insist upon the fuller measure of protection conferred by a legal mortgage, unless the advance is very temporary and is made to a customer of undoubted integrity. Nevertheless, practice on this matter differs considerably from bank to bank. Some banks which are most reluctant to take an equitable mortgage of land are content with an equitable mortgage of stocks and shares. There seems to be no logical justification for this. Unless "blank" transfers are obtained in support, a banker should never be content with an equitable mortgage in cases where the customer's occupation is likely to take him overseas. Failure to observe this rule may make it impossible to realise the securities should the customer default when he is abroad.

Disadvantages of Legal Mortgages of Stocks and Shares

15-43. The drawbacks of a legal, as opposed to an equitable, mortgage of stocks and shares apply for the most part to particular types of securities. They may be summarised as follows—

A. PARTLY-PAID SHARES

15-44. If partly-paid shares were transferred into the name of the bank's nominee company, that company would be liable for any calls made on the shares. Moreover, even if the nominee company sold the shares before a call was made, its liability would not necessarily be at an end. Section 212 of the Companies Act, 1948, provides in effect that, if a company is wound up, any one who was a shareholder during the previous year is liable for the unpaid amount on his shares, provided that (i) he is not liable to contribute in respect of any debt of the company contracted after he ceased to be a member, (ii) he is not liable to contribute unless the existing members are unable to satisfy the contributions required from them, and (iii) his liability is limited to the amount left unpaid on the shares by the present holder. In practice, therefore, bankers do not take legal

[33] *Ante*, paras. 15-23/25.

mortgages of partly-paid shares. Rare exceptions to this rule are made where the bank is satisfied that the customer is and will continue to be undoubted for the liability.

B. NO TRANSFER TO BANK'S NOMINEE COMPANY

15-45. Occasionally one finds that a company's articles provide that a limited company shall not be registered as a member. In this event, transfer of the securities into the name of the bank's nominee company will clearly be impossible, and, unless the bank is prepared to have them registered in the names of its officials, the only alternative is an equitable mortgage.

C. DIRECTOR'S QUALIFICATION SHARES

15-46. There is nothing in the Companies Act, 1948, making it obligatory for a director to hold any shares in the company on whose board he sits, but the articles very frequently require him to hold a specified share qualification. If, therefore, a director offers these shares as security, a transfer of them to the bank's nominee would deprive him of his directorship, and so the only course is to take an equitable mortgage.

D. FORGED TRANSFERS

15-47. The rule in *Sheffield Corporation* v. *Barclay* may involve the bank in loss unless precautions are taken. This rule is that a person who sends to a company a forged transfer and procures its registration is bound to indemnify the company, even though he acted in good faith. In *Sheffield Corporation* v. *Barclay*[34] two trustees, Timbrell and Honnywill, were the registered holders of a large amount of Sheffield Corporation stock. This stock was transferred by way of legal mortgage to Mr. E. E. Barclay as the nominee of Barclays Bank. Timbrell's signature to the transfer was genuine, but Honnywill's signature had been forged by Timbrell. Later, the stock was sold to third parties, and they were registered as holders. Timbrell's forgery was discovered, and Honnywill recovered judgment against Sheffield Corporation, whereby they were compelled to buy an equivalent amount of stock and register it in Honnywill's name. The corporation then brought an action against the bank, claiming an indemnity in respect of the loss, amounting to £11,169, which the corporation had suffered. It was held by the House of

[34] [1905] A.C. 392.

Lords, reversing the decision of the Court of Appeal, that the bank must indemnify the corporation, because the bank, by sending in the forged transfer for registration, impliedly contracted that it was genuine. The most satisfactory way of guarding against the possibility of forged transfers is for the banker to require the transferors to sign in his presence. Failing that, the bank should insist upon sending the transfer to the absent transferor by post. Under no circumstances should it be handed to the transferor who has just executed it, upon his promise to forward it to the other transferor.

E. ADMINISTRATIVE COSTS

15-48. Registration of the securities in the name of the bank's nominee company involves the bank in a certain amount of clerical work. When dividends are received by the nominee company, they have to be distributed to the bank's branches to be credited to the accounts of the customers concerned. In order to ease the burden of this work by decentralisation, some banks have created separate nominee companies for different areas.[35] Other banks overcome the difficulty by using personal nominees.

Stocks and Shares Deposited by Stockbrokers

15-49. It is not uncommon for stockbrokers to create a charge, in favour of their bankers, of securities to which their clients are beneficially entitled. This is perfectly proper, provided, of course, that it is done with the consent of the clients. The reason why money is borrowed in this way is because the clients are indebted to their brokers, and if the brokers did not borrow, the clients would have to do so in order to keep the brokers in funds.

15-50. At one time it was the practice of bankers to obtain confirmation from the beneficial owners that the securities could be charged in this way. However, it seems that this is no longer the practice. The rules of the Stock Exchange contain stringent provisions with regard to this type of borrowing. The client's written authority must be obtained by the broker; such authority must specify the period to which it relates and be renewed annually.[36] The rules also require that an independent accountant must inspect these authorities and report to the Council of the Stock Exchange that he has done so.[37]

[35] *Ante*, para. 15-9.
[36] Rule 79a, clause (1) (G).
[37] Rule 79a, clause (10) (A).

15-51. If stockbrokers hold securities on behalf of clients for safe custody, the securities must either be registered in the name of the client or in the name of the brokers' nominee company, or be deposited in a specially designated safe custody account with the brokers' bankers.[38]

Letters of Allotment as Security

15-52. The way in which a company normally issues shares was outlined in the previous chapter.[39] It will be recalled that, pending the issue of a share certificate, the shareholder is supplied with a letter of allotment. Occasionally these documents are offered to bankers as security. It is the invariable practice for letters of allotment to embody a form of renunciation which must be completed by the allottee of the shares if he wishes to transfer them before the date fixed for registration of the new shares. The banker should obtain his customer's signature to this form of renunciation, and the letter of allotment should be deposited at the bank together with the usual memorandum. This enables the bank to sell the shares if the customer fails to repay, or, alternatively, makes it possible for the bank to have the shares registered in the name of its nominee company, thus acquiring a legal mortgage. If, on the other hand, the bank has no intention of taking this course, it is sometimes good policy to obtain the customer's signature to "blank" transfers, provided always that the transfer is not required to be by deed. By so doing, the banker ensures that, when the share certificate is eventually issued in the customer's name, an effective equitable mortgage in the bank's favour will exist together with the power to sell the shares, if need arises. The bank should, of course, obtain possession of the share certificate immediately it is available. Normally, this can easily be arranged, because the certificate is issued in exchange for the letter of allotment, which has been deposited with the bank. Before agreeing to a transaction of this nature, the banker should examine the letter of allotment to find out the amounts of the instalments (if any) which will become due on the shares before they are fully paid; and it is a wise precaution to obtain the customer's written authority to pay such instalments and to debit his account therewith.

Shares in the Lending Bank as Security

15-53. From time to time customers who are also shareholders of the bank wish to borrow against the security of their shares. If the

[38] Rule 79a, clause (1) (G).
[39] *Ante*, paras. 14-7/8.

shares are partly paid—as a few bank shares are—the bank's articles
of association usually provide that the bank is to have a lien on the
shares for all sums owing by the shareholder to the bank. Therefore,
when such partly-paid shares are offered as security, it is unnecessary
to ask the customer to sign a memorandum of deposit. The share
certificate should be lodged with the bank, and notice of lien should
be given to the bank's registrar.

15-54. If the bank shares are fully paid, there will in practice be no
lien, because there is a Stock Exchange rule that an official quotation
will not be granted for any fully-paid shares on which the company
claims a lien.[40] Unless the bank's articles of association preclude the
bank from lending against the security of its own shares, the certificate should be deposited, a memorandum of deposit should be
executed and notice should be given in the usual way. If the articles
preclude the bank from lending against the security of its own shares,
it is the practice to ask the customer to lodge the certificate without
a memorandum of deposit. Notice is then given to the bank's
registrar. The lodging of the certificate under these circumstances
should be regarded only as evidence of means: the bank does not
obtain an effective security.

Stocks on the National Savings Stock Register

15-55. A person who purchases British Government stocks on the
Stock Exchange through the medium of a broker is registered as the
holder thereof in the books kept at the Bank of England and is
supplied with a stock certificate by the Bank. Instead of employing a
stockbroker, an investor may, if he wishes, purchase these stocks
through the National Savings Department. Application forms for
the purchase of stock may be obtained from any post office. If the
investor has an account with the National Savings Bank, the cost of
the stock and the commission will be debited to this account, if
he so desires. Alternatively, a remittance may be sent with the
application form. Not more than £5,000 stock may be purchased
at any one time.[41] An advantage of purchasing stock in this way is
that the commission charged by the department is very much lower

---

[40] See *ante*, para. 15-26.
[41] Post Office Register Regulations, 1925, r. 6 as amended by the Post Office Register
(Amendment) Regulations, 1969, r. 3 and Sched. The limitation does not apply in
certain cases, e.g. where stock is purchased (*a*) with moneys received by the investor
in respect of stock redeemed or savings certificates repaid, or (*b*) with moneys transferred to the investor from the account in a savings bank of a deceased depositor.

than that applicable to transactions on the Stock Exchange. Furthermore, interest on all securities held on the National Savings Stock register is paid gross, i.e., without deduction of income tax, though the stockholder may be liable to pay income tax and surtax thereon, depending upon his total income and allowances.

15-56. When the stock has been purchased, the holder's name is entered on the National Savings Stock register, which is quite distinct from the register at the Bank of England. Occasionally bankers are offered as security certificates relating to stock on the National Savings Stock register. A legal mortgage may be obtained by having the stock transferred into the name of the bank's nominee company. For this purpose a form of transfer should be obtained from the Director, National Savings Department, Savings Bank Division (Stock Branch), Harrogate, Yorkshire. All transfers of British Government stocks are exempt from stamp duty.[42]

15-57. If the advance is for a very short period and the customer is of high standing, the bank may be satisfied with an equitable mortgage. The stock certificate should be deposited with the usual form of memorandum. In addition, a banker sometimes asks his customer to sign an application form for the sale of the stock; these forms—like the applications for purchase—are obtainable from any post office. Then, if the customer defaults, it is a simple matter for the bank to realise the security. It is pointless to send notice of the deposit to the National Savings Department, because such notices will not be acknowledged or recorded. There are two disadvantages of taking an equitable mortgage of these stocks: (i) the holder can easily obtain a duplicate stock certificate and dispose of his stock, and (ii) the holder may, unknown to the bank, obtain a nomination form from the National Savings Department and nominate some person to receive the stock on his death. For these reasons some banks prefer not to take an equitable mortgage of stocks on the National Savings Stock register. An alternative course is to require the holder to have his stock transferred from that register to the corresponding register at the Bank of England. To do this the holder should complete the appropriate application form which may be obtained from the National Savings Department.[43]

Stocks on the Registers of Trustee Savings Banks

15-58. A person who has an account with a trustee savings bank may purchase British Government Stocks through that savings bank.

[42] Stamp Act, 1891, Sched. I.
[43] Post Office Register Regulations, 1925, r. 12.

The stock registers of trustee savings banks are a section of the National Savings Stock register. Commission on the purchase and sale of stock is the same as that which is charged by the National Savings Department, and interest is paid without deduction of income tax.

15-59. There are two possible ways of obtaining a legal mortgage of these stocks. If the lending bank is prepared to open an account with the trustee savings bank, the stock may be transferred into the name of the lending bank's nominee company. Alternatively, the stock may be transferred to the Bank of England register, and the holder may then transfer it into the name of the lending bank's nominee company. The advantage of the former method is that interest on the stock continues to be paid without deduction of income tax. Forms for the transfer of stock into the name of a nominee or to the Bank of England may be obtained from the trustee savings bank.

15-60. An equitable mortgage of these stocks may be obtained by deposit of the stock certificate, together with the usual form of memorandum. Some trustee savings banks acknowledge a notice of deposit, and if the stockholder attempts to dispose of the stock, they will notify the lending bank.

British Savings Bonds

15-61. These bonds, which are a Government security, used to be known as Defence Bonds, and later as National Development Bonds. Application must be made for five pounds of the bonds, or for a multiple of five pounds. There is no Bank of England issue, and, instead of issuing certificates, the National Savings Department supplies each investor with a bond book. When buying additional bonds of the same issue, the holder should produce this book. There is a limit to the amount of the bonds which an investor may hold. Interest is paid without deduction of income tax. The bonds have a maturity date, but they may be encashed before maturity on one month's notice. If the bonds are not encashed until maturity, a small premium is paid which is not subject to tax.

15-62. To obtain an equitable mortgage of the bonds, a banker secures the deposit of the bond book and obtains his customer's signature to the usual memorandum of deposit. It is also useful to ask the customer to sign an encashment notice, which may be obtained from any post office. Equitable mortgages of Savings Bonds are subject to the same disadvantages as equitable mortgages of other stocks on the National Savings Stock register.

15-63. A legal mortgage involves the transfer of the bonds into the name of the bank's nominee. Unfortunately, Savings Bonds are not transferable, except with the consent of the Director of Savings, and this consent is not forthcoming in the case of transfers by way of sale or mortgage. Thus, it is impossible to take a legal mortgage of these bonds.

National Savings Certificates

15-64. These are held solely on the National Savings Stock register. It is impossible to obtain a legal mortgage of the certificates, because they are not transferable, except in special circumstances and with the consent of the Director of Savings; but it has become a fairly common practice among bankers to obtain an equitable charge of the certificates by having them deposited with a repayment form duly signed by the holder and accompanied by the usual form of memorandum. The legality of this practice has been upheld by the Chief Registrar of Friendly Societies, to whom disputes concerning Savings Certificates are referred.[44] In the case in question[45] a customer of the Yorkshire Penny Bank deposited with the bank 500 Savings Certificates and a blank form for repayment signed by him. He also signed a memorandum of deposit. Subsequently, the customer was made bankrupt, and the bank notified the Director of Savings that it held the certificates as security. In reply the Director stated that the Postmaster-General could not recognise a charge on Savings Certificates and that no claim by any person other than the registered holder could be entertained. The trustee in bankruptcy also wrote to the Director claiming the certificates. The Director informed him that repayment of the certificates would be made on receipt of an application for repayment signed by him accompanied by the certificates. The bank referred the dispute to the Chief Registrar. At the hearing the bank argued that the owner of property has an inherent right to charge the property, unless there is a legal reason why the property in question cannot be charged. The trustee in bankruptcy contended that the bank's interest in the certificates was illegal under the Savings Certificates Regulations, 1933, and that the Regulations prohibited the Postmaster-General from recognising that interest. The Chief Registrar made his award in favour of the bank. "I can find nothing in the Regulations," he said, "which forbids the charging of the certificates."

---

[44] Savings Certificates Regulations, 1933, r. 27.
[45] *Yorkshire Penny Bank and the Postmaster General*, reported in the *Report of the Chief Registrar of Friendly Societies for the year 1952*, Part I, General, p. 51.

15-65. Although the legal position is clear, there are practical drawbacks which make Savings Certificates a somewhat unsatisfactory form of security. The holder can easily obtain duplicate certificates and encash them without the bank's knowledge. The banks used to give notice of the deposit to the National Savings Department, which acknowledged receipt and ensured that a certificate was not repaid or a duplicate issued before the bank had a chance to establish its interest. In 1950 the Director of Savings informed the banks that this facility must cease except as regards notices already accepted.[46] Another risk is that the holder may, unknown to the bank, obtain a nomination form from the National Savings Department and nominate some person to receive his certificates upon his death. In spite of these drawbacks, Savings Certificates are still accepted as cover for temporary advances.

Premium Savings Bonds

15-66. These are held solely on the National Savings Stock register.[47] It is impossible to obtain a legal mortgage of the bonds, because they are not transferable either during the lifetime of the registered holder or on his death.[48] Some banks, however, are prepared to take an equitable charge of the bonds by having them deposited with a repayment form signed by the holder and accompanied by the usual form of memorandum. The holder's name is not stated on the bonds, and it is therefore the practice of some banks to write to the Premium Savings Bond Office, Lytham St. Annes, Lancs., quoting the serial numbers of the bonds and enquiring whether the customer is the registered holder.

15-67. Premium Savings Bonds suffer from the same disadvantages as security as National Savings Certificates. In particular the holder might obtain duplicate bonds and encash them without the bank's knowledge. The terms upon which the bonds are issued expressly provide that no responsibility can be accepted in respect of their use as security for a loan.[49]

Units in a Unit Trust

15-68. Briefly, a unit trust operates as follows.[50] The savings of a large number of investors who subscribe to the initial issue are placed with the managers of the trust, who invest the funds, as a rule,

---

[46] See *Journal of the Institute of Bankers*, Vol. LXXI (1950), pp. 33–4.
[47] For a more detailed account of these bonds, see Vol. 1, para. 10-123.
[48] Finance Act, 1968, Sched. 18, para. 4.
[49] Ibid.
[50] For a more detailed account, see Vol. 1, paras. 10-112/15.

in a wide cross-section of securities. Every trust is divided into units, and each investor applies for a certain number of units. The issue is made at an advertised price per unit. Thereafter, it is still possible to apply for units, and the price of each unit depends upon the prices of the investments included in the portfolio. An investor may always realise his units, because the managers undertake to purchase all units offered to them. The price to be paid depends upon the prices of the underlying investments.

15-69. On principle it would appear to be impossible to create a legal mortgage of the units, because the holder himself has merely an equitable interest. Any mortgage which he creates must, it would seem, be equitable.[51] Two methods are available to an intending mortgagee of the units. The first, and most secure, is to ask the holder to transfer them into the name of the bank's nominee company. A form of transfer will generally be supplied by the managers of the trust. This should be completed in the usual way, stamped with the fixed duty of 10s. (50p) and sent to the managers, together with the customer's certificate and the appropriate registration fee. A new certificate in favour of the bank will then be issued. As in the case of registered stocks or shares, the bank will have its usual form of memorandum executed by the customer under hand.

15-70. The alternative method is to ask the customer to lodge the unit certificate with the bank and to sign a memorandum of deposit. The bank should give notice of its charge either to the managers or to the trustees (the latter are generally a trust corporation controlled by one of the large banks or insurance companies). This notice will be recorded in the register of unit holders without fee, and an acknowledgment will be sent to the bank. Section 117 of the Companies Act, 1948[52] (which precludes a company from entering on its register notices of trusts) has no application here, and, although many of the trust deeds of the fixed and flexible trusts declare that the trustees are not bound to take notice of any trusts or equities, it seems that these provisions are never enforced.

15-71. Finally, the bank may wish to be in a position to realise the units should the customer default. The correct course is to obtain the customer's signature to the form of renunciation which is generally printed on the back of the unit certificate. The date should not be filled in. If the customer defaults, the banker will merely insert the date and send the certificate to the managers of

---

[51] Yet in *Re Pain, Gustavson* v. *Haviland* [1919] 1 Ch. 38 (*post*, para. 28-5), it was held possible to have a *legal* assignment by way of mortgage of an *equitable* interest in a trust fund; but this decision has been criticised.

[52] *Ante*, para. 15-23.

the trust. No transfers are used when units are bought by the managers. Thus the customer's signature to the form of renunciation serves the same purpose as a "blank" transfer in the case of registered stocks and shares.

Inscribed Stocks as Security

15-72. The mode of transferring inscribed stocks used to be entirely different from that governing the transfer of registered stocks. Fortunately that system has come to an end, and inscribed stocks are now transferred in precisely the same manner as registered stocks.[53] This simplifies matters from the point of view of the lending banker, for it means that inscribed securities are transferable into the name of the bank's nominee company just as though they were registered securities. In this way the banker may obtain a legal mortgage.

15-73. A word of warning is necessary in relation to stock receipts. These are the memoranda issued to holders of inscribed stock, but (unlike stock certificates) they need not be produced when the stock is transferred. Even when the stock is redeemed, the owner is not asked for the stock receipt. It will be appreciated, therefore, that, if a banker was sufficiently incautious to take an equitable mortgage of inscribed stock by securing the deposit of the stock receipt, there would be nothing to prevent the customer from disposing of the stock without the bank's knowledge. Very occasionally a bank does consent to an equitable mortgage of these stocks and the customer signs an undertaking not to sell the stock without the bank's permission. Clearly the bank is completely at the mercy of the customer, and mortgages of this sort should be regarded as quite exceptional.

15-74. Many stocks which used to be inscribed have been converted into registered stocks; for example, inscribed stock for all British Government securities was abolished in 1943.[54] Accordingly, a customer who produces a stock receipt in respect of British Government stock issued to him prior to 1943 is not the owner of inscribed, but of registered, stock.[55] At any time he may, if he wishes, apply for a stock certificate, free of charge. If, therefore, the bank's advance against this security is likely to be temporary and it is not considered necessary for the stock to be transferred into the name of the bank's nominee company, the best course to take is to advise the

---

[53] *Ante*, para. 14-19.
[54] *Ante*, para. 14-20.
[55] The same applies to local authority stocks: *ante*, para. 14-20.

customer to make application for a stock certificate, which may then be lodged at the bank with a memorandum of deposit.

Discharging the Security

A. DISCHARGE OF LEGAL MORTGAGE

15-75. To vacate the security a transfer must be prepared transferring the stock from the bank's nominee company to the customer. As with the transfer in the opposite direction, the stamp duty is 10s. (50p). The memorandum which the customer signed may be destroyed or handed to him.

B. DISCHARGE OF EQUITABLE MORTGAGE

15-76. The stock or share certificate is returned to the customer, and the memorandum and blank transfer (if any) may be destroyed. If notice of the deposit was given to the company, it may be advisable to inform them that the bank has no further interest in the securities, because, although the company declined to accept notice of the deposit, it may have made some note thereof in its records. In those rare instances where the bank has served a notice in lieu of *distringas*, the company should always be advised when the security is discharged.

Enforcing the Security

A. LEGAL MORTGAGE

15-77. No special formalities need to be observed when it is desired to realise stocks and shares which have been transferred into the name of the bank's nominee company by way of legal mortgage. The memorandum which the customer signs when the mortgage is executed normally confers upon the bank an express power of sale at any time if the customer fails to repay upon demand.[56]

15-78. It is important to ensure that the demand is still effective at the time when the bank realises the shares. Thus if the bank demands repayment and then accepts further security in lieu of repayment, the right to sell the shares ceases to exist, because there is no longer any default in payment. If the bank then proceeds to sell the shares without making a fresh demand, the court will intervene at the instance of the mortgagor. This rule was applied by the House of

[56] *Ante*, para. 15-14.

Lords in *Hunter* v. *Hunter*[57] where Viscount Hailsham, L.C., stated[58] that "the right of sale is a very drastic remedy, and it is essential for the due protection of borrowers that the conditions of its exercise should be strictly complied with."

B. EQUITABLE MORTGAGE

15-79. If the bank is an equitable mortgagee of the securities, the mode of realisation depends upon whether or not the customer signed "blank" transfers which can be effectively filled in. If such transfers were obtained, the bank will complete its legal mortgage by transferring the securities into the names of its nominees, and the shares may then be sold out of their names; or if the name of the bank's nominees has not been inserted as transferee, a direct sale to a purchaser can be effected. The mere deposit of stock and share certificates with a lender accompanied by "blank" transfers confers an implied power of sale which may be exercised after reasonable notice.[59] It will probably be found, however, that express power to complete and register the transfers at any time is contained in the memorandum of deposit.

15-80. In cases where transfers have not been obtained, the first step towards realising the security is to call upon the customer to give instructions for sale. His attention should be drawn to that clause in the memorandum in which he agreed to execute any necessary transfer when called upon. If he declines, the bank may then apply to the court for either (i) an order for sale, or (ii) an order for transfer and foreclosure.[60]

---

[57] [1936] A.C. 222.
[58] At p. 247.
[59] *Stubbs* v. *Slater* [1910] 1 Ch. 632.
[60] For the meaning of foreclosure see *ante*, paras. 7-18/20. A banker would normally apply for sale. *Harrold* v. *Plenty* [1901] 2 Ch. 314, raised the question whether a person with whom a share certificate is deposited by way of security is entitled to foreclosure, or whether his only remedy is sale. Cozens-Hardy, J., decided that both remedies are available.

CHAPTER 16

Bearer Stocks as Security

16-1. BEARER securities are much less common to-day than they were before the Second World War. The Exchange Control Act, 1947, provided that no person in the United Kingdom might issue any bearer certificate or coupon without the permission of the Treasury.[1] However, the Finance Act, 1963, provided that the registered holder of British Government stock is entitled to exchange it for bearer bonds subject to certain conditions.[2] This provision was introduced for the benefit of foreign investors. Bearer securities have always been attractive to them.

Types of Bearer Securities

16-2. Many types of bearer documents have been recognised by our courts as being fully negotiable securities. In 1824 bonds of the King of Prussia were so recognised upon proof that they were sold in the English market and passed from hand to hand daily, like Exchequer bills, at a variable price, according to the state of the market.[3] This decision may be contrasted with a later case where certain Prussian bonds which were treated in Prussia as negotiable by delivery apart from the relevant coupons were held to be not negotiable in this way in England; no evidence was forthcoming that English merchants treated them as negotiable without the coupons attached.[4] In short the decisive factor is the usage of the *English* market. Among the other bearer securities which have been recognised as negotiable by our courts are Exchequer bills,[5] foreign government scrip,[6] the scrip of an English company,[7] bearer debentures of an English company,[8] and share warrants.[9]

---

[1] Sect. 10. See *ante*, para. 14-23.
[2] Sect. 71.
[3] *Gorgier* v. *Mieville* (1824) 3 B. & C. 45.
[4] *Picker* v. *The London and County Banking Co. Ltd.* (1887) 18 Q.B.D. 515
[5] *Wookey* v. *Pole* (1820) 4 B. & Ald. 1.
[6] *Goodwin* v. *Robarts* (1875) L.R. 10 Ex. 76 and in Ex. Ch. 337; affirmed by H.L. 1 App. Cas. 476.
[7] *Rumball* v. *The Metropolitan Bank* (1877) 2 Q.B.D. 194.
[8] *Bechuanaland Exploration Co.* v. *London Trading Bank Ltd.* [1898] 2 Q.B. 658.
[9] *Webb, Hale & Co.* v. *Alexandria Water Co. Ltd.* (1905) 93 L.T. 339; 21 T.L.R. 572. As regards share certificates, it has never been seriously contended that share certificates of an English company designating a named person as the owner of th6 shares are negotiable. In *Longman* v. *Bath Electric Tramways Ltd.* [1905] 1 Ch. 64e

Pledge of Bearer Securities

16-3. Being negotiable instruments, bearer securities are made available as security by way of pledge and not by mortgage.[10] A pledge occurs when goods (or the documents of title thereto) or bearer securities are delivered by one man to another to be held as a security for the payment of a debt or the performance of some other obligation, and upon the express or implied understanding that the subject-matter of the pledge is to be restored to the owner when the debt is discharged or the engagement has been fulfilled. The person depositing the goods or securities is termed the "pledgor," and the party with whom they are left is called the "pledgee."

16-4. A pledgee's rights over his security are to be distinguished from a mortgagee's rights over property mortgaged to him. A pledgee has what the courts have termed a "special property" in the thing pledged which enables him to sell it if the debt or other obligation is not discharged.[11] Where a definite time for payment has been fixed, the pledgee has an implied power of sale upon default, but, if there is no stipulated time for payment, the pledgee may demand payment and in default thereof may sell after giving notice to the pledgor of his intention to do so.[12] The pledgee must, of course, account to the pledgor for any surplus remaining after repayment of the debt. Although a pledgee is able to realise his security, he cannot (unlike a mortgagee) obtain a foreclosure.[13] A legal mortgagee (e.g. of life policies or of registered or inscribed stocks and shares) obtains more than a "special property" in the subject-matter of the mortgage: he gets the full legal title thereto, subject to the mortgagor's right to redeem. There is an exception in the case of land: a mortgagee of land is not permitted to-day to take an absolute conveyance of the legal estate subject to the mortgagor's right to redeem.[14] A further distinction between a pledge and a mortgage is that property pledged must be actually or constructively delivered to the pledgee, whereas in mortgage transactions possession of the property mortgaged does not necessarily pass to the mortgagee.

16-5. The mere deposit of bearer securities with the intention of pledging them is sufficient to confer upon a bank the rights of a

---

at p. 665, Romer, L.J., said " . . . it is to be remembered that a certificate of shares is not a negotiable instrument."

[10] Contrast *Carter* v. *Wake* (1877) 4 Ch. D. 605; 46 L.J. Ch. 841 (pledge of bearer bonds) with *Harrold* v. *Plenty* [1901] 2 Ch. 314 (equitable mortgage of shares).

[11] See Bowen, L.J.'s judgment in *Ex parte Hubbard* (1886) 17 Q.B.D. 690 at p. 698, quoted *post*, para. 22-10.

[12] *France* v. *Clark* (1883) 22 Ch. D. 830.

[13] *Harrold* v. *Plenty* [1901] 2 Ch. 314. For foreclosure, see *ante*, paras. 7-18/20.

[14] For the methods of mortgaging land, see *ante*, para. 4-3.

pledgee. Nevertheless, it is usual to ask the pledgor to sign a memorandum specifying the purpose of the deposit and conferring upon the bank an express power of sale if the overdraft is not repaid upon demand. Furthermore, the memorandum states that the bonds or warrants are deposited as a continuing security, thus excluding the operation of the Rule in *Clayton's* case.[15] If the memorandum is executed under hand, it is exempt from stamp duty.[16] The securities themselves should be examined to see that they are properly stamped and that they are not defaced in any way.[17] A rule of the Stock Exchange provides that "a bond or certificate is to be considered perfect, unless it be much torn or damaged, or a material part of the wording be obliterated."[18] If, as is usual, coupons are attached for the payment of interest or dividend, the banker should ensure that all unpaid coupons are present, and diary notes should be made to remit the coupons for collection on their due dates. Under the Exchange Control Act, 1947, most bearer securities have to be kept with an "authorised depositary."[19] Very often, when a customer requests an advance against bearer securities, those securities are already in his banker's custody in the latter's capacity as an authorised depositary. In such cases it is a simple matter to obtain the customer's signature to the necessary memorandum and to transfer the securities from the bank's safe-custody records to the appropriate security register.

Merits of Bearer Instruments as a Banking Security

16-6. The fact that most, if not all, bearer securities have been recognised as negotiable instruments makes them particularly suitable as cover for banking advances. It is an essential feature of every negotiable instrument that the property therein is capable of passing to a *bona fide* transferee for value even though the transferor may have no title or a defective title thereto. Before the end of the eighteenth century the courts had decided that a pledgee of a negotiable instrument was entitled to the same favourable treatment as a transferee for value.[20] The leading case illustrating this rule so far as it concerns a banker as pledgee is *London Joint Stock Bank* v. *Simmons*.[21] A stockbroker pledged to his bank certain foreign bonds with coupons attached which were payable to bearer and were

---

[15] (1816) 1 Mer. 572.
[16] See *ante*, para. 15-18.
[17] For stamp duty on bearer securities, see *post*, para. 33-6.
[18] Rule 135 (1).
[19] Sect. 15; see *ante*, para. 14-23.
[20] *Collins* v. *Martin* (1797) 1 B. & P. 648.
[21] [1892] A.C. 201. See also *Lloyds Bank Ltd.* v. *Swiss Bankverein* (1913) 108 L.T. 143,

clearly negotiable instruments. The bonds were the property of one of his clients, and the broker had no authority to deal with them in this way. The bank did not know whether or not the instruments belonged to him and made no inquiries. Eventually the broker absconded, and the bank realised these securities. When the client discovered what had taken place, he brought an action against the bank claiming that the bonds were his and that he was entitled to the proceeds of sale. The House of Lords, reversing the decision of the Court of Appeal, held that his claim must fail and that the bank, having acted in good faith, were entitled to retain and to realise the securities. Lord Herschell said[22]—

> The general rule of law is, that where a person has obtained the property of another from one who is dealing with it without the authority of the true owner, no title is acquired as against that owner, even though full value be given, and the property be taken in the belief that an unquestionable title thereto is being obtained . . .

But he stressed that there is an exception to the general rule in the case of negotiable instruments, and said[23]—

> It is surely of the very essence of a negotiable instrument that you may treat the person in possession of it as having authority to deal with it, be he agent or otherwise, unless you know to the contrary, and are not compelled, in order to secure a good title to yourself, to inquire into the nature of his title or the extent of his authority.

16-7. There are other advantages of bearer securities from the point of view of the lending banker. In particular, most of the formalities which are applicable when taking registered or inscribed stocks as security are avoided. For example, no question arises of having the securities transferred into the name of the bank's nominee company. This saves stamp duties. Furthermore, bearer securities can be easily realised if the customer defaults, and neither his co-operation nor an order of the court is required. Thus the bank is in a much stronger position than it is when it agrees to take an equitable mortgage of registered securities. The only drawback to bearer securities was that very occasionally bank officials realised how easy it was to sell them and fell into temptation. At the present day, however, it is more difficult than it was before the war to dispose of bearer securities because of the provisions of the Exchange Control Act, 1947.[24]

[22] [1892] A.C. at p. 215.
[23] [1892] A.C. at p. 217.
[24] See *ante*, para. 14-23.

Release of Bearer Securities

16-8. All that the banker needs to do is to cancel the memorandum and to enter the bearer securities again in his safe-custody records. On no account must the securities be delivered to the customer, for the 1947 Act requires them to be retained at all times by an authorised depositary, though the statute makes express provision for them to be transferred to another depositary if the owner so desires.[25] If they are to be sent to some other depositary by post, the risk of loss in transit should be covered by insurance.

American and Canadian Securities

16-9. The practice in the United States of America and in Canada relating to the issue of share certificates is somewhat different from that of this country. Share certificates of many American and Canadian companies are issued in favour of a specified registered holder, but they incorporate on the back a form of transfer and a power of attorney for execution in blank by the registered holder. The object of the power of attorney is to enable the holder to appoint an attorney to act for him in America or Canada, where alone a transfer can be registered. Thereafter the certificates are transferable by delivery and are in fact looked upon as bearer securities. In 1887 the question was raised whether certificates of this kind, issued by the Pennsylvania Railroad Company, were to be recognised by our courts as negotiable instruments.[26] The transfer forms on the reverse of the certificates had been signed by the registered holder, the names of the transferee and of the attorney both being left in blank. It was proved that, when signed in this way, such certificates, by the usage of English bankers and dealers in securities, were transferred by mere delivery and were dealt with like bearer bonds. Nevertheless, it was held that they were not negotiable. The learned judge stated briefly the requisites of a negotiable instrument, one of which is that it must be capable of being sued upon by the person holding it *pro tempore*. He observed[27]—

> Now it seems to me clear that this instrument could not be sued upon by the person holding it *pro tempore*, and could not therefore be negotiable, because when it was handed over by the transferor with this blank power of attorney, it could not be sued upon by that person until it was transferred on the register.

He also inclined to the view that—

[25] Sect. 15.
[26] *London and County Banking Company Ltd.* v. *London and River Plate Bank Ltd.* (1887) 20 Q.B.D. 232.
[27] 20 Q.B.D. at p. 239.

If the right of suing upon an instrument does not appear upon the face of it to be extended beyond one particular individual, no usage of trade, however extensive, will confer upon it the character of negotiability.

16-10. The usual practice in this country is for securities of this type to be registered in a recognised "marking name." This term came into use because, under the pre-war practice, the reverse of the certificate was "marked" with a rubber stamp when a dividend was paid. During the war the certificates were held abroad for safe custody, and the practice was discontinued. Nowadays the "marking names" usually pay dividends without marking the certificate, on the undertaking of the authorised depositary which holds the certificate to stamp it "all dividends claimed to . . ." before the certificate is released. Many banks, finance houses, and Stock Exchange firms have been given recognition as good "marking names." A full list of these names will be found in *The Stock Exchange Official Year Book*. The importance of having these securities registered in a recognised "marking name" arises from the fact that, by the Rules of the Stock Exchange, a member is not required to accept delivery of such securities in names other than "marking names" recognised by the market.[28] The dividends in respect of the shares are paid to the registered holder. Therefore, if the beneficial owner has had his shares registered in a recognised "marking name," he will have to apply to that institution or firm for the dividend. A small commission is usually charged for this service. Irrespective of whether or not the securities are registered in a "marking name," the certificates must be kept with an authorised depositary.[29]

American and Canadian Shares as Security

16-11. In most cases where shares of American and Canadian companies are offered as security for a proposed advance, it will be found that the certificates are already in the banker's custody in his capacity as authorised depositary. If the shares are not already registered in a good "marking name," this should be done forthwith, because where the shares are left in the name of a private individual they are not easily saleable, and furthermore there is always the possibility that they may be subject to a lien in favour of the company in respect of advances made by it to the registered holder. The firm or institution chosen for registration purposes should sign the transfer form in blank, and the customer should sign the bank's usual form of memorandum of deposit. In view of the fact that our courts have refused to recognise these certificates as negotiable instruments (even

---

[28] Rule 135 (3).
[29] Exchange Control Act, 1947, Sect. 15.

when the transfer forms are signed in blank),[30] the transaction is not a pledge but an equitable mortgage; but if the shares are registered in the name of the bank's nominee company (most of the nominee companies are good "marking names"), the mortgage will be legal.

16-12. Sometimes stockbrokers deposit these certificates with their bankers, and there is a risk that the securities may belong not to them but to one of their clients. Nevertheless, the bank's position will not be prejudiced, provided that there is nothing to put the bank upon inquiry as to the extent of the stockbrokers' authority to deal with the certificates. This was so decided in *Fuller* v. *Glyn Mills, Currie & Co.*,[31] where stockbrokers had mortgaged to their bank some Canadian Pacific Railway ordinary stock. The stock had been registered in the name of a Mr. Harmsworth, and the endorsed form of transfer had been signed by him. Eventually, the stockbrokers became bankrupt, and one of their clients, who was the owner of the stock, claimed its return from the bank. It was held, however, that, as there was nothing to put the bank upon inquiry, the plaintiff was estopped from setting up his title as against the bank, because he had left the certificates in the stockbrokers' hands in such a condition as to convey a representation to any person who took them from the stockbrokers that they had authority to deal with them.

[30] *Ante*, para. 16-9.
[31] [1914] 2 K.B. 168.

CHAPTER 17

Unquoted Shares as Security

17-1. UNQUOTED shares are those which are not quoted on any stock exchange.[1] The first problem with which a banker is faced when he is offered these shares as security is that of finding out their present worth. A useful approach is to inquire whether any of the shares have been valued recently for probate purposes. Another helpful course is to seek the assistance of the secretary to the company. As a matter of courtesy he will usually be prepared to inform the bank of the prices at which the company's shares have changed hands during the past twelve months. This information, coupled with details of the dividends paid by the company over the past two or three years, will probably be sufficient to enable one to place a value upon the shares.

17-2. In addition, it might be thought desirable to ask the customer to produce copies of the company's balance sheet for the past two or three years. When these are produced, one may try to value the assets on a break-up basis, deduct the company's liabilities and so arrive at the value of the shares. However, this method is usually far from reliable, largely because of the difficulty of valuing the assets. Sometimes it may be usefully employed in conjunction with one of the other methods outlined above.

17-3. If the banker is satisfied as to the value of the unquoted shares, the next task is to decide how to take them as security. Although there are some public companies whose shares are unquoted, most unquoted shares are those in private companies. Briefly, a private company is one which by its articles (*a*) restricts the right to transfer its shares; and (*b*) limits the number of its members to fifty (excluding present employees and past employees who obtained their shares whilst working for the company and have retained them since that time); and (*c*) prohibits any invitation to the public to subscribe for any shares or debentures of the company.[2] The restriction on the right to transfer the shares of a private company often makes it impossible to obtain a legal mortgage of such shares by having them transferred into the name of the bank's nominees. Furthermore, some public companies whose shares are unquoted have a similar

---

[1] See *ante*, para. 14-1.
[2] Companies Act, 1948, Sect. 28 (1).

restriction in their articles. In all such cases, one has to be content with an equitable mortgage. This will be effected in the way described in a previous chapter,[3] but it will often be found in practice that the shareholder objects to a notice of deposit being served on the company.

Disadvantages of Unquoted Shares as Security

17-4. First there is difficulty in valuing the shares.

17-5. Secondly, if it becomes necessary for the bank to realise them, the bank may be unable to find a purchaser. Even if a potential purchaser can be found, it may be that the directors, in the exercise of the powers conferred upon them by the articles, will decline to register a transfer in his favour. The best course is usually to offer the shares to the existing members: the articles of some companies require this to be done. A serious difficulty is that such members, being the only possible buyers, can often dictate their own price.

17-6. Thirdly, as already shown, it is often impossible to take a legal mortgage of the shares by having them registered in the name of the bank's nominees. Even if the directors say that they are prepared to register the bank's transfer, the articles should be carefully examined, because it has been decided that where a transfer is registered in breach of the articles, a member of the company and even the transferor, if the circumstances are such that he is not estopped from disputing the validity of the transfer, may obtain an order for rectification.[4]

17-7. Fourthly, by the Finance Act, 1940,[5] where a person has transferred any of his property to a company, the assets of the company are, in certain circumstances, deemed to be his property for the purposes of estate duty. The Act provides that the *company itself* is one of the parties liable for this duty.[6] This provision may seriously affect the company's financial postion and so reduce the value of its shares.

17-8. The drawbacks to unquoted shares as security are such that bankers often decline to accept them. In cases where they are taken, they are regarded as evidence of means, rather than as a security which can readily be turned into cash.

[3] *Ante,* paras. 15-19/22.
[4] *Hunter* v. *Hunter* [1936] A.C. 222.
[5] Sect. 46, as amended.
[6] Sect. 54.

Part Five

GUARANTEES

CHAPTER 18

The Nature of a Guarantee

18-1. A GUARANTEE is a promise by one person (called the "guarantor" or the "surety") to answer for the present or future debt of a second person (called the "principal debtor"), such promise being made to the person to whom the principal debtor is, or will become, liable. Thus, when a guarantor signs a guarantee in favour of a banker, he is saying in effect, "advance money to your customer, Mr. X, and if he does not repay, I will be responsible, provided that the amount of my liability shall not exceed (say) one thousand pounds."

18-2. A contract of guarantee should be distinguished from a contract of indemnity. An indemnity comes into existence where one man promises to save another harmless from the result of a transaction into which he enters at the instance of the promisor. Accordingly, if the promisor makes himself *primarily* liable, the contract is one of indemnity. The distinction is sometimes a very fine one, but it has important consequences in banking practice. For example, where a person wishes to become surety for someone who is under disability (e.g. minority), it should be made clear in the instrument which is drawn up that the so-called surety is to be liable as a principal. The instrument may, if desired, be worded both as a guarantee and as an indemnity, so that, if it only transpires subsequently that the so-called principal debtor was under disability with the result that sums advanced to him could not be made the subject of a guarantee, nevertheless the contract of indemnity will bind the promisor. The guarantee forms used by the banks incorporate a clause on these lines.[1]

18-3. Another distinction between a guarantee and an indemnity is that a guarantee is unenforceable by action unless evidenced by a memorandum in writing signed by the guarantor or by some other person duly authorised by him.[2] An indemnity, on the other hand, does not require a written memorandum. The point is of small practical importance to bankers, because, quite apart

---

[1] *Post*, para. 19-46.
[2] Statute of Frauds, 1677, Sect. 4. Where the guarantee is merely incidental to a larger contract and not the sole object of the parties to the transaction, the courts have held that the guarantee is not within the section. Such transactions will not be considered here because they do not affect bankers.

from the legal rule, no banker would contemplate lending money against the verbal promise of a third party to be responsible for its repayment.

18-4. Guarantees are subject to the ordinary rule of English law that all contracts, except those under seal, must be supported by consideration. But the Mercantile Law Amendment Act, 1856,[3] provides that it is unnecessary to set out the consideration in the written instrument. In point of fact, however, it is the invariable practice for the forms of guarantee used by the banks to contain a statement of the consideration.[4]

Effect of Mistake

18-5. Where a person signs a written document containing a contract that is fundamentally different in nature from that which he contemplated, the contract may be void for mistake. The classic illustration in the law of principal and surety is *Carlisle and Cumberland Banking Co.* v. *Bragg*.[5] In that case, a man named Rigg had an overdraft with the Carlisle and Cumberland Banking Co., and the bank required him to find a suitable person to guarantee the repayment of this debt. It would appear that they supplied him with one of their standard forms of guarantee, which he produced to a Mr. Bragg. He asked Mr. Bragg if he would sign it and gave him to understand that it related to some insurance matter. Relying upon this statement, Mr. Bragg signed the form of guarantee without reading it. Rigg then forged the signature of an attesting witness and returned the form to the bank. When eventually the bank brought an action against Mr. Bragg, it was held by the Court of Appeal that he was not liable. Kennedy, L.J., summed up the matter in the following words: "The principle involved, as I understand it, is that a consenting mind is essential to the making of a contract, and that in such a case as this there is really no *consensus*, because there was no intention to make a contract of the kind in question."[6] Counsel for the bank had argued that the fact that the defendant had not read the document was evidence of negligence and that he was estopped from alleging that the contents of the document did not represent his intention. The court rejected this argument on the ground that the defendant did not owe any duty to the bank to exercise care.

[3] Sect. 3.
[4] See *post*, paras. 19-12/13.
[5] [1911] 1 K.B. 489; see also *Gallie* v. *Lee* [1969] 2 W.L.R. 901.
[6] [1911] 1 K.B. at p. 497.

18-6. The rule of law illustrated by *Bragg's* case applies only where a person signs a document in the belief, induced by a misrepresentation, that it embodies a contract of a totally different nature from that which in fact it does.[7] If he was well aware of the type of transaction involved, but did not trouble to ascertain its contents, he could not evade liability.[8] Thus, if he signs a form of guarantee in the knowledge that it is a guarantee, he cannot plead absence of *consensus* on the ground that he failed to appreciate the significance of the numerous clauses embodied therein. Were it otherwise, the conduct of business affairs would become well-nigh impossible.

Disclosure of Information

18-7. There are certain contracts in our law which are said to be contracts *uberrimae fidei* (literally "of the utmost good faith") in which one or both of the parties is under an obligation to disclose to the other all material facts known to him which might influence the other when deciding whether or not he should enter into the contract. Failure to make full disclosure renders the contract voidable at the instance of the other party. Contracts of insurance fall within this category, and it is the duty of the intending assured to disclose to the underwriter all material facts known to him.[9]

18-8. The courts have decided that guarantees do not fall within this special class of contracts. In *Cooper* v. *National Provincial Bank Ltd.*[10] the plaintiff gave two guarantees in respect of the banking account of a customer of the National Provincial Bank named Mrs. Rolfs. He brought an action against the bank claiming to set aside the guarantees and have them declared void on the ground that the bank had failed to disclose (i) that Mrs. Rolfs' husband was an undischarged bankrupt, (ii) that the husband had authority to draw on the account, and (iii) that the account had been operated in an improper and irregular way because certain cheques had been drawn and then orders had been given not to pay. The bank contended that there was no legal obligation upon them to disclose any of these matters and counterclaimed for the amount of the guarantees with interest. Judgment was given in the bank's favour.

18-9. It is clearly established, therefore, that as a general rule a banker is under no duty to volunteer information which might

[7] *Muskham Finance Ltd.* v. *Howard* [1963] 1 Q.B. 904, at p. 912.
[8] *Howatson* v. *Webb* [1907] 1 Ch. 537; [1908] 1 Ch. 1.
[9] *London Assurance Co.* v. *Mansel* (1879) 11 Ch. D. 363, *ante*, para. 11-4.
[10] [1945] 2 All E.R. 641. See also *National Provincial Bank Ltd.* v. *Glanusk* [1913] 3 K.B. 335; *Lloyds Bank Ltd.* v. *Harrison* (1925) 4 L.D.B. 12; *Westminster Bank Ltd.* v. *Cond* (1940) 46 Com. Cas. 60.

influence the decision of a prospective guarantor. However, in exceptional circumstances the position may be different. Lord Campbell formulated the following proposition in a case decided over a hundred years ago[11]—

> I should think that this might be considered as the criterion whether the disclosure ought to be made voluntarily, namely, whether there is anything that might not naturally be expected to take place between the parties who are concerned in the transaction, that is, whether there be a contract between the debtor and the creditor, to the effect that his position shall be different from that which the surety might naturally expect; and, if so, the surety is to see whether that is disclosed to him. But, if there be nothing which might not naturally take place between these parties, then, if the surety would guard against particular perils, he must put the question, and he must gain the information which he requires.

This passage has been frequently cited, and the test formulated by Lord Campbell was, in fact, applied by the court in *Cooper's* case.

Rights of a Guarantor

18-10. A guarantor enjoys many rights if he does not expressly waive them. His rights may be considered under three headings: (*a*) those against the creditor, (*b*) those against the principal debtor, and (*c*) those against co-sureties, if any. However, as will be shown in the next chapter, bank forms of guarantee strip a guarantor of virtually all those rights which the law would otherwise confer upon him—at any rate where they might conflict with the bankers' interests.

A. GUARANTOR'S RIGHTS AS AGAINST THE CREDITOR

18-11. First, a guarantor is entitled, at any time during the currency of the guarantee, to call upon the creditor to inform him of the amount for which he is liable under the terms of his guarantee. A banker who is asked to supply this information will exercise care because the relationship between himself and his customer is a confidential one.[12] Under no circumstances should the bank supply the guarantor with a copy of the customer's account, unless, of course, the customer gives his consent. The information given should be strictly limited to a statement of the guarantor's present liability, i.e. on the assumption that the bank called upon him forthwith under the terms of the guarantee. Thus, if the debt exceeds the

---

[11] *Hamilton* v. *Watson* (1845) 12 Cl. & Fin. 109, at p. 119.
[12] *Tournier* v. *National Provincial Bank Ltd.* [1924] 1 K.B. 461. See Vol. 1, paras. 2-100/3.

amount of the guarantee, the guarantor should merely be told that he is liable for the full amount of his guarantee, whereas if the debt is less than the amount of the guarantee, the guarantor should be told the actual amount of the debt including bank charges. Furthermore, the guarantor should be reminded that, as a period of notice is required if he wishes to determine his liability,[13] the position may change before that period has expired.

18-12. Secondly, it has been suggested that, as soon as the guaranteed debt has become due and before the guarantor has been asked to pay it, he has a right to require the creditor to call upon the principal debtor to pay off the debt.[14] However, the existence of this right has been questioned.[15]

18-13. Thirdly, at any time after the debt has become due the guarantor may apply to the creditor and pay him off, and then, after giving an indemnity for costs, may sue the principal debtor in the creditors's name,[16] or even, so it would seem, in his own name, provided that he obtains an assignment of the guaranteed debt.[17]

18-14. Fourthly, if the guarantor is sued by the creditor for payment of the debt guaranteed, he may avail himself of any set-off arising out of the same transaction as the debt guaranteed which the principal debtor possesses against the creditor.[18]

18-15. Fifthly, if the guarantor pays off the debt, he is entitled to be subrogated to all the rights possessed by the creditor in respect of the debt.[19] The guarantor is entitled to the benefit of the creditor's remedies the moment he pays the debt. If, therefore, he offers to pay the debt on condition that those remedies are made over to him, but the creditor refuses, he is entitled to pay the money into court, and to bring an action for an assignment of the remedies.[20]

18-16. Thus, a guarantor paying off the debt has always been entitled to any securities which have been given for the debt by the principal debtor to the creditor.[21] This right is clearly based upon the obligation imposed on the principal debtor of indemnifying the guarantor, which makes it inequitable for the creditor to throw the whole liability on to the surety by electing not to avail himself of the

[13] See *post*, paras. 19-24/28.
[14] Halsbury's *Laws of England* (3rd ed., 1957), Vol. 18, p. 465.
[15] See Rowlatt, op. cit., pp. 173–8, where the authorities are exhaustively examined.
[16] *Swire* v. *Redman* (1876) 1 Q.B.D. 536.
[17] Law of Property Act, 1925, Sect. 136.
[18] *Bechervaise* v. *Lewis* (1872) L.R. 7 C.P. 372.
[19] Mercantile Law Amendment Act, 1856, Sect. 5.
[20] *Goddard* v. *Whyte* (1860) 2 Giff. 449.
[21] *Ex parte Crisp* (1744) 1 Atk. 133; Mercantile Law Amendment Act, 1856, Sect. 5.

securities for the guaranteed debt.[22] The right extends to all securities which the creditor has received from the principal debtor, before, contemporaneously with, or after the creation of the suretyship, and it makes no difference whether or not the guarantor knew of the securities at the time when he became surety.[23] If he guaranteed part only of the debt, he has, on payment of that sum, all the rights of the creditor in respect of that amount and is, accordingly, entitled to a proportionate share in any security held by the creditor for the whole debt.[24] However, bank guarantee forms are drafted in a way which prevents the guarantor from claiming any securities or any share therein unless he pays off the whole debt.[25]

18-17. Finally, the right of a guarantor to the securities deposited with the creditor extends, not only to those given by the principal debtor, but also to those given by any other person (whether a guarantor or not) for the purpose of securing the debt. Accordingly, a guarantor who has paid more than his due proportion of the common liability is entitled to have such securities assigned to him for the purpose of obtaining contribution.[26] For example, D owes money to C. The debt is secured by (i) a guarantee by G, and (ii) certain security deposited by S. If G pays off the debt, he will be entitled to have assigned to him the security deposited by S for the purpose of obtaining contribution from S.

B. GUARANTOR'S RIGHTS AS AGAINST THE PRINCIPAL DEBTOR

18-18. First, when the creditor acquires, as against the guarantor, a right to immediate payment of the debt, the guarantor is entitled to call upon the principal debtor to pay the amount of the debt guaranteed so as to relieve him from his obligation, even though he has, as yet, paid nothing under the guarantee and even though the creditor has not demanded payment from him or from the principal debtor.[27]

18-19. Secondly, as soon as the guarantor pays anything under his guarantee, he has an immediate right of action against the principal

---

[22] *Aldrich* v. *Cooper* (1803) 8 Ves. 382.
[23] *Forbes* v. *Jackson* (1882) 19 Ch. D. 615, at p. 621.
[24] *Goodwin* v. *Gray* (1874) 22 W.R. 312.
[25] See *post*, paras. 19-15/18.
[26] *Duncan, Fox & Co.* v. *North and South Wales Bank* (1880) 6 App. Cas. 1, at p. 19. See also the Mercantile Law Amendment Act, 1856, Sect. 5. For details of a surety's right to contribution, see *post*, para. 18-20.
[27] *Ranelaugh* v. *Hayes* (1683) 1 Vern. 189.

debtor.[28] But the guarantor cannot accelerate his remedy by paying the guaranteed debt before it becomes legally due.[29] If the principal debtor is bankrupt, the guarantor may prove in his estate for the amount which he has paid under the guarantee.[30] This right, however, is subject to the rule against double proof, whereby a surety cannot prove, in the bankruptcy of the principal debtor, upon a contract to indemnify him, whether express or implied, whilst the creditor is proving for the debt itself.[31]

C. GUARANTOR'S RIGHTS AS AGAINST HIS CO-SURETIES

18-20. First, one of several co-sureties who pays the debt, or more than his proportion of it, is entitled to contribution from the others in respect of the excess.[32] This is so whether they are bound jointly with him, or severally, or jointly and severally, and whether bound by the same instrument or by different instruments, and whether in the same amount or different amounts, and whether at the same time or different times, and whether or not the surety paying the debt knew of the existence of the co-sureties. The right to contribution is founded upon the rule that in equity the remedies of the creditor against the several guarantors should have been so applied as to apportion the burden, not necessarily equally, but rateably.[33] Thus the amount which the sureties are bound to contribute depends upon the proportions in which they are respectively liable.

18-21. It has been urged that a surety ought not to have a right to contribution from a co-surety unless the principal debtor is insolvent, or at any rate there is some impediment to suing him. It would be anomalous, so it is said, for the surety who pays to have an equity to contribution so long as the remedy against the principal debtor, which would relieve all the sureties, is available.[34] This would lead to a multiplicity of suits. The Court of Appeal has considered this argument and has laid down the rule that, when a guarantor brings an action against his co-sureties for contribution, he must make the

---

[28] *Davies* v. *Humphreys* (1840) 6 M. & W. 153. When the principal debtor has expressly agreed to indemnify the guarantor, the guarantor should sue on that agreement, and not for money paid to the use of the principal debtor under an implied contract of indemnity: *Toussaint* v. *Martinnant* (1787) 2 T.R. 100, at p. 104.

[29] *Coppin* v. *Gray* (1842) 1 Y. & C. Ch. Cas. 205, at p. 210.

[30] Bankruptcy Act, 1914, Sect. 30 (3) and (8).

[31] *Ex parte European Bank* (1871) 7 Ch. App. 99; and *In re Lennard* [1934] 1 Ch. 235.

[32] It has been said that the right to contribution may arise before the guarantor has made any payment, but there is very little authority to show the precise extent of the relief to which he is entitled: *per* Wright, J., in *Wolmershausen* v. *Gullick* [1893] 2 Ch. 514, at p. 520.

[33] *Deering* v. *Winchelsea* (1787) 2 B. & P. 270.

[34] Rowlatt, *op. cit.*, pp. 234–5.

principal debtor a party to that action, unless it is proved or can be inferred from the evidence before the court that the principal is insolvent, or that there is some other good reason why he should not be joined.[35]

18-22. If one guarantor pays the debt and takes over from the creditor securities given to the creditor by the principal debtor, he is obliged to allow for that security when seeking contribution from his co-sureties.[36] Similarly, if the guarantor paying the debt receives any payment from the principal debtor, he is bound to bring that into account and to give the other sureties the benefit of it rateably in relief of their contributions.[37]

18-23. Secondly, to aid him in recovering contribution from a co-surety, a guarantor is entitled to any securities given to the creditor by the co-surety.[38]

18-24. Thirdly, if one of the sureties is bankrupt and if the creditor proves for the whole debt, a co-surety paying more than his share is entitled, after the creditor has received twenty shillings in the pound, to the benefit of the creditor's proof and, in this way, he may receive dividends out of the bankrupt surety's estate up to, but not exceeding, the amount which he could have recovered as contribution.[39] If the surety paying proves in his own right for contribution, it seems that he can prove only for the actual sum recoverable.[40] Accordingly, a surety who pays the debt should ensure that a proof is made in the estate of any insolvent co-surety in the name of the creditor for the whole debt. For this purpose he is entitled, upon giving a proper indemnity, to the use of the creditor's name.[41]

Determination of a Guarantee

A. PAYMENT BY PRINCIPAL DEBTOR

18-25. The general rule is that if the principal debtor pays the debt, this discharges the surety from all liability; but, this is not so in a case where the payment amounts to a fraudulent preference.[42]

---

[35] *Hay* v. *Carter* [1935] 1 Ch. 397.
[36] *Re Arcedeckne* (1883) 24 Ch. D. 709.
[37] *Knight* v. *Hughes* (1828) 3 C. & P. 467.
[38] See *ante*, para. 18-17.
[39] *Re Parker, Morgan* v. *Hill* [1894] 3 Ch. 400.
[40] Ibid.
[41] See the Mercantile Law Amendment Act, 1856, Sect. 5, and *In re Parker* (*supra*).
[42] *Post*, paras. 19-51/55.

B. PAYMENT BY GUARANTOR

18-26. Similarly, payment of the debt by the guarantor puts an end to his liability. Normally, it is the creditor who calls upon the guarantor to fulfil his obligation by making payment, but occasionally the initiative is taken by the guarantor himself, who gives notice to the creditor that he wishes the contract to be determined. This notice need not by law be in writing, but it is often stipulated in guarantees that it must be so. Furthermore, it is frequently stipulated that the guarantee is to continue until a stated period after the notice has been given. The effect of a clause of this nature will be discussed later.[43]

C. MISREPRESENTATION

18-27. The guarantor may have the guarantee set aside if he had been induced to enter into it by a misrepresentation of an existing fact, even if made innocently.[44]

D. DEATH OF PRINCIPAL DEBTOR

18-28. There is a dearth of authority as to the effect of the death of the principal debtor. Being dead, he cannot incur further obligations, and so one may say that the guarantee is determined in the sense that the guarantor's liability has become crystallised. A practical problem, from a banker's point of view concerns cheques presented after the principal debtor's death but before the banker had notice thereof. There seems to be no ground for arguing that the indebtedness created by these cheques is not covered by the guarantee. Some bank guarantee forms expressly provide that the amount of such cheques is to be included in the sum guaranteed. Cheques presented after the bank has received notice of death are, of course, returned unpaid with the answer "drawer deceased."

E. NOTICE OF GUARANTOR'S DEATH

18-29. It appears to be established that, if a guarantee has been acted upon before the guarantor dies, his death does not put an end to the continuance of the security, unless and until it comes to the notice of the creditor.[45] As soon as it does come to his knowledge, the right to continue advances upon the security ceases, unless the guarantee contains a stipulation for notice by the deceased's personal

[43] *Post*, paras. 19-24/28.
[44] *Post*, para. 19-7.
[45] *Bradbury* v. *Morgan* (1862) 1 H. & C. 249. If the guarantee has not been acted upon before the guarantor's death, the legal position is obscure: see Rowlatt, op. cit., pp. 86–7.

representatives.[46] In other words, if the terms of the stipulation show that it can refer only to a notice given by the guarantor during his life (e.g. where it is to be under his hand), knowledge of the guarantor's death will determine the guarantee forthwith. The guarantee forms used by the banks have been drafted with this rule in mind.[47]

F. NOTICE OF GUARANTOR'S MENTAL INCAPACITY

18-30. The legal effect of the guarantor's mental incapacity is similar to that which follows his death: the guarantee is not determined until it comes to the notice of the creditor.[48] This was so held in a case where a bank had taken as security a continuing guarantee with a clause giving the guarantors, their executors, and administrators powers to determine it by three months' notice.[49] One of the guarantors became insane, and it was decided that, as soon as the bank received notice of the lunacy, it could no longer make advances for which the insane guarantor would be liable, though he remained responsible for debts already accrued due. Unfortunately, the bank did not break the current account, with the result that part of his liability was extinguished by the Rule in *Clayton's* case. Lawrence, J., observed that the notice clause made no provision for lunacy.[50] As a general rule, the guarantee forms used by the banks still make no provision for this contingency. Perhaps it is considered to be in bad taste to invite a guarantor to make provision for his possible mental incapacity.

G. THE GUARANTOR'S BANKRUPTCY

18-31. There is an old case which seems to be an authority for the view that the bankruptcy of the guarantor does not of itself revoke the guarantee.[51] Nevertheless, it is conceived that, under the present bankruptcy law, notice to the creditor of an act of bankruptcy by the guarantor or (in the absence of such notice) the making of a receiving order puts an end to the continuance of the security.[52] The creditor has, of course, a right to prove in the bankruptcy of the surety. If he

---

[46] *Coulthart* v. *Clementson* (1879) 5 Q.B.D. 42.
[47] *Post*, para. 19-24.
[48] There seems to be no authority concerning the principal debtor's mental incapacity. Presumably, it crystallises the guarantor's liability. Any advances to the debtor's receiver or committee should be the subject of a fresh arrangement.
[49] *Bradford Old Bank Ltd.* v. *Sutcliffe* (1918) 23 Com. Cas. 299 and, on appeal, [1918] 2 K.B. 833.
[50] 23 Com. Cas. at p. 301.
[51] *Boyd* v. *Robins* (1859) 5 C.B. (N.S.) 597.
[52] Bankruptcy Act, 1914, Sect. 30 (2) and (3).

decides to exercise this right and the guarantor eventually gets his discharge, it is submitted that the guarantee could no longer be relied on, should further advances be made to the principal debtor. A more difficult problem arises if the customer's account is in credit when the surety becomes bankrupt with the result that no proof is submitted. If the bankrupt obtains his discharge and his financial position improves, could the banker still rely upon the guarantee?[53] Although there is no clear authority on this point, it would be safer to assume that the contract is no longer in force; a fresh guarantee should be taken.

H. VARIATION OF TERMS OF PRINCIPAL CONTRACT

18-32. Any material variation of the terms of the contract between the creditor and the principal debtor will discharge the guarantor. A material variation means, for this purpose, any variation which cannot be seen without inquiry to be unsubstantial or one that cannot be otherwise than beneficial to the guarantor.[54]

I. AGREEMENT TO GIVE TIME TO PRINCIPAL DEBTOR

18-33. There is a rule that a binding agreement between the creditor and the principal debtor to give time to the debtor will discharge the guarantor from liability, if made without his consent and whether or not he is actually prejudiced thereby.[55] The reason given for this, as stated by Lord Eldon,[56] is that the creditor, by giving time to the principal debtor, has put it out of the power of the guarantor to consider whether he will have recourse to his remedy against the principal debtor or not, and because he in fact cannot have the same remedy against the principal debtor as he would have had under the original contract.

18-34. It is not surprising that this rule has been strongly criticised. Though sensible enough in cases where the guarantor is prejudiced, it is absurd that it should apply where he suffers no detriment. A learned writer has urged that "if we look at the situation with an unprejudiced eye, we shall perhaps see that the mere giving of time to the debtor does not generally injure the surety, but may on the contrary advantage him by saving the debtor's solvency."[57] Even so,

---

[53] Cf. *Questions on Banking Practice* (10th ed., 1965) p. 82, Question 154.
[54] *Holme* v. *Brunskill* (1878) 3 Q.B.D. 495.
[55] *Nisbet* v. *Smith* (1789) 2 Bro. C. C. 579; *Samuell* v. *Howarth* (1817) 3 Mer 272; and *Bolton* v. *Buckenham* [1891] 1 Q.B. 278.
[56] See *Samuell* v. *Howarth* (1817) 3 Mer. 272, at p. 278.
[57] Glanville L. Williams, *Joint Obligations* (1949), p. 123.

he is automatically discharged. The inflexibility of the rule was illustrated by Blackburn, J., in *Polak* v. *Everett*[58] where he observed that if the surety's right "be suspended for a day or an hour, not injuring the surety to the value of one farthing, and even positively benefiting him, nevertheless, by the principles of equity, it is established that this discharges the surety altogether." An eminent American judge ridiculed the legal position in the following words[59]—

> Without such an extension [i.e. of time], the surety would have the privilege, upon the maturity of the debt, of making payment to the creditor, and demanding immediate subrogation to the latter's remedies against the principal. He must, therefore, it is said, be deemed to have suffered prejudice if, by extension of the due date, the right has been postponed. . . . The law has shaped its judgments upon the fictitious assumption that a surety, who has probably lain awake at night for fear that payment may some day be demanded has in truth been smarting under the repressed desire to force an unwelcome payment on a reluctant or capricious creditor.

A well-drawn guarantee expressly excludes this rule by providing that the creditor may give time to the debtor without in any way affecting the guarantor's liability.[60]

J. RELEASE OF SECURITIES AND CO-SURETIES

18-35. As a result of the rules that a guarantor is entitled to contribution from every co-surety and to the benefit of every security held by the creditor, it has been decided that a guarantor will be discharged in whole or in part if a right of contribution or any security is lost by the action of the creditor.[61] The relief to which the guarantor is entitled upon the happening of such events is quite different from that enjoyed by him when his remedies upon the principal obligation are interfered with. In the latter case he is discharged absolutely, but if securities or co-sureties are released, he is only entitled to an allowance commensurate with the value of the protection lost to him. It is usual to insert a clause in the guarantee denying this right to the guarantor.[62]

K. CHANGE OF PARTIES

18-36. In the absence of agreement to the contrary, a guarantee is revoked, as to future transactions thereunder, by any change in the

---

[58] (1876) 1 Q.B.D. 669 at p. 674.
[59] B. N. Cardozo, *The Nature of the Judicial Process* (1932), pp. 152–4.
[60] *Post*, para. 19-21.
[61] *Carter* v. *White* (1883) 25 Ch. D. 666; and *Dale* v. *Powell* (1911) 105 L.T. 291.
[62] *Post*, para. 19-21.

constitution of the persons to or for whom the guarantee was given. The rule is an old one,[63] but it is now embodied, so far as changes in partnerships are concerned, in Sect. 18 of the Partnership Act, 1890, which provides that—

> A continuing guaranty or cautionary obligation[64] given either to a firm or to a third person in respect of the transactions of a firm is, in the absence of agreement to the contrary, revoked as to future transactions by any change in the constitution of the firm to which, or of the firm in respect of the transactions of which, the guaranty or obligation was given.

The statute does not, of course, apply to companies, but the same principle is applicable. Thus, where there is an amalgamation of two companies (as often happened in the case of banking companies) a guarantee given to either is generally invalidated as to future transactions.[65] In the history of English banking there have been many instances where a large bank has absorbed a smaller one. The legal position which arises here is rather different from that applicable to an amalgamation, for it seems clear that where one banking company absorbs another, the former can sue on guarantees previously received by it, but it cannot rely for the future on those given to the bank absorbed.[66] Guarantees given to the bank absorbed, however, can be made available in the hands of the absorbing bank so far as a definite amount is due at the date of absorption.[67] Sometimes, a private Act of Parliament is passed in order to deal, among other matters, with the question of the availability of guarantees and other securities when an amalgamation takes place.

L. RELEASE OF DEBT BY CREDITOR

18-37. Finally, a guarantor is discharged if the creditor releases the principal debtor from his liability.[68] Although this is obvious enough where the creditor expressly releases the principal debtor, it

---

[63] See, for example, *Wright* v. *Russel* (1774) 3 Wils. K.B. 530, and *Myers* v. *Edge* (1797) 7 T.R. 254.

[64] The Scottish equivalent of the English guarantee.

[65] See *Prescott, Dimsdale, Cave, Tugwell & Co. Ltd.* v. *Bank of England* [1894] 1 Q.B. 351, at pp. 364–5.

[66] Contrast *Capital and Counties Bank* v. *Bank of England* (1889) 61 L.T. 516, with *Prescott, Dimsdale, Cave, Tugwell & Co.* v. *Bank of England* [1894] 1 Q.B. 351. These cases were decided under the Bank Charter Act, 1844, Sects. 23 and 24, but the rules stated in the text above seem to follow by analogy.

[67] *Bradford Old Bank Ltd.* v. *Sutcliffe* [1918] 2 K.B. 833.

[68] "It is elementary law that . . . if the creditor releases the principal debtor, of course the surety is released too," *per* Sir H. H. Cozens-Hardy, M.R., in *Perry* v. *National Provincial Bank of England* [1910] 1 Ch. 464, at p.471.

is not so self-evident where the release is implied. Yet, in both cases, the guarantor is discharged. For example, it is established that a voluntary composition outside the bankruptcy law reducing the principal debtor's liability discharges the surety.[69] However, there is no reason why a contract of guarantee should not expressly provide that the creditor may compound with the principal debtor without affecting the guarantor's liability, and such a clause is, in practice, commonly inserted.[70] There is no necessity to make any special provision in the guarantee to cover the case where the principal debtor becomes bankrupt, because a discharge of the principal debtor after adjudication in bankruptcy does not affect the guarantor's liability. This is expressly provided for by the Bankruptcy Act, 1914,[71] which declares that "an order of discharge shall not release any person who at the date of the receiving order was . . . surety or in the nature of a surety" for the bankrupt. Similarly, the acceptance by a creditor of a composition does not release the surety.[72]

[69] *Ex parte Smith* (1789) 3 Bro. C.C.1; *Ex parte Glendinning* (1819) Buck. 517. On the other hand, a release of the principal debtor as part of an arrangement or composition under the Bankruptcy Act does not discharge a guarantor: *Ex parte Jacobs* (1875) 10 Ch. App. 211.

[70] *Post*, para. 19-21.

[71] Sect. 28 (4).

[72] Sect. 16 (20).

CHAPTER 19

Taking the Security

19-1. This chapter deals with some of the practical points to be considered when a guarantee is offered as security for an advance; and the clauses usually incorporated in the guarantee forms of the banks will be examined.

Financial Standing of the Guarantor

19-2. When a banker is offered a guarantee as security for an advance, it is necessary to ascertain the financial position of the proposed guarantor, for, as the late Mr. R. W. Jones observed, "the security behind a guarantee is the instant ability of the guarantor to pay when called upon."[1] Accommodation granted against a guarantee unsupported by collateral security should be regarded as an *unsecured* advance to the guarantor and to the customer. Evidently, the customer's financial position does not justify unsecured accommodation, and so the problem to be investigated is whether the proposed guarantor is the type of person to whom one would be prepared to make an unsecured loan.

19-3. If the proposed surety is also one of the bank's customers, it may not be difficult to answer this question, but if he banks elsewhere, it is customary to ask him for the name and address of his bankers and to tell him that it is proposed to write to them for their opinion as to his suitability as a guarantor for the amount of the proposed guarantee. Some banks, when making inquiries of this nature, state a figure in excess of the amount of the guarantee, presumably as a measure of caution. This practice is one which is strongly to be deprecated, if only because it gives the guarantor's bankers a misleading impression of the commitments entered into by their customer.

19-4. The reply is frequently the decisive factor in determining whether or not the overdraft should be granted, and it is, therefore, usual for the opinion to be given by a senior officer of the branch. For example, a reply worded "considered good for your figures and purpose" would undoubtedly justify the advance, whereas an

---

[1] R. W. Jones, *Studies in Practical Banking* (5th ed., 1960), p. 79.

opinion that "this customer is considered respectable and trust-worthy in the way of business, but we cannot speak for your figures" would probably lead to a refusal to lend, unless the guarantor could deposit some security in support of his guarantee. If the guarantee is executed, it is imperative to renew one's inquiry concerning the surety's standing at regular intervals, for example, every six months. The subsequent inquiries should be marked "renewal" so that the surety's bankers will not be misled into supposing that an additional guarantee is contemplated.

Execution of the Guarantee

19-5. When once one is satisfied as to the proposed surety's standing, the execution of the contract of guarantee is usually a simple, straightforward matter. The banker will, of course, have in mind the rule illustrated by *Carlisle and Cumberland Banking Co.* v. *Bragg*,[2] where the guarantor was able to evade liability on the ground that he believed that he was signing a contract of a fundamentally different nature. The usual practice is for the guarantor to come to the bank and to sign the guarantee in the presence of an officer of the bank, who will explain to him the effect of the document in general terms. If the guarantor resides some considerable distance from the bank, it is often possible to send the form of guarantee to a branch of the bank in his locality (or, if there is no branch in that district, to the bank's agent there) and to arrange for the guarantor to call at that office in order to sign the document. On no account should the form be handed to the customer for him to have the document executed, partly because he may induce the guarantor to sign by misrepresenting the nature of the instrument (as appears to have happened in *Bragg's* case) and partly because there is a risk that the guarantor's signature may be forged.

19-6. Sometimes a proposed guarantor, who calls at the bank for the purpose of signing the guarantee, asks questions concerning the way in which the customer's account has been conducted. This situation may be very embarrassing to the banker in view of the fact that he is under an implied duty to keep his customers' affairs confidential, save in certain exceptional cases.[3] One of these exceptional cases arises when the customer expressly or impliedly consents to the disclosure, and the late Sir John Paget expressed the view that the surety's questions might be answered on the ground that the customer had impliedly authorised disclosure by introducing the surety

---

[2] [1911] 1 K.B. 489, *ante*, para. 18-5.
[3] See *Tournier* v. *National Provincial and Union Bank of England* [1924] 1 K.B. 461, Vol. 1, paras. 2-100/3.

to the bank.[4] Lord Chorley, however, says that "this seems doubt-ful."[5] Clearly, it is safer to assume, in the absence of authority, that there is no implied consent by the customer to disclose his affairs under these circumstances. Without doubt, the safest course —and, indeed, the usual course—is to arrange a joint meeting be-tween the guarantor, the customer, and the banker at which the guarantor may, in the customer's presence, ask for information on any matters concerning the customer's affairs.

19-7. As a guarantee is not a contract *uberrimae fidei*, a banker is not, as a rule, under any obligation to volunteer information which might influence the decision of a prospective guarantor.[6] Neverthe-less, a situation could arise at the meeting between customer, guar-antor, and banker where the banker's silence on a particular point might amount to a misrepresentation and so entitle a guarantor to avoid his contract; for example, if the banker could see that the prospective guarantor had misunderstood a material fact, it would be the banker's duty to enlighten him. The effect of misrepresenta-tion was clearly explained by Lord Atkin when he said that "a con-tract of guarantee, like any other contract, is liable to be avoided if induced by material misrepresentation of an existing fact, even if made innocently."[7] And there is authority for the view that mere silence may, in certain cases, amount to a misrepresentation. It was Robert Louis Stevenson who wrote, "The cruelest lies are often told in silence,"[8] and our law appears to give recognition to this truth. Thus Lord Strathclyde expressed the view that a failure to disclose would be fatal to the bank's case "where a customer put a question or made an observation in the presence and hearing of the bank-agent, which necessarily and inevitably would lead anyone to the conclusion that the intending guarantor was labouring under a misapprehension with regard to the state of the customer's indebted-ness."[9] Another judge summed up the position by saying: "Very little said which ought not to have been said, and very little not said which ought to have been said, would be sufficient to prevent the contract being valid."[10] These considerations clearly show that, when the meeting takes place between customer, guarantor, and banker, the soundest policy is for the banker to explain briefly to the

[4] J. R. Paget, *Law of Banking* (7th ed., 1966), p. 583.
[5] Lord Chorley, *Law of Banking* (5th ed., 1967), p. 244.
[6] *Ante*, paras. 18-7/9.
[7] *MacKenzie* v. *Royal Bank of Canada* [1934] A.C. 468, at p. 475.
[8] *Virginibus Puerisque.*
[9] *Royal Bank of Scotland* v. *Greenshields* [1914] S.C. 259 at p. 268. This was a Scottish case, but there is no reason to think that English law differs on this point.
[10] *Per* Fry, J., in *Davies* v. *London and Provincial Marine Insurance Co.* (1878) 8 Ch.D. 469 at p. 475.

9—(B.855)

guarantor the nature of the liability which he is undertaking and then, if no questions are raised by him, to end the interview as rapidly as courtesy and good manners will permit.

19-8. If, as is usual, the guarantee is executed under hand, it is exempt from stamp duty.[11] A bank guarantee under seal will normally attract *ad valorem* duty of 2s. (10p) per cent on the amount of the guarantee, to be impressed within thirty days.[12]

Bank Guarantee Forms

19-9. In view of the fact that a contract of guarantee is a relatively simple transaction, it may be thought strange that the guarantee forms employed by the banks are such extremely lengthy documents. Even in recent years fresh clauses have been added to them. The highly-skilled legal advisers employed by the banks try to foresee every possible contingency but, alas, even they are not gifted with the wisdom of Solomon, with the result that very occasionally a guarantor is able to escape liability. When that happens, yet another clause is added and, in this fashion, the mesh around future guarantors is drawn tighter and tighter.

19-10. The forms should never be amended or added to in any way without legal advice. Even the most harmless-looking addition may produce unexpected consequences. This was clearly illustrated in *Westminster Bank Ltd.* v. *Sassoon*,[13] where a Mrs. Sassoon had guaranteed the account of the Marquis Guido Serra di Cassana for £1,700. She wanted to limit her liability to a period of twelve months, and so the following addition was made to the guarantee: "This guarantee will expire upon June 30, 1925." The bank argued that this was intended merely to limit Mrs. Sassoon's liability to advances made before 30th June, 1925. On that date the account was broken, and in October the bank called upon the guarantor to pay, whereupon she maintained that she was not liable in respect of any claims made under the guarantee after 30th June. Fortunately, from the bank's point of view, the Court of Appeal rejected her argument, on the ground that the guarantee was, in its terms, a continuing one and that there was nothing to limit its period in the manner contended for. Nevertheless, the case stands as a warning to those who feel disposed to amend the bank's printed forms. To meet the facts of this

[11] Finance Act, 1970, Sect. 32 and Sched. 7.

[12] Stamp Act, 1891, Sched. I, as amended by the Finance Act, 1970, Sect. 32 and Sched. 7. Not all guarantees under seal attract this rate of duty: *British-Italian Corporation Ltd.* v. *Commissioners of Inland Revenue* [1921] W.N. 220. The problem rarely arises in banking, because it is seldom, if ever, necessary to take a guarantee under seal.

[13] (1926), *The Times*, 27th November.

particular case and to avoid all ambiguity, the clause which ought to have been employed was: "This guarantee shall not cover any indebtedness incurred after 30th June, 1925."

19-11. It is now proposed to examine the clauses commonly found in the banks' forms of guarantee. From a purely practical point of view, the importance of understanding these clauses lies in the fact that an appreciation of their precise significance will very often assist one in deciding what steps can, and should, be taken if a customer whose account has been guaranteed is unable to repay. Many of the matters are highly technical, but it is hoped that the brief survey of certain aspects of the law of principal and surety in the previous chapter will render them more intelligible.

The Consideration Clause

19-12. Although the Mercantile Law Amendment Act, 1856,[14] provides that it is unnecessary to set forth the consideration in the written instrument embodying the guarantee, it is nevertheless usual to do so. In the case of a loan between private individuals, the repayment of which is to be guaranteed by a third person, it is quite usual to draft the consideration clause as follows: "In consideration of your lending to Mr. John Smith the sum of one thousand pounds, I hereby guarantee," etc. But this type of clause is quite unsuitable in a bank security form, because it seems likely that, unless the bank advanced *precisely* this sum, the guarantee would be of no effect. Some authority for this is to be found in *Burton* v. *Gray*,[15] where it was alleged that the owner of a certain property had deposited the title deeds with bankers as security for an advance to his brother. The owner was said to have signed a memorandum worded: "In consideration of your banking company lending to Mr. Frederick Burton, of, etc., the sum of £1,000 sterling . . . I deposit with you the several documents mentioned in the schedule hereunder written . . . as a security," etc. The principal debtor's account became overdrawn to an amount somewhat less than a thousand pounds, and it was held that the bankers had no valid charge on the deeds, because of non-compliance with the condition precedent; in other words, because they had not advanced the sum of one thousand pounds.

19-13. A typical consideration clause in a bank guarantee reads—

In consideration of the Bank making or continuing advances or otherwise giving credit or affording banking facilities for as long as the Bank may think fit or granting time to . . . (hereinafter called "the Principal")

[14] Sect. 3; see *ante*, para. 18-4.
[15] (1873) 8 Ch. App. 932.

19-14. The mere existence of an antecedent debt is not of itself valuable consideration for a guarantee, but subsequent advances are, of course, sufficient consideration. Furthermore, forbearance to sue or the granting of time to the debtor at the request of the guarantor constitutes consideration, and may perhaps be implied from the taking of the security.[16] Nevertheless, there is a risk in accepting a guarantee in respect of a dormant account. If no further advances are made, and if it cannot be proved that the bank granted time to the customer for repayment at the request of the guarantor, it may be held that there was no consideration to support the guarantee. There is a report of an Irish decision where a bank guarantee failed for want of consideration.[17] The bank should demand repayment of the dormant overdraft and the guarantor should sign a letter addressed to the bank asking the bank to grant time to the customer and offering to sign a guarantee. If the bank agrees to grant time, this is sufficient consideration for the giving of the guarantee. Alternatively, the guarantee could be executed under seal, in which case no consideration would be required.

The Operative Clause

19-15. The next clause usually defines the guarantor's liability and may be drafted as follows—

> I hereby guarantee to the Bank the payment of and undertake on demand in writing being made to me by the Bank to pay to the Bank all sums of money which may now be or which hereafter may from time to time become due or owing to the Bank anywhere from or by the Principal either as principal or surety and either solely or jointly with any other person upon current banking account bills of exchange or promissory notes or upon loan or any other account whatsoever or for actual or contingent liability including all usual banking charges
> Provided always that the amount for which I shall be liable under this guarantee shall not exceed [e.g. one thousand pounds] and interest on such amount or on such less sum as may be due from the date of the Principal's default until payment. Such interest shall be computed at two per cent over Bank rate for the time being and from time to time with a minimum of five per cent per annum

19-16. This clause calls for comment on several matters. The words "on demand in writing being made to me" are intended to overcome the difficulty which arose in *Parr's Banking Co.* v. *Yates*.[18] The defendant had signed a continuing guarantee which did not include

---

[16] See *Glegg* v. *Bromley* [1912] 3 K.B. 474, at p. 491.
[17] *Provincial Bank of Ireland Ltd.* v. *Donnell* [1934] N.I. 33.
[18] [1898] 2 Q.B. 460.

this phrase and, when the bank brought an action against him, he pleaded that the claim was barred by the Statute of Limitations, 1623,[19] on the ground that no fresh advances had been made to the principal debtor after the end of 1890, a period of more than six years before the date of the writ. The Court of Appeal accepted this argument. In the words of Vaughan Williams, L.J.[20]—

> . . . the cause of action on the guarantee arose as to each item of the account, whether principal, interest, commission, or other banking charge, as soon as that item became due and was not paid, and, consequently, the Statute of Limitations began to run in favour of the defendant in respect of each item from that date.

The decision has not escaped criticism,[21] but, unless and until it is overruled, it is safer to assume that it is good law. For this reason a well-drafted guarantee makes the cause of action arise when a demand in writing is served on the guarantor, and so time does not begin to run against the bank until that date. The efficacy of this clause was proved in *Bradford Old Bank Ltd.* v. *Sutcliffe*[22]—another decision of the Court of Appeal—when Pickford, L.J., said: "In my opinion there was no cause of action till after demand, and the plea of the Statute of Limitations therefore fails."[23]

19-17. It will be observed that, instead of the guarantee being worded as a guarantee for a named sum, it is expressed to be a guarantee for the *whole* of the customer's obligations, followed by a proviso limiting the surety's liability to a named sum. It might seem that the results in both cases are the same, but this is not so. There are two reasons for drafting the bank's form in this way.

19-18. The first reason is that if a surety guarantees *part only of the debt*, he has a right, upon payment of that sum, to a proportionate share in any security held by the creditor for the whole debt.[24] For example, G signs a guarantee for £500 in respect of a customer's overdraft. The account is overdrawn £1,500, but the bank holds other securities for this advance which are worth £1,000. If G pays to the bank the sum of £500 under his guarantee, he will prima facie be entitled to a proportionate share (one third) in the bank's security.

---

[19] 21 Jac. 1, c. 16. The present provision (also six years) is contained in the Limitation Act, 1939, Sect. 2 (1).
[20] [1898] 2 Q.B. at p. 467.
[21] See, e.g., J. R. Paget, *Law of Banking* (7th ed., 1966), p. 608.
[22] [1918] 2 K.B. 833. See also *Re Brown's Estate, Brown* v. *Brown* [1893] 2 Ch. 300.
[23] [1918] 2 K.B. at pp. 840–1. For another method which will prevent the limitation period from running, see *Wright* v. *New Zealand Farmers Co-operative Association of Canterbury Ltd.* [1939] A.C. 439.
[24] *Ante*, para. 18-16.

Clearly, no bank would care to see part of its security claimable by a guarantor, and so the guarantor is required to guarantee the repayment of the *whole debt* (with a limit to his liability), with the result—in the example quoted above—that he will not be entitled to any securities held by the bank unless he chooses to repay the entire advance of £1,500.

19-19. The second reason is that if the debtor is made bankrupt, the guarantor may prove in his estate for the amount which he has paid under the guarantee.[25] The advantage (from the bank's point of view) of expressing the guarantor's liability as in the clause quoted above is that, when the guarantor pays, he has no right to prove in the debtor's bankruptcy in competition with the creditor. This is illustrated by the leading case of *Re Sass*.[26] A Mr. Sass had an overdraft of £755 with the National Provincial Bank of England. The bank held a guarantee signed by a Mr. Stourton for the "whole amount" of the debt, with a proviso that his liability should not exceed £300 plus interest and other bank charges. Sass became bankrupt, and Stourton, on demand by the bank, paid to them £303. The bank placed this sum to the credit of a Securities Realised Account and tendered a proof against the bankrupt's estate for £755, being the whole amount due to them from the bankrupt. The trustee in bankruptcy rejected the proof, maintaining that it ought to be reduced by the £303 which the bank had received from Stourton. The court decided that the bank's proof was correct and so ought to have been admitted. Vaughan Williams, J., said[27]—

. . . the surety here became a surety for the whole of the debt. It is true that his liability was to be limited; but still, notwithstanding that, his suretyship was in respect of the whole debt, and he, having paid only a part of the debt, has in my judgment no right of proof in preference or priority to the bank to whom he became guarantor.

19-20. Some guarantee forms contain a clause dealing expressly with this matter, e.g.—

If the Principal shall become bankrupt the Bank may (notwithstanding payment to the Bank by me or any other person of the whole or any part of the amount hereby guaranteed) rank as creditors and prove against his estate for the full amount of the Bank's claim and the Bank may and shall receive and retain the whole of the dividends to the exclusion of all my rights as guarantor in competition with the Bank until the Bank's claim is fully satisfied

[25] *Ante*, para. 18-19.
[26] [1896] 2 Q.B. 12. See also *Re Houlder* [1929] 1 Ch. 205; and *Ulster Bank Ltd.* v. *Lambe* [1966] N.I. 161.
[27] [1896] 2 Q.B. at p. 15.

Power to Vary Securities, to Grant Time to, and to Compound with the Debtor

19-21. It will be recalled that (*a*) a guarantor is discharged in whole or in part if a right of contribution or any security is lost by the creditor's action,[28] (*b*) a binding agreement between the creditor and the principal debtor to grant time to the debtor discharges the guarantor from liability if made without his consent,[29] and (*c*) a voluntary composition outside the bankruptcy law reducing the principal debtor's liability discharges the guarantor.[30] Not unnaturally, bankers wish to be free to take any of these courses without affecting the guarantor's liability, and a clause on the following lines secures their freedom of action—

> I agree that the Bank shall have power without any further consent from me and without in any way affecting my liability under this guarantee to renew any advance and to hold over renew or give up in whole or in part any bills notes mortgages charges liens or other securities received or to be received from the Principal either alone or jointly with any other person or persons or from any other person or persons and to grant time to or compound with the Principal or any person or persons liable on any such bills notes mortgages charges liens or other securities or any person liable jointly with or as surety for the Principal or any other person or persons

19-22. The usefulness of a clause of this nature was demonstrated in *Perry* v. *National Provincial Bank of England*.[31] The plaintiff, as surety, had mortgaged certain property to the bank to secure the overdraft of a firm. The mortgage deeds contained a provision that the bank should be at liberty, without affecting their right under the mortgages "to vary exchange or release any other securities held or to be held by the bank for or on account of the moneys thereby secured or any part thereof . . . and to compound with give time for payment of and accept compositions from and make any other arrangements with the debtors." Subsequently, the firm became insolvent, a company was formed to acquire their property, and the bank agreed to take debentures from that company at the rate of twenty-five shillings' worth of debentures for every pound of debt not secured by mortgages of the firm's own property *in full satisfaction of the whole claim of the bank against the firm.* The plaintiff maintained that the bank had no claim upon his property, and he brought an action for reconveyance of the property to him on the ground that nothing was due under the mortgage. The bank (which had

[28] *Ante*, para. 18-35.
[29] *Ante*, paras. 18-33/34.
[30] *Ante*, para. 18-37.
[31] [1910] 1 Ch. 464.

been threatening to sell the property comprised in the plaintiff's mortgage) maintained that their rights against him had not been destroyed. The Court of Appeal gave their decision in the bank's favour, and the judgments delivered show that the decisive factor was the wording of the clause quoted above. Referring to the words employed in the instrument, Buckley, L.J., said[32]—

> There is there an agreement and declaration that the bank shall be at liberty to do certain things, including to compound with the debtor without forfeiting their rights under the instrument. The effect, I apprehend, is this. The surety mortgages his property to secure the principal debt, and the bank may, if they please, compound with [their customer], by which I understand that they may accept from [their customer] a sum less than the full amount of the debt upon the terms that they shall not sue [their customer] for the balance, and this deed provides that that may be done without affecting the bank's right against the surety.

It had been argued that the bank had no right as against the plaintiff on the ground that there could be no suretyship after the release of the principal debtor. However, as Sir H. H. Cozens-Hardy, M.R., said[33]—

> . . . the answer to that is that it is perfectly possible for a surety to contract with a creditor in the suretyship instrument that notwithstanding any composition, release, or arrangement the surety shall remain liable although the principal does not.

Guarantor Deprived of Power to Take Security

19-23. The late Sir John Paget once observed that "the main object of a guarantee should be to keep a free hand for the bank and a tight one on the guarantor."[34] There is probably no better illustration of this than the clause commonly included in bank guarantee forms whereby the guarantor undertakes not to protect himself by taking security from the principal debtor. The clause makes provision for what is to happen if the guarantor disregards his promise—

> I declare that I have not received any security from the Principal for the giving of this guarantee and I agree that I will not so long as any moneys remain owing by the Principal to the Bank take any security from the Principal in respect of my liability hereunder without first obtaining the Bank's written consent and I agree that in the event of my taking any such security the amount for which I am to be liable under this guarantee

[32] [1910] 1 Ch. at p. 478.
[33] [1910] 1 Ch. at p. 473.
[34] J. R. Paget, *Law of Banking* (7th ed., 1966), p. 579.

shall be increased by the amount by which the dividend payable by the Principal to the Bank is thereby diminished

The object of this clause is to ensure that, if the debtor becomes bankrupt and part of his overdraft is unsecured, his free assets will not be depleted to the detriment of the bank as the result of charges created in favour of the guarantor.

Written Notice to Determine the Guarantee

19-24. The legal effect of the next clause is a matter of controversy—

I agree that this guarantee shall be a continuing security to the Bank and shall not be determined except at the expiration of three calendar months' written notice given to the Bank of my intention so to do and in the event of my death the liability of my legal personal representatives and of my estate shall continue until the expiration of three calendar months' written notice given to the Bank of the intention of my legal personal representatives to determine this guarantee

19-25. There is, of course, no doubt as to the effect of the opening words of this clause. By agreeing that the guarantee is to be a "continuing security," the surety expressly excludes the operation of the Rule in *Clayton's* case.[35] If the Rule was not excluded, each sum paid into the principal debtor's account after the execution of the guarantee would reduce *pro tanto* the guarantor's liability, whilst each debit to the account would create a fresh advance for which the guarantor would not be liable.

19-26. It is the remainder of the clause stipulating for three months' notice to determine the guarantee which is the subject of conflicting opinions. Suppose that a surety executes a guarantee of a customer's banking account subject to the usual proviso that there shall be a limit to his liability of (say) £1,000. The guarantor gives notice to determine his guarantee when the customer's account is overdrawn only £500. If the banker allows the advance to increase to £1,000 during the next three months, will the guarantor be liable for that sum? As a matter of first impression, it is difficult to see why he should not be held to the terms of his bargain, yet the late Sir John Paget took the opposite view. The latest edition of his work discusses the problem thus[36]—

---

[35] (1816) 1 Mer. 572.

[36] J. R. Paget, *Law of Banking* (7th ed., 1966), p. 428. Paget gave a more detailed opinion in *Questions on Banking Practice* (9th ed., 1952) pp. 266–8. In the latest edition of *Questions on Banking Practice* (10th ed., 1965 at pp. 271–2), Paget's opinion is omitted. In the course of the substituted answer it is stated that "the legal effect of the clause requiring three months' notice of determination of the guarantee is beyond question; the account of the customer can be continued for the period of notice and the guarantor will be liable for the balance outstanding at the end of the period."

It would probably not be safe or right to make purely voluntary advances up to the expiration of the notice; advances or payments during the three months should, perhaps, be confined to the fulfilment of obligations express or implied incurred by the banker to the principal debtor prior to the receipt of the notice, such as the payment of outstanding cheques and the like. This view is based mainly on the duty of the guaranteed party to behave equitably towards the guarantor, recognised in *Holland* v. *Teed*,[37] and the difficulty of seeing where the object or sense of giving notice comes in, if the guaranteed person on receiving it is at liberty at once to run the amount up to the extreme limit.

19-27. On the other hand, a leading work on the law of principal and surety contains the following passage[38]—

It is often stipulated that the guarantee shall continue until a given period after notice of revocation shall have been given. In such cases the right of revocation, at any rate where the guarantee has been once acted upon, must be limited in accordance with the stipulation.

With this statement of the law the author would respectfully agree.

19-28. There is admittedly very little judicial authority on the subject, but there is an interesting *dictum* in a judgment of Bowen, J. He said[39]—

If, indeed, the contracting parties desire that on the death of the guarantor a special notice shall be necessary to determine the guarantee, they can so provide in the guarantee itself; and such a provision will, of course, bind the estate.

It is submitted that, when the learned judge said that the provision would be binding, this implies that it would cover advances made during the currency of the notice given by the guarantor's personal representatives. If this is the law, it would seem beyond doubt that the provision requiring a stipulated period of notice by the guarantor himself, if he wishes to determine the guarantee during his lifetime, is equally binding. In short, the author believes that the courts would construe the "notice clause" strictly and would hold the parties to the letter of their agreement.[40]

---

[37] (1848) 7 Hare 50.
[38] S. A. T. Rowlatt, *The Law of Principal and Surety* (3rd ed., 1936), pp. 84–5.
[39] *Coulthart* v. *Clementson* (1879) 5 Q.B.D. 42, at p. 48.
[40] To the same effect see the Gilbart Lecture of the late Mr. Bernard Campion, K.C., in the *Journal of the Institute of Bankers*, Vol. XLV (1924), p. 81. Lord Chorley makes an interesting suggestion. He says that "in the absence of direct authority, it may be considered advisable to provide expressly that the surety is to be liable for advances made within the limit of the guarantee, during the currency of a notice of revocation." Lord Chorley, *Law of Banking* (5th ed., 1967), p. 250.

19-29. If the guarantor dies and his personal representative is the debtor on whose behalf the guarantee was given, special care is necessary. There is a risk that the personal representative may deliberately refrain from giving notice to determine the guarantee in order that further advances may be made to him on his own account. It seems that the bank in these circumstances would not be entitled to the benefit of the guarantee for advances made after the guarantor's death.[41]

Guarantor's Power to Sue Debtor Restricted

19-30. As soon as a guarantor pays anything under his guarantee, he acquires an immediate right of action in respect thereof as against the principal debtor.[42] In certain cases this rule may prejudicially affect a bank. Suppose, for example, that a customer's account is overdrawn £800 and that a surety has guaranteed the repayment thereof with a limit to his liability of (say) £400. The surety, in response to a demand from the bank, pays to the bank the latter sum. Prima facie he would then be entitled to bring an action against the principal debtor for £400. Clearly, it is in the bank's interest for the guarantor to be denied that right, because part of the bank overdraft is still unpaid. The following clause effectively achieves this object—

> This guarantee shall be applicable to the ultimate balance that may become due to the Bank from the Principal and until repayment of such balance I will not take any steps to enforce any right or claim against the Principal in respect of any moneys paid by me to the Bank hereunder

A Sufficient Demand Defined

19-31. If a guarantor promises to pay the principal debt "on demand," a demand must be made upon him before he can be sued.[43] The main purpose of requiring the guarantor to undertake to pay "on demand" or "on demand in writing being made to me" is to overcome the difficulty which arose in *Parr's Banking Co.* v. *Yates*,[44] and, as stated previously, this formula is invariably employed in bank guarantee forms. However, the formula itself might give rise to yet another difficulty, because there might be difficulty in proving, to the satisfaction of the court, that a demand had been made upon

[41] *Harris* v. *Fawcett* (1873) 8 Ch. App. 866.
[42] *Davies* v. *Humphreys* (1840) 6 M. & W. 153, *ante*, para. 18-19.
[43] *Re Brown's Estate, Brown* v. *Brown* [1893] 2 Ch. 300. See also *Bradford Old Bank Ltd.* v. *Sutcliffe* [1918] 2 K.B. 833, *ante*, para. 19-16.
[44] [1898] 2 Q.B. 460, *ante*, para. 19-16.

the guarantor before the action was commenced. Of course, if the guarantor acknowledges receipt of the bank's letter, all is well; but it is not unknown for guarantors to omit to do so. The following clause is intended to cover this situation—

> A demand in writing shall be deemed to have been duly given to me or my legal personal representatives by sending the same by post addressed to me at the address herein written or at my last known address and shall be effectual notwithstanding any change of residence or death and such demand shall be deemed to be received by me or my legal personal representatives twenty-four hours after the posting thereof and in proving such service it shall be sufficient to prove that the letter containing the demand was properly addressed and put into the Post Office

Continuation of Account Notwithstanding Determination of Guarantee

19-32. When a guarantee is determined, the normal practice is to rule off the principal debtor's account. If this is not done and sums continue to be paid into the account, the Rule in *Clayton's* case[45] will apply and, prima facie, the payments in will reduce or extinguish the liability of the guarantor, whilst payments out of the account will create new advances for which the surety will, of course, not be liable. It seems clear, therefore, that, if by some oversight the creditor omits to break the account, he may well find that the guarantor will be able to escape liability. There is no better illustration of the ingenuity of the legal advisers of the banks than the clause which they have drafted to prevent this catastrophe. The object of the clause is to preserve the guarantor's liability even if the bank omits to break the customer's account.[46] It reads—

> In the event of this guarantee being determined either by notice by me or my legal personal representatives or by demand in writing by the Bank it shall be lawful for the Bank to continue the account with the Principal notwithstanding such determination and the liability of myself or my estate for the amount due from the Principal at the date when the guarantee is so determined shall remain notwithstanding any subsequent payment into or out of the account by or on behalf of the Principal

19-33. The efficacy of this clause was tested in *Westminster Bank Ltd.* v. *Cond.*[47] In that case the guarantee was determined by a demand in writing by the bank being served upon the guarantor on 29th August, 1933. The bank made no break in the customer's account and, after the lapse of almost six years (i.e. a few days before the

---

[45] (1816) 1 Mer. 572.
[46] For a suggested amendment of this clause to cover the determination of the guarantee by the guarantor's insanity, see *post*, para. 20-34.
[47] (1940) 46 Com. Cas. 60.

Statute of Limitations would have barred the bank's claim against the guarantor) the bank commenced an action against him. Various defences were raised, one of which was that the guarantor's liability had been discharged before the issue of the writ by reason of the fact that sums paid into the account subsequent to 29th August, 1933, had extinguished the then existing overdraft. Dealing with this defence, Tucker, J., said[48]—

> In the particular case with which I am now dealing the account was not ruled off, but it was one unbroken account . . . and, as at present advised—it is not necessary for me to give any decision on the matter— were it not for the terms of this particular guarantee I should be inclined to the view that the rule in *Clayton's* case might quite well have applied to the present circumstances . . . That being the position, and a position well known to all persons concerned with banking, this particular guarantee under which the bank are suing contains these words [His Lordship read the clause quoted above]. I think that those words are apt to prevent the application of the rule in *Clayton's* case. I cannot help thinking that they were designed expressly so to do, and I think they have achieved that object.

The other defences also failed, and judgment was given in favour of the bank.

Power to Open New Account Notwithstanding Determination of Guarantee

19-34. In spite of the decision in *Westminster Bank Ltd.* v. *Cond* (*supra*) recognising the validity of the type of clause described above, it still remains the usual practice for a bank to break the account of its customer when a guarantee is determined and to open a fresh account for future transactions. Some guarantee forms expressly authorise this to be done by a clause drafted thus—

> In the event of this guarantee being determined either by notice by me or my legal personal representatives or by demand in writing by the Bank it shall be lawful for the Bank to open a fresh account or accounts with the Principal and no moneys paid from time to time into any such account or accounts by or on behalf of the Principal and subsequently drawn out by the Principal shall on a settlement of any claim under this guarantee be appropriated towards or have the effect of payment of any part of the moneys due from the Principal at the date when the guarantee is determined

19-35. The decision in *Re Sherry*[49] seems to show that, strictly speaking, this clause is unnecessary, though the practice is still to

---

[48] At p. 73.
[49] (1884) 25 Ch. D. 692.

include it. A Mr. Sherry had signed two guarantees for £150 and
£400 respectively for the account of a Mr. Terry at the London and
County Bank. Sherry died, and the bank, on receiving notice of his
death, ruled off Terry's account (which was overdrawn £677) and
opened a new account for him, though the guarantee did not
expressly authorise them to do so. Except for the first day or two
after the opening of it, the new account was continually overdrawn,
but there were sufficient payments into it to discharge the dormant
debit balance on the old account. Terry then went bankrupt, and
the bank claimed against the executors of the surety, Sherry, for the
amount of the two guarantees, but the executors contended that they
were entitled to the benefit of the payments into the new account.
The Court of Appeal, reversing the decision of Bacon, V.-C., held
that the executors were still liable. Cotton, L.J., said[50]—

> The question is whether there is anything in the contract to prevent
> the bank from carrying these payments to the new account. There is
> certainly no express contract, and in my opinion there is no implied
> contract to that effect . . . The balance which the surety guarantees is
> the general balance of the customer's account, and to ascertain that, all
> accounts existing between the customer and the bank at the time when
> the guarantee comes to an end must be taken into consideration.

Additional Guarantees Given by Guarantor

19-36. It is a usual precaution to insert a clause to the effect that—

> This guarantee shall be additional to any other guarantee for the
> Principal signed by me that the Bank may at any time hold

19-37. Suppose, for example, that a surety signed a guarantee for
£200 and then, a few months later, executed another guarantee for
£300 in favour of the same principal debtor. In the absence of the
clause quoted above, he might be able to contend that the second
guarantee was intended by the parties to be in substitution for the
first.

19-38. Some banks make a practice of dealing with this problem by
inserting a specific clause in the second guarantee worded as follows:
"This guarantee is in addition to and not in substitution for the
guarantee signed by me on . . ." Such a clause strengthens the
bank's position in case the guarantor should subsequently maintain
that one of the bank's officials represented to him that the second
guarantee was to replace the earlier one. An even better way of

---

[50] At pp. 705–6.

guarding against this risk is to cancel the first guarantee and to obtain a fresh guarantee for the total amount.

Evidence as to Balance of Principal Debtor's Account

19-39. Unless some special provision is made in the guarantee, it is not always easy for a creditor to adduce the necessary evidence to obtain judgment against a guarantor. Although declarations made by a principal debtor during the transaction of the business for which the surety is bound are evidence against the surety, the admissions by the principal debtor, made subsequently, are no evidence against the surety, because the surety's contract is with the creditor and there is no privity between the principal debtor and the surety. As James, L.J., said, "it is perfectly clear that in an action against a surety the amount of the damage cannot be proved by any admissions of the principal."[51] In conformity with this rule, it has been held that a guarantor is not even bound by a judgment or award against the principal.[52]

19-40. For these reasons it is usual for a well-drawn guarantee to make express provision for the admission of certain evidence which would otherwise be inadmissible. A clause found in some bank guarantee forms runs as follows: "I agree that any acknowledgment in writing by the Principal or by any person authorised to draw on the Principal's account of the amount of the indebtedness of the Principal shall be conclusive evidence against me of the amount for the time being due to the Bank from the Principal." Although such a clause is obviously of considerable value, it is open to the objection that, to be effective, the co-operation of the principal debtor is required. The following type of clause is superior to that set out above because it enables the bank itself to supply the requisite evidence—

> I agree that a copy of the account of the Principal contained in the Bank's book of account or of the account for the preceding six months if the account shall have extended beyond that period signed by any officer of the Bank shall be conclusive evidence against me of the amount for the time being due to the Bank from the Principal

Possible Changes in Constitution of the Parties

19-41. In the absence of agreement to the contrary, a guarantee is revoked, as to future transactions, by any change in the constitution

[51] *Ex parte Young* (1881) 17 Ch. D. 668, at p. 671. See also *Evans* v. *Beattie* (1803) 5 Esp. 26.
[52] *Ex parte Young* (*supra*).

of the party for whom the guarantee was given.[53] A clause to exclude this rule may be drafted thus—

> Should the Principal be an unincorporate body committee partnership trustees or debtors on a joint account this guarantee shall remain effective notwithstanding any death retirement change accession or addition as fully as if the person or persons constituting such body committee partnership trustees or debtors on joint account at the date of the Principal's default or at any time previously was or were the same as at the date hereof

19-42. This clause makes it unnecessary to break the principal debtor's account so far as the guarantor's liability is concerned, though in practice the guarantor is often informed of the change in order that he may give notice to determine his liability, if he so desires. The principal debtor's account must be broken if it is desired to retain the liability of one of the former parties to the account, e.g. a retiring partner.

19-43. Similarly, the possibility that the bank may change its name or amalgamate with another bank is provided for as follows—

> I agree that this guarantee shall be enforceable notwithstanding any change in the name of the Bank or any change in the constitution of the Bank its successors or assigns or by its absorption of or by its amalgamation with any other bank or banks

Guarantor's Liability as Principal Debtor in Certain Cases

19-44. Suppose the customer whose account has been guaranteed is under some contractual incapacity—for example, minority—which makes it impossible for the bank to sue him for the debt. The question may arise whether the bank can enforce the guarantee against the surety. There was a dearth of authority in English law on this point until *Coutts & Co.* v. *Browne-Lecky and Others.*[54] In that case the repayment of an infant's overdraft had been guaranteed by two persons, both of whom were of full age. The fact that the borrower was under twenty-one was known to all parties.[55] Under Sect. 1 of the Infants Relief Act, 1874, the loan to the infant was "absolutely void," and Oliver, J., held that the guarantors could not be made liable in an action on the guarantee.[56] The learned judge

---

[53] *Ante,* para. 18-36.

[54] [1947] K.B. 104.

[55] The age of majority is now eighteen, instead of twenty-one: Family Law Act, 1969, Sect. 1.

[56] If a loan is made to an infant to purchase what the law regards as "necessaries," and the loan is actually spent for that purpose, the lender is subrogated to the rights of the seller and is allowed in equity the same right of recovery that the seller would

based his decision on two persuasive authorities, one of them being a Scottish case[57] and the other a quotation from the French jurist, Pothier. The citation from Pothier is quoted in de Colyar's *Law of Guarantees and of Principal and Surety*[58] and reads as follows—

> As the obligation of sureties is according to our definition an obligation accessory to that of a principal debtor, it follows that it is of the essence of the obligation that there should be a valid obligation of a principal debtor; consequently, if the principal is not obliged, neither is the surety, as there can be no accessory without a principal obligation.

19-45. The decision in *Browne-Lecky's* case was received by bankers with a certain amount of resentment, which was probably justifiable. It meant that two people who had solemnly agreed to be responsible for the debts of a third party, whom they knew to be a minor, were able to escape all liability.[59]

19-46. It now remains to investigate how the misfortune which befell Coutts & Co. can be avoided in the future. Clearly, what is required is a clause making it plain that, if the borrower is under any incapacity, the third party shall be treated as principal debtor and not as surety. The following clause (which some banks had inserted in their guarantee forms even before the *Browne-Lecky* case) appears to be effective[60]—

> I agree that all sums of money which may not be recoverable from me on the footing of a guarantee by reason of any legal limitation disability or incapacity on or of the Principal shall nevertheless be recoverable from me as sole or principal debtor

19-47. Pothier's explanation of the nature of a guarantee would seem to show that this type of clause is useful in relation to another kind of lending, namely, to unincorporated associations, such as many clubs, churches, committees, and societies. Lending money to an unincorporated body is often a risky transaction, partly because of the fact that it is difficult, if not impossible, to obtain redress against the association's funds, and partly because it is not easy to establish even the personal liability of any particular members of the association.[61] The value of taking a "guarantee" embodying the clause quoted above is that the person or persons executing it can be treated as primarily liable and sued accordingly.

---

have possessed had he not been paid: *Lewis* v. *Alleyne* (1888) 4 T.L.R. 560. Presumably, if the lender can sue the infant, a guarantor of the loan will also be liable.

[57] *Swan* v. *Bank of Scotland* (1836) 10 Bli. (N.S.) 627.

[58] 3rd ed. (1897), p. 210.

[59] For a criticism of the decision in *Browne-Lecky's* case, see E. J. Cohn, "Validity of Guarantees for Debts of Minors," *Modern Law Review*, Vol 10 (1947), pp. 40–51.

[60] Cf. *Yeoman Credit Ltd.* v. *Latter* [1961] 1 W.L.R. 828.

[61] Vol. 1, para. 11-416.

Guarantor's Liability for Ultra Vires Borrowing

19-48. A surety for the repayment of money borrowed by a company in excess of its borrowing powers may, it seems, be liable on his guarantee, at any rate if the contract was entered into in good faith and in the honest belief that it was legal. This rule rests chiefly upon the decision of Lawrence, J., in *Garrard* v. *James.*[62] The plaintiff provided £1,500 for the purchase of preference shares in a company. The company had agreed, under specified circumstances, to procure the repurchase of the shares at par, and two of the company's directors had joined in this arrangement as sureties, guaranteeing the due performance by the company of its part of the agreement. The company refused to honour this agreement on the ground that the performance of it would involve a purchase by the company of its own shares, which would be *ultra vires* and illegal. It was held that, as the contract was entered into in good faith and in the honest belief that it was legal, the plaintiff was entitled to judgment against the two sureties for £1,500. Lawrence, J., analysed the position as follows[63]—

> It seems to me immaterial whether the failure or omission by the company to perform its obligations is attributable to its financial inability or to statutory disability, as the liability of the defendants arises, whatever may be the cause of failure. The gist of the bargain entered into by the defendants, in my opinion, was: "If you, the plaintiff, will advance this £1,500, we, the defendants, will pay you, if the company does not pay."

19-49. If this decision is correct, it constitutes an exception to the rule laid down by Pothier and quoted above that "if the principal is not obliged, neither is the surety, as there can be no accessory without a principal obligation."[64] This anomaly was referred to by Oliver, J., in his judgment in *Coutts & Co.* v. *Browne-Lecky.*[65] "It may be," he said, "that the voidness of a contract to guarantee the debt of a company acting *ultra vires* is different in its consequences from the voidness brought about by the express and emphatic language of a statute, although . . . I cannot understand or express what the difference is."

19-50. Perhaps some day the Court of Appeal will have the opportunity of considering *Garrard* v. *James* (*supra*), and it would

---

[62] [1925] Ch. 616. Lawrence, J., followed the opinion of Blackburn, J., in *Chambers* v. *Manchester and Milford Railway Co.* (1864) 5 B. & S. 588, at p. 612, and the decision of Kay, J., in *Yorkshire Railway Wagon Co.* v. *Maclure* (1881) 19 Ch. D. 478; but in *Maclure's* case (1882) 21 Ch. D. 309, the Court of Appeal held that there was no *ultra vires* borrowing.
[63] [1925] Ch. at pp. 622–3.
[64] *Ante*, para. 19-44.
[65] [1947] K.B. 104, at p. 111.

not be surprising if they overruled it. It is all the more desirable, therefore, that bank guarantees should deal expressly with the possibility of *ultra vires* borrowing, even though, as the law stands at the moment, a surety is liable for such a loan, provided that the parties acted in good faith, honestly believing it to be legal. A clause commonly used reads—

> The Bank may recover against me notwithstanding that the Principal being a limited company may have exceeded its borrowing powers or that the borrowing from the Bank may have been *ultra vires*

Bankruptcy or Liquidation of the Principal Debtor

19-51. Some bank forms of guarantee contain a clause to this effect—

> No assurance security or payment which may be avoided under any enactments relating to bankruptcy or under Sections 320, 321 or 322 of the Companies Act 1948 or any statutory modification or re-enactment thereof and no release settlement or discharge which may have been given or made on the faith of any such assurance security or payment shall prejudice or affect the Bank's right to recover from me to the full extent of this guarantee as if such assurance security payment release settlement or discharge (as the case may be) had never been granted given or made

To understand the objects of this clause, some knowledge is required of (*a*) the law relating to floating charges created by limited companies, and (*b*) the law relating to fraudulent preference.

A. FLOATING CHARGES

19-52. One object of the type of clause set out above is to protect the bank where the customer is a limited company which creates a floating charge over its assets in favour of the bank.[66] There is a risk that the bank may not be fully protected by the charge if the company goes into liquidation within twelve months after the execution of the charge.[67] The clause provides in effect that if the guarantor is "released" in reliance upon the security of a floating charge and the charge is avoided under Sect. 322 of the Companies Act, 1948, the bank may still recover from the guarantor to the full extend of the guarantee. The efficacy of this provision has not as yet been tested in any reported case.

[66] For floating charges, see *post*, paras. 32-25/27.
[67] See Companies Act, 1948, Sect. 322, *post*, para. 32-33.

B. FRAUDULENT PREFERENCE

19-53. Another object of the clause set out above is to try to deal with some of the problems which arise under Sect. 44 of the Bankruptcy Act, 1914, and Sect. 320 of the Companies Act, 1948. Section 44 of the Bankruptcy Act, 1914, provides that any payment to a creditor made by a debtor unable to pay his debts as they become due, with a view to giving that creditor, *or any guarantor for the debt due to that creditor,* a preference over the other creditors is to be deemed fraudulent and void as against the trustee in bankruptcy, if the debtor is adjudged bankrupt on a bankruptcy petition presented within six[68] months thereafter. Section 265 of the Companies Act, 1929, (now replaced by Sect. 320 of the Companies Act, 1948) applied precisely the same rules to limited companies, i.e. if the company goes into liquidation, any payments made to prefer any particular creditor, *or any guarantor for the debt due to that creditor,* are to be deemed fraudulent and void as against the liquidator. It has been held that the term "preference" implies an act of free-will; if, therefore, the creditor brings pressure to bear on the debtor, e.g. by threatening legal proceedings, this will usually negative a fraudulent preference.[69] If, however, there is no pressure by the creditor, this does not necessarily mean that there is a dominant intention to prefer.[70]

19-54. An illustration drawn from one of the cases decided under Sect. 265 of the Companies Act, 1929, will help to clarify these provisions. In *Re M. Kushler Ltd.,*[71] Mr. and Mrs. Kushler were the sole directors and shareholders of a company to which Lloyds Bank Limited had granted an overdraft secured by the guarantee of Mr. Kushler and four policies of assurance on his life. On 10th May, 1941, the overdraft stood at £609. On 12th May the directors were advised that the company was insolvent and ought to be wound up. Between 12th May and 21st May payments were made into the bank as the result of which the overdraft was extinguished and Mr. Kushler was apparently relieved of liability under his guarantee. During the same period the company (with insignificant exceptions) paid none of its other creditors. On 23rd May a resolution was passed for the winding-up of the company. The liquidator

[68] Six months was substituted for three months by the Companies Act, 1947, Sect. 115 (3).
[69] *Butcher* v. *Stead* (1875) L.R. 7 H.L. 839; *Sharp* v. *Jackson* [1899] A.C. 419. It is sometimes very difficult to determine whether or not a bankrupt made a payment voluntarily; see *Re Cutts (a Bankrupt), Ex parte Bognor Mutual Building Society* v. *Trustee in Bankruptcy* [1956] 1 W.L.R. 728, where there was a division of opinion in the Court of Appeal.
[70] *Re F.L.E. Holdings Ltd.* [1967] 3 All E.R. 553.
[71] [1943] Ch. 248.

claimed that the payments to the bank constituted a fraudulent preference to the bank contrary to Sect. 265 of the Companies Act, 1929, and that the bank should repay these sums. The Court of Appeal upheld his claim. The result was, therefore, that, although Mr. Kushler's object in wiping out the company's overdraft was, no doubt, to relieve himself from personal liability, it was Lloyds Bank who had to make the refund.

19-55. Having refunded these sums, could Lloyds Bank then have recouped themselves out of the four life policies and by suing Mr. Kushler on his guarantee? It is submitted that the legal position relating to the guarantee was clear, but that the bank's interest in the policies was, in 1943, doubtful. As far as the guarantee was concerned, the law has been correctly stated as follows: "If a payment received by the creditor from the principal is afterwards, upon the bankruptcy of the principal, adjudged a fraudulent preference, and has to be restored to the estate by the creditor, the surety is liable for the amount where the creditor was not a party to the fraudulent preference."[72] Therefore Lloyds Bank could have sued Mr. Kushler upon his guarantee, had they thought it prudent to do so.

19-56. The clause quoted above[73] is intended to meet the case where the guarantor has been "released" on the faith of payments made to the credit of the account which have to be refunded on the ground that they constituted a fraudulent preference. In effect, the clause provides that the guarantor's liability is to remain, but it is unwise to be dogmatic as to its efficacy. If, in the *Kushler* case, Mr. Kushler had persuaded Lloyds Bank to write "cancelled" across the guarantee and if the guarantee had contained the above-mentioned clause, it seems very doubtful whether the bank would have succeeded in an action against Mr. Kushler. The safest course is not to cancel the instrument at all.[74]

19-57. The availability of the life policies to meet the sum refunded by the bank is an entirely different problem. In 1943—at the time of the decision in the *Kushler* case—the law on this point was obscure. The defect was remedied by Sect. 321 (1) of the Companies Act, 1948, which has the result of making the third party personally liable.[75] The section has not in any way affected a guarantor's

---

[72] S. A. T. Rowlatt, *The Law of Principal and Surety* (3rd ed., 1936), p. 123, citing *Pritchard* v. *Hitchcock* (1843) 6 M. & Gr. 151, and *Petty* v. *Cooke* (1871) L.R. 6 Q.B. 790.

[73] See para. 19-51.

[74] See *post*, para. 21-13.

[75] See *post*, para. 31-16.

liability. There is a useful provision in Sect. 321 (3), the result of which is that the creditor (i.e. the bank) can raise any question relating to the guarantor's liability and have it determined in the winding-up instead of having to bring separate proceedings.

19-58. Some banks have introduced additional provisions into their guarantee forms dealing expressly with the case where a guarantor deposits security in support of his guarantee. The object is to enable the bank to retain the security, initially for a period of six months after the customer's overdraft has been repaid. If during that period a bankruptcy petition is presented against the customer (or, in the case of a company, winding up commences), the bank is to be at liberty to retain the security for such further period as it thinks fit. The object of these provisions is to ensure that the guarantor's security will be available in case the customer's trustee in bankruptcy (or liquidator, as the case may be) succeeds in claiming payment of the sums which the customer paid to the bank, on the ground that the payments constituted a fraudulent preference of the bank or of the guarantor.

CHAPTER 20

Special Types of Guarantor

20-1. GUARANTEES given by certain persons or bodies of persons require special care, and these will be considered in this chapter.

Female Guarantors

20-2. It is sometimes erroneously supposed that the legal position of a female guarantor is potentially different from that of a man who enters into a similar obligation. One writer expressed the matter thus[1]—

> Notwithstanding the enlargement of woman's status economically and politically during the last half century, the presumption of law is that she is incapable of understanding a business transaction by the exercise of her own wit—when it is to her advantage not to understand. Thus, it is the practice of bankers, wherever possible, to arrange for a guarantee by a woman to be executed under the guidance of her solicitor, in order that she may not afterwards avoid her ability by asserting that she did not understand the implications of the document she executed.

There is, in fact, no presumption of law that a woman is incapable of understanding a business transaction, and, with the exception of certain cases where a woman signs a guarantee for her husband's account, it is no more necessary to have a female guarantor advised by her solicitor than it is to have such advice tendered to a man who is to execute a guarantee.[2] Before a woman puts her signature to the guarantee, the banker should explain to her the effect of the document in general terms. This precaution is equally important in the case of male guarantors.[3]

Wife's Guarantee of Husband's Account

20-3. There is one case, and one case only, where a female guarantor is (or, rather, may be) in a different legal position from that of a male guarantor, namely, when she guarantees the account of her

---

[1] R. W. Jones, *Studies in Practical Banking* (3rd ed., 1951), p. 83.

[2] Mr. Megrah rightly stresses that "the idea that women are in need of protection in regard to their business dealing dies hard." Maurice Megrah, *Gilbart Lectures on Banking*, 1950, p. 14.

[3] *Ante*, para. 19-5.

husband or of some company in which he is interested. Courts of equity have evolved a doctrine, known as the doctrine of undue influence, which has been concisely stated as follows[4]—

> In a court of equity, if A obtains any benefit from B, whether under a contract or as a gift, by exerting an influence over B which, in the opinion of the court, prevents B from exercising an independent judgment in the matter in question B can set aside the contract or recover the gift. Moreover, in certain cases the relation between A and B may be such that A has peculiar opportunities of exercising influence over B. If under such circumstances A enters into a contract with B, or receives a gift from B, a court of equity imposes upon A the burden, if he wishes to maintain the contract or gift, of proving that in fact he exerted no influence for the purpose of obtaining it.

Accordingly, contracts which are voidable for undue influence are of two kinds: (*a*) those in which there is a special relationship between the parties (e.g. between a trustee and his beneficiary, an agent and his principal, a solicitor and his client, a physician and his patient, a spiritual adviser and those under his control, a parent and a child who has recently come of age) where undue influence is *presumed* to exist, and (*b*) those in which there is no special relationship between the parties where undue influence must be proved as a fact.

20-4. It is now definitely established that the relationship of husband and wife is not among those fiduciary relations in which there is a *presumption* of undue influence.[5] Nevertheless, it may be proved as a fact that a husband did, in any particular case, and with respect to any particular transaction, stand to his wife in a relation of confidence or dominion, in which event a presumption of undue influence will arise and require to be rebutted by the party seeking to sustain the transaction. Thus, although there is no initial presumption of undue influence as between husband and wife, the very nature of the relationship between the parties makes it far more likely that undue influence may be proved than in a transaction between, say, two businessmen.

Independent Legal Advice

20-5. The question may arise whether a wife should receive independent legal advice before she signs a guarantee in favour of her

---

[4] *Ashburner's Principles of Equity* (2nd ed., 1933), p. 299.
[5] *Nedby* v. *Nedby* (1852) 5 De G. & Sm. 377; *Howes* v. *Bishop* [1909] 2 K.B. 390; *Bank of Montreal* v. *Stuart* [1911] A.C. 120; and *MacKenzie* v. *Royal Bank of Canada* [1934] A.C. 468.

husband or of a company in which he is interested. A brief consideration of the authorities enables one to appreciate the difficulty of giving a firm answer to this question. In *Bank of Montreal* v. *Stuart*[6] a Mrs. Stuart had signed a guarantee for $100,000 Canadian in favour of a company in which her husband was interested. She executed it at the office of Mr. Bruce, who was solicitor to the bank and to her husband, and was a director, secretary, shareholder, and creditor of the company. Subsequently, she signed a guarantee for $125,000 in substitution for the previous one, and, finally, she entered into other transactions the result of which was that she surrendered to the bank all her estate, real and personal, and was left without any means of her own. Upon no occasion did she receive independent legal advice.

20-6. In spite of the fact that she stated in evidence that she acted of her own free will to relieve her husband in his distress and that she would have scorned to consult any one, the Judicial Committee of the Privy Council held that the transactions could not stand. Delivering the judgment of the Privy Council, Lord Macnaghten said[7]—

> The evidence is clear that in all these transactions Mrs. Stuart, who was a confirmed invalid, acted in passive obedience to her husband's directions. She had no will of her own. Nor had she any means of forming an independent judgment even if she had desired to do so. . . . It may well be argued that when there is evidence of overpowering influence and the transaction brought about is immoderate and irrational, as it was in the present case, proof of undue influence is complete. However that may be, it seems to their Lordships that in this case there is enough, according to the recognised doctrine of Courts of Equity, to entitle Mrs. Stuart to relief.

Referring to the conduct of the solicitor, Lord Macnaghten observed[8]—

> His course was plain. He ought to have endeavoured to advise the wife and to place her position and the consequences of what she was doing fully and plainly before her. Probably if not certainly she would have rejected his intervention. And then he ought to have gone to the husband and insisted on the wife being separately advised, and if that was an impossibility owing to the implicit confidence which Mrs. Stuart reposed in her husband, he ought to have retired from the business altogether and told the bank why he did so.

20-7. This remarkable case may be contrasted with another decision of the Privy Council, namely *MacKenzie* v. *Royal Bank of Canada*.[9]

[6] [1911] A.C. 120.
[7] At pp. 136–7.
[8] At p. 139.
[9] [1934] A.C. 468.

A Mrs. MacKenzie signed a guarantee for $200,000 Canadian in favour of a company in which her husband was interested, and she also deposited certain shares as security for the same account. She signed the necessary documents at the bank's office. After she had done so, she was given a form to be taken to a lawyer and signed by him, intimating that he had given her independent advice, and that she fully understood the transaction, and a form to be signed by herself to the same effect. She then went over to the office of a Mr. Burritt, told him that she had already signed the guarantee, and that this document had been sent over as a matter of form. Apparently, Mr. Burritt accepted the position and signed, saying he did so as a matter of form, seeing that she had already signed the guarantee. He gave her no advice.

20-8. The judgment of the Privy Council was delivered by Lord Atkin, and, in so far as it relates to the principles under discussion, it may be summarised as follows: First, the Privy Council reiterated the rule that there is no presumption of undue influence in the relationship of husband and wife. Turning to the particular case, Lord Atkin said[10]—

> In their Lordships' view, the evidence falls far short of proof of undue influence by the husband. The plaintiff obviously possessed and exercised a will of her own. She was able generally to appreciate business conditions: and it is impossible to draw the inference that in the transactions in question her will was overborne by the stronger will of her husband.

20-9. Although the transactions could not be avoided on the ground of undue influence, it so happened that the bank had made a material misrepresentation to Mrs. MacKenzie at the time when she signed the documents. For that reason, the Privy Council held that she was entitled to avoid the contract of guarantee and to recover her securities.

20-10. It is not surprising that, when dealing with the alleged "independent advice" given by Mr. Burritt, the Privy Council said[11]—

> If it had been incumbent upon the bank to prove that the lady had had independent advice, their Lordships would have had the greatest difficulty in coming to the conclusion that the bank had discharged the onus. Independent advice to be of any value must be given before the transaction, for the question is as to the will of the party at the time of entering into the disputed transaction.

[10] [1934] A.C. at p. 475.
[11] [1934] A.C. at p. 474.

20-11. Clearly, a bank official may not find it easy to decide whether a prospective guarantor of her husband's account or of a company in which he is interested is (as Mrs. Stuart was) acting throughout in passive obedience to her husband's directions or whether, on the other hand, she is (as Mrs. MacKenzie was) possessed of a will of her own. And even if the bank official thinks he knows into which category she falls, he cannot be certain that a court of law will necessarily share his view, should the transaction be challenged subsequently. Therefore, even though there may well be cases where independent legal advice may be dispensed with, it seems prudent for bankers to make a general practice of ensuring that a wife does receive such advice prior to executing any guarantee for the benefit of her husband or of a company in which he is interested. The advice should be truly independent; that is to say, neither the bank's solicitor not the husband's solicitor should give it.

Guarantees by Minors and by Persons Just of Age

20-12. Persons under the age of eighteen are incapable of entering into a contract of guarantee.[12] Furthermore, if they purport to enter into such a contract, they cannot ratify it when they come of age.[13]

20-13. Immediately a person attains full age, he is endowed with full contractual capacity, but there is one type of guarantee given by such a person which requires special care—namely, where he or she becomes surety for a parent or for someone standing *in loco parentis*. This is one of those instances where, owing to the special relationship of the parties, undue influence is *presumed* to exist.[14] Even if the child is married and is no longer living at the parents' home, this does not necessarily put an end to the domination of the parents. Whether the parental domination has ceased is a question of fact depending upon the particular circumstances of each case. These rules were laid down by the Court of Appeal in 1934 in a case where a married daughter, aged twenty-two, was relieved from liability as surety for her mother in respect of an advance to the mother by moneylenders.[15] The only way to guard against this possibility is to insist that the proposed guarantor receives independent legal advice before executing the guarantee.

Guarantees by Partnerships

20-14. In the ordinary business transactions of a partnership each partner is an agent for the firm and his other partners. Section 5 of

[12] Infants Relief Act, 1874, Sect. 1; Family Law Reform Act 1969, Sect. 1.
[13] Infants Relief Act, 1874, Sect. 2.
[14] *Espey* v. *Lake* (1852) 10 Hare 260. See *ante*, para. 20-3.
[15] *Lancashire Loans Ltd.* v. *Black* [1934] 1 K.B. 380.

the Partnership Act, 1890, codified this rule of law in the following words—

> Every partner is an agent of the firm and his other partners for the purpose of the business of the partnership; and the acts of every partner who does any act for carrying on in the usual way business of the kind carried on by the firm of which he is a member bind the firm and his partners, unless the partner so acting has in fact no authority to act for the firm in the particular matter, and the person with whom he is dealing either knows that he has no authority, or does not know or believe him to be a partner.

Thus, unless it can be shown that the giving of guarantees is necessary for carrying on the business of a particular partnership in the ordinary way, one partner has no implied authority to bind the firm by executing a guarantee.[16] The practical result is, therefore, that, unless it clearly appears from the partnership deed or partnership agreement that the giving of guarantees is part of the ordinary business of the firm, a banker should either have the guarantee signed by all the partners on behalf of the firm, or, alternatively, have it executed by one partner with the express written authority of the others. The second alternative is seldom adopted in practice, chiefly because the authority ought to refer specifically to the execution of the bank's own form of guarantee, a copy of which should be attached to the authority. Instead of signing an authority of this nature, the partners might just as conveniently sign the guarantee itself.

20-15. The clauses employed in a guarantee given by partners are similar to those in a joint and several guarantee. In fact, some banks, instead of having a special form for guarantees by partners, make use of their ordinary "joint and several" form. Partners must expressly undertake joint and several liability, because, in the absence of express provision, they incur only joint liability for the debts and obligations of the partnership.[17]

Guarantees by Limited Companies

20-16. The general rule is that any contract entered into by a limited company to carry out an object not included among the objects of the company as specified in its memorandum of association is *ultra vires* ("beyond the powers of") the company and void. There are,

---

[16] *Brettel* v. *Williams* (1849) 4 Exch. 623.
[17] Partnership Act, 1890, Sect. 9. The same section provides that when a partner dies, his estate is severally liable for the debts of the firm, subject to the prior payment of his separate debts. For "joint" and "joint and several" liability, see *post*, para. 20-21.

however, certain powers which are implied in the case of every company, e.g. a power to appoint and act by agents.[18] Furthermore, a trading company has implied power to borrow and to give security for the purpose of its business.[19] But a power to execute guarantees cannot ordinarily be implied. If, therefore, a banker is offered a guarantee by a limited company, he should examine the company's memorandum to see whether it contains an express power to this effect.[20] In this connection no reliance should be placed upon the concluding words usually found in the objects clause to the effect that the company shall have power "to do all such other things as are incidental or conducive to the attainment of the above objects or any of them," for it seems very doubtful whether they really add anything to what the law itself implies as incidental to the specifically enumerated objects.[21]

20-17. If article 79, Table A, Companies Act, 1948, applies to the company, a further difficulty arises. That article provides in effect that the directors' powers to borrow money on behalf of the company and to issue securities on behalf of the company are limited.[22] The issue of securities extends not only to those to secure the company's liabilities, but also to those to secure the liabilities of third parties. The result is, therefore, that when the directors offer to execute a guarantee to secure the overdraft of a third party, attention must be directed to the provisions of article 79.

20-18. Unless a company's articles of association otherwise provide, the guarantee may be executed either under seal or under hand. The latter method is the more usual, an advantage being that a guarantee under hand is exempt from stamp duty, whilst a guarantee under seal normally attracts *ad valorem* duty of 2s. (10p) per cent on the amount of the guarantee.[23] Whichever method is adopted, the board of directors of the company should pass a resolution authorising certain officials to execute the instrument on the company's behalf, and the bank should be supplied with a certified copy of the resolution. It is a wise precaution for the bank to supply the company with a draft resolution worded as follows: "Resolved that the Chairman and Secretary be authorised to execute a guarantee for £1,000 in favour of the London Bank

---

[18] *Ferguson* v. *Wilson* (1866) 2 Ch. App. 77.
[19] *General Auction Estate and Monetary Co.* v. *Smith* [1891] 3 Ch. 432.
[20] In *Re Friary Holroyd and Healy's Breweries Ltd.* [1922] W.N. 293, an express power "to subsidise or otherwise assist" certain persons or companies was held to include the giving of a guarantee.
[21] *Simpson* v. *Westminster Palace Hotel Co.* (1860) 8 H.L.C. 712.
[22] See Vol. 1, para. 11-289.
[23] *Ante,* para. 19-8.

Limited on account of . . . in the form and terms of the specimen
guarantee attached hereto." The specimen should be initialled for
purposes of identification. This effectively precludes the company or
its liquidator from arguing upon some subsequent occasion that the
guarantee actually executed (containing all the special clauses found
in bank guarantees) was not specifically authorised by the directors.
Some banks achieve the same object by having a certified copy of
the resolution endorsed on the guarantee itself. The resolution is
worded: "Resolved that the Chairman and Secretary be authorised
to execute a guarantee for £1,000 in favour of the London Bank
Limited on account of . . . in the form and terms of the guarantee
produced to the board and on which guarantee a certified copy of
this resolution shall be inscribed."

20-19. Finally, when a company is proposing to execute a guarantee,
one must always ensure that the directors who pass the resolution are
not personally interested or that, if they are personally interested,
the appropriate steps are taken;[24] and that the guarantee will not
infringe the provisions of Sect. 54 or Sect. 190 of the Companies
Act, 1948.[25]

Guarantees by Two or More Persons

20-20. Sometimes, when a customer is casting around for suitable
security for a proposed advance, he will inform the bank that two
or more of his relations or friends are prepared to sign guarantees
on his behalf. He is making application for an overdraft of, say,
£600, and he states that three persons, G1, G2, and G3, are willing
to sign guarantees for £200 each. It is sound policy for the banker,
under these circumstances, to try to insist that all three sureties
join in signing one instrument for £600. The reason is not far to
seek: if and when the bank has to enforce the security, it may be
that G1 will be in a strong financial position, whereas G2 and G3
will not. The bank would demand the whole £600 from G1 and
leave it to him to claim contribution from his co-sureties. On the
other hand, it is not always good policy to take a joint and several
guarantee for a very large sum if one of the guarantors is of small
means; for example, most bankers would not think it proper for a
director of small means, who may be the "brains" of a company,
to join in signing a joint and several guarantee for £20,000 in respect
of the company's account.

20-21. Guarantees executed by two or more persons give rise to a
number of special problems. First, there are important differences

[24] See *post*, paras. 32-50/51.
[25] See *post*, paras. 32-73/77.

between joint liability on the one hand, and joint and several liability on the other. Where a surety is only bound jointly with his co-surety, and not severally also, his liability both for existing and for future debts of the principal comes to an end with his death, and the survivor or survivors alone become liable both at law and in equity.[26] This is known as the doctrine of "survivorship."[27] The process continues until there is but one survivor, when the obligation necessarily becomes several and, upon his death, devolves upon his personal representatives. Although this was clearly the position as established by the courts, it has been argued that the law was changed by the Law Reform (Miscellaneous Provisions) Act, 1934. The Act does not provide specifically for the case of joint obligations. It was passed to remedy the situation arising from the rule in tort, *actio personalis moritur cum persona* ("a personal action dies with the person"). Professor Glanville Williams considers that one effect of the Act is that the personal representatives of a deceased joint promisor are now in every case liable on the contract.[28] There is much force in this argument, but, until the point has been decided by the courts, it is perhaps safer to assume that the Act has not altered the law in this respect and, therefore, that when a joint surety dies his liability ceases.

20-22. Another disadvantage (from the creditor's point of view) of joint, as opposed to joint and several, liability, is that he has only one cause of action in respect thereof. In the event of joint and several liability, on the other hand, there are as many causes of action as there are parties. Bowen, L.J., stated the rule in the following words[29]—

> There is in the cases of joint contract and joint debt as distinguished from the cases of joint and several contract and joint and several debt, only one cause of action. The party injured may sue at law all the joint contractors or he may sue one . . . but whether an action in the case of a joint debt is brought against one debtor or against all the debtors . . . it is for the same cause of action—there is only one cause of action.

[26] *Other* v. *Iveson* (1855) 3 Drewr. 177.

[27] "Survivorship" here is the opposite of "survival." When one speaks of the "survival" of causes of action, this means that the obligation continues to bind the estate of the person formerly subject to it. But when there is "survivorship" of causes of action, the converse applies. See Glanville L. Williams, *Joint Obligations* (1949), p. 63.

[28] Glanville L. Williams, op. cit., p. 72. The Act provides in Sect. 1 (1) that "subject to the provisions of this section, on the death of any person after the commencement of this Act all causes of action subsisting against or vested in him shall survive against, or, as the case may be, for the benefit of, his estate."

[29] *Re Hodgson, Beckett* v. *Ramsdale* (1885) 31 Ch. D. 177, at p. 188.

20-23. In practice, bankers are seldom, if ever, prepared to accept the joint liability of guarantors—a result which is hardly surprising in view of the stronger position occupied by a creditor holding a joint and several guarantee.

Drafting of a Joint and Several Guarantee

20-24. To make it clear that the liability of the guarantors is to be joint and several, the words "we hereby jointly and severally guarantee . . ." should be used. The other clauses are similar to those inserted in guarantees executed by an individual.[30] However, the joining together of two or more persons as sureties in the same instrument makes it advisable to incorporate therein certain special provisions. Thus it is common to find a clause worded—

> The Bank shall be at liberty to release or discharge any of us from the obligations of this guarantee or to accept any composition from or make any other arrangements with any of us without thereby prejudicing or affecting the Bank's rights and remedies against the other or others of us

The value of this clause is that it excludes the rule that the release of a joint and several surety releases the other or others from liability.[31] A clear illustration of the danger of omitting the clause is provided by the decision in *Barclays Bank Ltd.* v. *Trevanion.*[32] Three directors of a limited company, Mr. Gladwell, Mr. Kell, and Mr. Trevanion, had signed a joint and several guarantee of the company's account with Barclays Bank up to a limit of £10,000. The company got into difficulties and, ultimately, when the account was overdrawn £3,607, the bank pressed the guarantors. Arrangements were made for the flotation of a new company, and the bank arranged with Mr. Gladwell and Mr. Kell to release them in consideration of the payment by each of them of £500 down or £600 by instalments spread over three years. This they assented to. Mr. Trevanion was offered the same terms of release, but he failed to come to a settlement with the bank, with the result that the bank commenced proceedings against him. Swift, J., rejected the bank's claim, and said—

> I cannot find in the written contract any words which entitle them to release two of the guarantors and to retain their rights against a third.

---

[30] Some banks make use of a form of guarantee which may be employed either for an individual or for a joint and several obligation.

[31] *Mercantile Bank of Sydney* v. *Taylor* [1893] A.C. 317. The same principle applies if one surety is released after joint and several judgment against the two: *Re E.W.A.* [1901] 2 K.B. 692.

[32] *The Banker*, Vol. XXVII (1933), p. 98.

In my view, when they released two, they altered the contract between themselves and the third guarantor in such a way as to prevent it being enforceable. They deprived him of his rights of contribution against his co-sureties, and I think that they then did something that released him from his bargain altogether.

20-25. Another clause which is usually found in a joint and several guarantee reads—

> We agree that this guarantee shall be a continuing security to the Bank and shall not be determined except at the expiration of three calendar months' written notice given to the Bank by each of us of our intention so to do and in the event of all or any of us dying the liability of our legal personal representatives and of our estates shall continue until the expiration of three calendar months' written notice to determine this guarantee given to the Bank by each of us and by the personal representatives of the person or persons so dying

The effect of a clause stipulating for a period of notice to determine a guarantee is a matter of controversy.[33] It is, however, beyond dispute that where a joint and several guarantee is worded as above, notice by one surety is insufficient to determine the guarantee. All must join in giving notice. This was established by the Judicial Committee of the Privy Council in *Egbert* v. *National Crown Bank*,[34] where a joint and several guarantee was to continue "until the undersigned, or the executors or administrators of the undersigned, shall have given the bank notice in writing to make no futher advances on the security of this guarantee." Lord Dunedin, in delivering the judgment of the Privy Council, said that the effect of the clause was that it was not open to any one of the guarantors to bring the guarantee to an end. "Their Lordships," he said, "are of opinion that this clause stipulates that the guarantee is to remain in force until there is notice given by each and all of the guarantors, the executors of any deceased co-signatory coming in his place."[35]

Status Inquiries: Joint and Several Guarantors

20-26. When status inquiries are addressed to the guarantors' bankers, it is advisable to inquire for the full amount of the guarantee in respect of each guarantor. It should be expressly stated, however, that there is to be a joint and several guarantee with a specified number of co-guarantors. This enables the bank which has been asked for its opinion to say, if it so desires, that its customer may be considered good for a stated proportion of the total liability.

---

[33] *Ante*, paras. 19-24/27.
[34] [1918] A.C. 903.
[35] [1918] A.C. at p. 907.

Execution of a Joint and Several Guarantee

20-27. When the various parties have expressed themselves as willing to undertake liability in a joint and several guarantee and the bank is satisfied as to their financial standing, all that remains is the execution of the instrument. It is unnecessary for the sureties to sign the guarantee in the presence of each other, though it is essential that all who have agreed to become sureties should actually sign the guarantee; otherwise, those who have already signed will not be bound. In *National Provincial Bank of England* v. *Brackenbury*[36] the bank suffered loss through the operation of this rule. A guarantee was, on its face, intended to be a joint and several guarantee by four guarantors. Three out of the four signed the guarantee, but the fourth did not sign. It was held that the three who had signed were not liable to the bank on the guarantee. In such a case, if the creditor is to be protected, it is for him to show that the sureties who have signed have consented to dispense with the execution of the document by the other or others. Probably the simplest method is for the bank to start afresh and have an entirely new guarantee prepared.

20-28. A closely related principle is that if one guarantor varies the terms of the guarantee without the consent of the other or others, none of the signatories will be bound. This is the curious result of the decision in *Ellesmere Brewery Company* v. *Cooper*.[37] Four persons, as sureties for a principal, had executed a joint and several bond of suretyship, by the terms of which the liability of two of them was limited to £50 each and that of the other two to £25 each. One of those whose liability was limited to £50, after the other three had executed the bond, executed it himself, but added to his signature the words "£25 only." The principal defaulted, and an action was brought against him and the four sureties. It was held that the effect of the added words was to make a material alteration in the bond, so that the first three signatories were discharged from their obligation, and that as the last signatory only executed the bond as a joint and several bond, he also was not bound by it. The strange result of the alteration made by the last signatory was to relieve himself as well as the others.

Determination of a Joint and Several Guarantee

20-29. The principal ways in which a contract of guarantee may come to an end were stated in a previous chapter.[38] There are, however, a

---

[36] (1906) 22 T.L.R. 797. See also *Evans* v. *Bremridge* (1855) 2 K. & J. 174; and *Hansard* v. *Lethbridge* (1892) 8 T.L.R. 346.

[37] [1896] 1 Q.B. 75.

[38] *Ante*, paras. 18-25/37.

number of special points to be noted in relation to joint and several guarantees—

A. NOTICE OF DEATH OF ONE GUARANTOR

20-30. It has been held that the death of one joint and several guarantor in a continuing guarantee for advances to be made does not, even when notified to the creditor, prevent the surviving guarantor or guarantors from remaining liable for further advances.[39] Accordingly, there is no necessity for the banker to take a fresh guarantee from the survivor or survivors. In practice, such a course is sometimes taken, but it is quite clearly a waste of time, except in those cases where it is desired to introduce a new guarantor to take the place of the deceased.

20-31. Although notice of the death of one of the guarantors does not determine the guarantee and so does not affect the survivors, it may be that the banker should break the principal debtor's account and pass future transactions through a new account if he wishes to retain the liability of the deceased surety's estate. His personal representatives should be notified forthwith so that they will not distribute the estate in ignorance of the liability. However, there are two reasons why it may be unnecessary to break the account—

(i) If the guarantee contains the type of clause which proved so useful in *Westminter Bank Ltd.* v. *Cond*,[40] the failure to break the account will not prejudice the bank's position—that is to say, the crystallised amount of the liability of the estate will not be reduced by subsequent payments to the credit of the account;

(ii) if the guarantee includes a stipulation that it is not to be determined except by notice given by each surety, including the personal representatives of a deceased surety, then the rule laid down in *Egbert* v. *National Crown Bank*[41] will apply. In that case the executors of the deceased guarantor did, in fact, write a letter to the bank purporting to revoke the guarantee. It was argued, first, that this notice brought the guarantee to an end as regards all the guarantors, and, second, that it brought it to an end, at least as regards the deceased guarantor. Both these arguments were rejected by the court. The guarantee remained in force until notice had been given by each guarantor.

20-32. If, therefore, a joint and several guarantee contains proper protective clauses, it should never be necessary to break the

[39] *Beckett & Co.* v. *Addyman* (1882) 9 Q.B.D. 783.
[40] (1940) 46 Com. Cas. 60, *ante*, para. 19-33.
[41] [1918] A.C. 903, *ante*, para. 20-25.

customer's account when one of the sureties dies, unless, of course, *all* the guarantors join in giving notice. In the latter event and in the absence of any special provision (such as that employed in *Cond's* case) the account should be broken when the notice expires.

B. NOTICE OF MENTAL INCAPACITY OF ONE
GUARANTOR

20-33. The legal effect of a guarantor's insanity is similar to that which follows his death.[42] Presumably, therefore, the mental incapacity of one joint and several guarantor in a continuing guarantee does not, even when notified to the creditor, prevent the other guarantor or guarantors from remaining liable for further advances. On the other hand, the decision in *Bradford Old Bank Ltd.* v. *Sutcliffe*[43] makes it clear that, as soon as the bank receives notice of the mental incapacity of one of the joint and several guarantors, it can no longer make advances for which the insane guarantor will be liable. The guarantee in *Sutcliffe's* case contained a stipulation that it should not be determined except by three months' notice in writing, but the clause made no express provision for mental incapacity. Thus it was held that the notice clause was inapplicable. The result was that, although the insane guarantor was liable for debts already accrued due, he was not responsible for advances made by the bank after they knew of his insanity. For some reason not stated in the report no action was brought against the sane guarantor.

20-34. As soon as the bank receives notice of the mental incapacity of a joint and several guarantor, the customer's account should be broken and future transactions passed through a new account. The bank in *Sutcliffe's* case omitted to do this, the consequence being that part of the liability of the insane guarantor was extinguished by the Rule in *Clayton's* case.[44] Not even the clause employed in the guarantee in *Westminster Bank Ltd.* v. *Cond*[45] would have prevented the operation of this Rule. That clause read: "In the event of this guarantee being determined either by notice by me or my legal personal representatives or by demand in writing by the Bank it shall be lawful for the Bank, etc." It would be a useful addition to this clause to insert the words "or by any other cause or reason whatsoever," thus covering the possibility of insanity.

[42] *Ante*, para. 18-30.
[43] (1918) 23 Com. Cas. 299 and, on appeal, [1918] 2 K.B. 833.
[44] (1816) 1 Mer. 572.
[45] (1940) 46 Com. Cas. 60, *ante*, para. 19-33.

C. BANKRUPTCY OF ONE GUARANTOR

20-35. If one joint and several guarantor is adjudicated bankrupt, the bank will have to decide whether to prove in his estate or to rely upon the liability of the solvent guarantor or guarantors. In the latter event it may be necessary to have a new guarantee signed by them. The general rule is that the release of a joint and several surety releases the other or others from liability, and, although most joint and several guarantee forms provide that *the bank* is to be at liberty to release any guarantor without affecting its rights against the other or others, it is arguable that a release obtained by discharge in bankruptcy, not being a release *by the bank*, would discharge the other sureties. There is, of course, no reason why a joint and several guarantee should not expressly provide that the bankruptcy of one surety is not to affect the liability of the others, but such a clause does not seem to be generally incorporated in the forms used by the banks.[46] Finally, if the bank decides to prove in the estate of the bankrupt guarantor, a formal demand in writing should be served upon him or his trustee and upon the other sureties. The customer's account should be broken and future transactions passed through a new account, unless the guarantee contains a clause similar to that employed in *Westminter Bank Ltd.* v. *Cond.*[47]

---

[46] See the clause *ante*, para. 20-24. Quite apart from express provision, it is possible that the court might extend the rule in *Beckett & Co.* v. *Addyman* (1882) 9 Q.B.D. 783, *ante*, para. 20-30 (death of a joint and several guarantor) to cases of bankruptcy.
[47] (1940) 46 Com. Cas. 60, *ante*, para. 19-33.

CHAPTER 21

Enforcing a Guarantee

21-1. A BANK usually refrains from calling upon a guarantor to honour his undertaking until every reasonable effort has been made to obtain payment from the customer. If a guarantor is required to pay, he experiences a natural feeling that the guaranteed party has "let him down." Unfortunately—and rather illogically—his animosity frequently extends to the bank as well. However, the time may arrive when the bank feels that the customer's position has deteriorated to such an extent that the only course available is to demand payment from the guarantor. This chapter is chiefly concerned with the practical steps to be taken in this respect and with the appropriation of payments received from guarantors.

The Demand for Payment

21-2. With the usual form of bank guarantee, the bank's right of action against the guarantor arises as soon as the customer has made default and the bank has served a written demand upon the guarantor.[1] Accordingly, if a bank wants to call upon a guarantor to pay, it should first address a demand to its customer, and, if this is not complied with, the bank should then demand payment from the guarantor. Very often a bank form of guarantee expressly provides that a demand is to be deemed to have been given to the guarantor if it is sent to him by post at the address specified in the guarantee or at his last known address.[2]

21-3. If the customer's overdraft exceeds the sum for which the guarantor has agreed to be responsible, the bank should simply demand payment of the latter amount, together with interest thereon at the rate stated in the guarantee until payment is made. If, on the other hand, the overdraft is less than the amount for which the guarantor agreed to be responsible, the account should be made up with interest and commission to date, and payment should be demanded of the aggregate amount, together with interest thereon at the specified rate until payment.

21-4. If the customer is still carrying on business and requires banking facilities, arrangements are sometimes made for a fresh

---

[1] *Ante*, paras. 19-15/17.
[2] *Ante*, para. 19-31.

account to be opened for him. Express power to open a new account is often included in the guarantee, but this power exists even in the absence of such a clause.[3] If a new account is not opened and sums are credited to the old account, the guarantor's liability will be *pro tanto* reduced, and amounts debited to the account will create a fresh advance for which the guarantor will not be responsible. However, this operation of the Rule in *Clayton's* case may be excluded by appropriate words in the guarantee.[4]

21-5. In the foregoing remarks it has been assumed that the customer is in default. There are, however, circumstances where the customer's account should be broken and a new account opened, although he has not defaulted. Thus in the event of the bankruptcy of the guarantor or in the event of his mental incapacity, the customer's account should be broken and a new account opened. The bank should notify the guarantor's trustee in bankruptcy or receiver, as the case may be, and details of any security deposited by the guarantor should be given. In many cases this is simply a formality necessary to safeguard the bank's position: the customer may be able to find alternative security, with the result that the guarantee may be cancelled.

21-6. The person upon whom the demand is made sometimes asks for a copy of the debtor's account going back several years. If the bank's form of guarantee contains the clause suggested in an earlier chapter,[5] it will never be necessary to provide anything more than a signed copy of the account for the last six months.

Notice to Determine Given by Guarantor or by his Personal Representatives

21-7. It is not always easy to decide what action the bank should take if the guarantor or, in the event of his death, his personal representative gives notice to determine the guarantee. Most bank forms of guarantee stipulate for a given period of notice, e.g. three months, and although the courts have never decided this point, it seems probable that this provision would be interpreted literally by the court with the result that advances made during the period of notice would be covered by the guarantee.[6] The correct course to take, therefore, when acknowledging the letter of the guarantor or his personal representatives, is to draw attention to the notice clause

---

[3] See *Re Sherry* (1884) 25 Ch. D. 692, *ante* para. 19-35.
[4] See *Westminster Bank Ltd.* v. *Cond* (1940) 46 Com. Cas. 60, *ante*, para, 19-33,
[5] *Ante*, para. 19-40.
[6] For a different view, see *ante*, para. 19-26.

and to point out that the final amount of the surety's liability cannot be calculated until the notice has expired. During the period of notice the bank will naturally try to arrange with its customer for the deposit of alternative security.

21-8. If one joint and several guarantor gives notice to determine his liability and the guarantee stipulates that it is not to be determined except by notice given by each surety, the bank will draw attention to this provision and decline to accept the letter as notice to determine.[7] In most cases it will be prudent to ask the customer whether he can put forward any proposal which would make it possible to release the guarantor concerned. If not, and unless each joint and several guarantor gives notice, the position remains unchanged and each surety will remain liable for the amount specified in the guarantee.

Guarantor's Right to Customer's Securities

21-9. If a guarantor repays the whole of the customer's overdraft, he is entitled to all securities held by the bank in respect thereof, whether deposited by the customer himself or by third parties.[8] The correct way of transferring or assigning the securities to the guarantor depends upon the nature of the securities. Thus, in the case of a legal mortgage of land or of a life policy the bank should execute a statutory receipt acknowledging the payment of a specified sum by the guarantor; this automatically transfers to the guarantor the benefit of the mortgage.[9] If the security is a legal mortgage of shares which have been transferred into the names of the bank's nominees, the shares should be transferred into the name of the guarantor. The principle in every case is that the bank must give to the guarantor the same rights as the bank possesses in relation to the security. The bank should notify the person who deposited the securities that they are being transferred or assigned to the guarantor.

21-10. Sometimes a guarantor offers to repay the whole debt even if its exceeds the amount of his liability under the guarantee, his object being to obtain an assignment of the securities held by the bank. There appears to be no reason why the bank should decline this offer.

---

[7] For a case involving notice by the personal representatives of a deceased joint and several guarantor, see *Egbert* v. *National Crown Bank* [1918] A.C. 903, *ante*, para. 20-25.

[8] *Ante*, para. 18-16.

[9] Law of Property Act, 1925, Sect. 115 (2), *ante*, para. 6-6.

Use of Securities Realised Account

21-11. If the sum paid by the guarantor is insufficient to repay the whole of the customer's indebtedness to the bank, the sum so paid should always be placed to the credit of a Securities Realised Account. This leaves undiminished the amount of the customer's debt so that, in the event of his bankruptcy, the bank may prove for the whole amount thereof. Bank guarantee forms are drafted in a way which permits the bank to do this, and the surety is prevented from proving in the bankruptcy for the amount paid by him. A clear illustration of this principle was provided by the decision of *Re Sass*.[10] If the bank, by proving in this way, eventually receives more than is required to repay the customer's debt, any surplus must be paid over to the guarantor. The legal position should be explained to the guarantor when he makes his payment to the bank. He should be reminded that, under the terms of the guarantee, he is precluded from taking any steps to enforce his rights against the principal debtor until the whole sum due to the bank has been repaid.

21-12. If the amount paid by the guarantor is sufficient to repay the advance to the customer, there is usually no necessity to place it to the credit of a Securities Realised Account, because there will be no need for the bank to make any proof in the customer's estate, should he become bankrupt. It is just possible, however, that certain payments into the customer's account prior to his bankruptcy may subsequently be claimed by the customer's trustee in bankruptcy (or liquidator in the case of company customers) as constituting a fraudulent preference of the bank or of the guarantor.[11] For this reason it is desirable to keep the sum paid by the guarantor in a suspense account until one is quite certain that no such claim will be made.

Retention of the Guarantee

21-13. When a guarantor pays the sum demanded from him, the guarantee should not be handed to him, nor should the bank write "cancelled" across it. An examination of the clauses discussed in Chapter 19 will show that some of them may still be useful to the bank even after the guarantor has paid. For example, under the "fraudulent preference" clause the bank may have occasion to demand payment of a further sum from him.[12] Furthermore, even

[10] [1896] 2 Q.B. 12, *ante*, para. 19-19.
[11] *Ante*, paras. 19-53/54.
[12] *Ante*, para. 19-55.

if the guarantor has paid every penny of the sum named in the guarantee as the limit of his liability, the cancellation of the instrument might nevertheless prejudice the bank. Thus, one of the clauses commonly stipulates that the guarantor must not enforce any right or claim against the principal debtor until the whole of his indebtedness to the bank has been discharged. It would not be easy for the bank to enforce this provision if the guarantee had been surrendered to the guarantor. The most prudent course, therefore, for the banker to take is to point out to the guarantor that certain clauses of the guarantee may still be operative and that the document will be retained by the bank.

21-14. There are instances where a bank cancels a guarantee either because the customer has deposited some other security or because he has no further need for overdraft facilities. In cases of this nature there is no objection to cancelling the instrument and handing it to the guarantor. If, however, the overdraft has been repaid very recently, this may indicate "fraudulent preference," and it would be unwise to cancel the guarantee.[13]

Payment by Joint and Several Guarantors

21-15. It is not unusual for a joint and several guarantor to take the view that he ought not to be called upon to pay more than a proportionate amount of the total liability under the guarantee. Suppose, for example, that a bank has obtained a joint and several guarantee executed by four persons limited to £200 and that the customer defaults when his account is overdrawn in excess of that sum. When the bank sends out formal demands for £200 to each guarantor, it is quite probable that some of them will offer to pay £50 each. There is, of course, no objection to accepting any sums thus tendered, which should be placed to the credit of a Securities Realised Account in the usual way. Nothing should be done which might suggest that the sureties who pay £50 each are discharged from further liability, e.g. by ruling out their names on the form of guarantee. One or more of the guarantors may be unable to pay, in which case the bank will wish to enforce payment against those who can, leaving them to seek contribution from their co-surety or co-sureties.

21-16. There are two reasons for placing to the credit of a Securities Realised Account any sums tendered by the guarantors. The first is to leave undiminished the amount of the customer's debt so that, in the event of his bankruptcy, the bank may prove for the whole

[13] *Ante*, paras. 19-53/54.

amount thereof.[14] The second reason is that one of the guarantors may become bankrupt; in this event it has been held by the Privy Council that money paid by another guarantor and placed to the credit of a Securities Realised Account, to be appropriated by the bank when it thinks fit towards payment *pro tanto* of the debt, need not be deducted when the bank proves in the bankruptcy of the bankrupt guarantor.[15]

Guarantor's Position in regard to Tax

21-17. When a customer pays interest to his bank, he may be entitled to obtain a repayment of tax on the amount of the interest, and for this purpose he will be supplied by his bank with a certificate stating the amount of interest paid.[16]

21-18. In *Holder* v. *Inland Revenue Commissioners*[17] guarantors paid very large sums to the Midland Bank Limited in respect of various guarantees, and they maintained that of those sums £17,861 represented interest added to the guaranteed accounts from 1920 to 1926. They therefore made a claim against the Commissioners of Inland Revenue for repayment of tax on £17,861. The House of Lords held that this claim must fail. Lord Dunedin stated[18] that, in his opinion—

> . . . interest payable on an advance from a bank means interest on an advance made to the person paying. The guarantor does not pay on an advance made to him, but pays under his guarantee. It is true that he pays a sum which pays all interest due by the person to whom the advance is made, but his debt is his debt under the guarantee, not a debt in respect of the advance made to him.

Clearly, therefore, when a guarantor pays off the debt, he should not be supplied with a certificate of payment of interest by the bank.

[14] See *ante*, paras. 19-19/20.
[15] *Commercial Bank of Australia Ltd.* v. *Official Assignee of the Estate of John Wilson & Co.* [1893] A.C. 181.
[16] Income and Corporation Taxes Act, 1970, Sects. 57–64.
[17] [1932] A.C. 624.
[18] [1932] A.C. at pp. 627–8.

Part Six

GOODS

CHAPTER 22

Introductory

22-1. THIS chapter deals first with the principal merits and demerits of goods as security for bankers' advances, and with the types of legal transaction involved. Then an account will be given of the documents with which a banker who makes advances of this nature should be familiar; C.I.F. and F.O.B. contracts will be considered; and, finally, some reference will be made to documentary credits. Succeeding chapters deal with the practice of bankers when lending against goods.

22-2. When a banker speaks of advances against goods or produce, he is thinking primarily of the finance of foreign trade: the import of raw materials, such as wool, cotton, wheat, and tea, and the export of manufactured products. The lending of money against the security of goods forms an important function of the banks.[1]

Advantages and Disadvantages of Goods as Security

22-3. The merits of goods as a banking security are as follows: (i) usually advances of this type are repaid rapidly, i.e. as soon as the buyer pays the purchase price, and rapidity of turnover is one of the first principles of sound lending; (ii) there are no heavy *ad valorem* stamp duties to pay when goods are made available as security; and (iii) it is reasonably certain that the banker will obtain a good title to the goods, provided that he acts in good faith and deals with merchants of high repute and wide experience.

22-4. Conversely, lending against goods has disadvantages, viz. (i) there is the difficulty of valuing the security, and, furthermore, in some

[1] On this subject generally, see *Banking and Foreign Trade* (being the lectures delivered at the Fifth International Banking Summer School, Christ Church, Oxford, July, 1952); *The Bill on London*, published for Gillett Brothers Discount Co. Ltd., (3rd ed., 1964); J. F. Stott, "Bankers' Advances Against Produce," *Journal of the Institute of Bankers*, Vol. LXXVI (1955), pp. 97–107, 222–33; James Dandy, "Finance for Overseas Trade," *Journal of the Institute of Bankers*, LXXIX (1958), pp. 31–40, 89–99; J. F. McClure, "Financing International Trade," *Journal of the Institute of Bankers*, Vol. LXXIX (1958), pp. 410–16, Vol. 80 (1959), pp. 152–6, 238–42, 324–8; Maurice Megrah, *The Legal Aspects of Goods as Banking Security* (being the Gilbart Lectures on Banking, 1959); *The City of London as a Centre of International Trade and Finance* (being the lectures delivered at the Fourteenth International Banking Summer School in the City of London and at Christ Church, Oxford, July, 1961); *The Finance of International Trade* (being the Ernest Sykes Memorial Lectures, 1965).

markets, there may be considerable fluctuation in prices; (ii) when a merchant is constantly buying and selling goods, the detailed records which a banker must keep involve much clerical work; (iii) insurance and storage charges are fairly heavy; and (iv) there is ample opportunity, in some types of transaction, for a dishonest customer to defraud his banker.

Mortgage, Pledge, and Hypothecation

22-5. There are three quite distinct methods of making goods available as security, namely, by way of mortgage, pledge, and hypothecation—

A. MORTGAGE

22-6. A mortgage is the conveyance of a legal or equitable interest in property as security for the payment of a debt or for the discharge of some other obligation.[2] Although mortgages of land and of certain types of personal property (such as life policies and stocks and shares) are very frequently taken as a banking security, mortgages of goods are almost unknown. This is so, largely because mortgages of goods are, in most cases, within the Bills of Sale Acts, and the mercantile community dislike bills of sale.[3] One serious drawback is that they have to be registered within seven days after execution.[4] The publicity which results is damaging to the borrower's credit: various trade protection papers publish the registration of bills of sale, with the result that other traders refuse to grant credit to the mortgagor. In fact, bills of sale seem to carry with them a kind of stigma. Furthermore, the Bills of Sale Act, 1882, Sect. 9, totally invalidates bills of sale given by way of security for money if they are not in the prescribed form, namely—

> . . . the said A.B. doth hereby assign unto C.D. his executors, administrators, and assigns, all and singular the several chattels and things specifically described in the schedule hereto annexed by way of security for the payment of the sum of £   , and interest thereon at the rate of
>
> per cent per annum

[2] *Ante*, para. 2-14.

[3] Originally, a bill of sale was a legal document assigning personal property. Under the Bills of Sale Acts such instruments are of two kinds: (i) absolute bills of sale, where chattels are sold absolutely to a purchaser, and (ii) bills of sale by way of security for the borrowing of money. On bills of sale generally, see *Stevens and Borrie's Elements of Mercantile Law* (15th ed., 1969), pp. 389–400, and C. H. M. Waldock, *The Law of Mortgages* (1950), pp. 75–126.

[4] Bills of Sale Act, 1878, Sects. 8 and 10; Bills of Sale Act (1878) Amendment Act, 1882, Sect. 8.

22-7. It is not surprising, therefore, that in practice bankers try to find some method of taking goods as security without having recourse to a bill of sale. For example, if a hotel proprietor offers his furniture as security, he would probably be asked to form a private limited company and to transfer his business assets, including the furniture, to the company which would then issue to the bank a debenture embodying a floating charge.[5] In this way the execution of a bill of sale would be avoided. Incidentally, hotel proprietors often obtain furniture under hire-purchase agreements, and care must be exercised in transactions of the kind outlined above.

22-8. Agricultural charges on farming stock and other agricultural assets may be created in favour of bankers under the provisions of the Agricultural Credits Act, 1928. These charges are mortgages within the meaning of the Law of Property Act, 1925.[6] They are subject to many special rules under the 1928 Act and are considered separately in Chapter 26. It is sufficient to say here that they do not require to be registered under the Bills of Sale Acts.[7]

B. PLEDGE

22-9. A pledge arises when goods (or documents of title thereto) or bearer securities are delivered by one person (called the "pledgor") to another person (called the "pledgee") to be held as a security for the payment of a debt or for the discharge of some other obligation, upon the express or implied understanding that the subject-matter of the pledge is to be restored to the pledgor as soon as the debt or other obligation is discharged. Where a definite time for payment has been fixed, the pledgee has an implied power of sale upon default, but if there is no stipulated time for payment, the pledgee may demand payment and in default thereof may exercise his power of sale after giving notice to the pledgor of his intention to do so.[8] Pledge is the characteristic mode of taking security over goods, and the practice in this connection is dealt with in the next chapter.

22-10. A pledge should be clearly distinguished from a mortgage. As Bowen, L.J., said[9]—

> There are two well-known and entirely distinct kinds of transaction. There is a mortgage of chattels, when there is no delivery of the chattels

---

[5] For securities by limited companies, see Chapter 32.
[6] Sect. 205 (1) (xvi).
[7] Agricultural Credits Act, 1928, Sect. 8 (1).
[8] *France* v. *Clark* (1883) 22 Ch. D. 830.
[9] *Ex parte Hubbard* (1886) 17 Q.B.D. 690, at p. 698.

to the mortgagee, but the general property in them passes to him by the mortgage deed. There is another entirely distinct transaction . . . the transaction of a pawn or pledge, where there must be a delivery of the goods pledged to the pledgee, but only a special property in them passes to him, in order that they may be dealt with by him, if necessary, to enforce his rights—the general property in the goods remaining in the pledgor. A special property in the goods passes to the pledgee in order that he may be able—if his right to sell arises—to sell them. In all such cases there is at Common Law an authority to the pledgee to sell the goods on the default of the pledgor to repay the money, either at the time originally appointed, or after notice by the pledgee.

Although, as Bowen, L.J., stated, there must always be a delivery of the goods pledged to the pledgee, they do not need to be physically transferred to the lender. Delivery of possession may be actual or constructive, the latter being the more usual in borrowing transactions among merchants. A further distinction between pledge and mortgage is that a pledgee (unlike a mortgagee) cannot obtain a foreclosure.[10]

C. HYPOTHECATION

22-11. Hypothecation is a legal transaction whereby goods may be made available as security for a debt without transferring *either* the property *or* the possession to the lender.[11] The way in which customers occasionally hypothecate goods to their banks is considered in Chapter 24. The term "hypothecation" is used in another sense, which is rather confusing. When a banker accepts a *pledge* of documents of title to goods, his customer usually signs a memorandum setting out the terms of the transaction, which is often referred to as a "letter of hypothecation." This is a loose use of the word, synonymous with "pledge" and should not obscure the fact that the transaction is not hypothecation in the strict legal sense.

Documents relating to Goods

22-12. When lending against the security of goods, a banker seldom handles, or even sees, the goods themselves. Instead, he is primarily concerned with various documents conferring certain rights in relation to the goods. The four main documents are (*a*) bills of lading, (*b*) marine insurance policies, (*c*) warehousekeepers' warrants, and (*d*) warehousekeepers' receipts. These will now be considered, as also will other documents which are used with them—

---

[10] *Harrold* v. *Plenty* [1901] 2 Ch. 314, *ante*, para. 16-3.
[11] Cf. H. L. Hart, *The Law of Banking* (4th ed., 1931), Vol. 2, p. 906.

A. BILL OF LADING

22-13. This is a document signed by the master of a ship or by his agent and given to the person shipping goods on board the vessel. The document performs three functions: (i) it is evidence of the terms of a contract of affreightment; (ii) it is evidence of the shipment of goods; and (iii) it is evidence that the holder of it has the property in the goods, i.e. it is a document of title. A bill of lading was the only document of title to goods known to the common law. It states that the goods will be delivered to "X or his assigns" or to "X or order" and, when endorsed in blank by X, it passes by delivery. Thus, the delivery of an endorsed bill "is equivalent to delivery of the goods themselves, and is effectual to transfer ownership if made with that intention. The bill of lading is the symbol of the goods."[12] In practice a document called a *"mate's receipt"* is usually issued upon shipment, and this is exchanged later for the bill of lading.

22-14. By virtue of the Bills of Lading Act, 1855,[13] the endorsee of a bill of lading to whom the property has passed under the endorsement becomes an assignee of the contract of carriage evidenced in the document. He may, therefore, become liable to pay freight, demurrage, and other charges. However, it was held by the House of Lords in *Sewell* v. *Burdick*[14] that this applies only to an endorsee who takes the full ownership, and not to a pledgee. Unfortunately, from a lender's point of view, the value of this case has been lessened by a later decision where it was held that if a pledgee presents the bill of lading in order to enforce his security by obtaining possession of the goods, he impliedly undertakes to fulfil the terms of the contract evidenced by it and so may become liable for freight, demurrage, and other charges independently of the Bills of Lading Act.[15]

22-15. The Act did not make bills of lading negotiable instruments. The essential characteristics of a negotiable instrument are:[16] (i) the property therein is capable of being transferred by delivery (either with or without endorsement according as to whether the instrument is in favour of order or bearer), (ii) a bona fide transferee for value obtains a title free from equities, and (iii) the holder can

---

[12] *Per* Lord Sumner, delivering the judgment of the Privy Council in *The Prinz Adalbert* [1917] A.C. 586, at p. 589.
[13] Sect. 1.
[14] (1884) 10 App. Cas. 74.
[15] *Brandt* v. *Liverpool, Brazil and River Plate Steam Navigation Co. Ltd.* [1924] 1 K.B. 575.
[16] Cf. Blackburn, J., in *Crouch* v *The Crédit Foncier Co.* (1873) L.R. 8 Q.B. 374, at p. 381.

sue on the instrument in his own name. The second characteristic
implies that a transferee who gives value in good faith may be able
to obtain a better title than his transferor had; for example, a bona
fide transferee for value of a bill of exchange can obtain a good title
from a thief. It is this quality that is lacking in the case of a bill of
lading. A transferee takes it subject to any defects in the title of
prior parties.[17]

22-16. Bills of lading are usually drawn in sets of three. They are
forwarded direct to the consignee by different mails in order to
reduce the risk of loss, or negotiated through a bank which has
agreed to finance the transaction. Lord Blackburn once said that he
had never been able to learn why merchants and shipowners continued the practice of making out bills of lading in parts.[18] However
that may be, the system of drawing them in sets of three certainly
enables a dishonest shipper to dispose of two or three parts to
different purchasers or pledgees. If this is done, the property in the
goods passes to the first person to obtain a transfer of one of the
parts, but the shipowner is entitled to deliver the goods to a person
who produces to him another part which has been taken subsequently, provided that the shipowner is acting bona fide without
notice of the earlier transaction. Although the shipowner is justified
in delivering the goods to that person, the legal ownership of the
goods as between the holders of the two bills remains unaffected,
i.e. the property therein is still vested in the party who first acquired
one of the parts.[19] No part of a bill of lading attracts any stamp
duty in this country, though many bills in respect of goods imported
are liable to duty in their country of origin.[20]

22-17. A "through" bill of lading is one which covers the carriage
of goods from one place to another by several shipowners or railway
companies. The person with whom the contract of carriage is made
in the first instance charges an inclusive rate for the sea voyage and
the land transit. "Through" bills of lading generally incorporate by
reference the usual form of bill of lading used by the shipowner,
which thus becomes a part of the contract, except to the extent that

[17] See Lord Campbell, C.J.'s remarks in *Gurney* v. *Behrend* (1854) 3 E. & B. 622,
at pp. 633–4. A bill of lading is sometimes said to be "*quasi*-negotiable" or "semi-
negotiable" in the sense that the unpaid seller's right of lien or stoppage *in transitu* is
defeated if the instrument comes into the hands of a bona fide purchaser: Sale of Goods
Act, 1893, Sects. 25 (2) and 47.
[18] *Glyn Mills, Currie & Co.* v. *The East and West India Dock Co.* (1882) 7 App. Cas.
591, at p. 605.
[19] *Barber* v. *Meyerstein* (1870) L.R. 4 H.L. 317; *Glyn Mills, Currie & Co.* v. *The
East and West India Dock Co.* (*supra*).
[20] The Finance Act, 1949, Sect. 35 and 8th Sched. abolished the stamp duty on bills
of lading.

its terms are inconsistent with the express terms of the "through" bill of lading.

22-18. A "received for shipment" bill of lading merely states that the goods specified are held awaiting a suitable vessel. The extent to which bills of this type are used depends principally upon conditions prevailing at the particular port; for example, they are more likely to be issued in ports where vessels call occasionally at irregular intervals than in busy ports with frequent sailings. The obvious weakness of a "received for shipment" bill is that the goods may have to wait on the quay for a considerable time and may deteriorate, or miss their market.

B. MARINE INSURANCE POLICY

22-19. Marine insurance is a contract of indemnity against losses incident to marine adventure accruing to a ship, cargo, freight, or other subject-matter of a policy during a given voyage or during a specified length of time.[21] The law relating to marine insurance was codified by the Marine Insurance Act, 1906, which enacts that a marine policy is assignable unless it contains terms expressly prohibiting assignment.[22] The assignee is entitled to sue thereon in his own name but is liable to be met by the same defences as would have been valid if the action had been brought by the person by whom the policy was effected; for example, the defendant may raise the defence of non-disclosure of material facts by the original insured.[23] The policy may be assigned by endorsement.[24] These provisions are important to a banker who is financing the shipment of goods, for he will normally require the policy to be endorsed in blank. A policy of marine insurance is exempt from stamp duty.[25]

C. WAREHOUSEKEEPERS' WARRANTS

22-20. These are documents issued by warehousekeepers stating that goods specified therein are deliverable to the person named or to his assigns by endorsement. They are now exempt from stamp duty.[26] Warehousekeepers' warrants may be subdivided into two

---

[21] On this subject generally, see Victor Dover and G. A. Calver, *The Banker's Guide to Marine Insurance of Goods* (1960).
[22] Sect. 50.
[23] Sect. 50.
[24] Ibid.
[25] Finance Act, 1970, Sect. 32 and Sched. 7.
[26] Finance Act, 1949, Sect. 35 and 8th Sched.

categories: (*a*) those issued under the provisions of private Acts of Parliament, and (*b*) those not so issued. The distinction between these two types of instrument is important.

A. Warrants Issued under Private Acts

22-21. Some warehousekeepers have statutory authority to issue warrants which are transferable. The various statutes differ slightly in their terms. Thus the Trafford Park Act, 1904, and the Liverpool Mineral and Metal Storage Company Limited (Delivery Warrants) Act, 1921, provide that the holder of warrants issued thereunder is to have "the same right to the possession and property of such goods as if they were deposited in his warehouse."[27] These warrants, although transferable, are not negotiable instruments which enable a transferee to obtain a better title than his transferor had. But the Port of London (Consolidation) Act, 1920, provides that warrants issued thereunder "shall be transferable by endorsement and shall entitle the person named therein or the last endorsee thereof named in the endorsement to the goods specified therein and the goods so specified shall for all purposes be deemed his property."[28] This would seem to enable an endorsee to acquire a better title to the goods than his endorser had. Accordingly, warrants of this type appear to be fully negotiable instruments.

B. Warrants Issued without Special Statutory Authority

22-22. There are many warehousekeepers who issue warrants without having the advantage of a private Act of Parliament. The endorsement and delivery of such a warrant is insufficient to pass the property in the goods.

22-23. The result is that warrants issued under private Acts are documents of title; the others are not.[29] A banker who is accepting a pledge of goods in a warehouse must always bear in mind this distinction.

D. WAREHOUSEKEEPERS' RECEIPTS

22-24. These are documents issued by a warehousekeeper stating that goods specified therein are held in his warehouse at the disposal of a named person. They are exempt from stamp duty.[30] Unlike

---

[27] 1904 Act, Sect. 34; 1921 Act, Sect. 4.

[28] Sect. 168. Another private Act which embodies a similar formula is the Mersey Docks Acts Consolidation Act, 1858.

[29] But they *are* documents of title for the purpose of the Factors Act, 1889, and the Sale of Goods Act, 1893; see Chapter 25.

[30] Finance Act, 1949, Sect. 35 and 8th Sched.

warehousekeepers' warrants, they are never transferable by endorsement. They are not documents of title,[31] and if the owner of the goods sells them, he will execute in the buyer's favour either a "transfer order" directing the warehousekeeper to hold the goods in the name of the purchaser or a "delivery order" directing the warehousekeeper to deliver the goods to the purchaser.

C.I.F. Contracts

22-25. These contracts are, as Lord Wright once observed, "more widely and more frequently in use than any other contract used for purposes of sea-borne commerce."[32] The letters "C.I.F." indicate that the price is to include cost, insurance, and freight. McCardie, J., explained the characteristics of this type of contract as follows—

> . . . the essential feature of an ordinary c.i.f. contract as compared with an ordinary contract for the sale of goods rests in the fact that performance of the bargain is to be fulfilled by delivery of documents and not by the actual physical delivery of goods by the vendor. All that the buyer can call for is delivery of the customary documents. This represents the measure of the buyer's rights and the extent of the vendor's duty. The buyer cannot refuse the documents and ask for the actual goods, nor can the vendor withhold the documents and tender the goods they represent.[33]

22-26. Although the buyer must pay when the documents are tendered, he can, of course, reject the goods upon their arrival and/or claim damages for breach of contract if they are not in accordance with the contract. This means that under a C.I.F. contract the seller is under two distinct obligations: (i) to deliver correct documents, and (ii) to deliver correct goods. In one of the most important judgments on this branch of the law in modern times, Devlin, J., said[34]—

> So far as the goods are concerned, [the seller] must put on board at the port of shipment goods in conformity with the contract description, but he must also send forward documents, and those documents must comply with the contract.

22-27. The documents which the seller is obliged to tender under a C.I.F. contract are (*a*) an invoice, (*b*) a marine insurance policy, and

[31] Except for the purposes of the Factors Act, 1889, and the Sale of Goods Act, 1893; see *post*, para. 25-5.
[32] *Smyth (Ross T.) & Co. Ltd.* v. *Bailey (T.D.), Son & Co.* [1940] 3 All E.R. 60, at p. 67. On this subject, see David M. Sassoon, *C.I.F. & F.O.B. Contracts* (1968).
[33] *Per* McCardie, J., in *Manbre Saccharine Co. Ltd.* v. *Corn Products Co. Ltd.* [1919] 1 K.B. 198, at p. 202.
[34] *Kwei Tek Chao* v. *British Traders and Shippers Ltd.* [1954] 2 Q.B. 459, at p. 480.

(c) the bill(s) of lading. These are the minimum: the parties may, of course, agree that additional documents must be supplied, e.g. a certificate of origin. The procedure to be followed was clearly explained by Hamilton, J. (subsequently Lord Sumner). A seller under a C.I.F. contract, said the learned judge[35]—

> . . . has firstly to ship at the port of shipment goods of the description contained in the contract; secondly to procure a contract of affreightment, under which the goods will be delivered at the destination contemplated by the contract; thirdly to arrange for an insurance upon the terms current in the trade which will be available for the benefit of the buyer; fourthly to make out an invoice . . . and finally to tender these documents to the buyer so that he may know what freight he has to pay and obtain delivery of the goods, if they arrive, or recover for their loss if they are lost on the voyage.

With one reservation, this correctly describes the practice to-day. In Lord Sumner's time—and indeed until the Second World War—it was customary for the buyer to pay the freight when the goods arrived, and for this reason the freight was deducted in the invoice. At the present day, it is the usual, though not the invariable, practice for the freight to be prepaid by the seller, with the result that no allowance in respect thereof is made in the invoice.

22-28. It should be emphasised that a seller under a C.I.F. contract must, in the absence of agreement to the contrary, tender the shipping documents specified above. At the present day, however, owing to changes in business practice, it is very frequently agreed that a seller need not tender a marine insurance policy. Few merchants to-day take out separate policies for each consignment of goods. Instead, they have a floating policy and make declarations in respect of each shipment. Thus, most C.I.F. contracts expressly provide for the tender of "policies and/or certificates and/or letters of insurance." If this provision is not inserted in the contract, the buyer is entitled to insist upon tender of a *policy*.[36] Similarly, the law has always regarded a bill of lading as an essential document: even a "received for shipment" bill is bad tender, because it does not acknowledge shipment.[37] Nevertheless, it is becoming quite common at the present day to provide that a delivery order shall be regarded as good tender, i.e. in place of a bill of lading.

---

[35] *Biddell Brothers* v. *E. Clemens Horst Co.* [1911] 1 K.B. 214, at p. 220.
[36] *Wilson, Holgate & Co.* v. *Belgian Grain & Produce Co.* [1920] 2 K.B. 1; *Diamond Alkali Export Corporation* v. *Fl. Bourgeois* [1921] 3 K.B. 433; *Scott (Donald H.) & Co. Ltd.* v. *Barclays Bank Ltd.* [1923] 2 K.B.1.
[37] *Diamond Alkali Export Corporation* v. *Fl. Bourgeois (supra).*

C. and F. Contracts

22-29. In these contracts the price of the goods includes cost and freight, but the insurance arrangements are left in the hands of the buyer. A considerable volume of this country's trade to Australia, New Zealand, and South Africa is transacted on these terms. Usually, the shippers declare their shipments to the marine insurance companies named by the buyers, and the premiums are then paid by the buyers.

F.O.B. Contracts

22-30. Under the original type of F.O.B. ("free on board") contract, the buyer's duty is to nominate the ship, and the seller's duty is to put the goods on board for account of the buyer and procure a bill of lading in the buyer's name.[38] The buyer is responsible for all freight and insurance charges. In modern times, however, the F.O.B. contract has become a flexible instrument. Sometimes the seller is asked to make the arrangements about the contract of carriage, and he will in fact take the bill of lading in his own name. In other cases the buyer engages his own forwarding agent at the port of loading to book space and to procure the bill of lading.[39]

Documentary Credits

22-31. A considerable volume of foreign trade is financed through the medium of documentary credits. A documentary credit is defined in the *Uniform Customs and Practice for Documentary Credits*[40] as "any arrangement, however named or described, whereby a bank (the issuing bank), acting at the request and in accordance with the instructions of a customer (the applicant for the credit), is to make payment to or to the order of a third party (the beneficiary) or is to pay, accept or negotiate bills of exchange (drafts) drawn by the beneficiary, or authorises such payments to be made or such drafts to be paid, accepted or negotiated by another bank, against stipulated documents and compliance with stipulated terms and conditions".

22-32. The necessity for a credit arises because the exporter naturally wishes to be assured that the goods which he has agreed to sell will be paid for, and the importer wishes to ensure that his money will

---

[38] In regard to F.O.B. contracts, see David M. Sassoon, *C.I.F. & F.O.B. Contracts* (1968).

[39] See *per* Devlin, J., in *Pyrene Co. Ltd. v. Scindia Navigation Co. Ltd.* [1954] 2 Q.B. 402. at p. 424.

[40] General Provisions and Definitions.

not be handed over until someone on his behalf has obtained documents which purport to represent a good title to the goods which he has agreed to buy. There are different types of documentary credit, one of which is described briefly below. Other types are outlined in a subsequent chapter.[41]

22-33. An importer who wants to have a credit opened addresses to his bank (the issuing bank) a written request—usually by completing a printed application form—asking that a credit be established. If his bank is willing to open the credit, it advises its agent or correspondent in the foreign centre that the credit has been established in favour of the named exporter; asks its correspondent to inform the exporter; and, sometimes, requests its correspondent to add its own "confirmation" to the credit. If the credit is "confirmed" in this way, the banker in the foreign centre places himself under a direct obligation to the seller.[42] The letter sent by the issuing bank to its foreign correspondent must be most precise in its terms. It must set out the quantity and exact description of the goods purchased and indicate the sum to be paid by the foreign correspondent to the exporter against delivery of specified documents before a given date. Often payment is authorised against the documents together with a draft drawn by the exporter, but sometimes no draft is required.

22-34. The credit is normally expressed to be "irrevocable"; that is to say, the issuing bank cannot lawfully cancel it without the consent of the foreign exporter, even if the bank's own customer (the importer) requests him to do so. If, indeed, he does cancel the credit, he will be liable in damages to the foreign exporter.[43] Occasionally, however, a credit is expressed to be "revocable." Such a credit, in the absence of some special provision, may be cancelled at any time and is of little protection to a seller. The usual reason for employing a revocable, rather than an irrevocable, credit is because an importer wants to protect himself against a seller whom he does not trust. However, Article 2 of the *Uniform Customs* provides that when a

---

[41] See *post*, paras. 23-11, 23-37, 23-39 and 23-48. On this subject generally, see H. C. Gutteridge and Maurice Megrah, *The Law of Bankers' Commercial Credits* (4th ed., 1968); A. G. Davis, *The Law Relating to Commercial Letters of Credit* (3rd ed., 1963); Maurice Megrah, *Documentary Credits—Some Aspects of the Law and Practice* (being the Gilbart Lectures on Banking, 1951), *Documentary Credit Problems* (being the Gilbart Lectures on Banking, 1952) and *Risk Aspects of the Irrevocable Credit* (being the Gilbart Lectures on Banking, 1958). A useful series of articles entitled "Documentary Credits" in *The Bankers' Magazine*, Vols. CLXXIV (1952) and CLXXV (1953) has been reprinted as a pamphlet.

[42] Cf. *Malas and Another (trading as Hamzeh Malas and Sons)* v. *British Imex Industries Ltd.* [1958] 2 Q.B. 127.

[43] See Article 3 of the *Uniform Customs;* and cf. *Urquhart Lindsay & Co. Ltd.* v. *Eastern Bank Ltd.* [1922] 1 K.B. 318.

revocable credit has been transmitted to and made available at a branch or other bank, its modification or cancellation is to become effective only upon receipt of notice thereof by such branch or other bank and is not to effect the right of that branch or other bank to be reimbursed for any payment, acceptance or negotiation made by it prior to receipt of such notice.[44]

22-35. Some confusion has been caused by treating the terms "irrevocable credit" and "confirmed credit" as synonymous. Thus, the Gilbart Lecturer in 1936, the late Mr. C. T. Le Quesne, K.C., said: "I believe I am right in saying that an irrevocable credit is the same thing as a confirmed credit."[45] This practice is strongly to be deprecated, and the author supports Mr. Megrah's plea that "a credit should be described as irrevocable when considered from the standpoint of the opening banker only; where it is advised to the beneficiary through another banker, who adds his own undertaking (which is irrevocable), the credit should be said to be 'confirmed' by that banker."[46] Thus, it will be apparent that a credit may be irrevocable and confirmed, or irrevocable and unconfirmed.

Transferable Credits

22-36. Article 46 of the *Uniform Customs* defines a transferable credit as one "under which the beneficiary has the right to give instructions to the bank called upon to effect payment or acceptance or to any bank entitled to effect negotiation to make the credit available in whole or in part to one or more third parties." For the purpose of understanding this type of credit, let it be assumed that a buyer (B) in this country is purchasing goods from abroad through a merchant or middleman (M), who in turn is buying them from a foreign seller (S). M wishes to prevent B and S from becoming known to each other, because this might encourage B and S to do business direct and so dispense with M's services. With this end in view, M asks B to arrange with a London banker for a confirmed transferable credit to be established in M's favour.[47]

22-37. The steps taken in a simple case are as follows. The credit established in M's favour is advised to him by the London banker, with a statement that it is transferable and an indication of the

---

[44] See also Article 38 of the *Uniform Customs, post* Appendix I.
[45] *Journal of the Institute of Bankers*, Vol. LVII (1936), p. 159. Mr Le Quesne quoted passages from the speeches of Lord Reading and Lord Sumner in support.
[46] Megrah, Gilbart Lectures, 1951, p. 53. See also Article 3 of the *Uniform Customs, post*, Appendix 1.
[47] For a fuller account than is possible here, see H. O. Nash, "Transferable Credits," *Journal of the Institute of Bankers*, Vol. LXXIII (1952) pp. 15–26. See also *Ian Stach Ltd.* v. *Baker Bosley Ltd.* [1958] 2 Q.B. 130, at p. 138 *per* Diplock, J.

monetary areas within which it may be transferred. The only variations which are normally permitted when the credit is transferred are as follows: (i) the amount may be reduced, thus allowing for M's profit, and (ii) the last date of validity is usually a few days earlier than in the original credit. When M's transfer instructions are received, the London banker issues a confirmed credit advice in favour of S and endorses M's credit with the amount transferred. The new credit in favour of S will state that it is opened on account of M, but it will not, of course, make any reference to B.

22-38. When S ships the goods, he presents the documents specified in the credit and, if they are in order, he receives payment. The bank informs M that his invoices are required immediately. These are substituted for S's invoices by the bank. The documents are passed on to B—except, of course, S's invoices, which are handed to M. To prevent the ultimate buyers and sellers from becoming acquainted, further precautions are generally taken. Thus the bills of lading usually show that shipment has been made by A, who is S's agent for this purpose. This prevents B from discovering S's identity by examining the bills of lading. Similarly, M will ensure that the bills do not name B as consignee.

22-39. In practice, there are many variations in the way these credits are handled as between one bank and another, but bankers generally are of the opinion that a word of warning should be given to any customer who asks a bank to open a transferable credit on his behalf. It has always been important that persons shipping goods should be merchants of repute, unlikely to ship goods differing materially from the description of them given in the documents. In the normal way when buyers and sellers are known to each other, there is not much risk, but it is otherwise when the ultimate buyer has no opportunity of finding out who is the actual shipper. The only prudent course for a buyer to take is to ensure that he deals with middlemen of good repute who would be unlikely to transact business with untrustworthy firms overseas.

CHAPTER 23

The Pledge of Goods

23-1. PLEDGE is the characteristic mode of taking goods as security. It arises when goods (or documents of title thereto) or bearer securities are delivered by one person (called the "pledgor") to another person (called the "pledgee") to be held as a security for the payment of a debt or for the discharge of some other obligation, upon the express or implied understanding that the subject-matter of the pledge is to be restored to the pledgor as soon as the debt or other obligation is discharged.[1]

Delivery of Possession

23-2. Delivery of possession may be either (*a*) actual or (*b*) constructive—

A. ACTUAL DELIVERY

23-3. If the pledgor has the goods in his physical possession, he can effect a pledge by actual delivery. X may borrow money from Y and hand over his watch by way of pledge. Lending of this type is usually regarded as the province of a pawnbroker rather than of a banker.

B. CONSTRUCTIVE DELIVERY

23-4. This can take place in various ways. For example, constructive delivery may be made, not by handing over the goods themselves, but by delivering the documents of title thereto, e.g. the bills of lading. This is sometimes called "symbolic delivery," because bills of lading are the symbols of the goods. It would seem that the delivery of some warehousekeepers' warrants issued under the provisions of private Acts of Parliament has the same legal effect as the delivery of bills of lading,[2] though Lord Wright appears to have taken the view that bills of lading are the only documents of title, the pledge of which amounts to a pledge of the goods themselves.[3]

---

[1] *Ante*, para. 22-9.
[2] *Ante*, para. 22-21.
[3] *Official Assignee of Madras* v. *Mercantile Bank of India Ltd.* [1935] A.C. 53, at pp. 58–9.

23-5. Again, possession may be delivered, while the goods are in the custody of a third person (e.g. a warehousekeeper), by the agreement of the pledgor and the pledgee, with the assent of that third person, that they are to be held in the name or on the account of the pledgee. The third party is said to "attorn" to the pledgee, and the transaction is sometimes referred to as "delivery by attornment."

Letter of Pledge

23-6. From a strictly legal point of view, there is no necessity for any written evidence of a pledge. In practice, however, a banker usually obtains his customer's signature to a document, sometimes called a "letter of pledge," a "letter of hypothecation," or a "letter of lien." Some banks require their customers to sign a document of this nature in respect of each transaction, in which case the documents of title to the goods are listed in a schedule thereto; other banks obtain the customer's signature to a document which covers all transactions. The clauses contained in both types of document are, of course, very similar. A document of the second type—sometimes called a general letter of pledge—commonly includes the following provisions—

(*a*) The customer agrees that the bank is to have a pledge upon all goods delivered by the customer or by his agents into the possession of the bank or of its agents and upon all bills of lading and other documents of title deposited by the customer or by his agents, with the bank or with its agents.

(*b*) The customer agrees that the goods and documents of title are pledged as a continuing security for the payment of all sums owed by the customer, either solely or jointly with any other person or persons, whether on balance of account or on guarantees or in respect of bills of exchange, and including interest with half-yearly rests and other banking charges.

(*c*) The customer agrees that in case of default in repayment of such sum or sums on demand, the bank may sell the goods or any part thereof.

(*d*) The customer agrees to keep the goods fully insured in such office as the bank may approve.

(*e*) The customer undertakes to pay all rent and other expenses of and incidental to the warehousing of the goods.

(*f*) The customer agrees that the bank is not to be responsible for the default of any broker employed to sell the goods.

23-7. In practice, letters of pledge are now probably exempt from stamp duty as agreements under hand. It may be, however, that they ought to be stamped as equitable mortgages; the definition of "equitable mortgage" for the purpose of the Stamp Act, 1891, is a very wide one,[4] and would seem to cover a memorandum of the pledge of goods.[5]

23-8. The most important aspect of a banker's work when lending against goods is the finance of the movement of goods from one country to another. The seller of goods in the country of their origin—whether they be primary commodities or manufactured goods—expects to receive payment as soon as he ships them, whereas the buyer does not usually expect to have to pay until the goods or the documents of title thereto have arrived. It is one of the functions of bankers to bridge, or at any rate to help to bridge, this "gap." A brief account will be given of the ways in which exports from this country and imports into this country are financed. Practice as between one bank and another varies to some extent in this field, and it should not be inferred that the methods described below are the only ones in common use.

Export of Goods

23-9. When an exporter in this country sells goods to an overseas buyer and the exporter is not prepared to agree that settlement shall take place on an "open account" basis, there are five principal methods available to the exporter to obtain payment, namely—

(*a*) The overseas buyer may arrange for the opening of an irrevocable documentary acceptance credit in London in favour of the exporter.

(*b*) A less satisfactory method, from the exporter's point of view, is the opening of a revocable credit in London in favour of the exporter.

(*c*) The exporter may make his own arrangements with an accepting house or bank for an acceptance credit.

(*d*) The exporter may draw bills upon the overseas buyer and negotiate them with a bank in London under a documentary credit opened by the overseas buyer.

(*e*) If no credit has been established by either party, the exporter will probably draw bills upon the overseas buyer and deliver them to his own bank, which may either (*i*) negotiate them, or (*ii*) make an advance against them, or (*iii*) merely take them for collection.

---

[4] *Post*, para. 33-30.
[5] Cf. E. G. Sergeant, *The Law of Stamp Duties* (5th ed., 1968), p. 167.

23-10. These methods will now be discussed, and from time to time reference will be made, to the *Uniform Customs and Practice for Documentary Credits* and to the *Uniform Rules for the Collection of Commercial Paper*. These two sets of rules were drawn up by the International Chamber of Commerce, and, in general, they are applied by the banks in the United Kingdom.[6] The *Uniform Customs* are reproduced in Appendix I of this book, and the *Uniform Rules* in Appendix II.

A. IRREVOCABLE DOCUMENTARY ACCEPTANCE CREDIT

23-11. At the request of an overseas buyer, a London bank gives an irrevocable undertaking to an exporter to accept bills of exchange drawn by him on the bank at (say) ninety days after sight for sums not exceeding a stated figure, provided that the bills drawn under the credit are in respect of a current shipment and are accompanied by certain specified shipping documents relating to the goods. When the documents are delivered to the bank, it obtains a pledge of the goods as security for its liability as acceptor of the bills of exchange. As soon as the exporter's bills have been accepted, he may offer them to a discount house, or to a bank, for discounting. The charge made for discounting the bills is calculated by applying the appropriate rate of interest to the lifetime of the bill.

23-12. The documents which are frequently called for under a credit are the ones which are required under a C.I.F. contract,[7] namely, an invoice, a marine insurance policy and the bill(s) of lading. It is, however, very common in modern practice to find that the credit permits an insurance certificate[8] as an alternative to a marine insurance policy. It is also quite usual for the credit to require the tender of certain additional documents, for example, a consular invoice, a certificate of analysis, a cargo declaration, a weight note, or a certificate of origin. These additional documents are required in order to protect the buyer. A documentary credit cannot give the buyer an absolute assurance that he will receive the goods which

[6] In regard to the *Uniform Customs*, see B. S. Wheble, "Documentary Credits: Uniform Customs and Practice," *Journal of the Institute of Bankers*, Vol. 84 (1963), pp. 27–46; Maurice Megrah, "Documentary Credit—A Common Code," *The Banker*, Vol. CXIII (1963), pp. 470–3; Maurice Megrah, "The Uniform Customs and Practice for Documentary Credits: the 1962 Revision and After," being the Gilbart Lectures on Banking, 1969. In regard to the *Uniform Rules*, see B. S. Wheble, "Uniform Rules for the Collection of Commercial Paper," *Journal of the Institute of Bankers*, Vol. 89 (1968), pp. 58–66.

[7] *Ante*, para. 22-27.

[8] *Ante*, para. 22-28.

he contracted to buy, because the bank makes payment against documents and not against the actual goods. Thus, a prudent buyer often stipulates for some additional document (e.g., a certificate of analysis) issued by a third party to provide independent evidence of the existence and quality of the goods.

23-13. Some account of the main points to look for when examining (i) the invoice, (ii) the marine insurance policy, and (iii) the bill(s) of lading, will be given. It should be added, however, that there are numerous reported decisions upon this branch of the law, and it is impossible to review them fully in this book.[9]

(i) *The Invoice*

23-14. This document should describe the goods in exactly the same way as they were described in the credit; in particular, if the credit contains a technical description of the goods in a foreign language, the invoice should describe the goods in the same language. Sometimes, the invoice contains certain information in addition to the description of the goods, and this is, of course, no reason for refusing the document; for example, the invoice very frequently sets out the shipping marks upon the goods.

23-15. Article 30 of the *Uniform Customs* provides—

> Unless otherwise specified in the credit, commercial invoices must be made out in the name of the applicant for the credit.
>
> Unless otherwise specified in the credit, banks may refuse invoices issued for amounts in excess of the amounts permitted by the credit.
>
> The description of the goods in the commercial invoice must correspond with the description in the credit. In the remaining documents the goods may be described in general terms.

(ii) *The Marine Insurance Policy*

23-16. The policy must insure the goods specified in the credit for the whole of the contractual journey or voyage,[10] and no other goods.[11] A documentary credit usually provides that the policy must be in favour of the exporter, who should endorse it in blank. In the absence of any provision to the contrary in the credit, the policy must be one which is "usual" in the trade in question. In one case it was held that a policy to pay "a total loss by total loss of vessel only"

---

[9] For a fuller account than is possible here, see *Halsbury's Laws of England* (3rd ed.), vol. 2, pp. 217–21; H. C. Gutteridge and Maurice Megrah, *The Law of Bankers' Commercial Credits* (4th ed., 1968); Victor Dover and G. A. Calver, *The Banker's Guide to Marine Insurance of Goods* (1960).

[10] *Landauer & Co.* v. *Craven & Speeding Brothers* [1912] 2 K.B. 94, at pp. 106–7.

[11] *May and Hassel Ltd.* v. *Exportles of Moscow* (1940) 45 Com. Cas. 128.

was inadequate in the meat trade in which it was customary to tender an "all risks" policy.[12]

23-17. In view of the doubts which may exist as to whether or not a particular type of policy is "usual," Article 27 of the *Uniform Customs* provides—

> Credits must expressly state the type of insurance required and, if any, the additional risks which are to be covered. Imprecise terms such as "usual risks" or "customary risks" shall not be used.
>
> Failing specific instructions, banks will accept insurance cover as tendered.

23-18. Dealing with "all risks" policies, Article 28 of the *Uniform Customs* provides—

> When a credit stipulates "insurance against all risks", banks will accept an insurance document which contains any "all risks" notation or clause, and will assume no responsibility if any particular risk is not covered.

23-19. As to the amount of the cover, Article 26 of the *Uniform Customs* provides—

> Unless otherwise specified in the credit, the insurance document must be expressed in the same currency as the credit.
>
> The minimum amount for which insurance must be effected is the C.I.F. value of the goods concerned. However, when the C.I.F. value of the goods cannot be determined from the documents on their face, banks will accept as such minimum amount the amount of the drawing under the credit or the amount of the relative commercial invoice, whichever is the greater.

In practice, a credit often stipulates for insurance cover for (say) five per cent above invoice price.

23-20. Marine insurance policies are exempt from stamp duty.[13] Cover notes issued by brokers should not be accepted, unless specifically authorised in the credit.[14]

(iii) The Bill(s) of Lading

23-21. The functions of bills of lading have already been stated.[15] When examining these documents, the following points should be considered—

23-22. Bills of lading are usually drawn in sets of three,[16] and the credit generally calls for a "full set." If it does so, "a tender of two

---

[12] *Borthwick* v. *Bank of New Zealand* (1900) 6 Com. Cas. 1.
[13] Finance Act, 1970, Sect. 32 and Sched. 7.
[14] Article 24 of the *Uniform Customs*.
[15] *Ante*, para. 22-13.
[16] *Ante*, para. 22-16.

bills accompanied by either an undertaking to produce the third or an indemnity for accepting less than three is not a sufficient tender."[17] In spite of this, the practice of taking an indemnity in such a case is quite a common one. If the credit does not call for a full set, it would seem that the tender of one of the set may be sufficient, as this is effectual to pass the property in the goods.[18] Nevertheless, it is not the usual practice of banks in this country to accept without indemnity anything less than a complete set of bills, even if the credit calls for "bill of lading" without specifying a full set.

23-23. As a rule, the credit calls for "clean" bills of lading, and even if it does not specify that the bills must be clean, the position is the same. "I think that in normal circumstances the ordinary business man who undertakes to pay against the presentation of bills of lading means clean bills of lading; and he would probably consider that that was so obvious to any other business man that it was hardly necessary to state it."[19] A clean bill of lading has never been exhaustively defined, but one learned judge said: "I incline to the view . . . that a clean bill of lading is one that does not contain any reservations as to the apparent good order or condition of the goods or the packing."[20] An unclean or "dirty" bill is one which does contain such a reservation; for example, it may show that the goods were received on board in a defective state or with packages broken.

23-24. Unless otherwise specified in the credit, "through"[21] bills of lading issued by steamship companies or their agents will be accepted, even though they cover several modes of transport.[22]

23-25. Unless otherwise specified in the credit, "received for shipment" bills of lading should not be accepted.[23] Article 18 of the *Uniform Customs* provides that loading on board may be evidenced

---

[17] *Donald H. Scott & Co.* v. *Barclays Bank Ltd.* [1923] 2 K.B. 1 at p. 12, *per* Bankes, L.J.

[18] *Barber* v. *Meyerstein* (1870) L.R. 4 H.L. 317; *Sanders Brothers* v. *Maclean & Co.* (1883) 11 Q.B.D. 327.

[19] *British Imex Industries Ltd.* v. *Midland Bank Ltd.* [1958] 1 Q.B. 542 at p. 551, *per* Salmon, J.

[20] Ibid., at p. 551, *per* Salmon, J., and see *Canada and Dominion Sugar Co. Ltd.* v. *Canadian National (West Indies) Steamships Ltd.* [1947] A.C. 46 at p. 54, *per* Lord Wright, delivering the opinion of the Privy Council. See also Article 16 of the *Uniform Customs.*

[21] *Ante*, para. 22-17.

[22] Article 17 of the *Uniform Customs.*

[23] Article 18 of the *Uniform Customs.* It was held in *Diamond Alkali Export Corporation* v. *Bourgeois* [1921] 2 K.B. 443 that a "received for shipment" bill, in the absence of agreement or custom to the contrary, was not a good tender under a c.i.f. contract for the sale of goods.

by an on-board bill of lading or by means of a notation to that effect dated and signed or initialled by the carrier or his agent, and that the date of this notation is to be regarded as the date of loading on board and shipment.

23-26. Article 20 of the *Uniform Customs* provides that banks will refuse a bill of lading showing the stowage of goods on deck, unless specifically authorised in the credit.

23-27. Unless otherwise stated in the credit, the bill of lading must be one which is "merchantable." Thus, a bank was held entitled to reject a bill of lading "to order" which did not name the shipper and was endorsed with an illegible signature.[24] In this connection, Article 21 of the *Uniform Customs* provides that banks may require the name of the beneficiary to appear on the bill of lading as shipper or endorser, unless the terms of the credit provide otherwise.

23-28. The bill of lading must cover the transit from the port of origin to the port of destination. The reason for this rule is that a buyer under a c.i.f. contract is entitled to have a bill of lading which gives him rights against the shipowner for the whole of the transit and not merely part of it.[25] Dealing with transhipment, Article 19 of the *Uniform Customs* provides—

> Unless transhipment is prohibited by the terms of the credit, bills of lading will be accepted which indicate that the goods will be transhipped en route, provided the entire voyage is covered by one and the same bill of lading.
>
> Bills of lading incorporating printed clauses stating that the carriers have the right to tranship will be accepted notwithstanding the fact that the credit prohibits transhipment.

23-29. If the credit stipulates that shipment must be made on or before a specified date, the bills of lading must show that the goods were shipped by that date.[26]

23-30. It is sometimes said that the bill of lading should not be "stale," a stale bill being one which is tendered so late (though during the currency of the credit) that it is impossible for the bank to which it is tendered to transmit it to reach the consignee before the arrival of the goods. The reason for this attitude is the belief that the bank is under a duty to the buyer to see that he is not put to

[24] *Skandinaviska Kredit A/B* v. *Barclays Bank Ltd.* (1925) 22 Ll.L. Rep. 523.
[25] *Landauer & Co.* v. *Craven and Speeding Brothers* [1912] 2 K.B. 94; *Hansson* v. *Hamel and Horley Ltd.* [1922] 2 A.C. 36.
[26] *Stein* v. *Hambros Bank of Northern Commerce* (1922) 10 Ll.L. Rep. 529.

any expense as a result of the arrival of the goods before the documents. The practice of banks in this country is not uniform in regard to stale bills of lading; it would seem that most banks prefer to use their discretion in each particular case.[27]

23-31. The bills of lading should be endorsed in blank by the party (usually the shipper) in whose favour they are drawn. Sometimes, however, the credit provides that the bills are to be in favour of the issuing bank; in this event, of course, the bills are not endorsed.

23-32. The effect of Article 30 of the *Uniform Customs* is that, although the description of the goods in the invoice must correspond with the description in the credit, the description in the remaining documents, including the bill of lading, may be in "general terms." Thus, in one case,[28] the credit referred to "Chilean Fish Fullmeal." The invoice described the goods in the same way, but the bills of lading simply referred to "Chilean Fishmeal." It was held that the bills of lading contained a sufficient general description of the goods.

23-33. In an earlier case where the *Uniform Customs* had no application,[29] the credit called for invoice and bills of lading evidencing shipment from Hongkong to Hamburg of "Hongkong duck feathers—85 per cent clean, 12 bales each weighing about 190 lb." The invoice set out the description in full and also the shipping mark. The bill of lading gave the same shipping mark and then "12 bales Hongkong duck feathers." There was no reference in the bill of lading to the weight of the bales or to "85 per cent clean." In fact, the bill contained a "weight and quality unknown" clause as follows: "Weight, measure, marks, numbers, quality, contents, and value if mentioned in the bill of lading are to be considered unknown unless the contrary has been expressly acknowledged and agreed to." The bank treated the invoice and bill of lading as being a sufficient compliance with the terms of the credit. Eventually, when the goods arrived, it was found that the feathers were "simply rubbish," and the customer maintained that the bank should have refused the bill of lading. The customer said, in effect, that by virtue of the "weight and quality unknown" clause, the bill of lading contained no description at all. Devlin, J., rejecting this argument, said[30]—

The clause is so well known and it is so almost universal to find a clause of this character in the bill of lading that I think it must be taken

---

[27] For a fuller discussion, see H. C. Gutteridge and Maurice Megrah, *The Law of Bankers' Commercial Credits* (4th ed., 1968), p. 89.
[28] *Soproma S.p.A.* v. *Marine & Animal By-Products Corporation* [1966] 1 Lloyd's Rep. 367.
[29] *Midland Bank Ltd.* v. *Seymour* [1955] 2 Lloyd's Rep. 147.
[30] Ibid., at p. 155.

that what the letter of credit requires is the description in the body of
the bill, whether or not it is accompanied by such a clause. . . . It is
sufficient that the description should be contained in the set of documents
as a whole and that the documents should each one be valid in itself and
each be consistent with the other; and, accordingly, it would not matter
for this purpose whether the description in the bill of lading is or is not
negatived by the clause in the bill of lading, since the description is
sufficiently contained in the invoice, which is one of the documents.

23-34. Another way of qualifying the quantity or weight of goods
shipped is by inserting in the bill of lading the words "said to." For
example, a bill of lading may acknowledge shipment of "a quantity
said to be 4,000 rods of iron, said to weigh 400 tons." Such a bill
would be a good tender. It should be noted, however, that the words
"said to" are qualifying merely the quantity and weight of the goods.
If the words qualified the description of the goods themselves, the
bill would probably be a bad tender. Thus, in one case, the bill of
lading acknowledged shipment of "28 packages said to contain
lorries," whereas it should have covered "28 new Chevrolet trucks";
the contention that the bill was defective was not challenged.[31]

23-35. Article 32 of the *Uniform Customs* provides—

> The words "about," "circa" or similar expressions are to be con-
> strued as allowing a difference not to exceed 10% more or 10% less,
> applicable, according to their place in the instructions, to the amount
> of the credit or to the quantity or unit price of the goods.
>
> Unless a credit stipulates that the quantity of the goods specified must
> not be exceeded or reduced, a tolerance of 3% more or 3% less will
> be permissible, always provided that the total amount of the drawings
> does not exceed the amount of the credit. This tolerance does not apply
> when the credit specifies quantity in terms of packing units or containers
> or individual items.

The 3% tolerance provision appears to depart from the rule
previously laid down by the court in *Moralice (London) Ltd.* v.
E. D. & F. Mann.[32] In that case a credit called for bills of lading
evidencing shipment of 500 metric tons of sugar in bags of 100 kilos,
i.e., a total of 5,000 bags, and it was held that documents relating to
4,997 bags of 100 kilos were not a good tender.

23-36. *Indemnities.* Occasionally, it will be found that there is some
irregularity in the documents presented under a credit. Strictly,
the documents should be rejected, but a sensible business course
is to communicate with the applicant for the credit and ask for further

---

[31] *Bank Melli Iran* v. *Barclays Bank (Dominion, Colonial and Overseas)* [1951] 2
T.L.R. 1057, at p. 1062.
[32] [1954] 2 Lloyd's Rep. 526.

instructions. Another course which is sometimes adopted is to make payment to the beneficiary against an indemnity, but this is a policy which should be pursued with caution because the applicant for the credit may reject the documents. Broadly speaking, therefore, this procedure should be adopted only in cases where the beneficiary's financial position is known to be undoubted for the amount of the transaction. Particular care should be taken if the bill of lading is unclean; for example, if it shows that the goods were received on board in a defective state or with packages broken. Normally, such bills should be rejected or further instructions sought from the applicant for the credit, but if, in exceptional circumstances, it is decided to pay against an indemnity, it is often sound policy to insist that the indemnity be executed not only by the beneficiary but also by his bank. Sometimes, it is no easy matter to decide whether to refuse payment altogether or to pay against an indemnity. Indeed, the art of handling documentary credit business successfully is the skilful use of discretion in taking documents which are not strictly in order from a legal point of view.

B. REVOCABLE DOCUMENTARY CREDIT

23-37. Sometimes, an overseas buyer arranges for the opening of a revocable documentary credit in London in favour of the exporter. This type of credit is less satisfactory, from the exporter's point of view, than an irrevocable credit.[33] Article 2 of the *Uniform Customs* provides—

> A revocable credit does not constitute a legally binding undertaking between the bank or banks concerned and the beneficiary because such a credit may be modified or cancelled at any moment without notice to the beneficiary.
>
> When, however, a revocable credit has been transmitted to and made available at a branch or other bank, its modification or cancellation shall become effective only upon receipt of notice thereof by such branch or other bank and shall not affect the right of that branch or other bank to be reimbursed for any payment, acceptance or negotiation made by it prior to receipt of such notice.

As in the case of an irrevocable documentary credit, a revocable documentary credit specifies the shipping documents which must accompany the bills of exchange drawn under the credit.

C. ACCEPTANCE CREDIT OPENED BY EXPORTER

23-38. Sometimes, an exporter makes his own arrangements with an accepting house or bank for an acceptance credit. The accepting

[33] See *ante*, para. 22-34.

house or bank will usually require security, such as the pledge to them of the shipping documents. They will forward these documents to their agent in the importer's country, to be released to the importer against payment.

D. NEGOTIATION OF BILLS UNDER A DOCUMENTARY CREDIT

23-39. The overseas buyer arranges for the London branch of his bank to negotiate bills drawn by the exporter *upon the importer*, provided that the bills are accompanied by the shipping documents. The exporter draws his bills on the importer and presents them, together with the documents, to the London branch, which purchases the bills in accordance with the credit. The bank then forwards the bills and the documents to the importer's country where the documents are surrendered to the importer either in exchange for cash or against acceptance of the bills.

E. NO CREDIT ESTABLISHED

23-40. If no credit has been established by either importer or exporter, the exporter will probably draw bills of exchange upon the importer and deliver them to his own bank which may either (*i*) negotiate them, or (*ii*) make an advance against them, or (*iii*) merely take them for collection.

(i) Negotiation of Bills without a Credit

23-41. If the exporter's bank is prepared to negotiate bills for a customer (and this will depend upon several factors, such as the standing of the exporter and of the buyer, and the marketability of the goods), the bank will decide whether to calculate forthwith the amount of interest to be deducted from the face value of each bill, or whether to handle the bills on a "charges after payment" basis. Whichever method is adopted, the bank will ask its customer to complete a printed form giving precise instructions concerning the bill. The *Uniform Rules* call this form a "remittance letter."[34]

23-42. The legal effect of the negotiation of the bill is that the negotiating bank becomes the holder in due course of the bill[35] and also holds the shipping documents by way of security. Thus the bank will be a pledgee of the goods and, if it holds a letter of pledge[36]

---

[34] See General Provision (c) of the *Uniform Rules*.
[35] Bills of Exchange Act, 1882, Sect. 29.
[36] *Ante*, para. 22-6.

signed by the customer, it will have the rights conferred upon it by that document.

23-43. If the bill is dishonoured, the negotiating bank will look primarily to its own customer as drawer to reimburse it in respect of the amount of the bill, together with interest and charges. In this connection, the Bills of Exchange Act, 1882[37] provides that the drawer of a bill engages that on due presentment it will be accepted and paid, and that if it is dishonoured he will compensate the holder, provided that the requisite proceedings on dishonour are duly taken. Furthermore, the bank as holder in due course, would also have the right to claim against the drawee if the latter had accepted the bill, but, as stated above, the bank looks primarily to its own customer for reimbursement.

23-44. Unless the goods have been surrendered to the drawee against his acceptance of the bill, they will be in a warehouse abroad or (one hopes) otherwise protected: warehouse space may not always be available. As a last resort, steps could be taken by the bank, as pledgee, to realise the goods to the best advantage, but this may not always be easy, especially if the market price of the goods is falling.

(ii) *Advance against Bills*

23-45. If the exporter's bank is not prepared to negotiate the bills drawn upon the importer, it may be willing to make an advance of a certain percentage of the face value of the bills. The bank will make a careful examination of the shipping documents which accompany the bills, and will request its customer to complete the usual form giving precise instructions, which will be passed forward, together with the bills and shipping documents, to the bank's overseas correspondent.

23-46. The bank becomes a pledgee of the goods, and, by virtue of the Bills of Exchange Act, 1882,[38] it is deemed to be a holder for value of the bills to the extent of the sum for which it has a lien, i.e., to the extent of the advance.

(iii) *Collection of Bills*

23-47. In this instance, the bank simply takes the bills on a collection basis without providing its customer with any finance at all. The customer completes the usual form giving instructions regarding the

[37] Sect. 55(1).
[38] Sect. 27 (3).

bills and the shipping documents. The bank sends these to its over-seas correspondent, and, when the proceeds are available, they are credited to the customer's account, after the deduction of collection charges. By collecting the proceeds in this way, the bank does not usually become holder for value of the bills, unless it has a lien over the bills arising out of some other transaction.

Import of Goods

23-48. As in the case of the export of goods, documentary credits are extensively used in order to finance imports into this country.[39] The importer usually completes a printed application form addressed to his own bank asking that a credit be established. This form describes the goods which are the subject of the shipment and sets forth the documents which must accompany the seller's drafts. Unless the credit is fully covered by cash, the bank will usually require a pledge of the goods concerned. The following are the terms frequently contained in an application to a bank in this country for a documentary credit without cash cover—

(i) The customer undertakes to provide the bank with funds to meet drafts drawn under the credit. In the case of sight drafts the funds must be provided on or before presentation of the drafts, and, in the case of acceptances, three days before maturity thereof.

(ii) The bank and its correspondents are not to be responsible for the genuineness, correctness or form of any document or documents or any endorsement thereon, or for any misrepresentation as to the quantity, quality or value of any goods comprised therein.

(iii) If the goods are not covered by insurance to the bank's satisfaction, the bank is authorised to insure them, and the customer undertakes to repay to the bank the amount of the premiums.

(iv) The goods which are the subject of the credit and the documents of title thereto are pledged to the bank as a continuing security for all advances made or to be made by the bank to the customer, and for all payments which may be made by the bank or its correspondents under the credit. In the event of a sale of the goods by the bank, the customer undertakes to pay on demand the amount of any deficiency on such sale, together with all usual commission and charges and expenses incidental thereto.

(v) The bank is not to be liable for any mistake or omission in the transmission of messages by cable.

[39] For a more detailed account, see Vol. 1, paras. 8-120/132.

(vi) The *Uniform Customs and Practice for Documentary Credits* (*1962 Revision*) are to apply.

23-49. Clause (iv) above is the security clause whereby the bank obtains a pledge of the goods which are the subject of the transaction. The question has been raised whether a customer could defeat the bank's security by rejecting the goods when they arrived in this country on the ground, for example, that the goods were not in conformity with the contract. In *Chao* v. *British Traders Ltd.*,[40] Devlin, J., considered this question, but on the facts of the particular case, he did not find it necessary to answer it, though he added that it was a matter to which attention might be paid by those who are concerned with it. Some banks have acted upon the suggestion made by the learned judge and have re-drafted this clause in their application forms.

23-50. When the overseas seller presents a complete set of documents, as required by the credit, to the English bank's correspondent in the foreign centre, the seller will either receive cash against the documents if it is a foreign currency credit, or will negotiate his draft drawn on the English bank if it is a sterling credit. The documents will be sent to the importer's bank in England. As a result of the "security clause" contained in the application form outlined above, that bank becomes the pledgee of the goods as soon as either (*a*) its foreign currency account has been debited abroad, or (*b*) it has honoured the beneficiary's sterling draft drawn on itself, as the case may be.

23-51. If the customer is able to provide his bank with funds to meet the drafts drawn under the credit, the bank will, of course, immediately release the documents to him so that he may collect the goods upon their arrival.[41] In some cases, however, the customer will be unable forthwith to provide the bank with funds to meet the drafts, and it remains to consider the steps which may be taken to facilitate disposal of the goods without prejudicing the bank's security.

Trust Receipts

23-52. One possible course would be for the bank to collect the goods from the ship in exchange for the bills of lading, warehouse them, and arrange for their sale. This procedure, however, would involve the bank in a considerable amount of work, and an even weightier

---

[40] [1954] 1 All E.R. 779, at p. 796.

[41] If the ship is lost and the goods never arrive, a claim will be made under the terms of the marine insurance policy.

objection is that customers strongly object to being deprived of the control of their goods in this way.

23-53. In suitable cases the bank will be prepared to release the bills of lading to the customer in exchange for a "trust receipt" or "trust letter" signed by the customer. By signing this document, the customer gives certain undertakings to the bank. Thus, he undertakes to hold the documents, the goods represented thereby, and the net proceeds thereof as trustee for the bank. If the intention is to warehouse the goods, the customer undertakes to warehouse them in the name of the bank, to deliver the warehousekeeper's warrants to the bank and to insure the goods. If the goods are to be sold, the customer undertakes to pay the proceeds of all sales to the bank, and to give to the bank on request authority to receive from the buyers the purchase moneys for the goods. As regards the stamp duty on the document, it is not certain whether the letter is exempt from stamp duty as an agreement under hand, or whether it should be stamped 10s. (50p) as a declaration of trust.[42] In practice it seems to be assumed that the document is exempt from duty.

23-54. MacKinnon, L.J., once described the system of obtaining trust receipts as a "very convenient business method."[43] The object is to maintain the original pledge, so that, if the customer becomes bankrupt, the goods will not be claimable by his trustee in bankruptcy for the benefit of his unsecured creditors. There is no doubt that it is effective for this purpose.[44] Of course, there are very obvious risks in permitting a customer to deal with the goods in this way: if he is dishonest, he may sell the goods and divert the proceeds of sale from his bank, or he may pledge the goods to some other lender, who will thereby obtain priority over the pledge in favour of the bank, provided that the second lender acts bona fide and without notice of the prior pledge.[45] In order to reduce the risk of loss to a minimum, the bank will naturally keep in close touch with the position. If the bills of lading are released in order that the goods may be warehoused in the bank's name, the bank will expect to receive a warehousekeeper's warrant within a reasonable period; and when documents are released in order that the goods may be sold, inquiry should be made, if the proceeds are not presently forthcoming. Most important of all, the bank should

---

[42] See *post*, para. 33-52.
[43] *Lloyds Bank Ltd.* v. *Bank of America National Trust and Savings Association* [1938] 2 K.B. 147, at p. 166.
[44] *North Western Bank Ltd.* v. *John Poynter, Son & Macdonalds* [1895] A.C. 56; *Re David Allester Ltd.* [1922] 2 Ch. 211.
[45] *Lloyds Bank Ltd.* v. *Bank of American National Trust and Savings Association* (*supra*). For the facts of this case see *post*, para. 25-4.

permit the system of trust receipts to be used only by customers whose integrity is undoubted; for, as a very distinguished judge wisely remarked, "mercantile genius consists principally in knowing whom to trust and with whom to deal, and commercial intercourse and communication is no more based on the supposition of fraud than it is on the supposition of forgery."[46]

Pledge of Goods Carried by Plane

23-55. Since the end of the Second World War, there has been a considerable increase in the volume of goods carried by plane, and it is not unnatural that merchants should expect the banks to be able to finance these movements of merchandise in much the same way as they finance the import and export of goods by sea.[47] When goods are sent by plane, the Carriage by Air Act, 1932,[48] provides that the carrier has the right to require the consignor to make out and hand over to him a document called an "air consignment note." This instrument is required to be in three original parts—

(i) The first part is for the carrier and is signed by the consignor. It constitutes the carrier's evidence of the contract of affreightment.

(ii) The second part is for the consignee, and is signed by both the consignor and the carrier. It is carried on the plane with the goods and is delivered to the consignee.

(iii) The third part is for the consignor. It is signed by the carrier and handed by him to the consignor after the goods have been accepted. This part acknowledges receipt of the merchandise and sets out the terms of the contract of carriage.

23-56. A bill of lading and an air consignment note have this in common: both acknowledge the receipt of goods, and both are evidence of the terms of a contract of affreightment. There the similarity ceases, for it is impossible to regard an air consignment note as a document of title to goods, whereas a bill of lading is a document of title.

23-57. The result is that a bank cannot obtain a valid pledge of goods by obtaining a deposit of an air consignment note; the deposit of such a note does not pass the constructive possession of the goods to the bank. Nevertheless, an air consignment note sometimes serves a limited purpose in bank security work. Thus, credits are occasionally

---

[46] *Per* Bowen, L.J., in *Sanders Brothers* v. *Maclean & Co.* (1883) 11 Q.B.D. 327, at p. 343.

[47] For articles on this subject, see W. W. Syrett, "The Air Consignment Note," *Journal of the Institute of Bankers*, Vol. LXX (1949), pp. 142–5, and F. R. Ryder, "Security over Produce. The Air Consignment Note," op cit., pp. 181–7.

[48] Sect. 1 and Sched. 1.

opened under which a London banker is instructed to obtain from an English merchant (who is exporting goods by plane) an invoice, an insurance policy, and the third part—the consignor's part—of the air consignment note. The bank is authorised to make payment against tender of these documents.

23-58. If a credit has not been opened and a customer of a bank in this country wishes to create a pledge over goods to be dispatched by him by plane, it would seem that the most satisfactory method is for the bank, by arrangement with its correspondent overseas, to require its customer to consign the goods to its correspondent. When the goods arrive, they will be delivered to or to the order of that bank, which will thus obtain possession of them. The bank in this country should hold a suitable letter of pledge whereby the customer agrees that his bank shall have a pledge upon all goods delivered by him or his agents into the possession of the bank or its agents.[49]

Goods in an Independent Warehouse

23-59. In the preceding paragraphs of this chapter attention has been directed to the financing of the movement of goods from one country to another. Occasionally, a bank is asked to lend money against the security of goods which are already warehoused in this country. Broadly speaking, the steps which should be taken depend upon whether the goods are stored on the customer's own premises or are warehoused in premises owned by some third party. In both cases the problem is basically the same, namely, to create a pledge of the goods in favour of the bank.

23-60. Let it be supposed, in the first place, that the goods are in an independent warehouse, that is to say, a warehouse which is neither owned by, nor let to, the customer; and let it be assumed that he has been given a warehousekeeper's receipt acknowledging that the goods are held on his behalf. This instrument is not a document of title to the goods;[50] and thus the mere deposit of the receipt with a bank will not create a valid pledge. The bank will, therefore, ask its customer to sign a transfer order directing the warehousekeeper to hold the goods in the name of the bank. The receipt and the transfer order should be lodged immediately with the warehousekeeper and a new receipt obtained in the bank's favour before the advance is granted. As soon as the warehousekeeper attorns to the bank, the

---

[49] *Ante*, para. 23-6.
[50] See *ante*, para. 22-24. But it *is* a document of title for the purpose of the Factors Act, 1889, and the Sale of Goods Act, 1893; see *post*, para. 25-5.

goods are within the constructive possession of the bank, and the pledge is complete.[51] Thereafter, the goods can be released only by the issue of a transfer order or a delivery order executed by authorised officials of the bank, whose specimen signatures should be supplied to the warehousekeeper.

23-61. There are several other steps which the bank should take. It is advisable, as it is in all cases of pledge, to hold a letter of pledge signed by the customer.[52] An endeavour should be made to limit the usual lien of the warehousekeeper for unpaid charges to those in respect of the particular goods specified on the receipt issued to the bank, otherwise the goods may be held until charges relating to other goods stored by the customer in the same warehouse have been paid. The difficulty is, however, that some warehousekeepers will not waive their general lien. It is, of course, for the customer to pay the warehouse charges, and the bank should verify that these payments are not allowed to fall into arrear. The goods should be kept fully insured, and notice of the bank's interest should be given to the insurance company.[53] If the goods are subject to considerable price fluctuation, the bank will naturally watch the market very closely and require the customer to maintain an adequate margin.

23-62. So far it has been assumed that the deposit of the customer's goods in the warehouse was acknowledged by the issue of a warehousekeeper's receipt. Let it be supposed that, instead of being given a receipt, the customer received a warehousekeeper's warrant. These warrants may be divided into two categories: (i) those which are transferable by virtue of the provisions of a private Act of Parliament, and (ii) those which are not.[54] Banks conducting business in one of our ports will, of course, familiarise themselves with the types of instrument issued by the various warehousekeepers in that port. Warrants in category (ii) are not documents of title,[55] and the only method of obtaining a pledge of the goods is by lodging the warrants with the warehousekeeper and obtaining a new warrant or receipt in favour of the bank. If, however, the bank is satisfied that the warrants are transferable under a private Act and are, therefore, documents of title, a valid pledge of the goods may be obtained by securing a deposit of the warrants. Nevertheless, unless the advance is for a very short period, it is the usual practice for the

[51] See *per* Lord Parker in *Dublin City Distillery (Great Brunswick Street Dublin) Ltd.* v. *Doherty* [1914] A.C. 823, at p. 852.
[52] *Ante*, para. 23-6.
[53] See *ante*, para. 3-66.
[54] *Ante*, paras. 22-20/23.
[55] Except for the purpose of the Factors Act, 1889, and the Sale of Goods Act, 1893; see *post*, para. 25-5.

bank to lodge the warrants with the warehousekeeper and to obtain a new warrant or receipt in its own favour.

Goods on Customer's Own Premises

23-63. At first sight it might seem impossible to obtain a pledge of goods which are stored on the customer's premises, because the essence of a pledge is that possession—either actual or constructive —must pass to the lender. There is, however, one way of overcoming this difficulty. The bank may take a lease at a nominal rent of part of the customer's premises, and the goods to be pledged may be stored therein. That part of the building is "sealed off," and the keys to it are handed to the bank. This certainly suffices to give the bank possession. If some of the goods are to be withdrawn, the attendance of a bank official is required, unless the bank is prepared to appoint the pledgor as its agent for this purpose. This method of obtaining a pledge is obviously not free from risk, and it should be used only in the case of customers of the highest standing. There is always the possibility that the customer may have a duplicate set of keys and may sell the goods to an innocent third party. Furthermore, in the event of the customer's bankruptcy, it is conceivable that the goods might be claimed by his trustee in bankruptcy as being within the "possession, order, or disposition" of the bankrupt.[56]

[56] Bankruptcy Act, 1914, Sect. 38.

CHAPTER 24

The Hypothecation of Goods

24-1. HYPOTHECATION is a legal transaction whereby goods may be made available as security for a debt without transferring *either* the property *or* the possession to the lender.[1] The law on this subject is complex, and there are some problems which still await solution by the courts. In this chapter it is intended first to indicate those cases where a banker may be asked to rely upon the hypothecation of goods as security for an advance, secondly to examine some of the errors which lenders have made in the past and, finally, to try to outline, in the light of the present authorities, the procedure which ought to be followed in order to create a valid hypothecation.

24-2. If a customer is in possession (whether actual or constructive) of goods, he will normally be able to pass that possession to his banker. Accordingly, he will usually be able to create a valid pledge of the goods. In some instances, however, it is impossible for a banker to be given the actual or constructive possession of goods, and it is in these cases that the possibility of hypothecating them must be considered. For example, the goods may be in a part of the customer's own warehouse which cannot be sealed off in such a way as to enable the banker to become a pledgee.[2]

The Lender's Risks

24-3. The risks of lending against the hypothecation of goods are twofold. First, there is the obvious practical consideration that, since the lender does not obtain actual or constructive possession of the goods, his measure of control over them is often very limited, with the result that the borrower will probably have ample opportunity of dealing with them fraudulently. The fact that the borrower may thereafter find himself in prison is but cold comfort to a lender who has lost money. The second type of risk arises from the extraordinary complexity of the Bills of Sale Acts. Many instruments used in connection with transactions of this sort require registration under these Acts and, if not registered, are void. If one knew precisely when an instrument requires registration, the position would be

[1] *Ante*, para. 22-11.
[2] See *ante*, para. 23-63.

easier, but, as the authorities stand at the moment, he would be a bold lawyer who would profess to say with absolute certainty whether any particular instrument does or does not fall within the Acts.

24-4. In *National Provincial and Union Bank of England* v. *Lindsell*[3] a bank failed to obtain a valid charge over goods because the charge had not been registered as a bill of sale. A customer of the bank was the owner of a car, which he delivered to a Mr. Lindsell, who was a motor engineer, for the purpose of being repaired. The customer wrote to Mr. Lindsell as follows: "This is to authorise you to hold the Sava car at present in your hands to the order of the National Provincial and Union Bank of England Ltd., Tunbridge Wells, or the proceeds when sold after deducting your own account. (Signed) K. Welding." He also forwarded a copy of the letter to the bank. Later, Mr. Lindsell sold the car on the customer's instructions and, after his own repairing charges had been satisfied, he had a balance of £235 which he ought to have paid over to the bank under the terms of the letter. The customer, however, falsely represented to him that "he had made it all right with the bank" and that the bank was content to receive £135 out of the proceeds. Mr. Lindsell, therefore, remitted this sum to the bank and handed the balance of £100 to the customer. The bank thereupon brought an action against Mr. Lindsell claiming a declaration that they were assignees of the proceeds of sale of the car and claiming payment from him of the £100 which he had paid to the customer. Judgment was given for the defendant. It was held that the letter signed by the customer was void, so far as it constituted a charge on the car, as being an unregistered bill of sale, and that, although the car had been sold and was represented by the proceeds in the repairer's hands, the invalid charge on the car could not be separated from the charge on the proceeds so as to make the latter valid.[4]

24-5. This case, therefore, stands as a warning to bankers. In order to perfect its security without the necessity of registering a bill of sale, the bank should have obtained a pledge of the car by arranging for the repairer to attorn to the bank. This would have given to the bank the constructive possession of the vehicle.[5] Thereafter the customer could have signed a letter addressed to the bank setting out

[3] [1922] 1 K.B. 21.
[4] Where a limited company executes a charge created or evidenced by an instrument which, if executed by an individual, would require registration as a bill of sale, such charge will be void if it is not registered under the Companies Act, 1948: see *post*, para. 32-4. For an example see *Dublin City Distillery (Great Brunswick Street, Dublin) Ltd.* v. *Doherty* [1914] A.C. 823.
[5] See *ante*, para. 23-5.

the terms of the transaction, and this letter would not have required registration as a bill of sale. The distinction may appear to be somewhat illogical, but the rule is that if goods have already passed out of the possession of the pledgor, documents subsequently executed evidencing the transaction are not bills of sale.[6]

Goods in Foreign Parts or at Sea

24-6. There are several exceptional cases where bills of sale do not require registration. One of these which is occasionally of importance to bankers relates to "bills of sale of goods in foreign parts or at sea."[7] In *R. v. Townshend*[8] a customer applied to his bankers for an advance against certain goods which had been consigned to him and were still at sea. The bank obtained from him an instrument which was referred to as a "hypothecation note" by which he undertook to hold the goods in trust for the bank and to hand over the proceeds in due course. There was no prior pledge of the goods. It was held that, although the instrument was a declaration of trust without transfer and was therefore a bill of sale, it did not require registration, because it fell within the exception stated above.

Goods in this Country

24-7. The question is whether it is possible to create a valid hypothecation of goods in this country by means of an instrument which does not require registration as a bill of sale. The Bills of Sale Acts of 1854 and 1878 exempt from their provisions any "transfers of goods in the ordinary course of business of any trade or calling" and also any "documents used in the ordinary course of business as proof of the possession or control of goods."[9] In several reported cases these exemptions have proved to be of assistance to lenders.

24-8. Thus, in *Ex parte North Western Bank*[10] a letter of hypothecation over wools of a bankrupt which were in his warehouse was held to create a good equitable charge in favour of bankers who had made advances; no delivery of the warrant for wools had been made; but it was held that the bankers had a good title against the

[6] *Ex parte Hubbard* (1866) 17 Q.B.D. 690, approved by the House of Lords in *Charlesworth* v. *Mills* [1892] A.C. 231.
[7] Bills of Sale Act, 1878, Sect. 4.
[8] (1884) 15 Cox C.C. 466.
[9] Sect. 7 of the 1854 Act; Sect. 4 of the 1878 Act.
[10] (1872) L.R. 15 Eq. 69.

trustee in bankruptcy. The equitable charge did not require registration, because the advance and charge had been made in the ordinary course of business.

24-9. The case was decided under the 1854 Act, but it was followed and approved in a decision under the Act of 1878, *Re Hamilton Young & Co.*,[11] where customers of a bank had obtained advances from their bank on the security of cloth belonging to them which was then in the hands of bleachers. The customers gave to the bank "letters of lien," accompanied by the bleachers' receipts for the goods. These letters were drafted as follows—

> We beg to advise having drawn a cheque on you for £ , which please place to the debit of our loan account No. 2, as a loan on the security of goods in course of preparation for shipment to the East. As security for this advance we hold on your account and under lien to you the undermentioned goods in the hands of [here followed list of goods and names of bleachers] as per their receipt enclosed. These goods when ready will be shipped to Calcutta, and the bills of lading duly endorsed will be handed to you.

The bank gave notice of their lien to the bleachers and, shortly afterwards, the customers were adjudicated bankrupt. The Court of Appeal decided that the charge in favour of the bank was valid. It was held that the letters of lien were not void for want of registration under the Bills of Sale Acts, because they were "documents used in the ordinary course of business as proof of the possession or control of goods" within the exception in the Act of 1878.[12] Furthermore, it was decided that the transaction could not be impeached on the ground that at the commencement of the bankruptcy the goods were "in the possession, order or disposition of the bankrupt" as "the reputed owner thereof" within the meaning of the Bankruptcy Act, 1883.[13] Although the bank gave notice of its lien to the bleachers, its rights did not depend upon the giving of notice. This was made clear in a subsequent case decided by the Privy Council.[14] Obviously, however, it is a wise precaution to take.

24-10. It is not easy to assess the precise value of the *Hamilton Young* case, particularly as a guide for the future. It is not that one doubts the correctness of the decision itself, for it has been cited by the Privy Council without any trace of disapproval;[15] the real

[11] [1905] 2 K.B. 772.
[12] Sect. 4.
[13] Sect. 44, now replaced by the Bankruptcy Act, 1914, Sect. 38.
[14] *Official Assignee of Madras* v. *Mercantile Bank of India Ltd.* [1935] A.C. 53, at p. 65.
[15] *Official Assignee of Madras, etc., supra.*

difficulty is to say with certainty whether any particular instrument would be held to be a document "used in the ordinary course of business as proof of the possession or control of goods." Bankers are well aware of this problem, and it is usual to adopt a form of instrument very similar to that which was upheld in the *Hamilton Young* case. Even so, it might still be necessary to satisfy the court, by adducing appropriate evidence, that instruments of the type in question are in general commercial usage. In the *Hamilton Young* case counsel for the trustee in bankruptcy argued in the Court of Appeal that the learned judge in the court below had held that the instruments were "documents used in the ordinary course of business as proof of the possession or control of goods" without any evidence having been adduced to that effect. Counsel then sought to introduce an affidavit by the trustee showing that no such practice prevailed in commerce. The Court of Appeal declined to admit this affidavit, because it had not been used in the court below and there had been no cross-examination upon it. One can only speculate as to what might have happened if the affidavit had been available in the lower court: the case might well have been decided against the bank. The possibility of this kind of development in any future case which comes before the courts should not be overlooked.

CHAPTER 25

Statutory Protection for Lenders

25-1. THERE is a general rule of the Common Law that a man cannot give a better title to property than he himself possesses. This is often expressed in the maxim *nemo dat quod non habet*. If, therefore, a customer steals certain property and pledges it to his banker as security for a loan, the banker—although acting in perfect good faith without any knowledge of the theft—will usually obtain no title thereto and will be obliged to return it to the person from whom it was stolen. As Blackburn, J., said: "At common law, a person in possession of goods could not confer on another, either by sale or by pledge, any better title to the goods than he himself had."[1] There are few exceptions to this general principle. The most important of them relates to negotiable instruments. A pledgee of such an instrument is entitled to the same favourable treatment as a transferee for value.[2] Goods, however, are not negotiable; neither are bills of lading or other documents of title.[3] Thus, the pledgee of stolen goods will nearly always be forced to restore them to the true owner, unless it can be proved that the goods have been sold in "market overt" after having been stolen;[4] or unless it can be shown that the true owner is estopped (i.e. precluded) from asserting his rights, as would be the case if he knowingly stood by when the pledge was made.

Pledges by Mercantile Agents

25-2. The maxim *nemo dat quod non habet* was also applicable in cases where factors or other similar agents pledged the goods of their principals without authority. Although it was quite common for factors who had received goods for disposal to advance sums to their principals and then to pledge the goods to provide themselves with funds, the courts consistently held that a pledge, as distinct from

---

[1] *Cole* v. *North Western Bank* (1875) 44 L.J.C.P. 233, at pp. 236–7.

[2] *Collins* v. *Martin* (1797) 1 B. & P. 648; *London Joint Stock Bank* v. *Simmons* [1892] A.C. 201; see *ante*, para, 16-6.

[3] Exceptionally, certain warehousekeepers' warrants issued under private Acts of Parliament would appear to be negotiable. See *ante*, para. 22-21.

[4] "Market overt" is the name applied to recognised markets throughout the country, or to any shop in the City of London. For the other requirements of a sale in "market overt," see *Stevens and Borrie's Elements of Mercantile Law* (15th ed., 1969), p. 184.

a sale, did not raise an estoppel against the principal so as to confer a good title on an innocent pledgee.[5] This "hard doctrine," as Lord Ellenborough once called it,[6] was eventually modified by Parliament. The relevant statutory provisions are obviously important to bankers and other lenders, though one should not lose sight of the fact that a practical banker relies more on his judgment of his customer than on this somewhat complicated legislation.

25-3. The Factors Act, 1889, defines a mercantile agent as one "having in the customary course of his business as such agent authority either to sell goods, or to consign goods for the purpose of sale, or to buy goods, or to raise money on the security of goods."[7] Section 2 of the Act provides that, where a mercantile agent is, with the consent of the owner, in possession of goods or of the documents of title to goods, any pledge made by him when acting in the ordinary course of business of a mercantile agent is to be as valid as if he were expressly authorised by the owner to make the pledge, provided, of course, that the pledgee acts in good faith and has no notice that the agent did not have authority to make the pledge. There is, however, a very important restriction in Sect. 4 of the Act, which declares, in effect, that the protection conferred by the Act upon pledgees does not apply where the debt due from the pledgor to the pledgee already existed at the date of the pledge.

25-4. Many decisions of the courts have been necessary to interpret some of the phrases used in Sect. 2 of the Act, but a detailed discussion of this branch of the law is beyond the scope of this work.[8] There is, however, one case in particular which deserves the careful consideration of bankers. In *Lloyds Bank Ltd.* v. *Bank of America National Trust and Savings Association*,[9] Strauss & Co. Ltd. pledged certain goods to Lloyds Bank as security for an advance. The company subsequently obtained possession of the documents of title by giving a trust receipt to the bank. In breach of good faith and in breach of their contract, the company pledged the goods to an American bank and thereby improperly obtained money upon the value of them. The question to be determined was which bank was entitled to the security. The Court of Appeal decided that Sect. 2 of the Factors Act was applicable to these transactions

---

[5] One of the earliest cases establishing this principle was *Paterson* v. *Tash* (1743) 2 Str. 1178.
[6] *Pickering* v. *Busk* (1812) 15 East 38, at p. 44.
[7] Sect. 1.
[8] The reader is referred to the standard textbooks, e.g. Benjamin's *Sale of Personal Property*.
[9] [1937] 2 K.B. 631; [1938] 2 K.B. 147.

and that the American bank, being an innocent pledgee, was fully protected. To reach this decision, it was held that the company were mercantile agents and, furthermore, that Lloyds Bank were the "owners" of the goods within the meaning of the section. Although some may feel that this involved giving a very wide meaning to the word "owner," there can be no doubt that the decision is in accordance with the spirit of the legislation, one of the main objects of which is to protect innocent pledgees.[10]

25-5. The Factors Act, 1889,[11] provides that, *for the purposes of the Act*, the expression "document of title" includes—

> any bill of lading, dock warrant, warehousekeeper's certificate and warrant or order for the delivery of goods, and any other document used in the ordinary course of business as proof of the possession or control of goods, or authorising or purporting to authorise, either by endorsement or by delivery, the possessor of the document to transfer or receive goods thereby represented.

Thus many instruments which are not documents of title in the normal way (e.g. warehousekeepers' receipts) are documents of title for the purpose of this legislation. Moreover, the Act declares that "a pledge of the documents of title to goods shall be deemed to be a pledge of the goods."[12] Thus, as Lord Wright stated[13]—

> . . . the curious and anomalous position was established that a mercantile agent, acting it may be in fraud of the true owner, can do that which the real owner cannot do, that is, obtain a loan on the security of a pledge of the goods by a pledge of the documents, without the further process being necessary of giving notice of the pledge to the warehouseman or other custodier and obtaining the latter's attornment to the change of possession.

In this respect, therefore, a banker or other pledgee is in a favoured position when dealing with mercantile agents. In practice, however, bankers always do give notice to the bailee of the goods and obtain his attornment, thus ensuring that the goods are not withdrawn without the bank's knowledge.

---

[10] The case should be contrasted with *Mercantile Bank of India Ltd.* v. *Central Bank of India Ltd.* [1938] A.C. 287, another example of fraudulent double-pledging. Here the *first* pledgee succeeded. The case concerned the pledge of railway receipts to two banks in India, and the special provision of the Factors Act had no application.

[11] Sect. 1. By Sect. 62, Sale of Goods Act, 1893, "document of title" has the same meaning in that Act.

[12] Sect. 3. It has been held that this section applies only to transactions within the Factors Act: *Inglis* v. *Robertson and Baxter* [1898] A.C. 616.

[13] *Official Assignee of Madras* v. *Mercantile Bank of India Ltd.* [1935] A.C. 53, at p. 06.

Pledges by Sellers in Possession

25-6. *Johnson* v. *Crédit Lyonnais Co.*[14] revealed a serious risk to which bankers were then exposed. A tobacco merchant named Hoffman had a quantity of tobacco lying in bond in the warehouses of the St. Katharine's Dock Company, and the usual dock warrants had been issued to him. The plaintiff bought the tobacco from Hoffman and paid for it, but he did not take the tobacco out of bond, as this would have involved paying duty forthwith. Instead, he left the dock warrants in Hoffman's possession and took no steps to have any change made in the books of the dock company as to the ownership of the tobacco. Hoffman, being the ostensible owner of the tobacco, fraudulently obtained advances from the Crédit Lyonnais Co. by pledging to them a portion of the tobacco. They acted in good faith and obtained fresh warrants from the dock company. On the then state of the law, the Court of Appeal held that the plaintiff was entitled to recover the value of the tobacco from the Crédit Lyonnais Co.

25-7. This result was manifestly unjust. Parliament acted swiftly. Shortly after the case had been heard in the Court of Appeal, and even before the court had given judgment, the law was altered by the Factors Act, 1877.[15] The provisions of that Act were substantially reproduced by Sect. 8 of the Factors Act, 1889, which declares that—

> Where a person having sold goods, continues, or is, in possession of the goods or of the documents of title to the goods, the delivery or transfer by that person, or by a mercantile agent acting for him, of the goods or documents of title under any sale, pledge, or other disposition thereof, or under any agreement for sale, pledge, or other disposition thereof, to any person receiving the same in good faith and without notice of the previous sale, shall have the same effect as if the person making the delivery or transfer were expressly authorised by the owner of the goods to make the same.[16]

This section appears to afford ample protection to a banker who lends against the security of goods which, unknown to him, have been sold to a third party.

Pledges by Buyers in Possession

25-8. An unpaid seller of goods has certain rights in relation thereto, which are set forth in the Sale of Goods Act, 1893.[17] Thus, if he is

---

[14] (1877) 3 C.P.D. 32.
[15] Sect. 3. But Sect. 6 declared that the Act applied only to acts done and rights acquired after it was passed: so it did not affect the parties in *Johnson's* case.
[16] Sale of Goods Act, 1893, Sect. 25 (1), contains a similar provision.
[17] Sect. 39.

still in possession he has a lien on them; if the buyer becomes insolvent as defined by the Act, the seller has the right of stopping the goods in transit after he has parted with the possession of them; and in certain cases specified in the Act, he has a right of re-sale. It is clearly of considerable importance to bankers to know to what extent the unpaid vendor's rights still subsist if the buyer pledges the goods to the bank. At one time the bank had no protection. Delivering judgment in a case in 1875, Blackburn, J., said: "It has been repeatedly decided that a sale or pledge of a delivery order or other document of title (not being a bill of lading) by the vendee does not defeat the unpaid vendor's rights . . ."[18]

25-9. The law was altered by the Factors Act, 1877,[19] and the provision in force at present is Sect. 9 of the Factors Act, 1889, which enacts that—

> Where a person, having bought or agreed to buy goods, obtains with the consent of the seller possession of the goods or the documents of title to the goods, the delivery or transfer, by that person or by a mercantile agent acting for him, of the goods or documents of title, under any sale, pledge, or other disposition thereof, or under any agreement for sale, pledge, or other disposition thereof, to any person receiving the same in good faith and without notice of any lien or other right of the original seller in respect of the goods, shall have the same effect as if the person making the delivery or transfer were a mercantile agent in possession of the goods or documents of title with the consent of the owner.[20]

Accordingly, a banker is fully protected if he takes a pledge of the goods, provided that he has no notice of the unpaid seller's rights.

[18] *Cole* v. *North Western Bank* (1875) 44 L.J.C.P. 233, at p. 242.
[19] Sect. 4.
[20] Sale of Goods Act, 1893, Sect. 25 (2), contains a similar provision.

CHAPTER 26

Agricultural Charges

26-1. A SUBSTANTIAL proportion of bankers' advances to farmers is unsecured. There are various reasons for this. First, many farmers do not own their own farms and therefore cannot mortgage them as security for a loan: it is said that sixty per cent of the farms of England and Wales are farmed by tenants.[1] Secondly, one frequently finds that a farmer's capital is nearly all invested in his stock, produce, and farming machinery. It is seldom that a farmer invests in stock exchange securities, though he is becoming increasingly "insurance minded," and sometimes an advance can be arranged against a mortgage of his life policy.

26-2. If a farming advance is to be unsecured, the bank will require from the farmer a statement of his assets and liabilities. Most banks use a printed form for this purpose with separate headings for live and dead stock, debtors, other assets, liabilities in respect of hire-purchase transactions, loans from friends and relations, other creditors, etc. It is a good plan to obtain these statements regularly from all farming customers who need accommodation, whether secured or unsecured. The most suitable time of the year to obtain the statement is during the winter, when growing crops and harvested stocks are lowest. If possible, a bank official should visit the farm personally; and unless the farmer is well known to the bank, the visit should be made without prior appointment, for it is not unknown for an unscrupulous farmer to invite a neighbour to feed his cattle on his land when a visit from the bank manager is expected. Visits of this nature are invaluable. Not only is one able to check the number of cattle and the other items in the balance sheet, but there is also the opportunity of examining the general condition of the farm as a whole. A little experience of this type of work will soon enable a bank official to form a fairly reliable opinion as to the ability and integrity of his customer. The supreme importance of the borrower's character was stressed by Mr. F. L. Bland in a lecture to the Institute of Bankers. "Your success as a country banker," he said, "will show itself in the extent to which your reading

---

[1] Shadrach G. Hooper, "Bankers and Farmers," *Journal of the Institute of Bankers*, Vol. LXXI (1950), p. 49. The same author's book, *The Finance of Farming in Great Britain* (1955), contains a wealth of information which is invaluable to bank officials who have farming customers.

of the farmer's character is correct, far more effectually than in the
accuracy with which you enumerate his sheep or put a price on his
milking cows and baby pigs, his implements or his stacks of corn."[2]

The Enfield Report, 1926

26-3. No one would question Mr. Bland's insistence on the importance of a borrower's character. Nevertheless, it is desirable that
farmers should be able to create a charge over their agricultural
assets. In 1926, Mr. R. R. (now Sir Ralph) Enfield, one of the
officers of the Ministry of Agriculture and Fisheries, prepared a
report on the whole question of agricultural credit.[3] He stated
that a farmer could make his crops and stock available as security
by executing a bill of sale, which would then require to be registered.
The various trade protection papers publish the registration of a bill
of sale, and "the usual effect of this," declared Mr. Enfield, "is to
dry up the fountain of credit from other sources. A bill of sale is
consequently regarded as an instrument which is only used as a
last extremity. . . . It is obvious, however, that to pledge a growing
crop as security for a loan is no more disgraceful than to pledge land
or buildings, and that . . . to do so might be a perfectly proper
and prudent act of a successful farmer."[4]

26-4. Mr. Enfield made the following recommendations[5]—

> Legislation should be enacted enabling a valid charge on certain
> assets, representing "temporary" agricultural wealth, to be given in
> favour of the banks, ranking in priority to all other charges except those
> in respect of rent, rates, and taxes. The charge would be in the form of
> a chattel mortgage, and the character of the commodities which could
> be charged should be defined by law. The execution of a mortgage
> chattel of this kind would be permitted for one purpose only—namely, to
> furnish security for money advanced to agriculturists or agricultural
> co-operative societies by the banks. By reason of the charge ranking in
> priority to other charges (with the above exceptions) a notification of
> the lien created in the property would be necessary only in the case of
> other banks. In these circumstances the problem of registration—the
> chief difficulty as regards the bill of sale—could be greatly simplified. It
> is recommended that provision should be made for the establishment of
> a *central bankers' register* open to inspection by all banks, but not open to
> inspection by the public, in which all mortgages executed under these
> provisions would be registered.

[2] *Journal of the Institute of Bankers*, Vol. LIX (1938), p. 208.
[3] Ministry of Agriculture and Fisheries. Economic Series No. 8. *Report on Agricultural Credit* (1926).
[4] Ibid., pp. 49–50.
[5] Ibid., pp. 51–2.

26-5. Mr. Enfield considered, also, the question of long-term and intermediate credit for the purchase of farms, and for the execution of improvements requiring a substantial outlay. He reported as follows[6]—

> To make long period loans is not part of the ordinary business of the joint stock banks; they prefer to keep their resources more mobile. For this purpose and for this purpose alone, it is therefore recommended that a special lending institution should be created.

With these recommendations as a background, the principal provisions of the Agricultural Credits Act, 1928, will be examined.

Agricultural Credits Act, 1928

26-6. Part I of this Act[7] provided for the incorporation of a company for the purpose of making loans on mortgages of agricultural land and of making loans under the Improvement of Land Acts, 1864 and 1899. This was the special lending institution which Mr. Enfield had envisaged. In due course, a company was registered called the Agricultural Mortgage Corporation Ltd., whose capital was subscribed by the Bank of England and the joint-stock banks. As a general rule, applications for loans are submitted to the Corporation through the banks.[8]

26-7. Part II of the Act enables a farmer to charge "all or any of the farming stock and other agricultural assets belonging to him" as security for an advance from his bank.[9] "Farming stock" is very widely defined and comprises crops or horticultural produce, whether growing or severed from the land; livestock, including poultry and bees, and the produce and progeny thereof; seeds and manures; agricultural vehicles, machinery, and other plant; and agricultural tenant's fixtures and other agricultural fixtures which a tenant is by law authorised to remove.[10]

26-8. An agricultural charge may be either fixed or floating or both.[11] The sum secured by either type of charge may be either a specified amount or a fluctuating amount advanced on current account.[12]

---

[6] Ministry of Agriculture and Fisheries. Economic Series No. 8. *Report on Agricultural Credit* (1926), p. 60.

[7] Sect. 1.

[8] For a useful account of the procedure to be adopted, see Shadrach G. Hooper, *The Finance of Farming in Great Britain*, pp. 90–3.

[9] Sect. 5 (1).

[10] Sect. 5 (7).

[11] Sect. 5 (2). For fixed charges, see *post*, paras. 26-11/12, and for floating charges see *post*, paras. 26-13/14.

[12] Sect. 5 (5).

The charge may be in such form as the parties desire.[13] It is exempt from stamp duty.[14]

26-9. The Act makes provision for the registration of agricultural charges at the Land Registry.[15] An unregistered charge is void as against any person other than the farmer. Registration is deemed to constitute actual notice, but where the charge is expressly made for securing a current account or other further advances, the bank is not deemed to have notice of another charge by reason only of its registration, provided that it was not registered at the time when the bank's own charge was created or when the last search (if any) by or on behalf of the bank was made, whichever last happpened.

26-10. The procedure for registration and for making the search is as follows. When the customer has executed the charge in favour of the bank, it must be registered within seven days, by completing Form A.C.1. This form requires the customer's signature. The fee for registration is 3s. (15p), and this is normally paid by affixing a Land Registry stamp to Form A.C.1, which should be forwarded to the Agricultural Credit Superintendent at the Land Charges Registry, Kidbrooke, London, S.E.3. To make quite sure that the customer has not created a charge in favour of another bank, application for an official search should be made on Form A.C.6, the fee being 3s. (15p). If the form is received by the Department after the morning mail has been attended to, an "expedited" search may be had the same day for an additional fee of 3s. (15p). The result of a search will be telegraphed or telephoned if desired; the additional fee for a telegram to any part of the country is a minimum of 9s. (45p), and for a reply by telephone a minimum of 6s. (30p). When eventually the banker wishes to cancel the entry in the register, he must send in Form A.C.3. The fee for cancellation is 3s. (15p).

Fixed Agricultural Charges

26-11. A fixed charge must specify the property charged, but may include the progeny of any livestock so specified and any agricultural plant subsequently substituted for that originally charged.[16] A fixed charge gives the bank the right, upon the happening of any event specified in the charge, to take possession of the property covered by the charge.[17] After an interval of five clear days or

[13] Sect. 5 (6).
[14] Sect. 8 (8).
[15] Sect. 9.
[16] Sect. 5 (3).
[17] Sect. 6.

such less time as may be allowed by the charge, the bank may sell the property either by auction or, if the charge so provides, by private treaty. The events usually specified are death, bankruptcy, composition or arrangement with creditors, dissolution of partnership, distress or execution against any of the property, and failure to repay the debt upon demand. Furthermore, the charge usually provides that if the farmer fails to repay the debt upon demand, the bank is to have power to appoint a receiver of the property. (If it becomes necessary to appoint a receiver, the bank generally appoints an auctioneer and estate agent.) Subject to these provisions, a farmer may sell any property comprised in the charge. He must then pay the proceeds to the bank immediately, except to such extent as the charge otherwise provides. He is under a similar obligation with respect to any money received by him under any policy of insurance on any of the property.

26-12. The Act does not confer upon the bank any power to inspect the property, and it is therefore usual to insert a clause in the form of charge giving the bank express power to do so. Another clause provides that the farmer undertakes to keep the property in good repair and condition and insured against loss or damage by fire and such other risks as the bank may require.

Floating Agricultural Charges

26-13. A floating charge covers "the farming stock and other agricultural assets from time to time belonging to the farmer, or such part thereof as is mentioned in the charge."[18] The essential feature of a floating charge is that it is a charge on a class of assets, both present and future. The farmer is under an obligation, as in the case of a fixed charge, to pay over to the bank amounts received by way of proceeds of sale or under policies of insurance. However, there is an important exception which applies only to floating charges. The Act provides[19] that—

> It shall not be necessary for a farmer to comply with such obligation if and so far as the amount so received is expended by him in the purchase of farming stock which on purchase becomes subject to the charge.

26-14. A floating charge becomes fixed upon the death or bankruptcy of the farmer, upon the dissolution of a partnership, or upon notice in writing to that effect being given by the bank on the happening of any event which by virtue of the charge confers upon

[18] Sect. 5 (4).
[19] Sect. 7.

the bank the right to give such a notice.[20] The events usually specified are failure to repay upon demand, composition or arrangement with creditors, and distress or execution against any of the property.

Priority of Agricultural Charges

26-15. Agricultural charges, in relation to one another, have priority in accordance with the times at which they are respectively registered.[21]

26-16. If a floating charge has been created, an instrument purporting to create a fixed charge on any of the property comprised in the floating charge is void as respects the property subject to the floating charge. Similarly, if a floating charge has been created, a bill of sale comprising any of the property covered by the floating charge is likewise void.[22]

26-17. If a farmer has mortgaged his land and later executes an agricultural charge over his crops, the rights of the bank under the charge in respect of the crops have priority to those of the mortgagee, irrespective of the dates of the mortgage and the charge.[23]

26-18. An agricultural charge is no protection in respect of property included in the charge which, but for the charge, would have been liable to distress for rent, taxes, or rates.[24]

Publicity Given to Agricultural Charges

26-19. Mr. Enfield had recommended that agricultural charges should be recorded in a register open to inspection by bankers only. The Act has not given effect to this proposal. It established a register open to search by any one who cares to complete Form A.C.6. Then, in a half-hearted attempt to avoid too much publicity, it declared that "it shall not be lawful to print for publication any list of agricultural charges or of the names of farmers who have created agricultural charges" and that "publication" means "the issue of copies to the public."[25] However, it expressly provided that the confidential notification by a trade association to its members in the district in which property subject to an agricultural charge is situated is not to be deemed to amount to publication. Moreover,

20 Ibid.
21 Sect. 8 (2).
22 Sect. 8 (3).
23 Sect. 8 (6).
24 Sect. 8 (7).
25 Sect. 10.

the Land Registry makes a practice of supplying certain banks and other organisations with particulars of the registrations and cancellations effected each week. There is no provision for this in the Act or in the rules made thereunder, but it is no doubt very convenient for the organisations concerned. Another result is that a farmer's credit is, in fact, often injured by the degree of publicity given to the charge which he has executed. In a very short time most of the merchants with whom he does business receive information about it.

Bankruptcy of Farmer

26-20. If a farmer is adjudged bankrupt on a bankruptcy petition presented within three months of executing an agricultural charge, whether fixed or floating, then, unless it is proved that he was solvent immediately after creating the charge, the Act provides that the amount which but for this provision would have been secured by the charge must be reduced by the sum owing to the bank prior to the giving of the charge.[26] The object of this provision is to prevent a banker from taking an effective charge from a farmer who is on the verge of bankruptcy to the detriment of the other creditors. The provision should be contrasted with that contained in Sect. 322 (1) of the Companies Act, 1948, with reference to floating charges created by limited companies.[27] In particular, the Rule in *Clayton's* case[28] cannot operate in favour of the bank in the case of agricultural charges, whereas it may do so in the case of floating charges created by companies.

Advantages of Agricultural Charges as Security

26-21. If a farmer is consistently making losses, the bank is in a position to call a halt and realise his agricultural assets before it is too late.

26-22. Agricultural charges are easy to take, they are exempt from stamp duty, and the registration and cancellation fees are very low.

26-23. Floating charges are quite safe in that they cannot be displaced by a fixed charge or by a bill of sale. Furthermore, an agricultural charge covering crops takes priority over the rights of a mortgagee of the land in respect of the crops.

[26] Sect. 8 (5).
[27] See *post*, para. 32-33.
[28] (1816) 1 Mer. 572.

12—(B.855)

Disadvantages of Agricultural Charges as Security

26-24. An agricultural charge is worth least when it is wanted most. In other words, trading losses reduce the value of the bank's security. The only sound policy for the bank to follow is to adopt a firm attitude before the value of the assets falls below the amount of the overdraft. Customers who are making losses are notoriously confident that they are "about to turn the corner," but this should not be allowed to dissuade the bank from calling in the overdraft and realising the security.

26-25. A farmer who is being pressed by his creditors sometimes sells some of the assets covered by the charge and pays the creditors with the proceeds, i.e. instead of placing the money to the credit of his account with the bank. If he does this with intent to defraud the bank, he may be sentenced to imprisonment for not more than three years,[29] but it is doubtful whether the penalty is sufficiently well known to act as a deterrent.

26-26. When a farmer's other creditors learn of the registration of the charge, they often look upon it as a danger signal and call in their loans.

26-27. Claims for rent, rates, and taxes normally take priority over an agricultural charge.

26-28. The periodical valuation by the bank of the farmer's agricultural assets involves much more time than, say, the valuation of a life policy or a portfolio of stocks and shares.

26-29. Because of these disadvantages, some banks rarely take agricultural charges. Other banks seem to place more reliance upon them. The published figures show that about three hundred charges are registered annually.[30]

[29] Agricultural Credits Act, 1928, Sect. 11.
[30] *Report to the Lord Chancellor on H.M. Land Registry for the Year 1968.*

Part Seven

OTHER TYPES OF SECURITY

CHAPTER 27

Mortgages of Ships

27-1. THE Merchant Shipping Act, 1894, provides that only (*a*) British subjects, and (*b*) "bodies corporate established under and subject to the laws of some part of Her Majesty's dominions, and having their principal place of business in those dominions," may own any share in a British ship.[1] The property in every such ship is divided into sixty-four shares.[2] This does not mean, of course, that there must be sixty-four owners: a private individual or a corporation may own any number of shares. No one is entitled to be registered as the owner of a fractional part of a share, but any number of persons (not exceeding five) may be registered as joint owners of any share or shares.[3]

27-2. The Act also provides that all British ships (with the exception of certain small vessels having a net tonnage not exceeding thirty tons) must be registered.[4] Registers are kept at most ports in the United Kingdom, as well as in many ports in British possessions overseas. Upon registration, the registrar issues a "certificate of registry" comprising the particulars respecting the ship entered in the register, with the name of her master.[5] This certificate is to be used "only for the lawful navigation of the ship."[6] The deposit of the certificate by way of security for a loan is illegal and void, the master or owner being entitled to recover it for the purpose of navigation.[7]

27-3. Ships or shares therein may be transferred only by completion of an instrument in the form prescribed in the Act. This instrument, when duly executed, has to be produced to the registrar at the port of registry, who enters the name of the transferee in the register.[8] It is expressly enacted that no notice of any trust, express, implied, or constructive may be entered in the register.[9]

[1] Sect. 1, as amended by the British Nationality Act, 1948, Sect. 31 and Sched. IV.
[2] Merchant Shipping Act, 1894, Sect. 5.
[3] Ibid.
[4] Sects. 2–3.
[5] Sect. 14.
[6] Sect. 15.
[7] *Wiley* v. *Crawford* (1861) 1 B. & S. 265.
[8] Sects. 24–6.
[9] Sect. 56.

Legal Mortgage of a Ship

27-4. The ships most usually mortgaged to a bank are trawlers and pleasure boats. Occasionally a professional valuation is obtained, but in most cases a banker prefers to rely primarily upon his knowledge of the ability and credit-worthiness of his customer. Probably ships are more difficult to realise than any other type of security: in times of depression, when the customer cannot make them pay, a banker will generally try in vain to find a market for them. A further point for consideration when lending against ships is the high rate of depreciation owing to normal wear and tear.

27-5. The mortgage must be in one of the two forms prescribed in the First Schedule to the Merchant Shipping Act, 1894, "or as near thereto as circumstances permit."[10] One form is used for the purpose of securing a principal sum and interest, and the other for securing an account current. Blank forms ready for use are sold by H.M. Stationery Office. The "account current" form is normally required by bankers, and two types are available: the first is for completion by individuals or joint owners, and the second for a body corporate.[11] In these forms one has to fill in, *inter alia*, the official number of the ship, her name, port of registry, and principal dimensions. The document must be signed and sealed by the mortgagor, and so a wafer seal should be affixed, unless the mortgagor is a company, which will, of course, use its own seal. The mortgage is exempt from stamp duty.[12] As soon as it has been executed, it should be registered.[13]

27-6. Although completion of the Stationery Office form, followed by registration, is all that is required to create a legal mortgage, bankers frequently obtain, in addition, a memorandum in which are embodied those special clauses usually found in bank mortgage forms. Thus, the mortgagor agrees that advances are to be repayable on demand, that the security is to be enforceable in the event of, say, one month's default, and that Sect. 93 of the Law of Property Act, 1925, is not to apply.[14] Furthermore, the mortgagor undertakes to keep the ship insured and to keep her in good repair so as to maintain her classification at Lloyd's. This memorandum, if executed

---

[10] Sect. 31.

[11] When ordering these forms, the reference numbers which should be quoted are (i) Customs and Excise Form No. 81, being Board of Trade Form No. 12, Mortgage to Secure Account Current (Individuals or Joint Owners), and (ii) Customs and Excise Form No. 81*a*, being Board of Trade Form No 12*a*, Mortgage to Secure Account Current (Body Corporate).

[12] Merchant Shipping Act, 1894, Sect. 721.

[13] See *post*, paras. 27-7/9.

[14] See *ante*, para. 4-28.

under hand, is exempt from stamp duty as an agreement under hand.[15] If the memorandum is executed under seal, it attracts a stamp duty of 10s. (50p).[16]

Registration of the Mortgage

27-7. The Merchant Shipping Act, 1894, provides for the registration of mortgages created thereunder in a register at the ship's port of registry. A banker who is accepting a mortgage of a ship should search the register at the port of registry, in order to ascertain whether any prior mortgages have been registered. He may make a personal search, the fee for which is 13s. (65p).[17] Alternatively, he may write to the registrar and obtain a copy of the entries in the register relating to the ship, upon paying a fee of £2 12s. (£2·60).[18] In order to protect the priority of his mortgage, he must have it registered. For this purpose, he will produce it to the registrar, who must record it in the register. Section 31 of the Act provides that—

> Mortgages shall be recorded by the registrar in the order in time in which they are produced to him for that purpose, and the registrar shall by memorandum under his hand notify on each mortgage that it has been recorded by him, stating the day and hour of that record.

27-8. The fee for registration of the mortgage is calculated as follows[19]—

> According to the gross tonnage represented by the ships or shares of ships mortgaged (e.g., the mortgage of 16/64 shares in a ship of 6,400 tons to be reckoned as the mortgage of 1,600 tons)
> Not exceeding 400 tons   £3 5s. (£3·25)
> For every 1,000 tons or part of 1,000 tons in excess of
> 400 tons   £1 12s. 6 (£1·62½)

27-9. If the mortgagor is a limited company, registration must also be effected at Companies House, in accordance with the Companies Act, 1948.[20]

Priority of Mortgages

27-10. The Merchant Shipping Act, 1894,[21] enacts that—

> If there are more mortgages than one registered in respect of the same ship or share, the mortgagees shall, notwithstanding any express, implied

---

[15] Finance Act, 1970, Sect. 32 and Sched. 7.
[16] Stamp Act, 1891, Sched. I.
[17] Merchant Shipping (Fees) Regulations, 1967, Sched. 18, Part 18.
[18] Ibid., Part 19.
[19] Ibid., Part 17.
[20] For details see *post*, para. 32-4.
[21] Sect. 33.

or constructive notice, be entitled in priority, one over the other, according to the date at which each mortgage is recorded in the register book, and not according to the date of each mortgage itself.

An unregistered mortgage is postponed to all registered mortgages, even though the registered mortgagees were aware of the prior unregistered mortgage.[22]

27-11. If a banker who is the first mortgagee of a ship receives actual notice of the execution of a second mortgage, he should rule off his customer's account in order to avoid the operation of the Rule in *Clayton's* case,[23] for it has been held that a first mortgagee of a ship whose mortgage is taken to cover future advances cannot claim, in priority over a second mortgagee, the benefit of advances made after he had notice of the second mortgage.[24] Lord Chorley and Dr. Giles take the view that, as every mortgagee is deemed to have notice of the contents of the register at the port of registry, the mere registration of a second mortage will have this postponing effect so far as the further advance on the first mortgage is concerned.[25] It has been argued, therefore, that the possibility of being prejudiced by constructive notice of a second mortgage makes it desirable that accommodation be taken by loan rather than by overdraft, no increase in the loan being permitted without a fresh search of the register.[26] As a counsel of perfection, no doubt this course is preferable, but in practice many advances on current account are made against the security of ships. Practical considerations make it extremely unlikely that a second mortgagee would fail to give express notice to the banker, who would then act accordingly.

27-12. The subject of priorities would be incomplete without a brief reference to maritime liens. A mortgagee of a ship may sometimes find himself seriously prejudiced by the operation of a maritime lien, because mortgagees are postponed to maritime liens. Broadly speaking, these liens may be classified under two headings, namely, those for remuneration or money due under some contract, and those for damage suffered from some tortious act.[27] In the first group are the liens created by bottomry and respondentia,[28] and for

---

[22] *Black* v. *Williams* [1895] 1 Ch. 408.

[23] (1816) 1 Mer. 572.

[24] *The Benwell Tower* (1895) 72 L.T. 664.

[25] Lord Chorley and O. C. Giles, *Shipping Law* (5th ed., 1963), p. 28.

[26] E. M. Butler, "The Ship's Mortgage as a Banking Security," *Journal of the Institute of Bankers*, Vol. LXX (1949), pp. 132–41.

[27] For a more detailed account of this subject, see Chorley and Giles, op. cit., pp. 33–41.

[28] A bottomry bond is a contract by which, in consideration of money advanced for the necessaries of the ship to enable her to proceed on her voyage, the ship and

salvage, for seamen's and master's wages, and their claims (if any) for wrongful dismissal, and for the master's disbursements, provided that he had authority to pledge the owner's credit. Under the second heading are maritime liens arising out of damage done by the ship as, for example, in collision. Usually, the risk in respect of most of these matters is covered by insurance, and a mortgagee should ensure that this has been done.

Insurance of the Ship

27-13. There are three main forms of insurance: marine, war risks, and club or mutual insurance. The principal risk against which a marine policy is intended to protect the assured is loss by perils of the sea. These perils are, of course, specified in the policy. The form of the policy has remained substantially the same since the latter part of the eighteenth century, though a few clauses have been added. As a result of the efforts of the London Institute of Underwriters, these clauses have been standardised. Thus, the "Running Down Clause" covers three-quarters of the liability for damage done to another ship in collision. This clause was introduced as a result of a decision which established the rule that payments made by the assured to a third party in consequence of a collision where the insured ship was partly or wholly to blame could not be recovered under the ordinary form of policy.[29]

27-14. Most marine insurance business passes eventually through the hands of Lloyd's underwriters, but brief reference must be made to club or mutual insurance. Shipowners carrying on business in a certain area form an association or a club, for the purpose of insuring themselves against a number of risks which Lloyd's and the various insurance companies either do not insure at all, or only on unfavourable terms. Thus, the associations provide cover in respect of the proportion uninsured under the R.D.C. clause and in respect of liability to cargo-owners for damage to cargo.

27-15. Having ensured that all the usual risks have been covered, a banker who is lending against the security of a ship should notify the underwriters and indemnity associations of his interest in the policies. A marine policy is usually assigned by an endorsement thereon, signed by the assured. It should then be held either by the banker himself, or by approved brokers subject to their undertaking

---

the cargo are made liable for the repayment of the money in the event of the safe arrival of the ship at her destination. A contract similar to this upon the cargo alone is called respondentia. Both are very rare at the present day.

[29] *De Vaux* v. *Salvador* (1836) 4 Ad. & E. 420.

Other Types of Security

to pay the proceeds of all claims to the bank. Finally, the banker must ensure that premiums are paid when due.

Discharge of Legal Mortgage

27-16. The Merchant Shipping Act, 1894, provides that, when the mortgage deed, with a receipt for the mortgage money endorsed thereon, duly signed and attested, is produced to the registrar, he must make an entry in the register to the effect that the mortgage has been discharged.[30] The receipt is exempt from stamp duty,[31] but a fee must be paid to the registrar. This fee is the same as the fee for registration of a mortgage of a ship.[32] The banker will, of course, inform the underwriters and indemnity associations that he no longer has any interest in the policies.

Realising the Security

27-17. By virtue of the Merchant Shipping Act, 1894, a registered mortgagee has power to dispose of the ship or share in respect of which he is registered and to give effectual receipts for the purchase money.[33] A second or subsequent mortgagee cannot sell without the concurrence of every prior mortgagee, unless he obtains an order of the court. When a mortgagee exercises his power of sale, he holds the proceeds of sale, after satisfying principal, interest, and costs, in trust for subsequent mortgagees (if any), and the owner. Instead of selling, a mortgagee of a ship or of a majority of shares in a ship may take possession of her and recoup himself out of the profits of running the vessel.[34] This alternative will not commend itself to bankers.

Equitable Mortgage of a Ship

27-18. It is only upon very rare occasions that a banker is content with an equitable mortgage of a ship. If a mortgage of a British ship is not registered in accordance with the provisions of the Merchant Shipping Act, it ranks merely as an equitable charge, and the lender may find himself postponed to a subsequent mortgagee who does register.[35] Practically the only case when a lender might be content with an equitable mortgage is where a foreign ship visiting

---

[30] Sect. 32. There is a suitable receipt printed on the Stationery Office forms.
[31] Sect. 721.
[32] Merchant Shipping (Fees) Regulations, 1967, Part 17.
[33] Sect. 35.
[34] *European and Australian Royal Mail Co. Ltd.* v. *Royal Mail Steam Packet Co.* (1858) 4 K. & J. 676.
[35] *Ante,* para. 27-10.

an English port needs a short-term advance; it might be considered undesirable to go to the trouble of registering a legal mortgage abroad.

Mortgage of an Unfinished Ship

27-19. A banker is sometimes asked to help to finance the construction of a ship. Steps must first be taken to find out who owns the property in the unfinished ship. In some cases the purchaser pays the price by instalments, and it is expressly agreed that the property in so much of the ship as has been constructed passes to him. In other cases the purchaser pays nothing until the ship has been completed, the legal property remaining meanwhile in the builder. Whoever owns the legal property can offer it as security for an advance, but the provisions of the Merchant Shipping Act are inapplicable to a security of this type, because a ship cannot be registered until she has been completed. As a rule both the purchaser and the builder will be limited companies, and whichever of them owns the unfinished ship will usually create a charge thereon by a debenture embodying a floating charge.[36]

[36] For debentures, see *post*, paras. 32-23/27.

CHAPTER 28

Mortgage of a Beneficiary's Interest Under a Trust

28-1. PROBABLY the most satisfactory definition of a trust is that of Professor Keeton, who defines it as "the relationship which arises wherever a person called the trustee is compelled in Equity to hold property, whether real or personal, and whether by legal or equitable title, for the benefit of some persons (of whom he may be one and who are termed *cestuis que trust*) or for some object permitted by law, in such a way that the real benefit of the property accrues, not to the trustee, but to the beneficiaries or other objects of the trust."[1]

28-2. The desire of a man to create a trust of his property for the benefit of some of his dependants is a very natural one. Sometimes, for example, he leaves his estate by will to his children for life, and then to his grandchildren absolutely. In this way his children will enjoy the income from the estate during their lives but are unable to spend the capital, which is thus preserved intact for the next generation. A person may, of course, create a trust during his life, though trusts created by will are far more numerous. The commonest type of trust is that whereby a husband or wife leaves his or her property by will in trust for the surviving spouse for life, and then to the children absolutely. One important advantage of disposing of one's property in this manner is that estate duty is payable once only, i.e. when the first spouse dies,[2] whereas, if one spouse left his estate absolutely to the other, estate duty would be payable twice, i.e. upon the death of each of them.

28-3. As a general rule there is no legal bar which prevents any beneficiary under a trust from mortgaging his interest as security for an advance, provided that he has attained the age of eighteen.[3] However, there are exceptional cases where it is declared in the trust deed or in the will that, if a beneficiary charges or alienates his interest in the trust fund, his interest will pass to someone else.

---

[1] G. W. Keeton, *The Law of Trusts* (9th ed., 1968), p. 5.
[2] Finance Act, 1894, Sect. 5 (2); Finance Act, 1898, Sect. 13; and Finance Act, 1914, Sect. 14 (*a*).
[3] The age of majority is now eighteen: Family Law Reform Act, 1969, Sect. 1.

These are known as "protective trusts," and an interest therein is clearly useless as security for a loan.[4]

Mortgage by a Life Tenant

28-4. Let it be assumed that a testator has devised and bequeathed a freehold estate, called Blackacre, and various stocks and shares to T1 and T2 upon trust for sale. L is to enjoy the income from this property during his life, and, upon his death, the property is to pass to R, the remainderman, absolutely: L has a life interest and R, a reversionary interest.

28-5. If L wishes to mortgage his life interest, the banker should examine the instrument creating the trust—in this example the will. If the property is held upon protective trusts, it will be quite unsuitable for security purposes.[5] In any event, L's interest will cease upon his death. Thus, as a general rule, it would only be acceptable as security if supported by a mortgage of an insurance policy on L's life. If this can be arranged satisfactorily, the bank's solicitors will examine the title deeds to Blackacre and the stock and share certificates, all of which are (and will remain) in the possession of T1 and T2, in whom vests the legal title to the property. The mortgage deed of L's interest will be prepared by the bank's solicitors, though some banks find it convenient to use a standard form for this purpose.[6] On general principles, it would seem that the mortgage will necessarily be equitable, because of the rule that "if the mortgagor has no legal estate but only an equitable interest, any mortgage he effects must necessarily be equitable."[7]

28-6. Steps must be taken to protect the bank's priority, for there is nothing to prevent L from creating a second mortgage of his life interest. The procedure to be followed depends upon what is known as the Rule in *Dearle* v. *Hall*,[8] as amended by Sect. 137 of the Law of Property Act, 1925. This rule ordains that priority depends upon the order in which *written* notice of the mortgages is received by the owner of the legal estate—in this case, by T1 and T2. Immediately prior to the execution of the mortgage, the bank or its solicitors

---

[4] See Trustee Act, 1925, Sect. 33.

[5] See *ante*, para. 28-3.

[6] For the special procedure relating to mortgages of equitable interests in registered land, see *ante*, para. 10-53.

[7] R. E. Megarry, *A Manual of the Law of Real Property* (4th ed., 1969), p. 469. Nevertheless, it has been held that, as a result of the Judicature Act, 1873, Sect. 25 (6) (replaced by the Law of Property Act, 1925, Sect. 136), it is now possible to have a legal assignment by way of mortgage of an *equitable* interest in a trust fund: *Re Pain, Gustavson* v. *Haviland* [1919] 1 Ch. 38. But the decision has been criticised.

[8] (1828) 3 Russ. 1.

will inquire of T1 and T2 whether they have already received any notices of prior incumbrances on L's interest. If the answer is in the negative, the mortgage will be executed, and notice thereof will be given to all the trustees. Notice to the solicitors acting for the trustees is not sufficient.[9] A formal acknowledgment of the notice should be requested.

28-7. There is one case where it is inappropriate to give notice of the bank's interest to the trustees, namely where a trust corporation has been nominated to receive notices of dealings affecting beneficial interests under the trust. In this connection, Sect. 138 (1) of the Law of Property Act, 1925, provides that "by any settlement or other instrument creating a trust, a trust corporation may be nominated to whom notices of dealings affecting real or personal property may be given . . . and in default of such nomination the trustees (if any) of the instrument, or the court on the application of any person interested, may make the nomination." These powers are seldom exercised, but, in order to safeguard its position, the bank should ask the trustees whether or not a trust corporation has been nominated to receive notices of dealings affecting beneficial interests under the trust. If such a nomination has been made, the bank should inquire of the trust corporation whether any notices of prior incumbrances on L's interest have been received. Formal notice of the bank's mortgage should be given to the trust corporation, and an acknowledgment should be requested.

28-8. If the customer defaults, the bank will have no right to the investments comprised in the trust fund, but only to the income arising therefrom. Alternatively, the bank could sell the customer's life interest to a third party.

Mortgage by a Remainderman

28-9. Mortgages of reversionary interests frequently involve long-term loans, which are not repaid until the life tenant dies. For this reason, they are not a suitable banking security and are seldom encountered in practice, except to support a weak position. Some insurance companies, however, are prepared to lend money against a mortgage of a reversionary interest. Another course open to the remainderman, if he wishes to anticipate his interest, is to sell it outright to one of the companies which specialise in the purchase of reversionary interests. Alternatively, there are one or two firms of auctioneers in London who make a practice of offering reversionary

---

[9] *Saffron Walden Second Benefit Building Society* v. *Rayner* (1880) 14 Ch.D. 406.

interests for sale by public auction. However, if the life tenant is very old, the bank may feel justified in making an advance to the remainderman against a mortgage of his interest.

28-10. In every case it is essential to ascertain whether the remainderman's interest is certain to take effect in possession at some future date. If, for example, the reversion is contingent upon his surviving the tenant for life, it would be unacceptable as security, unless it was supported by a mortgage of a life policy on the remainderman's life. The procedure to be followed when the mortgage is executed is similar to that outlined above with reference to mortgages of life interests. If the customer defaults, the bank will be entitled to sell R's interest in the trust fund. Alternatively, it may be thought desirable to hold it until it falls into possession.

CHAPTER 29

Assignments of Debts

29-1. THE assignment to a bank of a debt owed to a customer by a third party is a comparatively rare type of security. However, assignments of this kind and also assignments of debts which have not yet arisen are sometimes executed by customers.

Assignment of an Existing Debt

29-2. Occasionally an assignment of an existing debt may provide temporary cover for an advance, but as a general rule bankers look upon these propositions with disfavour. Clearly, the value of the security depends upon the ability of the third party to pay the debt, and furthermore its value may be reduced by any right of set-off which the third party may have against the customer. The assignment of an existing debt may be either (*a*) legal or (*b*) equitable—

A. LEGAL ASSIGNMENT

29-3. A legal assignment of a debt must comply with the requirements of Sect. 136 of the Law of Property Act, 1925, that is to say, it must be in writing (though a deed is not essential), and express notice in writing must be given to the debtor. No set form of words is required. The instrument of assignment, after reciting the parties, usually declares that the assignor (the customer) "assigns to the bank the debt of £ . . . due and owing to the customer by . . ." The document attracts stamp duty at the rate of 2s. (10p) per cent on the amount secured. The bank should forward a letter to the debtor stating that "Mr. . . . has, by an assignment dated . . ., assigned to the bank the debt of £ . . . due and owing by you to him." At the same time the bank should ask the debtor (i) to acknowledge receipt of the notice and to confirm the amount of the debt, (ii) whether he has any right of set-off against the assignor, and (iii) whether the debtor has received notice of any prior assignments.

29-4. There are five main reasons why written notice should always be given to the debtor—

    1. Notice in writing is necessary to entitle the banker to sue in his own name under the Law of Property Act, 1925.

2. If, in the absence of notice, the debtor pays the assignor he will be effectually discharged, whereas if the debtor pays after receiving notice of the assignment, the bank can still recover the debt from him.[1]

3. In the absence of notice the bank will be postponed to a subsequent assignee for value who has no notice of the previous assignment and gives written notice to the debtor.[2]

4. In the absence of notice the bank will be subject to any equities arising between the debtor and the creditor *after* the date of the assignment. The assignment is, of course, always subject to equities arising prior to that date.

5. In the absence of notice, if the assignor is adjudicated bankrupt the debt will generally be within his "order or disposition" under Sect. 38, Bankruptcy Act, 1914, and therefore it will be divisible amongst his creditors. The giving of notice to the debtor takes the debt out of the operation of the section.[3]

29-5. If the assignment is executed by a limited company, it must be registered at Companies House in accordance with the Companies Act, 1948.[4]

B. EQUITABLE ASSIGNMENT

29-6. Rarely will a banker be content with an equitable assignment of an existing debt. In general, an assignment which does not comply with the requirements of Sect. 136 of the Law of Property Act, 1925, will operate as an equitable assignment, e.g. if it is not in writing or if written notice is not given to the debtor. There are important differences between legal and equitable assignments of a debt. If an assignment is legal, the assignee can bring an action in his own name to enforce payment of the debt. If it is only equitable, the original creditor must usually be joined, as plaintiff if he consents, and if not, as defendant.[5] Moreover, if the assignment operates only in equity by virtue of the fact that written notice has not been given to the debtor, the other disadvantages noted above will apply.

Equitable Assignment of a Future Debt

29-7. It is not uncommon for a bank to agree to finance a customer who is carrying out a large contract, against the security of an

---

[1] *Brice* v. *Bannister* (1878) 3 Q.B.D. 569.
[2] *Marchant* v. *Morton, Down & Co.* [1901] 2 K.B. 829.
[3] *Rutter* v. *Everett* [1895] 2 Ch. 872.
[4] See *post*, para. 32-4.
[5] *Performing Right Society Ltd.* v. *London Theatre of Varieties Ltd.* [1924] A.C.1.

assignment of the progress payments which will become due under the contract. Clearly, this is a transaction which a banker will scrutinise very carefully, because there is always the possibility that the customer may fail to perform his part of the contract satisfactorily. It is impossible to execute a legal assignment of a future debt, but in equity such assignments, if made for valuable consideration, are treated as contracts to assign, of which specific performance will be granted.[6] Thus, a lender is fully protected, provided that he gives notice to the future debtor, and obtains an acknowledgment.

29-8. *Re Kent & Sussex Sawmills Ltd.*[7] is a case which illustrates this type of transaction and, at the same time, shows how disastrous it may be to omit to have the assignment registered at Companies House in the case of limited company customers. In June, 1944, the company entered into a contract with the Ministry of Fuel and Power to supply 30,000 tons of cut logs. To secure the company's overdraft at the Westminster Bank, the company addressed a letter to the Ministry which, after referring to the particular contract, proceeded as follows: "With reference to the above-mentioned contract, we hereby authorise you to remit all moneys due thereunder direct to this Company's account at Westminster Bank Ltd., Crowborough, whose receipt shall be your sufficient discharge. These instructions are to be regarded as irrevocable unless the said bank should consent to their cancellation in writing, and are intended to cover any extension of the contract in excess of 30,000 tons if such should occur." The letter was sent by the bank to the Ministry, and an acknowledgment was obtained. In May, 1945, the company entered into a further contract with the Ministry, and precisely the same procedure was followed as before. In 1946 the company went into liquidation. At that time £30,000 was owing to the company under the two contracts, and the company's overdraft amounted to over £83,000. It was held by the court that the two letters of authority constituted charges on the book debts of the company under Sect. 79 (2) (*e*) of the Companies Act, 1929,[8] and that, not having been registered under that section, they were void as against the liquidator. Thus the bank was deprived of security worth £30,000.

29-9. Sometimes, when a bank grants bridge-over facilities to a customer in connection with the sale of one house and the purchase

---

[6] *Tailby* v. *Official Receiver* (1888) 13 App. Cas. 523.

[7] [1947] 1 Ch. 177. See also *Independent Automatic Sales Ltd.* v. *Knowles & Foster* [1962] 1 W.L.R. 974.

[8] Now replaced by the Companies Act, 1948, Sect. 95 (2) (*e*), *post*, para. 32-4.

of another, an irrevocable authority is, at the bank's request, addressed by the customer to his solicitors. If the property which is being sold is mortgaged to a building society or other lender, the solicitors should be instructed to pay off the mortgage debt out of the proceeds of sale and then pay the net proceeds (after deduction of their costs and expenses) to the bank. These instructions should be expressed to be irrevocable, unless the bank consents to their cancellation.[9] The bank should send to the solicitors the letter containing their customer's instructions, and ask the solicitors to state (*a*) the completion date, (*b*) the sale price of the property, and (*c*) the net amount which is likely to be available after discharge of the mortgage debt (if any) and all costs and expenses. Sometimes the bank asks the solicitors to give their "undertaking" to pay the net proceeds to the bank, but this would seem to be unnecessary. Once the solicitors have been notified of the customer's irrevocable authority, this is binding upon them. It operates as an equitable assignment of the net proceeds of the sale, and if the solicitors disregard it and pay the net proceeds to their client, they will be liable to the bank for the amount so paid.

29-10. Some banks occasionally make short-term advances to farmers, against the security of an assignment by the farmer to the bank of sums which will become payable to the farmer by the Milk Marketing Board. In this connection Sect. 43 (1) of the Bankruptcy Act, 1914, provides as follows—

Where a person engaged in any trade or business makes an assignment to any other person of his existing or future book debts or any class thereof, and is subsequently adjudicated bankrupt, the assignment shall be void against the trustee as regards any book debts which have not been paid at the commencement of the bankruptcy, unless the assignment has been registered as if the assignment were a bill of sale given otherwise than by way of security for the payment of a sum of money, and the provisions of the Bills of Sale Act, 1878, with respect to the registration of bills of sale shall apply accordingly, subject to such necessary modifications as may be made by rules under that Act:

Provided that nothing in this section shall have effect so as to render void any assignment of book debts due at the date of the assignment from specified debtors, or of debts growing due under specified contracts, or any assignment of book debts included in a transfer of a business made bona fide and for value, or in any assignment of assets for the benefit of creditors generally.

---

[9] Strictly speaking, if the letters containing these instructions operate by way of security, they should be stamped as mortgages, i.e., at the rate of 2s. (10p) per cent on the amount secured. If the transaction is by a limited company, it should be registered at Companies House pursuant to Sect. 95, Companies Act, 1948: see *Re Kent & Sussex Sawmills Ltd.*, *supra*.

29-11. It would be very damaging to a farmer's credit to register an assignment under the Bills of Sale Act,[10] and so one must try to obtain as much protection as possible without resorting to registration. In practice the best course to follow is to ask the farmer to execute an assignment in the bank's favour of (*a*) all sums due or to become due to the farmer under his existing contract with the Milk Marketing Board, and (*b*) all sums which may become due to him under any other contract which he may make with the Board in the future.

29-12. The assignment in (*a*) would be valid in the event of the farmer's bankruptcy, because it would be a debt "growing due" under a specified contract. The assignment in (*b*) would, however, be void in the event of bankruptcy, unless it had been registered. Nevertheless, it is desirable to obtain an assignment of sums which may become due to a farmer under future contracts, because such an assignment will be valid, provided that the customer is not adjudicated bankrupt. It is not unknown in practice for a farmer who has borrowed all the money he can from one bank (largely on the faith of his Milk Marketing Board payments) to try to divert such payments to another bank. An assignment prevents him from doing this.

29-13. Many banks dispense with a formal assignment of sums payable to farmers under these contracts. Instead, the farmer is asked to sign an ordinary mandate authorising the Milk Marketing Board to remit the amount to the bank for the credit of his account. This authority can be revoked at any time, but in practice the Board notifies the bank of any change in the mandate, with the result that the bank knows immediately if an attempt is being made to divert payments to another bank. In the absence of an assignment, however, the bank cannot prevent the farmer from altering his mandate.

General Assignment of Existing and Future Debts

29-14. So far it has been assumed that debts due, or to become due, from specified debtors are assigned to a bank by way of security. Theoretically, it would be possible for a customer to execute a general assignment of debts as security. This is never done in practice, because of the provisions of Sect. 43 (1) of the Bankruptcy Act, 1914.[11]

[10] See *ante*, para. 26-3.
[11] See *ante*, para. 29-10.

CHAPTER 30

Credit Balances as Security

30-1. SOMETIMES a third party who has a credit balance at a bank is prepared to charge that balance as security for an advance to a customer.[1] It is impossible to envisage a more satisfactory security than this. It can never depreciate in value, and, if the customer defaults, the bank will be able to realise the security without trouble and without the expense of any legal proceedings.

30-2. It is essential to obtain from the third party a written agreement setting out the terms of the transaction. This stipulates that his credit balance is to be held by the bank as security for all sums owed by the customer, either solely or jointly with any other person or persons, whether on balance of account or on guarantees or in respect of bills of exchange, promissory notes, and other negotiable instruments, and including interest with half-yearly rests and other banking charges. It further provides that the bank may at any time, and without notice, transfer such portion of the credit balance as may be necessary to discharge the customer's liability. The document is exempt from stamp duty as an agreement under hand.[2]

30-3. If the third party creating the charge is a limited company, it would seem that registration should be effected at Companies House, in accordance with the Companies Act, 1948, on the ground that the transaction is "a charge on the book debts of the company."[3]

30-4. Instead of obtaining from the third party a specific agreement on the lines indicated, some banks achieve the same result by asking him to execute a guarantee at the time when he places the money on deposit. This should be done only where the form of guarantee contains a clause to the following effect—

> I agree that in respect of my liability hereunder the Bank shall have a lien on all securities belonging to me now or hereafter held by the Bank and on all moneys now or hereafter standing to my credit with the Bank on any current or any other account

The third party's balance should be held in a deposit account at notice. Then, if he gives notice to make a withdrawal, the banker

---

[1] The circumstances in which a banker may hold credit balances of a customer as cover for debit balances of the *same* customer, are examined in Vol. 1, paras. 2-55/72.

[2] Finance Act, 1970, Sect. 32 and Sched. 7.

[3] See *post*, para. 32-4.

has time to communicate with the debtor in order to try to make other security arrangements. When the notice expires, the bank will either consent to the withdrawal or notify the depositor that the sum is required under the terms of his guarantee.

30-5. A customer or a third party sometimes offers to deposit by way of security a pass book disclosing a balance with the National Savings Bank or with a Trustee Savings Bank. This is not a satisfactory security. Possession of the book does not confer on the holder any title to the deposit, not does it prevent an award being made for payment to the depositor without production of the book should the circumstances warrant it.[4] It has also been decided that deposits cannot legally be made the subject of an assignment.[5] In spite of these difficulties, it is not unknown for a joint-stock bank to take a deposit of such a pass book by way of security.

[4] See John Y. Watt, *The Law of Savings Banks* (3rd ed., 1948), Vol. 1, p. 81, citing the award in *Lucas*, No. 6, 1900.
[5] Op. cit, Vol. 1, p. 201, citing the award in *McMahon*, No. 21, 1895.

CHAPTER 31

Collateral Security

31-1. THE term "collateral security" has three meanings. First, it is sometimes used to describe impersonal security, such as land, life policies, or stocks and shares. In this sense it may be contrasted with personal security, e.g. a guarantee. This use of the term is more common in the United States of America than it is in this country.

31-2. Secondly, collateral security has a technical meaning in the law relating to stamp duties. There it means "secondary" security (as opposed to "primary") and "additional" security (as opposed to "original"). Collateral security, in this sense, attracts a lower rate of duty than primary or original security.[1]

31-3. Thirdly, collateral security means any form of security deposited by someone other than the customer himself. It is to be contrasted with "direct" security, which is any type of property owned by the customer and charged by him by way of security. Thus, a guarantee is always collateral security, whereas land, life policies, stocks and shares, etc., may be either direct or collateral, depending upon whether they are lodged by the customer himself or by a third party. Throughout the rest of the chapter, collateral security is used in this sense.

Advantage of Collateral Security

31-4. The advantage of collateral, as compared with direct, security, is that the former type of security may be disregarded when proving in the customer's bankruptcy. The importance of this will be apparent from the following examples. First, let it be supposed that X has been granted a loan of £1,000 partially secured by stocks and shares worth £800, which X himself has deposited. In the event of X becoming bankrupt, the bank must either (*a*) surrender its security for the benefit of the unsecured creditors as a whole and prove for the total amount of the debt—a most unlikely course, or (*b*) realise its security and prove for the balance of the debt, or (*c*) value its security and prove for the balance.[2] In the

---

[1] See *post*, para. 33-34.
[2] Bankruptcy Act, 1914, Sect. 32 and Sched. II.

illustration, therefore, the bank would prove as an unsecured creditor for £200. If a dividend of 20p in the pound was paid in respect of X's estate, the bank would receive £40 and incur a bad debt of £160.

31-5. Secondly, let it be supposed that the stocks and shares had been deposited by a third person, Y, instead of by X, the customer. In other respects the facts are as stated above. Under these circumstances the bank is allowed to disregard its security when proving in the bankrupt's estate, i.e. it may prove for £1,000.[3] In the result the bank, having proved for £1,000, receives a dividend of £200—assuming, as before, a dividend of 20p in the pound. This leaves a balance of £800 outstanding. The bank thereupon realises the stocks and shares (which are worth £800) and incurs no loss. It is seldom that the figures work out as neatly as this in everyday practice, but the illustrations serve to show that, as a general rule, £800 of collateral security may be of greater value to a banker than £800 of direct security. The only case when it would make no difference whether the security was direct or collateral would be where the debtor was bankrupt and had no assets at all for distribution to his creditors. Under these circumstances the banker would sustain a loss of £200 in both the examples given above.

31-6. The joint estate of partners is considered as different from the separate estate of any partner. Therefore, a partnership creditor, who has a security for his debt belonging to the separate estate of one partner, need not value it when proving in the joint estate,[4] and, conversely, a creditor of one partner is not obliged to value a security belonging to the joint estate. An experienced banker bears these rules in mind when trying to arrange security for an advance. It is particularly useful, for example, to have a partnership overdraft secured by property belonging to the separate estates of the partners. In this connection, however, a word of warning may not be out of place. Property may appear, at first, to be a partner's own property, but, when the firm's balance sheet is examined, it may be found that it is an asset of the partnership. Obviously, this must be treated as direct security for a loan to the firm. Similarly, one sometimes discovers that property which appears to belong to a director of a limited company is, in fact, the property of the company.

Collateral Security Forms

31-7. The security forms used by the banks when taking collateral security differ from those applicable to direct security, though

---

[3] Bankruptcy Act, 1914, Sect. 167.
[4] *Ex parte Caldicott* (1884) 25 Ch. D. 716.

some clauses are common to both. For example, in direct security forms it is usual to embody a "consolidation clause" to exclude the operation of Sect. 93 of the Law of Property Act, 1925.[5] A similar clause is included in collateral security forms, the intention being to deny to the third party those rights which he might otherwise enjoy under Sect. 93.

31-8. In the collateral forms the consideration clause usually states that the third party is depositing the security in consideration of the bank making or continuing advances or otherwise affording banking facilities to its customer. Clauses are then inserted which have the effect of allowing the utmost latitude to the bank and of denying to the third party any rights, the exercise of which might conflict with the best interests of the bank. These provisions are similar to those in a well-drawn guarantee. For example, the third party agrees that the bank may vary the securities held for the debtor's account, and may grant time to and compound with the debtor. He further agrees that he will not take security from the debtor and that, if he does so, he will hold such security for the benefit of the bank. Another clause deprives the third party of his right to prove in the customer's bankruptcy in competition with the bank. It is usually worded as follows—

> Although my liability hereunder cannot exceed the value of the mortgaged securities yet this security shall be construed and take effect as a guarantee of the whole and every part of the principal moneys and interest owing and to become owing as aforesaid and accordingly I am not to be entitled as against the Bank to any right of proof in the bankruptcy of the Principal unless and until the whole of such principal moneys and interest shall have first been completely discharged and satisfied

31-9. The third party also agrees that a specified period of notice is necessary to determine the security. This provision is drafted on the same lines as the notice clause in a guarantee—

> I agree that this security shall be binding as a continuing security on me and my legal personal representatives until the expiration of three calendar months' written notice to the contrary from me or my legal personal representatives

31-10. As soon as the period of notice has expired, the bank should rule off the customer's account and pass future transactions through a new account. This is necessary in order to avoid the operation of the Rule in *Clayton's* case.[6] For the same reason the account should

---

[5] See *ante*, paras. 4-28, 12-20, 27-6.
[6] (1816) 1 Mer. 572.

be broken if the bank receives notice of the bankruptcy or insanity of the person depositing the collateral security.

31-11. There is an alternative method of making third-party security available for an advance to a customer. The bank may ask the third party to sign a guarantee for a named sum and to deposit the security in support thereof on a direct security form. All such forms expressly provide that the security is given in respect, *inter alia*, of liability on guarantees. To take collateral security in this roundabout fashion is normally quite unnecessary, but there are occasions when it may usefully be done. For example, suppose that a third party offers highly speculative stocks and shares, worth about £500, as security for an advance of £500 to a customer. If the stocks and shares are taken as collateral security and then they depreciate in value, the third party will not be liable to make up the difference. But if the bank insists upon a guaratee for £500 supported by a deposit of the stocks and shares, a fall in their value will not reduce the liability of the third party. A word of warning, however, is necessary here. The consideration clause in direct security forms often states that the security is deposited in consideration of the bank making or continuing advances or otherwise affording banking facilities to the person depositing the security. In this case it is unwise to take a direct security form over security held in support of a guarantee executed by a person *who is not himself a customer of the lending bank*. Either the consideration clause should be amended by the bank's solicitors, or, better still, the third party should deposit the security on a collateral form and sign a guarantee as well.

31-12. Again, it is often very convenient to use a guarantee to "pick up" security which a customer has previously deposited to secure his own account. For example, customer X mortgaged land, valued at £500, to secure his own account. That overdraft has been repaid, and he is now offering to mortgage the land to the bank to secure a proposed overdraft to be granted to his friend, Y. One method would be to discharge the present mortgage and to ask X to create a fresh one as collateral security for Y's account. This trouble and expense may be avoided by requesting X to sign a guarantee in respect of Y's account. This "picks up" the security which X had previously deposited, and, if Y defaults, the bank may have recourse to the security, should that be necessary.

31-13. If a wife offers to deposit collateral security for her husband's account or for the account of some company in which he is interested, the banker should always insist that the wife receives independent legal advice before she enters into the transaction.

This precaution is taken so that she will not be able to prove, at a later date, that she signed under the undue influence of her husband. The considerations involved are similar to those where a wife signs a guarantee for her husband's account.[7] Apart from this type of case, collateral security may be accepted from women, whether married or single, without any special formalities.

Releasing Collateral Security

31-14. When a customer repays his overdraft, any third party who had deposited security in respect thereof is entitled to have it released and returned to him. The procedure to be followed depends upon the nature of the security. Thus, a legal mortgage of land is usually discharged by endorsing thereon a receipt for the money secured by the mortgage, a legal mortgage of stocks and shares is discharged by transferring them back into the name of the third party, and so on.

31-15. It is not unknown for a customer who is on the verge of bankruptcy to realise such assets as he possesses and pay the proceeds into his banking account, thus extinguishing his overdraft. His object in doing this is to persuade the bank to release to his relatives and friends any security which they have deposited, i.e. before bankruptcy supervenes. This may amount to a "fraudulent preference," with the result that the bank may be obliged to repay the sums in question to the customer's trustee in bankruptcy.[8] In this respect the case of *Re Conley*[9] is instructive. Mr. Conley had overdrafts at Barclays Bank and Lloyds Bank, in respect of which collateral security had been deposited by his wife and his mother. Shortly before 16th November, 1934, by various means Mr. Conley paid large sums into his accounts so that on that day the accounts were in credit. Soon after that day his wife and mother demanded the release of the securities and obtained them. On 30th November, Mr. Conley's business was closed down, and he was immediately made bankrupt. These facts were assumed in the court of first instance and again in the Court of Appeal. It was held by the Court of Appeal that Mr. Conley's wife and mother were sureties or guarantors within the meaning of Sect. 44 of the Bankruptcy Act, 1914, and that, if the facts were as assumed, the payments by Mr. Conley into his banking accounts amounted to a fraudulent preference. The case was remitted to the court below for further hearing. It is understood that no subsequent hearing took place

---

[7] See *ante*, paras. 20-3/11.
[8] For fraudulent preference see *ante*, paras. 19-53/55.
[9] [1938] 2 All E.R. 127. See also *In re Kushler Ltd.* [1943] Ch. 248, *ante*, paras. 19-54/57.

and that the banks concerned repaid the sums claimed by the trustee in bankruptcy. Furthermore, although the Court of Appeal was not required to decide whether the banks could claim any part of the moneys from the bankrupt's wife and mother, one of the judges indicated that, in his opinion, the banks could not claim reimbursement from them.[10]

31-16. This state of affairs was manifestly unjust: the very people whom Mr. Conley wished to prefer—his wife and mother—were apparently able to escape all liability, whilst the banks were obliged to refund the sums paid in and to suffer the loss themselves. The Cohen Committee recommended that the law should be amended.[11] Their recommendation was embodied in the Companies Acts of 1947 and 1948,[12] the result being that the depositor of the collateral security is now subject to the same liabilities "as if he had undertaken to be personally liable as surety for the debt to the extent of the charge on the property or the value of his interest, whichever is the less." This is a useful safeguard from the banking standpoint. If a banker is compelled to refund sums to liquidators or trustees in bankruptcy, on the ground of fraudulent preference, he is entitled to claim reimbursement from those who had deposited collateral security, even though they were smart enough to remove their securities prior to the liquidation or bankruptcy of the customer.

[10] [1938] 2 All E.R. at p. 139, *per* Luxmoore, J. sitting in the Court of Appeal.
[11] *The Report of the Committee on Company Law Amendment*, Cmd. 6659 (1945), para. 147.
[12] The Companies Act, 1947, Sect. 115 (4) applies to bankruptcy, and the Companies Act, 1948, Sect. 321 (1) applies to the winding up of companies.

Part Eight

SECURITIES GIVEN BY COMPANIES

CHAPTER 32

Securities Given by Companies

32-1. In modern times most of the large borrowers from the banks are limited companies. When a company wishes to borrow money, a number of preliminary legal questions must be resolved, for example, whether the company has power to borrow, how and by whom the power may be exercised, and whether there is any limitation on the amount which may be borrowed. These questions are considered in Volume 1 of this work.[1] The purpose of this chapter is to consider some of the problems relating to securities given by limited companies.

32-2. Many of the principles applicable to securities created by private individuals apply also to securities created by companies. However, there are certain matters affecting companies which do not arise in the case of other borrowers. Thus, most charges created by companies must be registered with the Registrar of Companies. Again, an important advantage enjoyed by companies, but denied to most individual borrowers, is the ability of a company to create a special type of charge known as a floating charge.[2]

32-3. Some security forms, e.g., a form of legal mortgage, must be executed under seal. The company's own seal should be used. If, however, a document under hand is sufficient, the board of directors should pass a resolution on the following lines authorising certain officials, probably the chairman and the secretary, to execute the instrument on the company's behalf: "Resolved that the Chairman and Secretary be authorised to execute [here describe the document] in favour of the London Bank Limited in the form and terms of the specimen attached hereto." The specimen should be initialled, and a certified copy of the resolution should be supplied to the bank.

Registration and Searching at Companies House

32-4. By virtue of Sect. 95 of the Companies Act, 1948, particulars of the following charges created by limited companies together with

---

[1] Paras. 11-276/94.
[2] A farmer seems to be the only individual borrower who may create a floating charge, and then only over his agricultural assets: see *ante*, para. 26-13. Industrial and provident societies also have certain statutory powers to create floating charges: see Vol. 1, paras. 11-386/87.

the instruments, if any, by which the charges are created or evidenced must be registered with the Registrar of Companies, Companies House, 55–71, City Road, London, E.C.1., within twenty-one days of the date of their creation—

(*a*) a charge for the purpose of securing any issue of debentures;[3]

(*b*) a charge on uncalled share capital of the company;

(*c*) a charge created or evidenced by an instrument which, if executed by an individual, would require registration as a bill of sale;[4]

(*d*) a charge on land, wherever situate, or any interest therein, but not including a charge for any rent or other periodical sum issuing out of land;[5]

(*e*) a charge on book debts of the company;[6]

(*f*) a floating charge on the undertaking or property of the company;[7]

(*g*) a charge on calls made but not paid;

(*h*) a charge on a ship or any share in a ship;

(*i*) a charge on goodwill, on a patent or a licence under a patent, on a trademark or on a copyright or a licence under a copyright.

32-5. Registration is not required in the following cases—

(*a*) where a negotiable instrument is given to secure the payment of any book debts of a company, and the instrument is deposited for the purpose of securing an advance to the company;[8]

(*b*) where a company assigns, by way of security, its interest in a policy issued by the Exports Credits Guarantee Department of the Board of Trade;[9]

(*c*) where a company mortgages shares, or assigns a life policy by way of security, or pledges goods.[10]

32-6. Subject to the special provisions relating to debentures in Sect. 95 (8) of the Companies Act, 1948, the particulars required by the Registrar are set out in Sect. 98 (1) (*b*) as follows:

---

[3] For debentures, see *post*, paras. 32-23/24.

[4] For bills of sale, see *ante*, para. 22-6.

[5] A sub-charge on land requires registration, either as a charge on land under Sect. 95 (2) (*d*), or as a charge on a book debt under Sect. 95 (2) (*e*); see *Re Molton Finance Ltd.* [1968] Ch. 325.

[6] For an illustration, see *Re Kent and Sussex Sawmills Ltd.* [1947] Ch. 177, *ante*, para. 29-8.

[7] For floating charges, see *post*, paras. 32-26/27.

[8] Companies Act, 1948, Sect. 95 (6).

[9] *Paul & Frank Ltd. and another* v. *Discount Bank (Overseas) Ltd. and another* [1967] Ch. 348.

[10] These are not among the registrable charges listed in Sect. 95.

(i) if the charge is a charge created by the company, the date of its creation, and, if the charge was a charge existing on property acquired by the company, the date of the acquisition of the property;

(ii) the amount secured by the charge;

(iii) short particulars of the property charged; and

(iv) the persons entitled to the charge.

32-7. Section 95 (8) of the Companies Act, 1948, provides that, in the case of a series of debentures containing or giving by reference to any other instrument, such as a trust deed, any charge to the benefit of which the debenture holders are entitled *pari passu*, it is sufficient if within twenty-one days after the execution of the deed containing the charge, or if there is no such deed, after the execution of any debentures of the series, the following particulars are filed—

(*a*) the total amount secured by the whole series;

(*b*) the dates of the resolutions authorising the issue of the series and the date of the covering deed, if any, by which the security is created or defined;

(*c*) a general description of the property charged; and

(*d*) the names of the trustees, if any, for the debenture holders;

together with the deed containing the charge, or, if there is no such deed, one of the debentures of the series.

32-8. Registration pursuant to Sect. 95 is effected by lodging the mortgage, debentures, or other instrument of charge with the Registrar, together with the Board of Trade Form No. 47.[11] Fees are no longer payable for entries in the register of charges kept by the Registrar.[12] Primarily it is the duty of the company to register the charge, but the Companies Act, 1948, expressly provides that registration may be effected on the application of any person interested therein.[13] In practice, when a registrable charge is created in favour of a bank, registration is effected by the bank or by its solicitors. As the charge must be stamped before it is registered,[14] and as registration has to be effected within twenty-one days of the creation of the charge, there is no time to lose. When registration has been effected, the Registrar must issue a certificate of registration, which he sends to the applicant, at the same time returning to him the instrument of charge. The certificate states the

---

[11] Companies (Forms) Order, 1949.

[12] Companies (Fees) Regulations, 1967. The fee of 1s. (5p) for inspecting the register of charges remains payable.

[13] Sect. 96 (1).

[14] Stamp Act, 1891, Sect. 17.

amount thereby secured; it is conclusive evidence that the requirements of the Act as to registration have been complied with.[15]

32-9. Thus in *Re C. L. Nye Ltd.*,[16] a company wanted to buy
certain premises, and negotiated a loan from the Westminster Bank
on the security of the premises. On 28th February, 1964, the transfers
of the premises, sealed by the vendors, were handed over to the bank,
or possibly to a solicitor acting for the bank, together with a charge
sealed by the company. The transfers and the charge were undated.
By an oversight, the charge was not registered with the Registrar of
Companies. On 18th June, 1964, the oversight was noticed, and on
3rd July the solicitor acting for the bank applied for registration of
the charge. He inserted 18th June in the charge, and on 3rd July, he
presented an application for registration of particulars of the charge.
The application stated, incorrectly, that the charge had been executed
on 18th June, 1964. The particulars were registered by the Registrar
on 3rd July, that is to say, within twenty-one days of 18th June (the
date inserted in the charge), but not within twenty-one days of 28th
February (the actual date of execution of the charge). In July, 1964,
the company went into liquidation. On 16th November, 1967, the
Registrar issued a certificate of registration. The liquidators sought
a declaration that the charge was void on account of non-registration
within twenty-one days from the date of its creation. The bank
contended that the certificate of registration was conclusive evidence
that the requirements of the Companies Act, 1948, had been complied with. Plowman, J., held that the charge was void, since it had
not been registered in due time, but the Court of Appeal reversed
his decision on the ground that once the Registrar's certificate had
been granted, Sect. 98 (2) of the Companies Act, 1948, applied and
so the certificate was conclusive evidence that all the requirements
of the Act had been complied with. Thus the charge in favour of the
bank was valid.

32-10. The register of charges kept by the Registrar is open to
inspection by any person on payment of a fee of 1s. (5p).[17] As a rule,
a bank searches the register before making any overdraft arrangements with a company. This is done, even though the charge which
the bank proposes to take does not require registration, e.g. a mortgage of shares. The asset concerned may already be the subject of a
charge in a debenture, and all debentures have to be registered. As
regards the method of searching, there are no search forms issued
for postal applications. Banks outside the Central London area
normally request either their Head Office or one of their nearby

15 Companies Act, 1948, Sect. 98 (2).
16 [1969] 2 All E.R. 587; on appeal, [1970] 3 W.L.R. 158.
17 Companies (Fees) Regulations, 1967.

London branches to search for them. Alternatively, if the bank's solicitors are attending to the matter, they usually ask their London agents to make the search.

32-11. If a registrable charge is not registered within twenty-one days of its creation, it is void against the liquidator and any creditor of the company.[18] Furthermore, the company and every officer of the company who is in default are liable to a fine of £50.[19] When a charge becomes void for want of registration, the money secured by the charge becomes payable immediately.[20] If the omission to register a charge is accidental or is not of a nature to prejudice the position of creditors or shareholders, the court may order that the time for registration shall be extended.[21] In practice, in those very rare cases where a bank omits to register a charge within twenty-one days of its creation, the bank usually obtains a fresh charge from the company and registers that charge.

32-12. Some companies are reluctant to create a registrable charge, because they consider that when it becomes known that they have created a charge, this can be harmful to their business. The provisions concerning registration cannot be evaded by taking an undated charge, for it has been held that if a company executes a charge which is undated, and, some months later, when accommodation is required, the date is filled in and the charge is registered, it is void for want of registration.[22] Nor can the provisions concerning registration be evaded by taking an oral charge, e.g. where the directors deposit title deeds as security without a memorandum. Section 95 (1) expressly provides that particulars of the charges specified therein "together with the instrument, if any," whereby the charges are created or evidenced must be registered. Clearly, the registration of purely oral charges is required.[23]

32-13. If a company enters into a contract to purchase land and agrees with its bank to deposit the title deeds on completion by

---

[18] Companies Act, 1948, Sect. 95 (1). A subsequent registered charge takes priority over an earlier unregistered charge, even though the subsequent chargee has express notice of the prior unregistered charge when he takes his security: see *Re Monolithic Building Co., Tacon* v. *Monolithic Building Co.* [1915] 1 Ch. 643, a decision on Sect. 93 of the Companies (Consolidation) Act, 1908, now replaced by Sect. 95 of the 1948 Act.

[19] Sect. 96 (3).

[20] Sect. 95 (1).

[21] Sect. 101. For an example of a case where time was extended see *Re Kris Cruisers Ltd.* [1948] 2 All E.R. 1105.

[22] *Esberger & Son Ltd.* v. *Capital and Counties Bank* [1913] 2 Ch. 366. *Quaere* whether this case would now be decided differently having regard to *Re C. L. Nye Ltd., ante*, para. 32-9.

[23] In *Re F. L. E. Holdings Ltd.* [1967] 3 All E.R. 553, an oral charge had been registered. However, as the date of the charge had been incorrectly stated, the charge was void for want of due registration.

way of security, the company thereby creates a charge over its equitable interest in the land arising from the contract, and so registration is necessary. If, however, a company agrees with its bank to create a charge in the future upon the happening of some contingency, no registration is required, because the agreement does not create a present security.[24] Sometimes, a company borrows money and gives an undertaking to execute a debenture "whenever called upon." Bankers are well advised to avoid this type of arrangement. If the charge is not created until the company is insolvent and about to wind up, the debenture, although registered before the winding up, may be set aside as fraudulent, provided that less than six months has elapsed between the issue of the debenture and the commencement of the winding up.[25]

Registration at the Company's Own Office

32-14. Every company must keep at its registered office a register of charges and enter therein all charges on any of the company's assets. The register must give, in each case, a short description of the property charged, the amount of the charge, and, except in respect of securities to bearer, the names of the persons entitled thereto.[26] The company must also keep a copy of the instruments creating the charges.[27] If any officer of the company knowingly and wilfully authorises or permits the omission of any entry in the register, he is liable to a fine not exceeding £50.[28] However, the mere non-registration of a charge in the company's register does not affect the validity of the security. The register of charges and the copies of those charges which require registration at Companies House are open to inspection by any creditor or member of the company without fee, and the register of charges is open to inspection by any other person on payment of such fee, not exceeding 1s. (5p) for each inspection as the company may prescribe.[29]

32-15. It is doubtful whether it is worth his while for a banker to search this register. Theoretically, a search might prove useful, because some charges which are not registrable at Companies House should be entered in the company's own register. In practice,

---

[24] See *per* Buckley, J. in *Re Jackson and Bassford Ltd.* [1906] 2 Ch. 467 at pp. 476–7; *Re Gregory Love & Co.* [1916] 1 Ch. 203.
[25] *Re Jackson and Bassford Ltd., supra; Re Eric Holmes (Property) Ltd.* [1965] Ch. 1052.
[26] Companies Act, 1948, Sect. 104 (1).
[27] Sect. 103.
[28] Sect. 104 (2).
[29] Sect. 105 (1).

however, many companies—particularly the smaller ones whose officers are little acquainted with company law—do not keep the register up to date, and too much reliance should not be placed upon it.

32-16. Where any liability of a company is secured, otherwise than by operation of law, on any assets of the company, the balance sheet must include a statement that the liability is so secured, but it is unnecessary to specify the assets on which the liability is secured.[30] Thus an examination of the company's balance sheet should disclose information about secured liabilities, but in practice this cannot always be relied upon.

Inadequacy of the System of Registration

32-17. A defect in the system of registration of charges created by companies was revealed in *National Provincial and Union Bank of England* v. *Charnley*.[31] A company had created in favour of a bank a mortgage over a leasehold factory and a charge over certain chattels. The bank sent the deed creating the security to the Registrar of Companies for registration. In the particulars on Form No. 47, the deed was described merely as a mortgage of the leasehold premises, no mention being made of the chattels. The Registrar copied this into the register, omitting all mention of the charge on the chattels. Subsequently the sheriff, in execution of a judgment recovered by the defendant against the company, seized certain chattels of the company upon the premises. The bank claimed these chattels under its charge, and obtained from the Registrar a certificate that the mortgage or charge was registered pursuant to Sect. 93 of the Companies (Consolidation) Act, 1908. That section provided (as does Sect. 98 (2) of the 1948 Act, which is now in force) that such certificate was conclusive evidence that the requirements of the Act as to registration had been complied with. The Court of Appeal held that, as the certificate identified the instrument of charge, and stated that the mortgage or charge thereby created had been duly registered, it must be understood as certifying the due registration of all the charges created by the instrument, including that of the chattels, even though the register, in omitting to mention them, was not merely defective but misleading.

32-18. Accordingly, a banker or other lender cannot rely exclusively upon the information available to him as a result of inspecting the

---

[30] Sect. 149 (2) and Sched. VIII.
[31] [1924] 1 K.B. 431; followed in *Re Eric Holmes (Property) Ltd.* [1965] Ch. 1052; and *Re Mechanisations (Eaglescliffe) Ltd.* [1966] Ch. 20.

register kept by the Registrar of Companies and the register kept by the company itself. If such inspection reveals the existence of a prior mortgage or charge, it is prudent in many cases to call for a copy of the instrument creating the prior charge.

Mortgages of Land by Companies

32-19. When a private individual mortgages land, the lender should always search the registers in the Land Charges Department, but registration of the mortgage is necessary only in those cases where the title deeds are not deposited with the lender.[32] With regard to limited companies, however, the register at Companies House should be searched and the mortgage must always be registered there, irrespective of whether or not the deeds are deposited, and irrespective of whether or not the land has a registered title. The Land Charges Act, 1925,[33] provided that, in the case of a land charge created by a company for securing money, registration under the Companies Act was sufficient in place of registration under the Land Charges Act, and that it was to have effect as if the land charge had been registered thereunder. However, the law was amended by the Law of Property Act, 1969,[34] which enacts that the provision in the Land Charges Act, 1925, is not to apply to any charge created by a company other than one created as a floating charge.[35] In practice, therefore, when a company mortgages land, the bank should search the registers kept in the Land Charges Department, but registration of the mortgage in that Department is necessary only in those cases where the title deeds are not deposited with the bank. Failure to register a charge at Companies House renders it void against a liquidator and any creditor of the company;[36] failure to register in the Land Charges Department renders it void against a purchaser. Since a purchaser of the property affected by a charge includes a mortgagee[37] and a mortgagee is also a creditor, it follows that a mortgagee is not bound by a charge registered in the Land Charges Department, unless it is also registered at Companies House. Floating charges still do not require to be registered in the registers kept in the Land Charges Department.[38]

---

[32] *Ante*, para. 3-62.
[33] Sect. 10 (5).
[34] Sect. 26.
[35] The law was amended so that advantage could be taken of the terms of Sect. 4 (2), Law of Property (Amendment) Act, 1926: see *ante*, para. 3-35.
[36] See *ante*, para. 32-11.
[37] Land Charges Act, 1925, Sect. 20 (8).
[38] The Law Commission recommended the exclusion of floating charges "primarily in order to reduce the work which might otherwise be imposed on the Land Charges Registry and on lenders and their advisers." See Law Com. No. 18, para. 72.

32-20. If title to the land has been registered, it is advisable to send the land certificate to the District Land Registry[39] to be brought up to date, in addition to searching at Companies House. When the mortgage has been executed, the same procedure should be followed as in the case of a mortgage created by a private individual; that is to say, if the mortgage is a legal one, it must be registered at the land registry[40] or, if equitable, notice of deposit of the land certificate must be given.[41] Whether the mortgage is legal or equitable, it must be registered at Companies House. It matters little which registration is effected first, though in practice it is safer to register at Companies House first, so as to ensure that registration there is made within twenty-one days. Rule 145 of the Land Registration Rules, 1925, provides that, when a charge is registered at the land registry, the certificate of registration issued by the Registrar of Companies should be produced. However, this is not obligatory. If the certificate is not produced, a note is made in the register that the charge is subject to the provisions of the Companies Act.

32-21. If the land is situated in Yorkshire (but outside the City of York), one should search (a) at Companies House; (b) in the appropriate local deeds registry at Northallerton, Beverley, or Wakefield (the Law of Property Act, 1969, contains provisions which will eventually lead to the closure of these local deeds registries[42] but until they are closed, a search there may reveal restrictive covenants, equitable easements, or estate contracts, which are not, of course, registrable at Companies House); and also (c) in the Land Charges Department in London. If the mortgage is a legal one, irrespective of whether or not it is protected by deposit of the deeds, it should be registered locally at Northallerton, Beverley, or Wakefield, as well as at Companies House. If the mortgage is equitable and the deeds are deposited, registration at Companies House alone is sufficient. If the mortgage is equitable and the deeds are not deposited, it seems that by virtue of Sect. 10 (5) and (6) of the Land Charges Act, 1925, registration at Companies House used to be sufficient.[43] However, such registration is no longer sufficient,

[39] See *ante*, para. 10-15.
[40] See *ante*, para. 10-26.
[41] See *ante*, para. 10-32.
[42] See *ante*, para. 3-63.
[43] Sect. 10 (6), as amended by Sect. 7 and Sched., Law of Property (Amendment) Act, 1926, provides that "in the case of a general equitable charge . . . affecting land within any of the three ridings . . . registration shall be effected in the prescribed manner in the appropriate local deeds registry" instead of being registered in the Land Charges Register in London. But Sect. 10 (5) modified this as regards companies by enacting that registration under the Companies Act was sufficient in place of registration under the Land Charges Act and was to have effect as if the land charge had been registered thereunder.

because the Law of Property Act, 1969,[44] enacted that the provision in Sect. 10 (5) of the Land Charges Act, 1925, is not to apply to any charge created by a company other than a floating charge.

32-22. Finally, the registers kept by the district, borough and county councils, should be searched, if the nature of the property offered as security seems to render this desirable.[45]

Debentures

32-23. The Companies Act, 1948, gives a very wide meaning to the term debenture. It provides that "debenture" includes debenture stock, bonds and any other securities of a company whether constituting a charge on the assets of a company or not.[46] When a business man or a lawyer speaks of a debenture, he is usually referring to the type of instrument which does create a charge on the company's assets, or some of them. In this narrower and more usual meaning, a debenture may be defined as an instrument executed by a company in favour of a bank or other lender, which normally gives a specific or fixed charge on the company's fixed assets (e.g. its freehold and leasehold properties) and what is known as a "floating charge" on the rest of its undertaking.[47]

32-24. A debenture may be expressed to be a security for all sums owed by the company to the lender (an "all-moneys" debenture), or it may be a security for a fixed sum (a "fixed-sum" debenture). The fixed-sum type of debenture has certain disadvantages as a banking security, and is seldom used for that purpose. Thus, the amount of a fixed-sum debenture has to be disclosed when the debenture is registered at Companies House. Directors usually prefer to execute an all-moneys debenture, because no amount is thereby disclosed upon registration. Again, if a fixed-sum debenture is used and if the company wants to borrow more money, additional fixed-sum debentures have to be issued, stamped and registered at Companies House. This is avoided if an all-moneys debenture is used; it is merely necessary to increase the stamp duty on the original document within thirty days of granting the additional accommodation.

Fixed and Floating Charges

32-25. A debenture in favour of a bank usually creates a fixed charge on certain assets of the company, and a floating charge over

[44] Sect. 26; see *ante*, para. 32-19.
[45] *Ante*, paras. 3-56/58.
[46] Sect. 455 (1).
[47] For fixed and floating charges, see *post*, paras. 32-25/27.

the remainder of the assets. Thus, a fixed first charge is usually created on the company's goodwill and on its uncalled capital; and a fixed first charge by way of legal mortgage is created on its freehold and leasehold property, and on its fixed plant and machinery, with the result that the company is prevented from disposing of these assets without the permission of the debenture holder. Finally, a first floating charge is created over all the other property and assets of the company.

32-26. A floating charge does not prevent the company from dealing in the ordinary course of business with the assets which are the subject of the charge. Thus, a floating charge is a charge on assets which are continually changing in the ordinary course of the business of the company and, until some legal step is taken by the debenture holder to determine the position, the company is entirely free to deal with those assets, for example, by selling them and using the proceeds to purchase fresh assets, which themselves are then subject to the floating charge. In the words of Lord Macnaghten[48]—

> A floating security is an equitable charge on the assets for the time being of a going concern. It attaches to the subject charged in the varying condition in which it happens to be from time to time. It is of the essence of such a charge that it remains dormant until the undertaking charged ceases to be a going concern, or until the person in whose favour the charge is created intervenes.

32-27. A floating charge ceases to float and becomes "fixed" or "crystallised" if—

(i) The company makes default in payment of interest or in repayment of part of the principal or commits some other breach of the terms of the debenture, *and the lender thereupon takes some step to crystallise the charge.* The usual step which he takes is to appoint a receiver. The mere fact that a company fails to meet the written demand of the lender for repayment does not of itself convert the floating charge into a fixed charge.[49]

(ii) The company goes into liquidation. A floating charge crystallises automatically at the commencement of the winding up of the company, whether or not the company is in default to the holder of the charge.[50] The licence given by the holder of a floating charge to a company to deal with its assets in the ordinary course of business is on the implied condition that the company

---

[48] *Governments Stock and Other Securities Investment Co. Ltd.* v. *Manila Railway Co. Ltd.* [1897] A.C. 81, at p. 86.
[49] *Nelson & Co.* v. *Faber & Co.* [1903] 2 K.B. 367, at p. 376; *Evans* v. *Rival Granite Quarries Ltd.* [1940] 2 K.B. 979.
[50] *Hodson* v. *Tea Company* (1880) 14 Ch. D. 859.

carries on business; and so, if the company ceases to carry on business, the licence is automatically determined and the charge becomes fixed and fastens upon the assets.

(iii) The company ceases to carry on business without going into liquidation.[51] This rarely happens in practice.

Disadvantages of Floating Charges

32-28. Although floating charges are undoubtedly a useful form of company security—especially when used in conjunction with a specific charge over a company's fixed assets—they do suffer from a number of disadvantages from a banker's point of view. The following are the principal weaknesses of this form of security—

A. REDUCTION IN VALUE OF THE ASSETS

32-29. A floating charge is often worth least when a lender seeks to rely upon it. As a company which executes a floating charge is free to deal with its assets in the ordinary course of business, it may, unknown to the bank, realise its stocks and collect money from trade debtors in order to meet pressing unsecured creditors, with the result that when the bank appoints a receiver, the value of the remaining assets may be very small. The outstanding trade debtors may consist very largely of doubtful or slow payers, and some debtors may refuse to pay on the ground that they have claims against the company. Work-in-progress may be unsaleable except as scrap, unless it is completed. Moreover, when a company is short of cash, repairs and replacements are often deferred, and this inevitably reduces the value of the assets concerned. Finally, the cost of realising the assets is frequently substantial. The receiver has to be remunerated for his services, and in many cases there are fees payable to agents employed by him.

B. PRIORITY OF PREFERENTIAL CREDITORS

32-30. Certain classes of creditors are, by law, treated preferentially, either in the event of the company being wound up, or in the event of a receiver being appointed.[52] These preferential creditors, as they are usually called, have priority over creditors holding a floating charge and over unsecured creditors, but not over creditors who hold a fixed charge on the company's assets. The various classes of

---

[51] *Nelson & Co.* v. *Faber & Co.* (*supra*), at p. 376.
[52] Companies Act, 1948, Sects. 94 (1) and 319 (1).

preferential creditors are listed in Volume 1 of this work.[53] The largest preferential creditor is frequently the Inland Revenue.

32-31. In the result, if a company is being wound up and the free (i.e. uncharged) assets are insufficient to pay the preferential creditors, their claims must be met out of any property comprised in a floating (but not a fixed) charge in priority to the claims of the debenture holder. Likewise, if a company is *not* being wound up but a receiver is appointed, preferential debts which have accrued up to the date of his appointment must be paid out of the assets comprised in a floating (but not a fixed) charge in priority to the claims of the debenture holder;[54] any such payments, however, may be recouped, as far as may be, out of the assets of the company available for payment of the general creditors.[55] In modern conditions of heavy taxation, it not infrequently happens that a large proportion of the proceeds of realisation of a company's assets has to be applied by the receiver to satisfy the demands of the Revenue. Little remains for the debenture holder.

C. PRIORITY OF OTHER CREDITORS

32-32. If a bank is relying on a floating charge and the company is being hard pressed by its creditors, there is a risk that certain creditors may obtain priority over the bank. For example, if a company's landlord levies a distress for rent before the bank appoints a receiver under its floating charge, this will be valid as against the bank.[56] Again, if a creditor obtains judgment against a company, and goods covered by a floating charge are seized and sold by the sheriff to satisfy the judgment, it seems that this will be valid as against the holder of the floating charge, provided that the proceeds are paid by the sheriff to the creditor before the charge is crystallised by the appointment of a receiver.[57] Finally, if a creditor obtains a garnishee order absolute attaching a credit balance of the company in the hands of some third party, this will be valid as against the holder of a floating charge, provided that the order absolute is made before a receiver is appointed.[58]

D. LIQUIDATION WITHIN A YEAR

32-33. The Companies Act, 1948,[59] provides that a floating charge created during the twelve months prior to the commencement of

[53] Para. 11-299.
[54] Companies Act, 1948, Sect. 94 (1).
[55] Sect. 94 (5).
[56] *Re Roundwood Colliery Co., Lee* v. *Roundwood Colliery Co.* [1897] 1 Ch. 373.
[57] *Re Opera Ltd.* [1891] 3 Ch. 260; *Taunton* v. *Sheriff of Warwickshire* [1895] 2 Ch. 319; *Evans* v. *Rival Granite Quarries Ltd.* [1910] 2 K.B. 979.
[58] *Evans* v. *Rival Granite Quarries Ltd.* (*supra*).
[59] Sect. 322 (1).

winding up is invalid, except to the extent of cash paid to the company "at the time of or subsequently to the creation of, and in consideration for, the charge," together with interest thereon at five per cent, or such other rate as may for the time being be prescribed by the Treasury.[60] It is further enacted, however, that the charge is valid if it can be proved that, immediately after its creation, the company was solvent. In order to prove solvency for this purpose, it is necessary to prove that the company was able to pay its debts as they became due.[61]

32-34. Sometimes there is a delay of a few days, or even a week or two in the execution of the charge. It has been held by the courts that the question whether or not a payment is made "at the time of" the creation of the charge is one of fact, and so a payment made shortly *before* and in anticipation of the charge, and in reliance on a promise to execute it, is within the words used in the section.[62]

32-35. The Rule in *Clayton's* case[63] may operate in favour of a bank if a company goes into liquidation within twelve months of the creation of a floating charge. All moneys paid into a company's bank account after a floating charge is executed are deemed to have been appropriated to reduce the debt outstanding at the time of execution, and all subsequent drawings amount to new lendings secured by the charge. Therefore, if the amount so paid in equals or exceeds the debt outstanding at the time of execution, the charge will be fully effective, even if the company goes into liquidation within the year.[64]

E. POSSIBLE PRIORITY OF SUBSEQUENT FIXED CHARGE

32-36. A company which has created a floating charge may at a later date execute in favour of another lender a fixed mortgage or charge on some of the assets comprised in the floating charge, and,

---

[60] Companies Winding Up (Floating Charges) (Interest) Order, 1949, prescribed a rate of four per cent, but this order was revoked by the Companies Winding Up (Floating Charges) (Interest) Order, 1952, so the rate of interest is now five per cent.
[61] *Re Patrick and Lyon Ltd.* [1933] 1 Ch. 786.
[62] *Re Collumbian Fireproofing Co. Ltd.* [1910] 2 Ch. 120; *Re Stanton (F. and E.) Ltd.* [1929] 1 Ch. 180.
[63] (1816) 1 Mer. 572.
[64] *Re Thomas Mortimer Ltd.* (1925) [1965] 1 Ch. 187 (Note), a case decided under Sect. 212, Companies (Consolidation) Act, 1908; *Re Yeovil Glove Co. Ltd.* [1965] Ch. 148.

unless proper precautions are taken in the first instance by the holder of the floating charge, the subsequent fixed charge may take priority over the floating charge. The reason why the subsequent fixed charge may take priority over the earlier floating charge is because the specific charge is regarded as having been completed under implied licence from the holder of the floating charge. In the result, the fixed charge will take priority over the floating charge, whether or not the specific chargee had notice of the floating charge, and whether his charge is legal or equitable.[65] In order to avoid this result, it is usual to insert a clause in the debenture containing the floating charge whereby the company undertakes not to create any mortgage or charge on any of its assets to rank in priority to or *pari passu* with the floating charge. This restrictive clause, however, will not be binding upon a subsequent chargee unless he has notice of it; and the mere registration of a floating charge at Companies House is not notice that the charge contains a restrictive clause.[66] There are two ways of overcoming this difficulty. The more usual course is to recite the restrictive clause in Form 47 when registering the debenture at Companies House. The alternative method is to persuade the company to pass a special resolution authorising the execution of the floating charge and incorporating the restrictive clause. Every special resolution must be filed at Companies House,[67] and a subsequent lender would probably be affected with notice of its terms.

Form of Debenture

32-37. Banks have their own printed form of debenture which is suitable for use in most cases. The following are the principal clauses commonly incorporated in an "all-moneys" debenture—

(i) The company covenants to repay upon demand[68] all moneys owing, including interest and commission charges.

(ii) By way of security the company normally creates a fixed first charge on its goodwill and on its uncalled capital; a fixed first charge by way of legal mortgage on its freehold and leasehold property, and on its fixed plant and machinery; and a floating charge over all its other property and assets.

[65] *Re Hamilton's Windsor Ironworks, Ex parte Pitman and Edwards* (1879) 12 Ch. D. 707; *Re Castell & Brown Ltd., Roper* v. *Castell and Brown Ltd.* [1898] 1 Ch. 315.
[66] *Re Valletort Sanitary Steam Laundry Co. Ltd., Ward* v. *Valletort Sanitary Steam Laundry Co. Ltd.* [1903] 2 Ch. 654; *Re Standard Rotary Machine Co.* (1906) 95 L.T. 829.
[67] Companies Act, 1948, Sect. 143.
[68] In some forms a short period after demand, e.g. 7 or 14 days after demand, is stipulated for.

(iii) The company covenants not to create any mortgage or charge to rank in priority to or *pari passu* with the floating charge.[69]

(iv) The moneys secured by the debenture are declared to become immediately payable upon the happening of certain specified events, such as a demand in writing by the bank, the commencement of winding-up proceedings, or the cessation of business by the company.

(v) At any time after the bank has demanded payment of any moneys secured by the debenture and whether or not they have become due, the bank is authorised to appoint by writing a receiver, with power to take possession of the property charged and to carry on the company's business. It is stipulated that the receiver is to be the company's agent, so as to make the company responsible for his acts and defaults. The company irrevocably appoints the bank and any receiver jointly and also severally its attorney and attorneys for the purpose of executing deeds.

(vi) The company undertakes to supply the bank half-yearly or oftener if required with a balance sheet, profit and loss and trading account showing the true position of the company's affairs not more than one month previously, certified by the auditors of the company.

(vii) Finally, there is the usual undertaking to insure the property and to produce the premium receipts.

Completing the Security

32-38. Some of the matters detailed below must receive attention in every case when debentures are taken as security, but others arise only occasionally—

A. SEARCHES

32-39. In every case a search should be made at Companies House, and if land is charged, other searches may be necessary.[70]

B. RE-ISSUE OF DEBENTURES

32-40. If a company has redeemed any debentures previously issued, it may re-issue them, unless (*a*) there is any provision to the contrary in the company's articles or in any contract entered into by the company, or (*b*) the company has resolved that the debentures are to be cancelled.[71] Particulars of any redeemed debentures which

---

[69] See *ante*, para. 32-36.
[70] See *ante*, para. 32-19.
[71] Companies Act, 1948, Sect. 90 (1).

a company has power to re-issue must be given in the company's balance sheet.[72] On a re-issue of redeemed debentures the person entitled to them has the same priorities as if they had never been redeemed.[73] Accordingly, when a banker finds that a company has power to re-issue redeemed debentures, he should insist that they be cancelled. Alternatively, if they are a suitable security from the banking standpoint, they could be re-issued to the bank. For the purposes of stamp duty, the re-issue of a debenture is treated as the issue of a new debenture.[74] The re-issue of debentures to the bank is particularly useful if some of the debentures of the same series are still current and are in the hands of other lenders, because the bank thereby obtains a security ranking *pari passu* with the other debentures. It is also enacted—and this too is of practical importance to bankers—that, whenever a company deposits any of its debentures to secure advances from time to time on current account or otherwise, the debentures are not to be deemed to have been redeemed by reason only of the company's account having ceased to be in debit whilst the debentures remained so deposited.[75]

C. DEPOSIT OF DEEDS, ETC.

32-41. When taking debentures as security a bank should always obtain the deposit of any title deeds, stock and share certificate, or life policies comprised in the security. If the company was left in possession of these documents, it might mortgage them to another lender. This does not necessarily mean that the second lender would obtain priority over the bank, even if the assets concerned were merely covered by a floating charge in favour of the bank; a bank usually safeguards its priority by inserting a restrictive clause in the debenture *and* having it entered on the register at Companies House.[76] The object, therefore, of having these documents deposited is the purely practical one of making it impossible, so far as one can, for the company to contract secured loans from other sources without the bank's knowledge.

D. VALUATION OF THE SECURITY

32-42. The value of a debenture as a security depends upon the assets on which it is charged. The assets—land and buildings, stock, debtors (less provision for doubtful debts), stock exchange securities,

---

[72] Companies Act, 1948, Sched. VIII.
[73] Sect. 90 (2).
[74] Sect. 90 (4).
[75] Sect. 90 (3).
[76] See *ante*, para. 32-36.

etc.—are valued in the usual way, and any prior charges are deducted. In relation to floating charges, certain creditors of the company may have preferential rights and will rank before the floating charge.[77] Debentures should be re-valued at regular intervals. In many cases it is sufficient to re-value then annually, i.e. when the company forwards to the bank a copy of its balance sheet. However, whenever current assets are relied upon substantially, quarterly or even monthly figures are often called for.

E. SEALING, STAMPING AND REGISTRATION

32-43. When the debenture has been sealed by the company, it must be stamped at the rate of 2s. (10p) per cent on the amount secured,[78] which is the amount of the debenture where it is for a fixed sum, or the maximum amount of the advance where it is an "all-moneys" debenture. Fixed-sum debentures (which are rarely taken as security[79]) are registered in the name of the bank's nominee company, and are accompanied by a memorandum of deposit. This memorandum states that the debenture is to be a continuing security for all sums due or to become due, that the bank may charge interest on the overdrawn account at its usual fluctuating rate (instead of the rate specified in the debenture), and that the bank, on the company's default, may sell the debenture.[80] The memorandum is exempt from stamp duty, if it is executed under the hand of duly authorised officials.[81]

32-44. All debentures must be registered at Companies House.[82] Moreover, if land is comprised in the security, registration elsewhere may also be required.[83]

F. DEBENTURE OF NEWLY CONSTITUTED COMPANY

32-45. Special precautions are sometimes necessary when a bank is asked to lend to a newly constituted company and the company

---

[77] See *ante*, para. 32-32.

[78] See *post*, para. 33-24.

[79] See *ante*, para. 32-24.

[80] This memorandum is sometimes known as the "Buckley Agreement." It is so called because Mr. H. B. Buckley, Q.C. (later Lord Wrenbury), expressed the opinion that, in the absence of such agreement, the bank's rights might be restricted to those of an outside debenture holder. As there would be no link between the banking account and the debenture, the bank might possibly be unable to sue on the overdraft as opposed to the debenture.

[81] Finance Act, 1970, Sect. 32 and Sched. 7.

[82] See *ante*, para. 32-4.

[83] See *ante*, paras. 32-20/21.

executes a debenture or mortgage to secure the advance. *Re Simms*[84] illustrates the risk attaching to this type of transaction. Mr. Simms, a builder, with a view to obtaining accommodation from Lloyds Bank, converted his business into a private limited company. He transferred substantially the whole of his assets to the company, which also undertook responsibility for his liabilities. Debentures for £12,500 were issued to Lloyds Bank to secure an overdraft of about £7,000. Mr. Simms did not inform any of his creditors of the transfer of his assets to the company. Very soon some of the creditors became alarmed and began to press for their money. Mr. Simms was unable to comply with a bankruptcy notice, and, as a result of this act of bankruptcy, he was adjudicated bankrupt. The title of a trustee in bankruptcy relates back to the *first* act of bankruptcy committed during the three months preceding the presentation of the bankruptcy petition.[85] It was held that the transfer of Mr. Simms' assets to the company was a "fraudulent transfer" within the meaning of the Bankruptcy Act, 1914,[86] and was therefore an act of bankruptcy. Thus, the trustee's title related back to the date of that transfer, with the result that all the assets transferred to the company had to be handed over to the trustee. The debentures given to the bank to secure the company's overdraft were almost worthless, because there were practically no assets remaining in the company's hands.

32-46. To guard against this kind of risk, a banker should make sure that all the creditors have either been paid or have agreed to accept the new company as their debtor. Naturally, one must use discretion; if the financial position of the person who has transferred his assets to the new company is known to be undoubted, it would serve no useful purpose, and in fact would give offence, to make such inquiries.

G. DIRECTOR PERSONALLY INTERESTED

32-47. When lending to limited companies it is often sound policy to try to arrange that the advance be secured not only by a debenture embodying a fixed charge and a floating charge, but also by the personal guarantee of the directors. This applies particularly to small family concerns where the directors hold most, if not all, of

---

[84] [1930] 2 Ch. 22.

[85] Bankruptcy Act, 1914, Sect. 37.

[86] Sect. 1 (1). "Fraudulent," in this connection, does not necessarily connote moral fraud. There need be no more than a design to defeat or delay creditors, generally by some act which will prevent the distribution of the debtor's property in accordance with the bankruptcy laws: *Re Sinclair, Ex parte Chaplin* (1884) 26 Ch.D. 319.

the share capital. The guarantee is taken as proof of the confidence which the directors have in the future of their company, and it tends to ensure their personal active interest in the company's affairs. When assessing the financial status of the directors as guarantors one must, of course, bear in mind that this may be related to the success of the company.

32-48. It is advisable to have the debenture issued at the time when the guarantee is executed, or else to have the debenture issued first. If the guarantee precedes the issue of the debenture, there is a risk that the debenture may be void as against the liquidator of the company, unless proper precautions are taken. In *Victors Ltd.* v. *Lingard*[87] all five directors of a company guaranteed the company's overdraft at the Midland Bank. Some eighteen months later the directors resolved that the company should issue to the bank £30,000 first debentures by way of additional security. The company's articles provided that no director should be disqualified from entering into contracts with the company, but added that "no director shall vote as a director in regard to any contract, arrangement, or dealing in which he is interested or upon any matter arising thereout, and if he shall so vote his vote shall not be counted, nor shall he be reckoned for the purpose of constituting a quorum of directors." Romer, J., stated that the object of this article was "to ensure to the company that its directors should not be placed in a position in which their personal interests might be in conflict with the duty they owed to the company, and that in all transactions entered into by them on behalf of the company, the company should be able to rely upon their unbiased and independent judgment."[88] In the circumstances it was to the personal advantage of the directors to issue the debentures, because it tended to relieve them from liability under their guarantee. Thus, it was held that the resolution providing for the issue of the debentures was a nullity. Fortunately for the bank, however, it was also held that, having regard to the subsequent history of the proceedings between the company and the bank, the company was estopped from alleging the invalidity of the debentures.

32-49. Although *Victors Ltd.* v. *Lingard* was concerned with the issue of debentures, the principle is of much wider application. It applies to all types of direct security taken from companies subsequent to the execution of a guarantee by the directors or the deposit of security by them for the company's account; it applies where one company guarantees the account of another company

[87] [1927] 1 Ch. 323.
[88] [1927] 1 Ch. at pp. 329–30.

and a director who votes on the resolution authorising the giving of the guarantee is a director or shareholder of the company for whose benefit it is given; and presumably it applies if a director is merely a shareholder in the bank receiving the guarantee. In all these cases, a director is personally interested.

32-50. The procedure which should be adopted in order to avoid loss is as follows. First, the company's articles must be examined. They will not necessarily contain a clause similar to that in *Victors Ltd. v. Lingard.* Sometimes, articles contain an express provision that the directors may vote in regard to contracts in which they are interested. If the articles are silent on this point, Table A will apply. The relevant articles of Table A in the various Companies Acts differ slightly;[89] and, for the first time, Table A in the 1948 Act expressly permits a director to vote upon "any arrangement for the giving by the company of any security to a third party in respect of a debt or obligation of the company for which the director himself has assumed responsibility in whole or in part under a guarantee or indemnity or by the deposit of a security." In the absence of such an article, the problem is governed by the general rule of law that no man, acting as an agent, can be allowed to put himself in a position in which his interest and duty will be in conflict.[90] In short, such a director must not vote.

32-51. Secondly, one should ascertain how many directors are precluded from voting by virtue of this rule. If there are sufficient directors to form a "disinterested" quorum, they may pass the resolution authorising the issue of the debentures. The quorum is usually specified in the articles. Article 99, Table A, Companies Act, 1948, provides: "The quorum necessary for the transaction of the business of the directors may be fixed by the directors, and unless so fixed shall be two." If it is impossible to obtain a disinterested quorum (as was the case in *Victors Ltd. v. Lingard,* where all the directors had signed the guarantee), the resolution should be passed, not by the directors, but by the company in general meeting. The only alternative is for the company to alter its articles, conferring upon the directors the power to vote on contracts in which they are interested. Sometimes one finds that there are no shareholders apart from the directors themselves. Even in this case, however, it is advisable for the directors, in their capacity as shareholders, to pass this resolution at a *general* meeting, rather than at a directors' meeting.[91]

---

[89] See article 57, 1862 Act; article 77, 1908 Act; article 72, 1929 Act; articles 84 and 88, 1948 Act.

[90] *Parker* v. *McKenna* (1874) 10 Ch. App. 96, at p. 118.

[91] This is certainly the normal practice, though it is doubtful whether it is strictly essential for the directors to act in general meeting, provided that they are unanimous.

32-52. After security has been taken from a company, it is sometimes discovered that the rule laid down in *Victors Ltd.* v. *Lingard* has been violated, the resolution authorising the giving of the security having been passed by interested directors. The remedy is to persuade the company to pass a resolution in general meeting ratifying the arrangements made by the directors. By passing an ordinary resolution, shareholders can ratify any contract which comes within the powers of the company.[92]

32-53. Finally, irrespective of whether or not directors are permitted to vote on contracts in which they are interested, their attention may usefully be drawn to Sect. 199 (1) of the Companies Act, 1948, which provides that it is the duty of a director "who is in any way, whether directly or indirectly, interested in a contract or proposed contract with the company to declare the nature of his interest at a meeting of the directors of the company." Any director who fails to declare his interest is liable to a fine not exceeding £100.[93]

Notice of Second Charge

32-54. If a company which has executed a debenture in favour of its bank creates a second charge over some or all of the assets comprised in the security given to the bank, the company's account must be broken as soon as the bank receives notice of the second charge. This is essential in order to avoid the operation of the Rule in *Clayton's* case.[94]

32-55. If the second lender registers his charge at Companies House, but fails to give express notice to the bank, is the bank deemed to have notice of the charge merely by reason of the fact that it has been registered? There is no answer to this question in the Companies Act, but Eve, J., expressed the view that registration amounts to constructive notice.[95] The opinion given by the learned judge was admittedly not necessary to enable him to arrive at his decision and is, therefore, a dictum possessing merely persuasive authority. Furthermore, it was expressed in a case which did not involve the priority of a lender on current account. If his view is correct, and if it applies to persons who lend money on current account, then, once a second charge has been registered, any further advances by the bank must rank after it. It is quite impossible for bankers to search the register at Companies House every few days in order to

---

[92] *Grant* v. *United Kingdom Switchback Railways Co.* (1888) 40 Ch. D. 135.
[93] Sect. 199 (4).
[94] (1816) 1 Mer. 572.
[95] *Wilson* v. *Kelland* [1910] 2 Ch. 306, at p. 313.

find out whether their company customers have created any further charges on their assets. It is, however, a wise precaution to examine regularly one of the commercial gazettes in which such matters are published.

Appointment of a Receiver

32-56. In most cases a company duly repays its indebtedness to the bank. However, if a company which has executed a debenture gets into financial difficulties, the bank will have to decide whether or not to appoint a receiver. Sometimes the directors themselves realise that nothing can be done to save the company and they may invite the bank to appoint a receiver. In most cases, however, they are anxious to continue to trade, and accordingly they usually press the bank to honour their cheques, and especially their weekly wages cheques. The bank has a difficult decision to make. On the one hand, if it declines to provide cash for wages, then in the absence of any other source of finance, the employees will leave and the company will have to close down. On the other hand, if the bank does provide cash for wages, the company will probably continue to trade, but if it is already trading at a loss, those losses may be increased. With these considerations in mind, the bank will have to decide whether or not the time has come to appoint a receiver. It will almost certainly do so if it learns that other creditors are taking legal action to recover the amounts due to them.

32-57. As a general rule, a receiver is appointed by a debenture holder pursuant to a power contained in the debenture. The debenture usually provides that a receiver may be appointed "at any time after the bank shall have demanded payment of any moneys hereby secured and whether or not they shall have become due." It is usual to appoint as receiver an accountant who is experienced in this work. A receiver who is appointed pursuant to an express power in a debenture will not be displaced by the court in the event of the subsequent winding-up of the company by the court.[96] The power of a debenture holder to appoint a receiver may be exercised even after the company has gone into liquidation, and, where a receiver is so appointed, the court will not, if the appointment is valid, displace the receiver by appointing the liquidator in his place.[97] However, if a receiver does not take possession of the company's property before the winding-up order is made, he must apply to the court for leave to do so. A liquidator may be appointed to act also

[96] *Re Stubbs (Joshua) Ltd., Barney* v. *Stubbs (Joshua) Ltd.* [1891] 1 Ch. 475.
[97] *Re Stubbs (Joshua) Ltd. (supra).*

as receiver in respect of the assets charged by the bank's debenture, but this is rarely done because of a possible conflict of interests.

32-58. If a debenture does not confer upon the holder express power to appoint a receiver, application must be made to the court for the appointment. This is rarely necessary. Whether he is appointed by the court or by the debenture holder, a receiver may apply to the court for directions in respect of any particular matter arising in connection with the performance of his functions.[98]

32-59. The appointment of a receiver by a bank is made by writing under hand or seal, as required by the debenture. The document recites that the moneys secured by the debenture are due and payable, and appoints some third party (usually an accountant) to be receiver of the property charged by the debenture. The express powers of the receiver are often stated: these may include a power to carry on the business of the company, power to borrow money on the property charged by the debenture, and power to sell any of the assets charged. The receiver is made the agent of the company so that the company, and not the bank, will be responsible for his acts.

32-60. Any person who obtains a court order for the appointment of a receiver or who himself appoints a receiver must have the appointment registered at Companies House within seven days; and, if he fails to do so, he is liable to a fine not exceeding five pounds for every day during which the default continues.[99] Notice of the appointment should be given on Board of Trade Form No. 53.

Remuneration of Receiver

32-61. When a receiver is appointed by the court, his remuneration is fixed by the court. If he is appointed out of court, his remuneration is usually fixed by agreement under an express provision in the debenture.[100] Even when he is appointed out of court, the court may, on an application by the liquidator of the company, fix the amount to be paid to him; moreover, if he has been paid in respect of any period before the making of the order any amount in excess of the sum so fixed for that period, he or his personal representatives may be required to account for the excess or such part thereof as may be specified in the order.[101]

---

[98] Companies Act, 1948, Sect. 369 (1), reproducing Sect. 87 (1) of the 1947 Act.
[99] Companies Act, 1948, Sect. 102.
[100] See Sect. 109 (6), Law of Property Act, 1925, and *Re Greycaine Ltd.* [1946] Ch. 269, *ante*, para. 7-15.
[101] Companies Act, 1948, Sect. 371 (1) and (2).

Powers and Duties of Receiver

32-62. It is beyond the scope of this book to give a detailed account of the powers and duties of a receiver. However, as banks sometimes find it necessary to appoint a receiver, it is desirable that bank officers should possess a general knowledge of this branch of the law. Accordingly, a brief account of the subject will be given here.

32-63. If substantially the whole of a company's property is included in a charge and a receiver is appointed, he must notify the company of his appointment and the company must send to him a statement of the company's affairs in a prescribed form within fourteen days of such notice.[102]

32-64. The receiver must within two months after the receipt of this statement send (i) to the Registrar of Companies, a copy of the statement and of any comments which he sees fit to make thereon, and also a summary of the statement; and (ii) to the company, a copy of any such comments or a notice that he does not think fit to make any comment; and (iii) to the debenture holders, a copy of the summary.[103]

32-65. The receiver must within two months (subject to extension by the Board of Trade) after the expiration of twelve months from the date of his appointment and of every subsequent twelve months and within two months after he ceases to act, send to the Registrar of Companies, to the company, and to the debenture holders an abstract of his receipts and payments in a prescribed form.[104]

32-66. The receiver enjoys the statutory powers conferred by Sect. 109 of the Law of Property Act, 1925.[105] Moreover, when a bank as debenture holder appoints a receiver, the receiver has the powers set out in the bank's form of debenture; for example, the receiver will often be given power to carry on the company's business. In essence, therefore, the receiver's duties are to carry on the company's business if that seems desirable, and to realise the company's assets with a view to collecting the maximum amount possible in order to discharge the company indebtedness to the bank. In cases where a receiver is appointed in respect of the whole of a company's assets and the receiver is given power to carry on the company's business, the directors become, for all practical purposes, *functus officio.* In such cases the company will probably be wound up if any unsecured creditors think it worth their while to present a petition. In practice,

---

[102] Companies Act, 1948, Sect. 372.
[103] Ibid.
[104] Ibid.
[105] *Ante,* para. 7-16.

they will only do this if there is a reasonable prospect of any funds being available for the payment of their debts. If the unsecured creditors petition for the winding up of the company and a liquidator is appointed, his task is to act as a watchdog over the receiver until the receiver's duties are completed. The liquidator will then deal with any remaining assets of the company.

32-67. The receiver must pay preferential creditors before he pays the unsecured creditors and any creditors holding a floating charge.[106]

32-68. When a receiver appointed under the powers contained in any instrument ceases to act, he must notify the Registrar of Companies.[107] Notice should be given on Board of Trade Form No. 57 A. Usually, he ceases to act because there is nothing more to receive, all the property having been realised. Very occasionally, however, a company regains its financial stability, and the receiver can retire. An interesting question arises in regard to the crystallisation of floating charges. If the company recovers and the receiver retires, does a crystallised charge commence to "float" again? Probably it does, on the basis that the debenture holder has again restored the company's licence to deal with its assets, unless this is inconsistent with the terms of the debenture.[108]

Releasing Company Securities

32-69. The procedure which should be followed when releasing a mortgage or charge executed by a limited company depends upon the type of property involved. Thus, when a life policy is re-assigned, the bank should give notice to the insurance company that the policy has been released; a discharge of a legal mortgage of stocks and shares is effected by transferring them from the bank's nominee company to the customer. In general, the same procedure is followed as in the case of securities given by private individuals.

32-70. In the case of charges which have been registered at Companies House, the register must be amended when the security is released. To do this, the company must complete Board of Trade Form No. 49.[109] This form, usually known as a "memorandum of satisfaction," embodies a formal notice (which must be under the company's seal)

---

[106] *Ante*, para. 32-30.
[107] Companies Act, 1948, Sect. 102 (2).
[108] See L. C. B. Gower, *The Principles of Modern Company Law* (3rd ed., 1969), p. 436; for a different view see *Kerr on Receivers* (13th ed., 1963), p. 327.
[109] Companies (Forms) Order, 1949.

that the charge has been satisfied. There is also a statutory declaration to be made by the secretary and one of the directors, verifying the truth of the particulars given. This must be made before a Commissioner for Oaths, a Notary Public, or a Justice of the Peace. When the form has been completed, it must be sent to the Registrar of Companies. A fee of 5s. (25p) is payable. The Registrar may then make the appropriate entry in the register and must, if required, furnish the company with a copy thereof.[110] The Registrar does not usually notify the person in whose favour the charge had been registered, but it is understood that some banks have made a special arrangement with the Registrar whereby, as a matter of courtesy and without obligation, the Registrar will notify the bank concerned, in whose favour a charge had been registered, that an entry of satisfaction has been made.

32-71. Sometimes part only of the property charged is to be released. In this event, Board of Trade Form No. 49A should be completed by the company and sent to the Registrar, who will make an entry in the register that a specified part of the property or undertaking of the company has been released from the charge.[111]

32-72. If, at any time, the bank has received notice that any of the property comprised in its charge has been the subject of a second mortgage executed by the company, the deeds or other documents of title must be delivered to the second mortgagee. Where the bank has not received express notice of any second mortgage, it is doubtful whether or not search should be made at Companies House to make quite sure that no second mortgage has been registered there. The question whether registration amounts to constructive notice has not yet been decisively answered.[112]

Loans to Company Directors

32-73. Sometimes a banker is asked to grant accommodation to a director of a company and is offered, as cover for the advance, the guarantee of, or some other security deposited by, the company itself. These proposals must usually be declined. Sect. 190 of the Companies Act, 1948, provides that—

> It shall not be lawful for a company to make a loan to any person who is its director or a director of its holding company, or to enter into any guarantee or provide any security in connection with a loan made to such a person as aforesaid by any other person.

[110] Companies Act, 1948, Sect. 100.
[111] Companies Act, 1948, Sect. 100.
[112] See *ante*, para. 32-55.

32-74. There are exceptions laid down by the Act.[113] Thus, the prohibition has no application "in the case of a company whose ordinary business includes the lending of money or the giving of guarantees in connection with loans made by other persons"; for example, there is nothing to prevent a banking company from making loans, in the ordinary course of business, to its own directors. Furthermore, the prohibition does not extend to a loan made to a director "to meet expenditure incurred or to be incurred by him for the purposes of the company or for the purpose of enabling him properly to perform his duties as an officer of the company"; such transactions, however, require the approval of the company in general meeting.

Loans for Purchase of a Company's Shares

32-75. Section 54 of the Companies Act, 1948, provides that, subject to certain exceptions, it is unlawful for a company to give, whether directly or indirectly, and whether by means of a loan, guarantee, the provision of security or otherwise, any financial assistance for the purchase of, or subscription for, its own or its holding company's shares. The following are illustrations of transactions which must be declined on the ground that they would infringe the provisions of the section—

(i) X asks for accommodation to enable him to buy shares in a company, the overdraft to be secured by the guarantee of, or some other security deposited by, the company. X's intention is often to secure control of the company by making a take-over bid for its shares.[114]

(ii) X Company Ltd. proposes to buy some shares in Y Company Ltd., and X Company Ltd. asks its bankers for accommodation for this purpose, the overdraft to be secured by the guarantee of, or some other security deposited by, Y Company Ltd.

(iii) X Company Ltd., as in the previous example, wishes to buy some shares in Y Company Ltd., and X Company Ltd. asks its bankers for a short-term advance, which is to be repaid out of the proceeds of a loan by Y Company Ltd. to X Company Ltd.

32-76. There are certain exceptions to the general rule laid down in Sect. 54, the most important of which is that the prohibition does not apply where the lending of money is part of the ordinary business

---

[113] Sect. 190.

[114] Cf. *Selangor United Rubber Estates Ltd.* v. *Cradock* (No. 3) [1968] 1 W.L.R. 1555. In this case a bank suffered loss, even though X did not ask the bank for accommodation. The bank knew that the company's own funds were being used to finance a take-over bid by X. Both the company and X had their accounts at the bank.

of a company; for example, a bank may make loans to its customers for the purchase of shares in the bank.

32-77. If the provisions of the section are infringed, the company and every officer of the company concerned are liable to a fine not exceeding one hundred pounds. It does not follow, however, that a transaction which infringes the section is necessarily invalidated. It has been held that, upon its true construction, the section does not invalidate a security given by the company in contravention of the section.[115] However, this rule only benefits an innocent lender, i.e., a lender who does not know that the provisions of Sect. 54 are being contravened.

[115] *Victor Battery Co. Ltd.* v. *Curry's Ltd.*, [1946] Ch. 242.

Part Nine

STAMP DUTIES

CHAPTER 33

Stamp Duties

33-1. THE general rule is that an instrument which has been executed in any part of the United Kingdom or which relates to any property situated in the United Kingdom may not be given in evidence in a court of law (except in criminal proceedings), or be available for any purpose whatever, unless it is duly stamped in accordance with the law in force at the time when it was first executed.[1] It is enacted, however, that if an unstamped instrument is produced as evidence in any civil court and if the instrument is one which may legally be stamped after execution, it may be received in evidence upon payment to the officer of the court whose duty it is to read the instrument of (*a*) the amount of the unpaid duty, (*b*) the penalty payable on stamping the same, and (*c*) a further sum of one pound.[2] When a banker finds that he has a document in his possession which, owing to some oversight, has not been stamped, he should not wait until legal proceedings are contemplated. His correct course is to write immediately to the Commissioners of Inland Revenue, Bush House (South West Wing), London, offering to pay the duty and penalty. In genuine cases the authorities are very lenient in regard to stamping up under penalty.

33-2. It is obviously essential for bank officers to be familiar with the rates of stamp duty applicable to the very wide variety of documents which they handle. In this chapter the various duties which apply to most of the instruments encountered in security work are summarised in alphabetical order. The rules relating to "collateral" stamping are very important, and these are explained under the heading of "Mortgages." Except where otherwise indicated, all the duties specified below must be denoted by impressed stamps only.[3]

Agreements under Hand

33-3. An agreement under hand only, and not otherwise specifically charged with any duty, is exempt from duty.[4] Instruments of this

---

[1] Stamp Act, 1891, Sect. 14 (4).
[2] Sect. 14 (1).
[3] Sect. 2.
[4] Finance Act, 1970, Sect. 32 and Sched. 7.

nature used by bankers include guarantees, charges on credit balances, and letters of set-off.

Agricultural Charges

33-4. Exempt from duty.[5]

Assignments of Debts

33-5. A legal assignment is stamped as a mortgage at the rate of 2s. (10p) per cent. If the assignment is of a future debt and therefore necessarily equitable, the letter addressed by the assignor to the debtor, being by way of mortgage, requires stamping as a mortgage. Furthermore, if a second letter is addressed by the assignor to the bank, this will usually require to be stamped as an equitable charge at the rate of 1s. (5p) per cent on the amount secured.[6]

Bearer Securities

33-6. Share warrants and stock certificates to bearer issued by English companies must usually bear a duty of an amount equal to three times the transfer duty, i.e. the amount of the *ad valorem* stamp duty which would be chargeable on a deed transferring the shares or stock specified in the warrant or certificate, if the consideration for the transfer were the market value of such shares or stock; most overseas bearer securities are liable to duty of an amount equal to twice the transfer duty.[7]

Bills of Lading

33-7. Exempt from duty.[8]

Charges on Credit Balances

33-8. See "Agreements under Hand."

Conveyances or Transfers

33-9. Subject to certain exceptions, a conveyance or transfer on sale of any property attracts duty as specified in the following table.[9]

---

[5] Agricultural Credits Act, 1928, Sect. 8 (8).
[6] See *post*, para. 33-30.
[7] Stamp Act, 1891, Sched. I; Finance Act, 1963, Sect. 59.
[8] Finance Act, 1949, Sect. 35 and Sched. VIII.
[9] Stamp Act, 1891, Sched. I; Finance (1909–10) Act, 1910, Sect. 73; Finance Act, 1947, Sect. 52; Finance Act, 1959, Sect. 31; Finance Act, 1963, Sect. 55 (1) and Sched. XI; Finance Act, 1970, Sect. 32 and Sched. 7.

This table of duties is the one applicable to such transactions as the transfer, by way of sale, of registered or inscribed stocks and shares (except transfers of Government stocks and transfers of stock issued by a local authority in the United Kingdom, which are exempt from duty), the conveyance of freehold property, and the assignment of leaseholds.

Where the amount or value of the consideration does not exceed £5	1s. (5p)
Exceeds £5 but does not exceed £100	2s. (10p) for every £10 or part of £10 of the consideration
Exceeds £100 but does not exceed £300	4s. (20p) for every £20 or part of £20 of the consideration
Exceeds £300	10s. (50p) for every £50 or part of £50 of the consideration

33-10. There are certain reliefs in the case of conveyances or transfers (not being transfers of stock or of marketable securities or of units under a unit trust scheme) where the consideration does not exceed £7,000. Thus the reduced rates apply to sales of freehold and lease-hold properties. If the consideration does not exceed £5,500, no duty is payable; it it exceeds £5,500 but does not exceed £7,000, the duty is at the rate of 5s. (25p) per £50.[10]

Debentures

33-11. See "Mortgages."

Floating Charges

33-12. See "Mortgages."

Guarantees

33-13. A guarantee under hand is exempt from duty.[11]

33-14. A guarantee under seal in favour of a bank normally attracts *ad valorem* duty at the rate of 2s. (10p) per cent on the amount of the guarantee to be impressed within thirty days.[12]

[10] Finance Act, 1958, Sect. 34; Finance Act, 1963, Sect. 55 (1) and Sched. XI; Finance Act, 1967, Sect. 27.
[11] Finance Act, 1970, Sect. 32 and Sched. 7.
[12] Stamp Act, 1891, Sched. I, as amended by Finance Act, 1947, Sect. 52; Finance Act, 1963, Sect. 57; Finance Act, 1970, Sect. 32 and Sched. 7. But see *ante*, para. 19-8.

Letters of Pledge

33-15. In practice these documents are regarded as exempt from duty as "Agreements under Hand". It may be, however, that they ought to be stamped as equitable mortgages; the definition of "equitable mortgage" for the purpose of the Stamp Act, 1891, is a very wide one,[13] and would seem to cover a memorandum of the pledge of goods.[14]

Letters of Set-off

33-16. These are exempt from duty as "Agreements under Hand."

Life Policies

33-17. Policies of life insurance must be stamped according to the following scale[15]—

Where the amount insured exceeds £50 but does not exceed £1,000	1s. (5p) for every £100 or part of £100 of the amount insured
Where the amount insured exceeds £1,000	10s. (50p) for every £1,000 or part of £1,000 of the amount insured

33-18. The "sum insured" does not include ordinary bonuses. But in the case of an endowment policy with bonuses, if the company guarantees that the bonuses shall amount to a certain sum upon maturity of the policy, duty is payable on the aggregate amount of the sum insured together with the guaranteed amount of bonus.[16]

Life Policy, Mortgage of

33-19. See "Mortgages."

Marine Insurance Policies

33-20. Policies of marine insurance are exempt from duty.[17]

---

[13] *Post*, para. 33-30.
[14] Cf. E. G. Sergeant, *The Law of Stamp Duties* (5th ed., 1968), p. 168.
[15] Stamp Act, 1891, Sched. I; Finance Act, 1970, Sect. 32 and Sched. 7.
[16] E. N. Alpe, *Law of Stamp Duties* (25th ed., 1960), p. 334.
[17] Finance Act, 1970, Sect. 32 and Sched. 7.

Memoranda of Deposit

A. OF STOCKS AND SHARES

33-21. If the memorandum is executed under hand, it is exempt from duty.[18] But if it is executed under seal, it must be stamped as a mortgage at the rate of 2s. (10p) per cent.

B. OF A LIFE POLICY OR TITLE DEEDS

33-22. If the memorandum is under hand, it requires stamping as an equitable mortgage at the rate of 1s. (5p) per cent.[19] If executed under seal, the memorandum would have to be stamped at the rate of 2s. (10p) per cent.

Mortgages

A. LEGAL MORTGAGES

33-23. Mortgages, bonds, and debentures must be stamped according to the scale given below. The term "mortgage" is very widely defined by the Stamp Act, 1891,[20] with the result that most legal mortgages and equitable mortgages under seal fall within the category.

33-24. Common examples of documents which require stamping at this rate are legal mortgages of land, or of life policies, debentures created by limited companies, and assignments of debts.[21] The scale is as follows[22]—

For the payment or repayment of money—

Not exceeding £300	1s. (5p) for every £50 or part of £50 of the amount secured
Exceeding £300	2s. (10p) for every £100 or part of £100 of the amount secured

33-25. It is not always easy to decide what is the correct amount of duty payable, particularly in view of the fact that there is some controversy concerning the law on this subject. In *Re Waterhouse's Policy*[23] a customer of the Bank of Ireland mortgaged to the bank

---

[18] Finance Act, 1970, Sect. 32 and Sched. 7.
[19] Sect. 86 (2) and Sched. I.
[20] Sect. 86 (1).
[21] But mortgages of ships are exempt. See "Ships, Mortgages of."
[22] Stamp Act, 1891, Sched. I, as amended by Finance Act, 1947, Sect. 52; Finance Act, 1963, Sect. 57; Finance Act, 1970, Sect. 32 and Sched. 7.
[23] [1937] 1 Ch. 415.

his life policy for £500 with profits. At that time, his overdraft amounted to £596. The mortgage was stamped for an amount which was sufficient to cover an advance of £500, the face value of the policy. When the policy matured, the profits thereon amounted to £463, making a total of £963 payable by the company. The sum owing by the customer to the bank was then £619. The company informed the bank that, subject to their receiving from the bank a certificate that the total amount advanced under the mortgage deed had not exceeded £500 (the amount covered by the stamp), they were prepared to pay to the bank all sums due under the policy. The bank informed the company that it was not in a position to give the company the certificate asked for, but that the customer, by a letter enclosed, authorised payment being made to the bank and that if the company were not satisfied with such authorisation the bank would be content for the company to pay them £500, the amount which the mortgage was stamped to cover, and that the balance of the sum falling due might be paid to the customer. The company refused to pay £500 to the bank and the balance to the customer, insisting that the mortgage was insufficiently stamped. The bank commenced legal proceedings.

33-26. It was held by Farwell, J., that the bank was justified in claiming £500 against the company. The learned judge said that, in his opinion, if a bank chooses to take security for an overdraft, and stamps that security with a stamp which is only sufficient to cover a limited sum, the result is that the bank is precluded from claiming that the security which it has is a security for any greater sum than that which the stamp on it covers. Nevertheless it is a perfectly good security for the amount covered by the stamp.

33-27. The effect of this decision was clearly summarised by Mr. H. B. (now Sir Henry) Lawson in the following words—

> If a banker or other person lends money, and takes a security unlimited in amount, he is entitled to stamp the security, with stamp duty to cover any sum which he may choose, without regard to the actual amount of the debt. In other words, if the mortgagee values the security at, say, £500, whereas the debt is already £1,000 (possibly the mortgagee holds a guarantee or other security), he is at liberty to stamp the security to cover £500 only.[24]

The Board of Inland Revenue, however, take a different view. In a letter, dated 17th July, 1937, addressed to the Institute of Bankers, they say that they do not "understand the judgment as stating that

---

[24] H. B. Lawson, "Stamping of Unlimited Securities," *Journal of the Institute of Bankers*, Vol. LVIII (1937), pp. 458–64.

an unlimited security upon which (e.g.) £700 is owing at the time
when it is presented for stamping, or has at some prior time been
owing, can be 'duly stamped' to cover (e.g.) £500."[25]

33-28. It is difficult to reconcile this opinion of the Board with the
decision in the *Waterhouse* case, and the author shares Sir Henry
Lawson's view that a lender is entitled to stamp a security to cover
any sum which he may choose, irrespective of the amount of the
debt. Nevertheless, the usual practice is for unlimited securities to
be stamped up to keep pace with the debt as it increases, because, as
Sir Henry Lawson points out, a mortgagee cannot tell to what extent
it may be necessary for him eventually to look to the security, which
may increase in value. There are exceptional cases when one may
deviate from this general rule. To take an extreme case, suppose
that an overdraft of £10,000 is to be secured by a guarantee of
£9,000 and by a mortgage of land valued at £1,000. In the author's
opinion, the mortgage should be stamped to cover, say, £1,500, i.e.
in order to allow a margin for appreciation. According to the *Waterhouse* case it is quite unnecessary to stamp the mortgage to cover the
full amount of the debt, namely, £10,000.

33-29. The foregoing note is confined to unlimited securities. It is
possible to include in a mortgage a "limiting clause" prescribing
that the amount recoverable shall not exceed a stated sum. In this
event the Stamp Act, 1891,[26] expressly provides that the document
should be stamped to cover only the sum specified. One of the
Clearing banks embodies a limiting clause in most of its security
forms.

B. EQUITABLE MORTGAGES

33-30. It is most important to note precisely what constitutes an
equitable mortgage for the purpose of the Stamp Act, 1891. It is
therein provided[27] that—

> For the purpose of this Act the expression "equitable mortgage" means
> an agreement or memorandum, under hand only, relating to the deposit
> of any title deeds or instruments constituting or being evidence of the
> title to any property whatever (other than stock or marketable security),
> or creating a charge on such property.

[25] Op. cit., p. 460.
[26] Sect. 88 (1).
[27] Sect. 86 (2).

An equitable mortgage attracts duty at the rate of 1s. (5p) for every £100, or fractional part of £100, of the amount secured.[28]

33-31. It will be noticed that this duty applies only to instruments under hand. Equitable mortgages under seal must be stamped according to the scale (2s. (10p) per cent) in paragraph 33-24. For equitable mortgages of stocks and shares, see "Memoranda of Deposit."

C. PAYMENT OF ADDITIONAL DUTY

33-32. It is generally advisable for unlimited securities to be stamped up to keep pace with the debt as it increases.[29] This applies just as much to the stamping of equitable mortgages as it does to legal mortgages. Suppose, for example, that a customer executed a mortgage of land to secure an overdraft of £4,000 and that the mortgage was stamped to cover an advance of that amount. If the overdraft subsequently increases to, say, £5,000, additional duty should be paid: £1 if the mortgage is legal, 10 × 2s. (10p); 10s. (50p) if the mortgage is equitable, 10 × 1s. (5p). The additional duty must be paid within thirty days from the date when the advance first exceeded the amount originally covered.[30] After that period one may only stamp up under penalty, and for this reason a very careful watch must be kept on the amounts for which the bank's securities have been stamped.

33-33. When a mortgage, whether legal or equitable, is sent to the Stamp Office for additional stamps to be impressed, it must be accompanied by a certificate in the following terms signed on behalf of the bank—

> I hereby certify that the amount at any time owing by   .   .   .   to the City Bank Limited
> (*a*) did not exceed £   .   .   . until   .   .
> OR (*b*) has not at any time exceeded the sum of £   .   .   .
> and I request that further stamp duty may be impressed on the instrument of   .   .   . day of   .   .   . 19   , to cover a total advance of £   .   .   .

D. COLLATERAL STAMPING

33-34. This applies where two or more mortgages under seal (whether or not executed by the same mortgagor) are held as security for the same debt. The earliest in point of time is considered

---

[28] Stamp Act, 1891, Sched. I, as amended by Finance Act, 1947, Sect. 52, and Finance Act, 1963, Sect. 57.
[29] See *ante*, para. 33-28.
[30] Stamp Act, 1891, Sects. 15 and 88 (2).

as the primary security and this must be stamped at the full rate of 2s. (10p) per cent.[31] The others are regarded as "collateral" security, that is to say, as "secondary" or "additional" security. They may be stamped at the reduced rate of 1s. (5p) per £200, with a maximum of 10s. (50p) duty payable on any one instrument.[32] For example, if a mortgagor executes a legal mortgage of Blackacre on 1st April, a legal mortgage of Whiteacre on 4th April, and a legal mortgage of Greenacre on 10th April (all mortgages to secure the same debt of £5,000), the mortgage of Blackacre must be stamped £5 as the primary security, 50 × 2s. (10p), and the other two mortgages should each be stamped 10s. (50p).

33-35. In addition to the red stamps showing the duty actually paid on them, documents stamped collaterally used to bear blue stamps denoting the duty paid on the primary security.[33] For this purpose the primary security had to be exhibited to the stamping authorities at the time when the collateral was presented for stamping. If several mortgages under seal were executed at the same time, any one of them might be chosen as the primary security to be fully stamped. This system was modified as from 1st October, 1968, as the result of an agreement between the Board of Inland Revenue and the Committee of London Clearing Bankers, with the approval of the Council of the Law Society. The revised procedure is as follows. When a collateral mortgage is presented, with the relevant primary security, for first stamping, it is normally stamped initially only with the amount of duty (red stamps) and with the blue "duty paid" stamp (to establish its status as a collateral), but it is not stamped with blue stamps denoting the amount of duty paid on the primary document. Furthermore, it will not thereafter normally be presented for denoting stamping until discharge or transfer of the primary or collateral, whereupon cumulative denoting will be effected on request. It is, of course, still necessary to present collaterals for stamping with red duty stamps up to the maximum of 50p. The revised procedure is not applied in any case where, either because a guarantor/surety arrangement is involved or because of other special circumstances, it appears desirable that the collateral documents should at all times be denoted to reflect the amount of stamp duty impressed on the primary document.

33-36. When a loan is secured by several mortgages under seal and the sum advanced subsequently exceeds the amount covered by the

---

[31] See the scale, *ante*, para. 33-24.
[32] Stamp Act, 1891, Sched. I; Revenue Act, 1903, Sect. 7; Finance Act, 1947, Sect. 52; Finance Act, 1963, Sect. 57; Finance Act, 1970, Sect. 32 and Sched. 7.
[33] Stamp Act, 1891, Sect. 11.

stamps, additional stamps to cover the excess must be impressed on the primary security within thirty days. The certificates set out in the text above should be completed. If the collateral securities have not reached the limit of 10s. (50p), further stamps must be impressed thereon at the rate of 1s. (5p) per £200. If they already bore stamps to the limit of 10s. (50p), they used to be presented to have additional blue stamps added (free of charge) to correspond with the increased stamp duty on the primary security. However, under the revised procedure referred to above, banks normally present existing collaterals for further denoting stamping only when the primary security is discharged or transferred, or when the collateral is itself discharged or transferred.

33-37. If the primary security is the first to be discharged, the earliest dated collateral security takes its place and will be regarded as the primary document. The blue stamps on that document indicate the amount for which the security is available.

33-38. It is important to note that the collateral rate of 1s. (5p) per £200, with a maximum of 10s. (50p), applies only where the primary security has been stamped at the rate of 2s. (10p) per cent. It applies, for example, where the primary security is a legal mortgage of land or of a life policy, an equitable mortgage under seal or a guarantee under seal. Equitable mortgages under hand must always be stamped at the rate of 1s. (5p) per cent. Thus, if the first security taken is a mortgage under seal and the second security is an equitable mortgage under hand (or vice versa), no advantage can be taken of the reduced collateral rate. Similarly, the reduced rate does not apply to two or more equitable mortgages under hand.

E. FORMER RATES OF DUTY

33-39. Prior to 1st August, 1947, the rates of duty on mortgages were 2s. 6d. per cent (mortgages under seal), 1s. per cent (equitable mortgages under hand), and 6d. per cent (the collateral rate). The Finance Act, 1947,[34] doubled those rates, and the Finance Act, 1963,[35] restored them to what they were prior to 1st August, 1947. The Finance Act, 1970,[36] reduced the rate of duty on mortgages under seal to 2s. (10p) per cent, left the rate of duty on equitable mortgages under hand unchanged, and re-stated the collateral rate as 1s. (5p) per £200.

[34] Sect. 52.
[35] Sect. 57.
[36] Sect. 32 and Sched. 7.

Powers of Attorney

33-40. The general charge upon a letter or power of attorney is 10s. (50p); however, instruments for certain special purposes are otherwise charged.[37]

Reconveyance, Release, or Discharge of Mortgage

A. RELEASE OF LEGAL MORTGAGES

33-41. A reconveyance, release, discharge, or surrender of a legal mortgage, bond or debenture is liable to duty at the rate of 1s. (5p) for every £200, or fractional part of £200, of the total amount or value of the money at any time secured, with a maximum duty of 10s. (50p).[38]

33-42. Where there is a release of part only of the security (whether or not on payment off of part of the mortgage debt), the *ad valorem* duty does not apply, and the release must be stamped 10s. (50p). But in practice, where the total amount at any time secured is less than £1,000, the Commissioners of Inland Revenue limit the charge to the *ad valorem* rate.[39]

33-43. Releases by building societies are exempt from stamp duty by the Building Societies Act, 1874.[40]

B. RELEASE OF EQUITABLE MORTGAGES

33-44. In the normal way, when an equitable mortgage is discharged, no stamp duty is payable.[41]

Set-off, Letters of

33-45. See "Letters of Set-off."

Share Warrants

33-46. See "Bearer Securities."

[37] Stamp Act, 1891, Sched. I.
[38] Stamp Act, 1891, Sched. I, as amended by Finance Act, 1947, Sect. 52, and Finance Act, 1963, Sect. 57; Finance Act, 1970, Sect. 32 and Sched. 7.
[39] *Munro* v. *Inland Revenue Commissioners* (1895) 23 Court of Sess. Cas. 4th series, 232, 233, footnote; [1896] W.N. 149.
[40] Sect. 41.
[41] See *ante*, para. 6-16.

Ships, Mortgages of

33-47. Exempt from duty.[42]

Stocks and Shares, Transfer of

33-48. A transfer on sale of registered or inscribed stocks and shares must be stamped in accordance with the scale of duties applicable to "Conveyances or Transfers."

33-49. If securities are transferred, by way of legal mortgage, to a lender or to his nominee, a nominal figure (say, 25p) should be inserted in the transfer as the consideration. The transfer may then be stamped with a 10s. (50p) stamp, instead of the usual *ad valorem* duty.[43] The same procedure should be followed when the securities are re-transferred into the name of the borrower. The person registering the transfers will naturally wish to be satisfied that they are genuinely entitled to the benefit of the lower duty. The Commissioners of Inland Revenue have stated that it is sufficient, where a bank or its nominee is a party to the transfer, for an accredited representative of the bank to sign a certificate to the effect that "the transfer is excepted from Sect. 74 of the Finance (1909–10) Act, 1910." Alternatively, the certificate may set forth the facts of the transaction. The certificate is usually endorsed on the transfer.

33-50. All transfers of Government stocks and of stocks issued by a local authority in the United Kingdom are exempt from stamp duty.[44]

33-51. For the duty payable upon an equitable mortgage of stocks and shares, see "Memoranda of Deposit."

Trust Letters or Trust Receipts

33-52. In practice these documents are regarded as exempt from duty, as agreements under hand. It may be, however, that the ought to be stamped 10s. (50p). The Schedule to the Stamp Act, 1891, lays down this duty for a "declaration of any use or trust of or concerning any property by any writing, not being a will, or an instrument chargeable with *ad valorem* duty as a settlement."

Warehousekeepers' Receipts and Warrants

33-53. Exempt from duty.[45]

---

[42] Merchant Shipping Act, 1894, Sect. 721.

[43] Stamp Act. 1891, Sched. I; Finance (1909–10) Act, 1910, Sect. 74 (6); and see *Inland Revenue Circular relating to Stamp Duties*, August, 1949.

[44] Stamp Act, 1891, Sched. I; Finance Act, 1967, Sect. 29 (2) (b).

[45] Finance Act, 1949, Sect. 35,

APPENDIX I

Uniform Customs and Practice for Documentary Credits

(1962 Revision)

General Provisions and Definitions

(*a*) These provisions and definitions and the following articles apply to all documentary credits and are binding upon all parties thereto unless otherwise expressly agreed.

(*b*) For the purposes of such provisions, definitions and articles the expressions "documentary credit(s)" and "credit(s)" used therein mean any arrangement, however named or described, whereby a bank (the issuing bank), acting at the request and in accordance with the instructions of a customer (the applicant for the credit), is to make payment to or to the order of a third party (the beneficiary) or is to pay, accept or negotiate bills of exchange (drafts) drawn by the beneficiary, or authorises such payments to be made or such drafts to be paid, accepted or negotiated by another bank, against stipulated documents and compliance with stipulated terms and conditions.

(*c*) Credits, by their nature, are separate transactions from the sales or other contracts on which they may be based and banks are in no way concerned with or bound by such contracts.

(*d*) Credit instructions and the credits themselves must be complete and precise and, in order to guard against confusion and misunderstanding, issuing banks should discourage any attempt by the applicant for the credit to include excessive detail.

(*e*) When the bank first entitled to avail itself of an option which it enjoys under the following articles does so, its decision shall be binding upon all the parties concerned.

(*f*) A beneficiary can in no case avail himself of the contractual relationships existing between banks or between the applicant for the credit and the issuing bank.

Form and Notification of Credits

Article 1

Credits may be either (*a*) revocable, or (*b*) irrevocable.

All credits, therefore, should clearly indicate whether they are revocable or irrevocable.

In the absence of such indication the credit shall be deemed to be revocable, even though an expiry date is stipulated.

Article 2

A revocable credit does not constitute a legally binding undertaking between the bank or banks concerned and the beneficiary because such a credit may be modified or cancelled at any moment without notice to the beneficiary.

When, however, a revocable credit has been transmitted to and made available at a branch or other bank, its modification or cancellation shall become effective only upon receipt of notice thereof by such branch or other bank and shall not affect the right of that branch or other bank to be reimbursed for any payment, acceptance or negotiation made by it prior to receipt of such notice.

Article 3

An irrevocable credit is a definite undertaking on the part of an issuing bank and constitutes the engagement of that bank to the beneficiary or, as the case may be, to the beneficiary and bona fide holders of drafts drawn and/or documents presented thereunder, that the provisions for payment, acceptance or negotiation contained in the credit will be duly fulfilled, provided that all the terms and conditions of the credit are complied with.

An irrevocable credit may be advised to a beneficiary through another bank without engagement on the part of that other bank (the advising bank), but when an issuing bank authorises another bank to confirm its irrevocable credit and the latter does so, such confirmation constitutes a definite undertaking on the part of the confirming bank either that the provisions for payment or acceptance will be duly fulfilled or, in the case of a credit available by negotiation of drafts, that the confirming bank will negotiate drafts without recourse to drawer.

Such undertakings can neither be modified nor cancelled without the agreement of all concerned.

Article 4

When an issuing bank instructs a bank by cable, telegram or Telex to notify a credit and the original letter of credit itself is to be the operative credit instrument, the issuing bank must send the original letter of credit, and any subsequent amendments thereto, to the beneficiary through the notifying bank.

The issuing bank will be responsible for any consequences arising from its failure to follow this procedure.

Article 5

When a bank is instructed by cable, telegram or Telex to issue, confirm or advise a credit similar in terms to one previously established and which has been the subject of amendments, it shall be understood that the details of the credit being issued, confirmed or advised will be transmitted to the beneficiary excluding the amendments, unless the instructions specify clearly any amendments which are to apply.

Article 6

If incomplete or unclear instructions are received to issue, confirm or advise a credit, the bank requested to act on such instructions may give preliminary notification of the credit to the beneficiary for information only and without responsibility; and in that case the credit will be issued, confirmed or advised only when the necessary information has been received.

Liabilities and Responsibilities

Article 7

Banks must examine all documents with reasonable care to ascertain that they appear on their face to be in accordance with the terms and conditions of the credit.

Article 8

In documentary credit operations all parties concerned deal in documents and not in goods.

Payment, acceptance or negotiation against documents which appear on their face to be in accordance with the terms and conditions of a credit by a bank authorised to do so, binds the party giving the authorisation to take up the documents and reimburse the bank which has effected the payment, acceptance or negotiation.

If, upon receipt of the documents, the issuing bank considers that they appear on their face not to be in accordance with the terms and conditions of the credit, that bank must determine, on the basis of the documents alone, whether to claim that payment, acceptance or negotiation was not effected in accordance with the terms and conditions of the credit.

If such claim is to be made, notice to that effect, stating the reasons therefor, must be given by cable or other expeditious means to the bank from which the documents have been received and such notice must state that the documents are being held at the disposal of such bank or are being returned thereto. The issuing bank shall have a reasonable time to examine the documents.

Article 9

Banks assume no liability or responsibility for the form, sufficiency, accuracy, genuineness, falsification or legal effect of any documents, or for the general and/or particular conditions stipulated in the documents or superimposed thereon; nor do they assume any liability or responsibility for the description, quantity, weight, quality, condition, packing, delivery, value or existence of the goods represented thereby, or for the good faith or acts and/or omissions, solvency, performance or standing of the consignor, the carriers or the insurers of the goods or any other person whomsoever.

Article 10

Banks assume no liability or responsibility for the consequences arising out of delay and/or loss in transit of any messages, letters or documents, or for delay, mutilation or other errors arising in the transmission of cables, telegrams or Telex, or for errors in translation of interpretation of technical terms, and banks reserve the right to transmit credit terms without translating them.

Article 11

Banks assume no liability or responsibility for consequences arising out of the interruption of their business by strikes, lock-outs, riots, civil commotions, insurrections, wars, Acts of God or any other causes beyond their control. Unless specifically authorised, banks will not effect payment, acceptance or negotiation after expiration under credits expiring during such interruption of business.

Article 12

Banks utilising the services of another bank for the purpose of giving effect to the instructions of the applicant for the credit do so for the account and at the risk of the latter.

They assume no liability or responsibility should the instructions they transmit not be carried out, even if they have themselves taken the initiative in the choice of such other bank.

The applicant for the credit shall be bound by and liable to indemnify the banks against all obligations and responsibilities imposed by foreign laws and usages.

Documents

Article 13

All instructions to issue, confirm or advise a credit must state precisely the documents against which payment, acceptance or negotiation is to be made.

Terms such as "first class," "well known," "qualified" and the like shall not be used to describe the issuers of any documents called for under credits and if they are incorporated in the credit terms banks will accept documents as presented without further responsibility on their part.

DOCUMENTS EVIDENCING SHIPMENT OR DISPATCH (SHIPPING DOCUMENTS)

Article 14

Except as stated in Article 18, the date of the Bill of Lading, or date indicated in the reception stamp or by notation on any other document evidencing shipment or dispatch, will be taken in each case to be the date of shipment or dispatch of the goods.

Article 15

If the words "freight paid" or "freight prepaid" appear by stamp or otherwise on documents evidencing shipment or dispatch they will be accepted as constituting evidence of the payment of freight.

If the words "freight prepayable" or "freight to be prepaid" or words of similar effect appear by stamp or otherwise on such documents they will not be accepted as constituting evidence of the payment of freight.

Unless otherwise specified in the credit or inconsistent with any of the documents presented under the credit, banks may honour documents stating that freight or transportation charges are payable on delivery.

Article 16

A clean shipping document is one which bears no superimposed clause or notation which expressly declares a defective condition of the goods and/or the packaging.

Banks will refuse shipping documents bearing such clauses or notations unless the credit expressly states clauses or notations which may be accepted.

MARINE BILLS OF LADING

Article 17

Unless specifically authorised in the credit, Bills of Lading of the following nature will be rejected—

(*a*) Bills of Lading issued by forwarding agents.

(*b*) Bills of Lading which are issued under and are subject to the conditions of a Charter-Party.

(*c*) Bills of Lading covering shipment by sailing vessels.

However, unless otherwise specified in the credit, Bills of Lading of the following nature will be accepted—

(*a*) "Port" or "Custody" Bills of Lading for shipments of cotton from the United States of America.

(*b*) "Through" Bills of Lading issued by steamship companies or their agents even though they cover several modes of transport.

Article 18

Unless otherwise specified in the credit, Bills of Lading must show that the goods are loaded on board.

Loading on board may be evidenced by an on-board Bill of Lading or by means of a notation to that effect dated and signed or initialled by the carrier or his agent, and the date of this notation shall be regarded as the date of loading on board and shipment.

Article 19

Unless transhipment is prohibited by the terms of the credit, Bills of Lading will be accepted which indicate that the goods will be transhipped en route, provided the entire voyage is covered by one and the same Bill of Lading.

Bills of Lading incorporating printed clauses stating that the carriers have the right to tranship will be accepted notwithstanding the fact that the credit prohibits transhipment.

Article 20

Banks will refuse a Bill of Lading showing the stowage of goods on deck, unless specifically authorised in the credit.

Article 21

Banks may require the name of the beneficiary to appear on the Bill of Lading as shipper or endorser, unless the terms of the credit provide otherwise.

OTHER SHIPPING DOCUMENTS, ETC.

Article 22

Banks will consider a Railway or Inland Waterway Bill of Lading or Consignment Note, Counterfoil Waybill, Postal Receipt, Certificate of Mailing, Air Mail Receipt, Air Transportation Waybill, Air Consignment Note or Air Receipt, Trucking Company Bill of Lading or any other similar document as regular when such document bears the reception stamp of the carrier or issuer, or when it bears a signature.

Article 23

When a credit calls for an attestation or certification of weight in the case of transport other than by sea, banks will accept a weight stamp or any other official indication of weight on the shipping documents unless the credit calls for a separate or independent certificate of weight.

INSURANCE DOCUMENTS

Article 24

Insurance documents must be as specifically described in the credit, and must be issued and/or signed by insurance companies or their agents or by underwriters.

Cover notes issued by brokers will not be accepted, unless specifically authorised in the credit.

Article 25

Unless otherwise specified in the credit, banks may refuse any insurance documents presented if they bear a date later than the date of shipment as evidenced by the shipping documents.

Article 26

Unless otherwise specified in the credit, the insurance document must be expressed in the same currency as the credit.

The minimum amount for which insurance must be effected is the CIF value of the goods concerned. However, when the CIF value of the goods cannot be determined from the documents on their face, banks will accept as such minimum amount the amount of the drawing under the credit or the amount of the relative commercial invoice, whichever is the greater.

Article 27

Credits must expressly state the type of insurance required and, if any, the additional risks which are to be covered. Imprecise terms such as "usual risks" or "customary risks" shall not be used.

Failing specific instructions, banks will accept insurance cover as tendered.

Article 28

When a credit stipulates "insurance against all risks," banks will accept an insurance document which contains any "all risks" notation or clause, and will assume no responsibility if any particular risk is not covered.

Article 29

Banks may accept an insurance document which indicates that the cover is subject to a franchise, unless it is specifically stated in the credit that the insurance must be issued irrespective of percentage.

COMMERCIAL INVOICES

Article 30

Unless otherwise specified in the credit, commercial invoices must be made out in the name of the applicant for the credit.

Unless otherwise specified in the credit, banks may refuse invoices issued for amounts in excess of the amount permitted by the credit.

The description of the goods in the commercial invoice must correspond with the description in the credit. In the remaining documents the goods may be described in general terms.

OTHER DOCUMENTS

Article 31

When other documents are required, such as Warehouse Receipts, Delivery Orders, Consular Invoices, Certificates of Origin, of Weight, of Quality or of Analysis, etc., without further definition, banks may accept such documents as tendered, without responsibility on their part.

Miscellaneous Provisions

QUANTITY AND AMOUNT

Article 32

The words "about," "circa" or similar expressions are to be construed as allowing a difference not to exceed 10% more or 10% less, applicable, according to their place in the instructions, to the amount of the credit or to the quantity or unit price of the goods.

Unless a credit stipulates that the quantity of the goods specified must not be exceeded or reduced, a tolerance of 3% more or 3% less will be permissible, always provided that the total amount of the drawings does not exceed the amount of the credit. This tolerance does not apply when the credit specifies quantity in terms of packing units or containers or individual items.

PARTIAL SHIPMENTS

Article 33

Partial shipments are allowed, unless the credit specifically states otherwise.

Shipments made on the same ship and for the same voyage, even if the Bills of Lading evidencing shipment "on board" bear different dates, will not be regarded as partial shipments.

Article 34

If shipment by instalments within given periods is stipulated and any instalment is not shipped within the period allowed for that instalment, the credit ceases to be available for that or any subsequent instalment, unless otherwise specified in the credit.

VALIDITY AND EXPIRY DATE

Article 35

All irrevocable credits must stipulate an expiry date for presentation of documents for payment, acceptance or negotiation, notwithstanding the indication of a latest date for shipment.

Article 36

The words "to," "until," "till" and words of similar import applying to the expiry date for presentation of documents for payment, acceptance or negotiation, or to the stipulated latest date for shipment, will be understood to include the date mentioned.

Article 37

When the stipulated expiry date falls on a day on which banks are closed for reasons other than those mentioned in Article 11, the period of validity will be extended until the first following business day.

This does not apply to the date for shipment which, if stipulated, must be respected.

Banks paying, accepting or negotiating on such extended expiry date must add to the documents their certification in the following wording—

"Presented for payment (or acceptance or negotiation as the case may be) within the expiry date extended in accordance with Article 37 of the Uniform Customs."

Article 38

The validity of a revocable credit, if no date is stipulated, will be considered to have expired six months from the date of the notification sent to the beneficiary by the bank with which the credit is available.

Article 39

Unless otherwise expressly stated, any extension of the stipulated latest date for shipment shall extend for an equal period the validity of the credit.

Where a credit stipulates a latest date for shipment, an extension of the period of validity shall not extend the period permitted for shipment unless otherwise expressly stated.

SHIPMENT, LOADING OR DISPATCH

Article 40

Unless the terms of the credit indicate otherwise, the words "departure," "dispatch," "loading" or "sailing" used in stipulating the latest date for shipment of the goods will be understood to be synonymous with "shipment."

Expressions such as "prompt," "immediately," "as soon as possible" and the like should not be used. If they are used, banks will interpret them as a request for shipment within thirty days from the date on the advice of the credit to the beneficiary by the issuing bank or by an advising bank, as the case may be.

PRESENTATION

Article 41

Documents must be presented within a reasonable time after issuance. Paying, accepting or negotiating banks may refuse documents if, in their judgment, they are presented to them with undue delay.

Article 42

Banks are under no obligation to accept presentation of documents outside their banking hours.

DATE TERMS

Article 43

The terms "first half," "second half" of a month shall be construed respectively as from the 1st to the 15th, and the 16th to the last day of each month, inclusive.

Article 44

The terms "beginning," "middle" or "end" of a month shall be construed respectively as from the 1st to the 10th, the 11th to the 20th, and the 21st to the last day of each month, inclusive.

Article 45

When a bank issuing a credit instructs that the credit be confirmed or advised as available "for one month," "for six months" or the like, but does not specify the date from which the time is to run, the confirming or advising bank will confirm or advise the credit as expiring at the end of such indicated period from the date of its confirmation or advice.

Appendix I
Transfer

Article 46

A transferable credit is a credit under which the beneficiary has the right to give instructions to the bank called upon to effect payment or acceptance or to any bank entitled to effect negotiation to make the credit available in whole or in part to one or more third parties (second beneficiaries).

A credit can be transferred only if it is expressly designated as "transferable" by the issuing bank. Terms such as "divisible," "fractionable," "assignable" and "transmissible" add nothing to the meaning of the term "transferable" and shall not be used.

A transferable credit can be transferred once only. Fractions of a transferable credit (not exceeding in the aggregate the amount of the credit) can be transferred separately, provided partial shipments are not prohibited, and the aggregate of such transfers will be considered as constituting only one transfer of the credit. The credit can be transferred only on the terms and conditions specified in the original credit, with the exception of the amount of the credit, of any unit price stated therein, and of the period of validity or period for shipment, any or all of which may be reduced or curtailed. Additionally, the name of the first beneficiary can be substituted for that of the applicant for the credit, but if the name of the applicant for the credit is specifically required by the original credit to appear in any document other than the invoice, such requirement must be fulfilled.

The first beneficiary has the right to substitute his own invoices for those of the second beneficiary, for amounts not in excess of the original amount stipulated in the credit and for the original unit prices stipulated in the credit, and upon such substitution of invoices the first beneficiary can draw under the credit for the difference, if any, between his invoices and the second beneficiary's invoices. When a credit has been transferred and the first beneficiary is to supply his own invoices in exchange for the second beneficiary's invoices but fails to do so on demand, the paying, accepting or negotiating bank has the right to deliver to the issuing bank the documents received under the credit, including the second beneficiary's invoices, without further responsibility to the first beneficiary.

The first beneficiary of a transferable credit can transfer the credit to a second beneficiary in the same country, but if he is to be permitted to transfer the credit to a second beneficiary in another country this must be expressly stated in the credit. The first beneficiary shall have the right to request that payment or negotiation be effected to the second beneficiary at the place to which the credit has been transferred, up to and including the expiry date of the original credit, and without prejudice to the first beneficiary's right subsequently to substitute his own invoices for those of the second beneficiary and to claim any difference due to him.

The bank requested to effect the transfer, whether it has confirmed the credit or not, shall be under no obligation to make such transfer except to the extent and in the manner expressly consented to by such bank, and until such bank's charges for transfer are paid.

Bank charges entailed by transfers are payable by the first beneficiary unless otherwise specified.

© International Chamber of Commerce

Uniforms Customs and Practice for Documentary Credits has been published by the International Chamber of Commerce, 38 Cours Albert—1er 75 Paris VIII (British National Committee of the I.C.C., High Holborn House, 52/54 High Holborn, London, W.C. 1) in English-French, German-English, Spanish-Portuguese editions. This publication may be obtained from International Headquarters of the I.C.C. and from the various National Committees.

APPENDIX II

Uniform Rules for the Collection of Commercial Paper

General Provisions and Definitions

(*a*) These provisions and definitions and the following articles apply to all collections of commercial paper and are binding upon all parties thereto unless otherwise expressly agreed or unless contrary to the provisions of a national, state or local law and/or regulation which cannot be departed from.

(*b*) For the purpose of such provisions, definitions and articles:

(i) "commercial paper" consists of clean remittances and documentary remittances.

"Clean remittances" means items consisting of one or more bills of exchange, whether already accepted or not, promissory notes, cheques, receipts, or other similar documents for obtaining the payment of money (there being neither invoices, shipping documents, documents of title, or other similar documents, nor any other documents whatsoever attached to the said items).

"Documentary remittances" means all other commercial paper, with documents attached to be delivered against payment, acceptance, trust receipt or other letter of commitment, free or on other terms and conditions.

(ii) The "parties thereto" are the principal who entrusts the operation of collection to his bank (the customer), the said bank (the remitting bank), and the correspondent commissioned by the remitting bank to see to the acceptance or collection of the commercial paper (the collecting bank).

(iii) The "drawee" is the party specified in the remittance letter as the one to whom the commercial paper is to be presented.

(*c*) All commercial paper sent for collection must be accompanied by a remittance letter giving complete and precise instructions. Banks are only permitted to act upon the instructions given in such remittance letter.

If the collecting bank cannot, for any reason, comply with the instructions given in the remittance letter received by it, it must advise the remitting bank immediately.

Presentation

Article 1

Commercial paper is to be presented to the drawee in the form in which it is received from the customer, except that the collecting bank is to affix any necessary stamps, at the expense of the customer unless otherwise instructed.

Remitting and collecting banks have no obligation to examine the commercial paper or the accompanying documents if any, and assume no responsibility for the form and/or regularity thereof.

Article 2

Commercial paper should bear the complete address of the drawee or of the domicile at which the collecting bank is to make the presentation. If the address is incomplete or incorrect, the collecting bank may, without obligation and responsibility on its part, endeavour to ascertain the proper address.

Article 3

In the case of commercial paper payable at sight the collecting bank must make presentation for payment without delay.

In the case of commercial paper payable at a usance other than sight the collecting bank must, where acceptance is called for, make presentation for acceptance without delay, and must, in every instance, make presentation for payment not later than the appropriate maturity date.

Article 4

In respect of a documentary remittance accompanied by a bill of exchange payable at a future date, the remittance letter should state whether the documents are to be released to the drawee against acceptance (D/A) or against payment (D/P).

In the absence of instructions, the documents will be released only against payment.

Payment

Article 5

In the case of commercial paper expressed to be payable in the currency of the country of payment (local currency) the collecting bank will only release the commercial paper to the drawee against payment in local currency which can immediately be disposed of in accordance with the instructions given in the remittance letter.

Article 6

In the case of commercial paper expressed to be payable in a currency other than that of the country of payment (foreign currency) the collecting bank will only release the commercial paper to the drawee against payment in the relative foreign currency which can immediately be remitted in accordance with the instructions given in the remittance letter.

Article 7

In respect of clean remittances partial payments may be accepted if and to the extent to which and on the conditions on which partial payments are authorized by the law in force in the place of payment. The clean remittance will only be released to the drawee when full payment thereof has been received.

In respect of documentary remittances partial payments will only be accepted if specifically authorized in the remittance letter, but unless otherwise instructed the collecting bank will only release the documents to the drawee after full payment has been received.

In all cases where partial payments are acceptable, either by reason of a specific authorization or in accordance with the provisions of this Article, such partial payments will be received and dealt with in accordance with the provisions of Article 5 or 6.

Acceptance

Article 8

The collecting bank is responsible for seeing that the form of the acceptance appears to be complete and correct, but is not responsible for the genuineness of any signature or for the authority of any signatory to sign the acceptance.

Protest

Article 9

The remittance letter should give specific instructions regarding legal process in the event of non-acceptance or non-payment.

In the absence of such specific instructions the banks concerned with the collection are not responsible for any failure to have the commercial paper protested (or subjected to legal process in lieu thereof) for non-payment or non-acceptance.

The collecting bank is not responsible for the regularity of the form of the protest (or other legal process).

Case-of-need (Customer's Representative) and Protection of Goods

Article 10

If the customer nominates a representative to act as case-of-need in the event of non-acceptance and/or non-payment the remittance letter should clearly and fully indicate the powers of such case-of-need.

Whether a case-of-need is nominated or not, in the absence of specific instructions the collecting bank has no obligation to take any action in respect of the goods represented by a documentary remittance.

Advice of Fate, etc.

Article 11

The collecting bank is to send advice of payment or advice of acceptance, with appropriate detail, to the remitting bank without delay.

Article 12

The collecting bank is to send advice of non-payment or advice of non-acceptance, with appropriate detail, to the remitting bank without delay.

Article 13

In the absence of specific instructions the collecting bank is to send all advices or information to the remitting bank by quickest mail.

If, however, the collecting bank considers the matter to be urgent, it may advise by other quicker methods at the expense of the customer.

Charges and Expenses

Article 14

If the remittance letter includes an instruction that collection charges and/or expenses are to be for account of the drawee and the drawee refuses to pay them, the collecting bank, unless expressly instructed to the contrary, may deliver the commercial paper against payment or acceptance as the case may be without collecting charges and/or expenses. In such a case collection charges and/or expenses will be for account of the customer.

Article 15

In all cases where in the express terms of a collection, or under these Rules, disbursements and/or expenses and/or collection charges are to be borne by the customer, the collecting bank is entitled to recover its outlay in respect of disbursements and expenses and its charges from the remitting bank and the remitting bank has the right to recover from the customer any amount so paid out by it, together with its own disbursements, expenses and charges.

Liabilities and Responsibilities

Article 16

Banks utilising the services of another bank for the purpose of giving effect to the instructions of the customer do so for the account of and at the risk of the latter.

Banks are free to utilise as the collecting bank any of their correspondent banks in the country of payment or acceptance as the case may be.

If the customer nominates the collecting bank, the remitting bank nevertheless has the right to direct the commercial paper to such nominated collecting bank through a correspondent bank of its own choice.

Article 17

Banks concerned with a collection of commercial paper assume no liability or responsibility for the consequences arising out of delay and/or loss in transit of any messages, letters or documents, or for delay, mutilation or other errors arising in the transmission of cables, telegrams or telex, or for errors in translation or interpretation of technical terms.

Article 18

Banks concerned with a collection of commercial paper assume no liability or responsibility for consequences arising out of the interruption of their business by strikes, lock-outs, riots, civil commotions, insurrections, wars, Acts of God, or any other causes beyond their control.

Article 19

In the event of goods being despatched direct to the address of a bank for delivery to a drawee against payment or acceptance or upon other terms without prior agreement on the part of that bank, the bank has no obligation to take delivery of the goods, which remain at the risk and responsibility of the party despatching the goods.

© International Chamber of Commerce

Uniform Rules for the Collection of Commercial Paper has been published by the International Chamber of Commerce, 38 Cours Albert—1ᵉʳ, 75 Paris VIII (British National Committee of the I.C.C., High Holborn House, 52/54 High Holborn, London, W.C. 1) in French-English, German-English, Japanese-English and Turkish editions. This publication may be obtained from International Headquarters of the I.C.C. and from the various National Committees.

Index

All references are to paragraph numbers of the text